MW01505781

PLOTINUS

VI

LCL 445

PLOTINUS

ENNEADS VI. 1–5

WITH AN ENGLISH TRANSLATION BY
A. H. ARMSTRONG

HARVARD UNIVERSITY PRESS
CAMBRIDGE, MASSACHUSETTS
LONDON, ENGLAND

ISBN 0-674-99490-6

Printed on acid-free paper and bound by
Edwards Brothers, Ann Arbor, Michigan

CONTENTS

PREFACE

TO LOEB PLOTINUS VI–VII

The text of these volumes corresponds to that of the third volume of the revised *editio minor* of Henry and Schwyzer (*Plotini Opera* III, Oxford Classical Texts, 1982), with correction of printers' errors and a few changes in punctuation, except in the following places, where the changes are indicated in the critical notes:

vol. VI	vol. VII
VI. 1. 12. 38	VI. 7. 1. 48–9
VI. 2. 5. 5	VI. 7. 7. 25
VI. 2. 9. 21	VI. 7. 7. 26–8
VI. 3. 4. 36	VI. 8. 1. 7
VI. 4. 3. 15	VI. 8. 14. 19
VI. 5. 8. 29–31	VI. 8. 18. 29
VI. 5. 10. 44	VI. 8. 21. 23
VI. 5. 12. 6	

Indices have not been provided. The availability of the recently published *Lexicon Plotinianum* (by J. H. Sleeman and Gilbert Pollet: Leiden and Leuven 1980) makes the provision of a selective word-index unnecessary and likely to be misleading; and the *Index Fontium* in *Plotini Opera* III (see above), while not complete, is very extensive and must be referred to by anyone seriously interested in the sources of Plotinus; work on its revision and expansion is continuing.

PREFACE

The preparation of Volumes VI and VII for publication has been assisted by grants from the British Academy and the Leverhulme Trust, which are gratefully acknowledged.

A. H. ARMSTRONG.

SIGLA

A	=	Laurentianus 87, 3.
A^1	=	Codicis A primus corrector.
E	=	Parisinus Gr. 1976.
E	=	exemplum alterum tractatus VI. 5 in codice E a posteriore scriba scriptum.
B	=	Laurentianus 85, 15.
R	=	Vaticanus Reginensis Gr. 97.
J	=	Parisinus Gr. 2082.
U	=	Vaticanus Urbinas Gr. 62.
C	=	Monacensis Gr. 449.
Q	=	Marcianus Gr. 242.
L	=	Ambrosianus Gr. 667.
w	=	AE
x	=	RJ
z	=	QL
mg	=	in margine
ac	=	ante correctionem
pc	=	post correctionem
H-S^1	=	Henry-Schwyzer, editio maior
H-S^2	=	Henry-Schwyzer, editio minor (= OCT)

ORDO ENNEADVM COMPARATVR
CVM ORDINE CHRONOLOGICO

Enn.	chron.	Enn.	chron.	Enn.	chron.
I 1	53	II 1	40	III 1	3
I 2	19	II 2	14	III 2	47
I 3	20	II 3	52	III 3	48
I 4	46	II 4	12	III 4	15
I 5	36	II 5	25	III 5	50
I 6	1	II 6	17	III 6	26
I 7	54	II 7	37	III 7	45
I 8	51	II 8	35	III 8	30
I 9	16	II 9	33	III 9	13

Enn.	chron.	Enn.	chron.	Enn.	chron.
IV 1	21	V 1	10	VI 1	42
IV 2	4	V 2	11	VI 2	43
IV 3	27	V 3	49	VI 3	44
IV 4	28	V 4	7	VI 4	22
IV 5	29	V 5	32	VI 5	23
IV 6	41	V 6	24	VI 6	34
IV 7	2	V 7	18	VI 7	38
IV 8	6	V 8	31	VI 8	39
IV 9	8	V 9	5	VI 9	9

ORDO CHRONOLOGICVS COMPARATVR
CVM ORDINE ENNEADVM

chron.	Enn.	chron.	Enn.	chron.	Enn.
1	I 6	19	I 2	37	II 7
2	IV 7	20	I 3	38	VI 7
3	III 1	21	IV 1	39	VI 8
4	IV 2	22	VI 4	40	II 1
5	V 9	23	VI 5	41	IV 6
6	IV 8	24	V 6	42	VI 1
7	V 4	25	II 5	43	VI 2
8	IV 9	26	III 6	44	VI 3
9	VI 9	27	IV 3	45	III 7
10	V 1	28	IV 4	46	I 4
11	V 2	29	IV 5	47	III 2
12	II 4	30	III 8	48	III 3
13	III 9	31	V 8	49	V 3
14	II 2	32	V 5	50	III 5
15	III 4	33	II 9	51	I 8
16	I 9	34	VI 6	52	II 3
17	II 6	35	II 8	53	I 1
18	V 7	36	I 5	54	I 7

PLOTINUS

ENNEAD VI. 1–5

SVMMARIVM

Τάδε ἔνεστι Πλωτίνου φιλοσόφου ἐννεάδος ἕκτης·

3

ENNEAD VI. 1–3

VI. 1–3. ON THE KINDS OF BEING

Introductory Note

THE work on the *Categories* (Nos. 42–44 in the chronological order) was composed late in Plotinus' writing life, towards the end of the six years during which Porphyry was with him (*Life* ch. 5). It is difficult not to feel as one reads it that he did not find the subject very congenial. In the first of the three treatises into which Porphyry has divided the work (Porphyry's editorial divisions correspond exactly here to the real divisions of the subject-matter, as they do not always do elsewhere) Plotinus seems to be doing his duty as a Platonic philosopher by making his contribution to the traditional polemic which some Platonists had been engaged in since, probably, the first century B.C. against the category-doctrine of Aristotle and the Peripatetics and to the joint attack by Peripatetics and Platonists on Stoic category-doctrine which had been going on since about the same period. (There were other Platonists, notably Alcinous (or Albinus) in the second century A.D. who took a more positive attitude which finally prevailed in the Platonic school, with Porphyry and Iamblichus.)

In the first twenty-four chapters of VI. 1 Plotinus seems to be very much dependent on the polemic against the Aristotelian categories of the Platonist of the second century A.D. Nicostratus (who took over the work of an otherwise unknown Lucius), about which we know something from the *Commentary on the Categories* of Simplicius: the passages of this which are relevant to the text of Plotinus are printed in the *editio maior* of Henry and

Schwyzer.[1] In the last six chapters of the treatise it is likely that he is making use of the anti-Stoic polemic of the Peripatetic Andronicus, the editor of Aristotle in the first century B.C. and his pupil Boethus. Ancient philosophers are not at their best in polemic, and Plotinus and his Platonic and Peripatetic sources are no exceptions. Very much of the criticism is carping, superficial and tendentious, and there is very little attempt to understand the positions of Aristotle and the Stoics or to discover what they are really trying to do. The philosophical point of view is throughout that of Platonism as Plotinus understood it. Aristotle is treated as if he were a bad and metaphysically unintelligent Platonist, and the Stoics as gross and crude materialists. (Plotinus can sometimes understand Aristotle at a very much deeper level, and, even when he is criticising him, develop genuinely Aristotelian thoughts: and his own thought in some areas is much influenced by Stoicism, in ethics and in his understanding of the organic unity of the universe.)

VI. 2 is on a considerably higher level and must rank as one of the major works of Plotinus on the One-Being, the Divine Intellect, Νοῦς. Here he turns from polemic against opponents to expound the true Platonic doctrine of the Categories of the Intelligible World. These are the "greatest genera" of Plato *Sophist* 254D–257A, Being, Rest, Motion, Same and Other. Plotinus uses them in a remarkable and original way, of which this treatise gives the fullest account to be found in the *Enneads.* It has not perhaps very much to do with logic in any ordinary Aristotelian or modern sense: the "categories" are not really used as logical categories or classes. Bréhier, in his *Notice* to VI. 1–3 in his edition (p.37), puts it very well when he speaks of it as a "reflective analysis which brings to light different aspects of the same whole." The ultimate

[1] On Nicostratus see further K. Praechter "Nikostratos der Platoniker" in *Hermes* 57 (1922), 481–517 and J. Dillon *The Middle Platonists* (London 1977), 233–6.

appeal, as always when Plotinus is speaking of the intelligible world and its source, is to a direct awareness or vision, for which discursive reasoning can only prepare us. This is very apparent in Chapter 8 and in the last three chapters of the treatise, especially Chapter 21.

In VI. 3 Plotinus returns from the intelligible to the sensible world, and does his best to provide it with a suitable Platonic set of categories. His attitude to Aristotle at this point becomes a good deal more positive, and this part of the work is more a critical adaptation than a refutation of Peripatetic doctrine. But he finds it difficult to arrive at any certain conclusions, and is more imprecise and undogmatic than usual. This is particularly apparent in the last eight lines of Chapter 3, where he suggests, though he does not pursue the suggestion, that we might be able to manage here below with only two categories, quasi-substance and relation, and in the rather impatiently agnostic last words of Chapter 27. We can see clearly in this treatise how a Platonist, who, following the *Timaeus*, does not believe that any certain and unchanging knowledge of the sense-world is possible, can be much more open and uncommitted to any particular account of the nature and structure of material things than an Aristotelian, who, while still believing that certain and unchanging knowledge is possible, must find its objects predominantly in the world of sense.

(Only Substance, Quantity, Quality, Motion and, incidentally, Relation are discussed in VI. 3. It is possible, but not certain, that Plotinus meant to continue with a fuller discussion of other categories than the summary remarks in the last chapter.)

ON THE KINDS OF BEING

Synopsis

VI. 1

Earlier opinions on the number of beings and kinds of being summarily considered. Do the ten Aristotelian categories apply to both sensible and intelligible worlds (ch. 1)? Substance: criticisms of Aristotelian doctrine: there cannot be one category of substance for both sensible and intelligible worlds (chs. 2–3). Quantity: difficulties about numbers and magnitudes, discontinuous and continuous quantity (ch. 4). Speech and time should not be classed as quantitative (ch. 5). Relation: difficulties of the Aristotelian doctrine. Relations are not only in our thinking (chs. 6–9). Quality: difficulties about the Aristotelian account and the classification of qualities (chs. 10–12). When. Why make it a separate category: are not "whens" parts of time (ch. 13)? Where. Again, as with the "when", perversity of making a separate category, and putting place and what is in place in different categories (ch. 14). Action (or doing and making): critical discussion of the Aristotelian account (chs. 15–19). Affection (or passivity). Difficulties about making it a separate category, sharply distinguished from Action (chs. 20–21). Action-Affection as Relation (ch. 22). Having: is this category really necessary (ch. 23)? The same applies to Position (ch. 24).

The Stoic Categories: absurdity of the Stoic highest genus, "something": confusion in their materialistic account of substance-subject (ch. 25). Attack on Stoic materialism (chs. 26 and 27). The great Stoic mistake is reliance on sense-perception (ch. 28). Criticism of the materialistic Stoic account of Quality (ch. 29). Summary dismissal of the Stoic categories of State and Relation (ch. 30).

ON THE KINDS OF BEING

The Platonic genera. Genera and Principles. Being and Becoming (again, absurdity of the Stoic "something") (ch. 1). Being is one and many: its co-equal genera are also principles (ch. 2). The transcendent One cause of the genera: the genera in the unity of the One-Being: inadequacy of discursive reason to apprehend this (ch. 3). Bodily and intelligible being: Soul as a handy example of the intelligible (ch. 4). The unity and multiplicity of Soul, and of the One-Being (chs. 5 and 6). Movement as life in Soul and Intellect. Necessity also of the genus Rest (ch. 7). The discernment by direct vision of Being, Motion and Rest in Intellect: this brings with it the discernment of Same and Other (ch. 8). Are there more genera? Why the transcendent One is not a genus (ch. 9). Why the One in the One-Being is not a genus: how this One is in Being (chs. 9–11). All things, including mathematical entities, which appear to be soulless, strive towards the One and Good (chs. 11–12). Quantity and number are posterior to and derived from the five Platonic genera (ch. 13). So is quality: in the intelligible world it is the activity of substance (ch. 14). Being and the other four Platonic genera (ch. 15). There is no place for the other Aristotelian categories in the intelligible (ch. 16). The Good is not a genus: the activity, life or movement of the One-Being towards the transcendent Good is its good (ch. 17). The Beautiful belongs to Substance, Knowledge is Movement. Intellect is not a genus, but all that truly exists: and the virtues are its activities (ch. 18). The genera and their species: universal and particular in Intellect (chs. 19–20). The great vision of Intellect, in which, deriving from and along with the primary genera, Quality, Quantity, number and figure are discerned. The all-inclusiveness of Intellect (ch. 21). Exegesis of *Timaeus* 39E (the Complete Living Creature) in terms of this doctrine, with confirmatory texts from the *Parmenides* and *Philebus* (ch. 22).

ON THE KINDS OF BEING

VI. 3

Are the categories of the sense-world the same, analogously, as those of the intelligible, or different? Problems of classification in the sense-world (ch. 1). Sensible substance: matter, form and composite: the Platonic intelligible categories cannot be applied, even analogously, to sensible substance (ch. 2). Discussion of matter, form and composite continued: relation of other categories to them. Seven, five, or possibly only two categories of the sensible world (ch. 3)? What have matter, form and composite in common to make us put them in the category of "substance" (ch. 4)? Substance and substrate (chs. 4–5). What does "is" mean in the sense-world (ch. 6)? It is not matter from which things here below derive their being (ch. 7). Sensible substance as a combination of qualities and matter (ch. 8). How should the genus "sensible substance" be divided into species (chs. 9–10)? Quantity in the sense-world (chs. 11–15). Quality in the sense-world (chs. 16–20). Movement in the sense-world (chs. 21–26). Stillness in the sense-world is to be distinguished from the Platonic category Rest in the intelligible (ch. 27). Summary conclusion, with a few remarks on Relation (ch. 28).

VI. 1. (42) ΠΕΡΙ ΤΩΝ ΓΕΝΩΝ ΤΟΥ ΟΝΤΟΣ ΠΡΩΤΟΝ

1. Περὶ τῶν ὄντων πόσα καὶ τίνα ἐζήτησαν μὲν καὶ
οἱ πάνυ παλαιοί, ἕν, οἱ δὲ ὡρισμένα, οἱ δὲ ἄπειρα
εἰπόντες, καὶ τούτων ἕκαστοι οἱ μὲν ἄλλο οἱ δὲ ἄλλο τὸ
ἕν, οἱ δὲ τὰ πεπερασμένα καὶ αὖ τὰ ἄπειρα εἰπόντες· καὶ
5 τοῖς μετ᾽ αὐτοὺς ἐξετασθεῖσαι αὗται αἱ δόξαι ἱκανῶς
ἀφετέαι ἡμῖν. ὅσα δ᾽ ἐξετάσαντες τὰ ἐκείνων ἔθεντο ἐν
γένεσιν ὡρισμένοις αὐτοί, περὶ τούτων ἐπισκεπτέον, οἳ
οὔτε ἓν θέμενοι, ὅτι πολλὰ καὶ ἐν τοῖς νοητοῖς ἑώρων,
οὔτε ἄπειρα, ὅτι μήτε οἷόν τε μήτ᾽ ἐπιστήμη ἂν γένοιτο,
10 τά τε πεπερασμένα εἰς ἀριθμὸν αὐτῶν, ὅτι τὰ[1]
ὑποκείμενα οὐκ ὀρθῶς οἷον στοιχεῖα, γένη δή[2] τινα
οὗτοι εἰρήκασιν, οἱ μὲν δέκα, οἱ δὲ ἐλάττω· εἶεν δ᾽ ἂν
τινες οἱ πλείω τούτων. ἔστι δὲ καὶ ἐν τοῖς γένεσι

---

[1] αὐτῶν, ὅτι τὰ] αὐτῶν. ὅτι ⟨δὲ⟩ τὰ H–S[1].
[2] Theiler: δὲ Enn.: del. Volkmann, H–S[1].

---

[1] The "extremely ancient philosophers" are the Pre-
Socratics. As usual, Plotinus takes his information about
them from Aristotle and dismisses them very summarily.
"One being": Thales, Anaximenes, Heraclitus; "a definite
number": Empedocles; "an infinite number": Anaxagoras,
Democritus.

[2] Aristotle and the Stoics.

[3] The reference may be to Peripatetic discussions of the
Categories by Andronicus, Boethus, and their followers

VI. 1. ON THE KINDS
OF BEING I

1. The extremely ancient philosophers investigated beings, how many there were and what they were: some said there was one being, some a definite number, and some an infinite number; and in each of these groups, some said the one being was one thing and some another, and the same applies to those who said the number of beings was limited and those who said that it was infinite.[1] And since these views have been sufficiently examined by those who came after them, we can let them go. But since these later philosophers,[2] after examining the views of the earlier ones, themselves placed beings in a number of definite kinds, we must consider them and see how many the kinds are; these philosophers did not posit one being, because they saw many even in the intelligible realm, nor an infinite number, because this was impossible and knowledge could not occur, and some of them posited ten of their numerically limited kinds and some fewer (they have said that the foundations of being are not rightly thought of as a sort of elements, but as genera of some kind); but there might have been some who posited more than these ten.[3] But there are differences in their genera

(first century B.C.): cp. Dexippus *In Categ.* I 37, p. 32,10–34.2. But the wording is vague, and Plotinus clearly did not know much about these people and was not very interested in them.

διαφορά· οἱ μὲν γὰρ τὰ γένη ἀρχάς, οἱ δὲ αὐτὰ τὰ ὄντα
τῷ γένει τοσαῦτα.

15 Πρῶτον τοίνυν τὴν διαιρουμένην εἰς δέκα τὰ ὄντα
ληπτέον ἀνασκοποῦντας, πότερα δέκα γένη δεῖ νομίζειν
αὐτοὺς λέγειν κοινοῦ ὀνόματος τυχόντα τοῦ ὄντος ἢ
κατηγορίας δέκα. ὅτι γὰρ οὐ συνώνυμον τὸ ὂν ἐν ἅπασι,
λέγουσι καὶ ὀρθῶς λέγουσι· μᾶλλον δὲ ἐκεῖνο πρῶτον
20 ἐρωτητέον, πότερα ὁμοίως ἔν τε τοῖς νοητοῖς ἔν τε τοῖς
αἰσθητοῖς τὰ δέκα, ἢ ἐν μὲν τοῖς αἰσθητοῖς ἅπαντα, ἐν
δὲ τοῖς νοητοῖς τὰ μὲν εἶναι, τὰ δὲ μὴ εἶναι· οὐ γὰρ δὴ
ἀνάπαλιν. οὗ δὴ ἐξεταστέον, τίνα κἀκεῖ τῶν δέκα, καὶ εἰ
τὰ ἐκεῖ ὄντα ὑφ᾽ ἓν γένος ὑπακτέον τοῖς ἐνταῦθα, ἢ
25 ὁμωνύμως ἥ τε ἐκεῖ οὐσία ἥ τε ἐνταῦθα· ἀλλ᾽ εἰ τοῦτο,
πλείω τὰ γένη. εἰ δὲ συνωνύμως, ἄτοπον τὸ αὐτὸ
σημαίνειν τὴν οὐσίαν ἐπί τε τῶν πρώτως ὄντων καὶ τῶν
ὑστέρων οὐκ ὄντος γένους κοινοῦ, ἐν οἷς τὸ πρότερον
καὶ ὕστερον. ἀλλὰ περὶ τῶν νοητῶν κατὰ τὴν διαίρεσιν
οὐ λέγουσιν· οὐ πάντα ἄρα τὰ ὄντα διαιρεῖσθαι
30 ἐβουλήθησαν, ἀλλὰ τὰ μάλιστα ὄντα παραλελοίπασι.

2. Πάλιν οὖν ἆρα γένη νομιστέον εἶναι; καὶ πῶς ἓν
γένος ἡ οὐσία; ἀπὸ γὰρ ταύτης πάντως ἀρκτέον. ὅτι μὲν
ἓν ἐπί τε τῆς νοητῆς ἐπί τε τῆς αἰσθητῆς κοινὸν εἶναι

as well: for some of them make the genera principles of being, others the beings themselves, generically the same in number.

First, then, we must take the opinion which divides beings into ten, and see whether we think the philosophers are saying that there are ten genera which fall under the common name of "being", or ten categories. For they say, and say rightly, that being does not mean the same thing in all ten; but we should rather ask them this first, whether the ten are there in the same way in the intelligible beings and the beings perceived by sense, or whether they are all in the beings of the sense-world, but in the intelligibles some are there and some not: for it certainly cannot be the other way round. At this point we must examine which of the ten are also there in the intelligible, and if the things there can be brought under one genus with those here below, or whether the term "substance" is used ambiguously of that there and this here. But if this is so, then there are more than ten genera. But if "substance" is used in the same sense there as here, it will be absurd for it to mean the same thing when applied to primary beings and those which come after them, since there is no common genus of things among which there is priority and posteriority. But in their classification they are not speaking about the intelligible beings: so they did not want to classify all beings, but left out those which are most authentically beings.

2. Again, then, are they really to be considered as genera? And how is substance one genus? For we must in any case begin with this. That there cannot be one common substantiality applying to both

PLOTINUS: ENNEAD VI. 1.

ἀδύνατον τὸ τῆς οὐσίας, εἴρηται. καὶ προσέτι ἄλλο τι
5 ἔσται πρό τε τῆς νοητῆς καὶ πρὸ τῆς αἰσθητῆς, ἄλλο τι
ὂν κατηγορούμενον κατ' ἀμφοῖν, ὃ οὔτε σῶμα οὔτε
ἀσώματον ἂν εἴη· ἔσται γὰρ ἢ τὸ σῶμα ἀσώματον, ἢ τὸ
ἀσώματον σῶμα. οὐ μὴν ἀλλὰ ἐπ' αὐτῶν τῶν τῇδε
οὐσιῶν ζητητέον, τί κοινὸν ἐπὶ τῆς ὕλης καὶ τοῦ εἴδους
10 καὶ τοῦ ἐξ ἀμφοῖν. πάντα γὰρ ταῦτα οὐσίας λέγουσιν
εἶναι, καὶ οὐ τὸ ἴσον εἰς οὐσίαν ἔχειν, ὅταν μᾶλλον
λέγηται τὸ εἶδος οὐσία ἢ ἡ ὕλη· καὶ ὀρθῶς· οἱ δ' ἂν
εἴποιεν τὴν ὕλην μᾶλλον. αἱ δὲ πρῶται λεγόμεναι οὐσίαι
πρὸς τὰς δευτέρας τί ἂν ἔχοιεν κοινόν, ὁπότε παρὰ τῶν
15 προτέρων ἔχουσιν αἱ δεύτεραι τὸ οὐσίαι λέγεσθαι; ὅλως
δὲ τί ἐστιν ἡ οὐσία εἰπεῖν οὐκ ἔστιν· οὐδὲ γάρ, εἰ τὸ
ἴδιόν τις ἀποδοίη, ἤδη ἔχει τὸ τί ἐστι, καὶ ἴσως οὐδὲ
τὸ "ἓν καὶ ταὐτὸν ἀριθμῷ δεκτικὸν τῶν ἐναντίων" ἐπὶ
πάντων ἁρμόσει.

3. Ἀλλ' ἆρα μίαν τινὰ κατηγορίαν λεκτέον ὁμοῦ
συλλαβοῦσι τὴν νοητὴν οὐσίαν, τὴν ὕλην, τὸ εἶδος, τὸ ἐξ
ἀμφοῖν; οἷον εἴ τις τὸ τῶν Ἡρακλειδῶν γένος ἕν τι
λέγοι, οὐχ ὡς κοινὸν κατὰ πάντων, ἀλλ' ὡς ἀφ' ἑνός·
5 πρώτως γὰρ ἡ οὐσία ἐκείνη, δευτέρως δὲ καὶ ἧττον τὰ
ἄλλα. ἀλλὰ τί κωλύει μίαν κατηγορίαν τὰ πάντα εἶναι;
καὶ γὰρ καὶ τὰ ἄλλα πάντα ἀπὸ τῆς οὐσίας τὰ λεγόμενα

---

[1] This seems to be a polemical reference to the widest
Stoic category τι ("sort of something"), which included
both corporeals (the only realities) and incorporeals
(which existed only in thought): cp. *SVF* II 117, 329, 331–3;
cp. ch. 25, 1–10.

[2] A critical reference to Aristotle *Categories* 5. 4a10–11.

intelligible and sensible substance has been said already. And besides, there will [if this is so] be something else before both intelligible and sensible substance, which *is* something else and is predicated of both, and this could not be either body or bodiless: for [if it is] body will be bodiless, or the bodiless body.[1] Of course we must also investigate this point about the substance here below themselves, what there is common to matter and form and the composite of both. For they say that all these are substances, but that they are not equal in respect of substance, when it is said that form is more substance than matter—quite correctly; but there are those who would say that matter is more substance. But what could the substances which they call primary have in common with the secondary ones, when the secondary ones derive their name of substances from those prior to them? But in general it is impossible to say what substance is: for even if one gives it its "proper characteristic", it does not yet have its "what it is", and perhaps not even the definition "that which is one and the same in number which is receptive of the opposites" will fit all cases.[2]

3. But ought we really to call substance one category, collecting together intelligible substance, matter, form and the composite of both? This would be like saying that the genus [or clan] or the Hera-clids was a unity, not in the sense of a unity common to all its members, but because they all come from one ancestor: for the intelligible substance would be so primarily, and the others secondarily and less. But what prevents all things from being one category? For everything else which is said to exist

εἶναι. ἢ ἐκεῖνα μὲν πάθη, αἱ δ' οὐσίαι ἐφεξῆς ἄλλως.

ἀλλὰ γὰρ καὶ οὕτως οὔπω ἔχομεν ἐπερείσασθαι τῇ
10 οὐσίᾳ, οὐδὲ τὸ κυριώτατον λαβεῖν, ἵν' ἀπὸ τούτου καὶ
τὰς ἄλλας. συγγενεῖς μὲν δὴ οὕτως ἔστωσαν πᾶσαι αἱ
λεγόμεναι οὐσίαι ἔχουσαί τι παρὰ τὰ ἄλλα γένη. τί ἄρα
γε αὐτὸ τοῦτο τὸ "τὶ" καὶ τὸ "τόδε" καὶ τὸ
"ὑποκείμενον" καὶ μὴ ἐπικείμενον μηδ' ἐν ἄλλῳ ὡς ἐν
15 ὑποκειμένῳ μηδὲ ὅ ἐστιν ἄλλου ὄν, οἷον λευκὸν ποιότης
σώματος καὶ ποσὸν οὐσίας, καὶ χρόνος κινήσεώς τι καὶ
κίνησις τοῦ κινουμένου; ἀλλ' ἡ δευτέρα οὐσία κατ'
ἄλλου. ἢ ἄλλον τρόπον τὸ "κατ' ἄλλου" ἐνταῦθα, ὡς
γένος ἐνυπάρχον καὶ ἐνυπάρχον ὡς μέρος καὶ τὸ "τὶ"
ἐκείνου· τὸ δὲ λευκὸν κατ' ἄλλου, ὅτι ἐν ἄλλῳ. ἀλλὰ
20 ταῦτα μὲν ἴδια ἄν τις λέγοι πρὸς τὰ ἄλλα καὶ διὰ τοῦτο
εἰς ἓν οὕτω συνάγοι καὶ οὐσίας λέγοι, ἓν δέ τι γένος οὐκ
ἂν λέγοι, οὐδὲ δηλοῖ πω τὴν ἔννοιαν τῆς οὐσίας καὶ τὴν
φύσιν. καὶ ταῦτα μὲν ἐνταῦθα κείσθω· ἐπὶ δὲ τὴν τοῦ
ποσοῦ ἴωμεν φύσιν.

4. Ἀριθμὸν δὴ πρῶτον ποσὸν λέγουσι καὶ τὸ
συνεχὲς ἅπαν μέγεθος καὶ τόπον καὶ χρόνον, τὰ δ' ἄλλα

18

derives from substance. Now those other existents are affections [of substances] and substances are in successive order in a different way. But besides that, in this way we are not yet able to put any weight on substance or grasp the most essential thing about it, in order that the others may come from it. Let all the so-called substances, certainly, be akin in this way and have something over and above the other genera. But what *is* this very "something" and "this here", and the "substrate" and the not resting upon or being in something else as in a substrate, nor being what it is as belonging to another, as white is a quality of body and quantity belongs to substance, and time is something belonging to motion, and motion belongs to the moved? But second substance is predicated of something else. Now here it is predicated of something else in a different way, in the sense of an immanent genus, immanent as a part, and the "what it is" of that first substance; but the [quality] white is predicated of something else because it is in something else. But one might say that these are peculiar properties of substances as compared with other things, and for this reason one might collect them into one and call them substances, but one would not be speaking of one genus, nor would one yet be making clear the concept and nature of substance. Let this discussion rest here, and let us go on to the nature of the quantum.[1]

4. They say that the first quantum is number, also all continuous magnitude and place and time, and they refer all the other things they call quanta back

[1] Plotinus returns to the discussion of sensible "substance" at length in VI. 3.

εἰς ταῦτα ἀναφέρουσιν, ὅσα ποσὰ λέγουσι, καὶ τὴν
κίνησιν ποσὸν τῷ τὸν χρόνον, καίτοι ἴσως ἀνάπαλιν τοῦ
5 χρόνου τὸ συνεχὲς παρὰ τῆς κινήσεως λαβόντος. εἰ μὲν
δὴ τὸ συνεχὲς ᾗ συνεχὲς ποσὸν φήσουσιν εἶναι, τὸ
διωρισμένον οὐκ ἂν εἴη ποσόν· εἰ δὲ κατὰ συμβεβηκὸς
τὸ συνεχές, τί κοινὸν ἀμφοτέροις ἔσται τὸ ποσοῖς εἶναι;
τοῖς μὲν γὰρ ἀριθμοῖς τὸ ποσοῖς εἶναι ὑπαρχέτω· καίτοι
10 τοῦτο τὸ λέγεσθαι ποσοῖς ὑπάρχει, οὔπω δέ, τίς ἡ φύσις
καθὸ λέγεται, δηλοῦται· ἀλλὰ γραμμή γε καὶ ἐπίπεδον
καὶ σῶμα οὐδὲ λέγεται, ἀλλὰ μεγέθη μὲν λέγεται, ποσὰ
δὲ οὐ λέγεται, εἴπερ τότε προσλαμβάνει τὸ ποσὸν
λέγεσθαι, ὅταν εἰς ἀριθμὸν ἀχθῇ δίπηχυ ἢ τρίπηχυ· ἐπεὶ
15 καὶ τὸ σῶμα τὸ φυσικὸν μετρηθὲν γίγνεται ποσόν τι,
καὶ ὁ τόπος κατὰ συμβεβηκός, οὐχ ᾗ τόπος. δεῖ δὲ μὴ
τὸ κατὰ συμβεβηκὸς ποσὸν λαμβάνειν, ἀλλὰ τὸ καθ᾽
αὐτό, οἷον ποσότητα· ἐπεὶ οὐδὲ τοὺς τρεῖς βοῦς ποσόν,
ἀλλὰ τὸν ἐπ᾽ αὐτοῖς ἀριθμόν· βόες γὰρ τρεῖς δύο
κατηγορίαι ἤδη. οὕτως οὖν καὶ γραμμὴ τοσήδε δύο
20 κατηγορίαι, καὶ ἐπιφάνεια τοσήδε δύο, καὶ ἡ ποσότης
μὲν αὐτῆς ποσόν, αὐτὴ δὲ ἡ ἐπιφάνεια διὰ τί ποσόν;
περατωθεῖσα γοῦν οἷον τρισὶ γραμμαῖς ἢ τέτρασι λέγεται
εἶναι ποσόν. τί οὖν; μόνον τοὺς ἀριθμοὺς φήσομεν
ποσόν; ἀλλ᾽ εἰ μὲν τοὺς καθ᾽ αὐτοὺς ἀριθμούς, οὐσίαι
25 λέγονται οὗτοι καὶ μάλιστα τῷ καθ᾽ αὐτοὺς εἶναι. εἰ δὲ

---

[1] These are the Platonic Ideal Numbers, which Plotinus
discusses in VI. 6.

to these, and they say that movement is quantified by the quantum of time, though perhaps, conversely, time takes its continuity from movement. But now, if they are going to say that the continuous is a quantum in so far as it is continuous, the discontinuous would not be a quantum; but if the continuous is a quantum incidentally, what is this being quantitative which is common to both? Now let us agree that numbers have the property of being quanta; yet this only gives them the property of being called quanta, and it is not yet made clear what their nature is in virtue of which they are called quanta; but a line and a surface and a body are not even called quanta, but are called magnitudes but not quanta, granted that they receive the additional appellation of quanta when they are brought to a number, two cubits or three cubits: since the natural body also becomes a quantum when it is measured, and place is so incidentally, not in so far as it is place. But one must not take what is incidentally a quantum, but the quantitative in itself, like quantity: since even the three oxen are not a quantum, but their number is: for three oxen are already two categories. In this way, therefore, a line of a certain length is two categories, and a surface of a certain area is two categories, and its quantity is a quantum, but why is the surface itself a quantum? It is, at any rate, only when it is limited, by three or four lines for instance, that it is said to be a quantum. Well then, shall we assert that only the numbers are quantitative? But if we mean the numbers in and by themselves,[1] these are called substances, and are called so particularly because they are in and by themselves. But if we mean the num-

τοὺς ἐν τοῖς μετέχουσιν αὐτῶν, καθ᾽ οὓς ἀριθμοῦμεν, οὐ
μονάδας, ἀλλὰ ἵππους δέκα καὶ βοῦς δέκα, πρῶτον μὲν
ἄτοπον δόξει εἶναι, εἰ ἐκεῖνοι οὐσίαι, μὴ καὶ τούτους,
ἔπειτα δέ, εἰ μετροῦντες τὰ ὑποκείμενα ἐνυπάρχουσιν ἐν
30 αὐτοῖς, ἀλλὰ μὴ ἔξω ὄντες ὥσπερ οἱ κανόνες καὶ τὰ
μέτρα μετροῦσιν. ἀλλ᾽ εἰ ἐφ᾽ ἑαυτῶν ὄντες λαμβάνονται
εἰς τὸ μετρεῖν καὶ μὴ ἐν τοῖς ὑποκειμένοις, οὔτε ἐκεῖνα
ποσὰ τὰ ὑποκείμενα μὴ μετέχοντα ποσότητος, αὐτοί τε
διὰ τί ποσόν; μέτρα γάρ· τὰ δὲ μέτρα διὰ τί ποσὰ ἢ
35 ποσότης; ἢ ὅτι ἐν τοῖς οὖσιν ὄντες, εἰ μηδεμιᾷ τῶν
ἄλλων ἁρμόττουσι, τοῦτο, ὃ λέγονται, ἔσονται καὶ ἐν τῇ
λεγομένῃ ποσότητι κείσονται. καὶ γὰρ ἡ μονὰς αὐτῶν
ὁρίζει ἕν, εἶτ᾽ ἔπεισι καὶ ἐπ᾽ ἄλλο, καὶ ὁ ἀριθμὸς ὅσα
μηνύει, καὶ μετρεῖ τὸ πλῆθος ἡ ψυχὴ προσχρωμένη.
40 μετροῦσα οὖν οὐ τὸ τί ἐστι μετρεῖ· ἓν γὰρ λέγει καὶ δύο,
κἂν ὁποιαοῦν καὶ ἐναντία ᾖ· ἀλλ᾽ οὐδὲ ἥντινα διάθεσιν
ἔχει, οἷον θερμὸν ἢ καλόν, ἀλλ᾽ ὅσα. τοῦ ποσοῦ ἄρα, εἴτε
καθ᾽ αὑτόν, εἴτ᾽ ἐν τοῖς μετέχυυσι θεωροῖτο, αὐτός, οὐ
τὰ μετέχοντα. οὐ τὸ τρίπηχυ τοίνυν, ἀλλὰ τὰ τρία. διὰ
45 τί οὖν καὶ τὰ μεγέθη; ἆρα, ὅτι ἐγγὺς τοῦ ποσοῦ, καὶ οἷς
ἂν ἐγγίνηται, ποσὰ αὐτὰ λέγομεν, οὐ τῷ κυρίως ποσῷ,

22

bers in the things which participate in them, the numbers by which we count, not just units, but ten horses or ten oxen, first of all it will seem absurd that, if the numbers in themselves are substances, these [counting] numbers should not be so as well, and then [it will also seem absurd] if when they measure their subjects they exist in them, and do not exist outside them and measure them like rulers and measuring-pots. But if it is as existing on their own and not in their subjects that they are taken for measuring, those subjects will not be quanta since they will not participate in quantity, and why are the numbers themselves quantitative? For they are measures: but why are measures quanta or quantity? Presumably because, since they are among the things that exist, if they do not fit into any of the other categories, they will be what they are called and will be placed in the category called quantity. For their unit marks off one thing, and then goes on to another, and number indicates how many there are, and soul measures the multiplicity using number to help it. Therefore when it measures it does not measure what a thing is: for it says "one" and "two", whatever they are and even if they are opposites; but it does not measure what state a thing is in either, warm or beautiful for instance, but how many things there are. Number itself then, whether it is regarded in itself or in the things which participate in it, is quantitative, but its participants are not. So not the "three cubits long" but the "three". Why, then, are magnitudes also quantitative? Is it because they are near the quantum, and we call the things in which they occur quanta, not because they are quanta in the proper sense, but we call something big as if on

ἀλλὰ μέγα λέγομεν, ὥσπερ πολλοῦ μετέχον ἀριθμοῦ,
καὶ μικρόν, ὅτι ὀλίγου; ἀλλὰ τὸ μέγα αὐτὸ καὶ τὸ
μικρὸν οὐκ ἀξιοῦται ποσὰ εἶναι, ἀλλὰ πρός τι· ἀλλὰ
ὅμως πρός τι λέγουσι, καθόσον ποσὰ δοκεῖ εἶναι.
50 σκεπτέον δὲ ἀκριβέστερον. ἔσται τοίνυν οὐχ ἕν τι γένος,
ἀλλ' ὁ ἀριθμὸς μόνος, τὰ δὲ δευτέρως. οὐ κυρίως τοίνυν
ἓν γένος, ἀλλὰ κατηγορία μία συνάγουσα καὶ τὰ ἐγγύς
πως τὰ πρώτως καὶ δευτέρως. ἡμῖν δὲ ζητητέον, πῶς οἱ
καθ' αὐτοὺς ἀριθμοὶ οὐσίαι ἢ καὶ αὐτοὶ ποσόν τι·
55 ὁποτέρως δ' ἂν ἔχωσιν, οὐκ ἂν κοινόν τι ἔχοιεν πρὸς
τούτους ἐκεῖνοι, ἀλλ' ἢ ὄνομα μόνον.

5. Ὁ δὲ λόγος καὶ ὁ χρόνος καὶ ἡ κίνησις πῶς;
πρῶτον δὲ περὶ τοῦ λόγου, εἰ βούλει [μετρεῖται μὲν
γάρ].[1] ἀλλὰ λόγος ὢν τοσόσδε ἐστί[ν]—⟨μετρεῖται μὲν
γάρ⟩—ᾗ δὲ λόγος, οὐ ποσόν· σημαντικὸν γάρ, ὥσπερ
5 τὸ ὄνομα καὶ τὸ ῥῆμα. ὕλη δ' αὐτοῦ ὁ ἀήρ, ὥσπερ καὶ
τούτων· καὶ γὰρ σύγκειται ἐξ αὐτῶν· ἡ δὲ πληγὴ
μᾶλλον ὁ λόγος, καὶ οὐχ ἡ πληγὴ ἁπλῶς, ἀλλ' ἡ
τύπωσις ἡ γιγνομένη, ὥσπερ μορφοῦσα· μᾶλλον οὖν
ποίησις καὶ ποίησις σημαντική. τὴν δὴ κίνησιν ταύτην
κατὰ[2] τὴν πληγὴν ποίησιν μᾶλλον ἂν εὐλόγως τις
10 θεῖτο, τὴν δὲ ἀντικειμένως πάθος, ἢ ἑκάστην ἄλλου μὲν
ποίησιν, ἄλλου δὲ πάθος, ἢ ποίησιν εἰς τὸ ὑποκείμενον,
πάθημα δ' ἐν τῷ ὑποκειμένῳ. εἰ δὲ μὴ κατὰ τὴν πληγὴν

---

[1] transposuimus.
[2] coniecimus: καὶ Enn.

the ground that it participates in a great deal of number, and small, because it participates in a little? But the big itself and the small are not considered to be quanta, but relations; but, all the same, they call them relations in so far as they appear to be quanta. But we must consider this more precisely. There will, then, not be one genus, but only number, and the other things as quanta secondarily. There is not, then, one genus in the proper sense, but one category which gathers in also the things that are somehow near quanta in a primary and secondary sense. But we [Platonists] must investigate how the numbers in and by themselves are substances, or whether they too are a kind of quantum; but, whichever way they are, those numbers would have nothing in common with these numbers here below, except the name alone.

5. But how are [articulate] speech and time and movement quanta? First of all, if you like, about speech. But it is speech and is of a certain quantity—for it is certainly measured—yet in so far as it is speech it is not a quantum: for it is something significant, like noun and verb. Like theirs, its matter is the air: for in fact it is composed of them; but it is rather the impact which is speech, and not just simply the impact but the resulting impression which so to speak shapes the air: it is therefore an action, and a significant action. Certainly one would more reasonably class this movement according to the impact as an action and the corresponding movement as an affection, or say that each of them was an action of one thing and an affection of another, or an action upon the substrate and an affection in the substrate. But if the voice is not considered in terms

25

ἡ φωνή, ἀλλὰ καὶ κατὰ τὸν ἀέρα, δύο ἂν εἴη καὶ οὐ μία ἡ
κατηγορία ἐκ τῆς σημαντικῆς, εἰ ⟨τὸ σημαντικὸν
ταύτης, τὸ δὲ⟩[1] συσσημαντικὸν ἐκείνης τῆς
15 κατηγορίας. ὁ δὲ χρόνος, εἰ μὲν κατὰ τὸ μετροῦν
λαμβάνοιτο, τί ποτε τὸ μετροῦν ληπτέον· ἢ γὰρ ψυχὴ ἢ
τὸ νῦν. εἰ δὲ κατὰ τὸ μετρούμενον, κατὰ μὲν τὸ τοσόσδε
εἶναι, οἷον ἐνιαύσιος, ἔστω ποσόν, κατὰ μέντοι τὸ
χρόνος εἶναι φύσις τις ἄλλη· τὸ γὰρ τοσόνδε ἄλλο ὂν
20 τοσόνδε ἐστίν. οὐ γὰρ δὴ ποσότης ὁ χρόνος· ἡ δὲ
ποσότης οὐκ ἐφαπτομένη ἄλλου αὐτὸ τοῦτο ἂν εἴη τὸ
κυρίως ποσόν. εἰ δὲ τὰ μετέχοντα πάντα τοῦ ποσοῦ
ποσὰ θεῖτο, καὶ ἡ οὐσία ἔσται τὸ αὐτὸ καὶ ποσόν. τ ὸ δ ὲ
ἴ σ ο ν κ α ὶ ἄ ν ι σ ο ν ἴ δ ι ο ν εἶν α ι τ ο ῦ π ο σ ο ῦ ἐ π ᾿
αὐτοῦ ληπτέον, οὐ τῶν μετεχόντων, ἀλλ᾿ ἢ κατὰ
25 συμβεβηκός, οὐχ ᾗ αὐτὰ ἐκεῖνα, ὥσπερ ὁ τρίπηχυς
ποσός, συνηρημένος καὶ οὗτος οὐκ εἰς γένος ἕν, ἀλλ᾿ ὑφ᾿
ἓν καὶ μίαν κατηγορίαν.

6. Τὸ δὲ πρός τι οὕτως ἐπισκεπτέον, εἴ τις κοινότης
γενικὴ ἐν αὐτῷ ὑπάρχει ἢ ἄλλον τρόπον εἰς ἕν, καὶ
μάλιστα ἐπὶ τούτου, εἰ ὑπόστασίς τις ἡ σχέσις ἐστὶν

---

[1] Igal.

of the impact but of the air, there would be two categories and not one to be extracted from the significant action, if the significant thing is to be placed in this category and the co-significant in that.[1] As for time, if it is understood in its measuring capacity, we must grasp what it is that measures: for it is either soul or the "now". But if it is understood as measured, let it be a quantum in respect of being of a certain length, a year's length for instance; but in respect of being time it is some different nature: for the so much is a something else which is so much. Quite certainly time is not quantity; but it is just exactly quantity which has no hold on anything else which is the quantum in the strict and proper sense. But if one classes all the things which participate in the quantitative as quanta, then substance will be the same thing as quantum. But that "equal and unequal are characteristic of the quantum"[2] must be understood of the quantum itself, not of the things which participate in it, except incidentally, not in so far as they are those things which they are, as the man three cubits tall is; he too is not brought together into one genus, but under one genus and one category.

6. As regards relation, we should enquire about it in this way: whether there is any generic community in it, or whether it comes together in another way into one. And it is particularly important when dealing with this category to ask whether this state of being related has any substantial existence, for

[1] We adopt here Igal's conjecture, which gives good sense and accords with Simplicius *In Categ.* 6, p. 131. 8–10.

[2] Aristotle *Categories* 6. 6a26–7

αὕτη, ὥσπερ ὁ δεξιὸς καὶ ἀριστερὸς καὶ τὸ διπλάσιον
5 καὶ τὸ ἥμισυ, ἢ ἐπὶ μὲν τῶν ἐστιν, ὥσπερ ἐπὶ τοῦ
ὕστερον λεχθέντος, ἐπὶ δὲ τοῦ πρότερον λεχθέντος
οὐδεμία, ἢ οὐδαμοῦ τοῦτο. τί δὴ ἐπὶ διπλασίου καὶ
ἡμίσεος καὶ ὅλως ὑπερέχοντος καὶ ὑπερεχομένου, καὶ
αὖ ἕξεως καὶ διαθέσεως, ἀνακλίσεως, καθίσεως,
10 στάσεως, καὶ αὖ πατρὸς υἱέος, δεσπότου δούλου, καὶ
πάλιν ὁμοίου ἀνομοίου, ἴσου ἀνίσου, ποιητικοῦ τε αὖ
καὶ παθητικοῦ, καὶ μέτρου καὶ μετρουμένου; καὶ
ἐπιστήμη καὶ αἴσθησις, ἡ μὲν πρὸς ἐπιστητόν, ἡ δὲ
πρὸς αἰσθητόν. ἡ μὲν γὰρ ἐπιστήμη ἔχοι ἂν πρὸς
ἐπιστητὸν μίαν τινὰ κατ᾽ ἐνέργειαν ὑπόστασιν [πρὸς τὸ
15 τοῦ ἐπιστητοῦ εἶδος],[1] καὶ ἡ αἴσθησις πρὸς αἰσθητὸν
ὡσαύτως, τό τε ποιητικὸν πρὸς τὸ παθητικὸν κἂν ἔργον
ἓν ἀπεργάσαιτο, καὶ τὸ μέτρον πρὸς τὸ μετρούμενον
τὴν μέτρησιν. ὅμοιον δὲ πρὸς ὅμοιον τί ἂν ἔχοι
ἀπογεννώμενον; ἢ οὐκ ἀπογεννώμενον, ἀλλὰ ὑπάρχον,
τὴν ταυτότητα τὴν ἐν τῷ ποιῷ. ἀλλὰ παρὰ τὸ ἐν
20 ἑκατέρῳ ποιὸν οὐδέν. οὐδὲ τὰ ἴσα· τὸ γὰρ ταὐτὸν ἐν τῷ
ποσῷ προϋπάρχει πρὸ τῆς σχέσεως. ἡ δὲ σχέσις τί ἄλλο
ἢ ἡμετέρα κρίσις παραβαλλόντων τὰ ἐφ᾽ ἑαυτῶν ὄντα ἃ
ἐστι καὶ λεγόντων "τοῦτο καὶ τοῦτο τὸ αὐτὸ μέγεθος
ἔχει καὶ τὴν αὐτὴν ποιότητα" καὶ "οὗτος πεποίηκε
25 τοῦτον καὶ οὗτος κρατεῖ τούτου"; κάθισίς τε καὶ στάσις
παρὰ τὸ καθήμενον καὶ ἑστηκὸς τί ἂν εἴη; ἢ δ᾽ ἕξις [καὶ
διάθεσις][2] ἡ μὲν κατὰ τὸ ἔχον λεγομένη ἔχειν ἂν μᾶλλον

---

[1] del. Dörrie.
[2] del. Kirchhoff.

instance the right and the left and the double and the half, or whether it is so in some cases, for instance the one last mentioned, but there is no substantiality in the first mentioned, or whether it is nowhere so. What, then, about double and half and in general exceeding and exceeded, and again about habitual state and [changeable] disposition, and lying, sitting, standing, and again about father, son, master, slave, and further about like, unlike, equal, unequal, and active also and passive, and measure and measured? And knowledge and sense-perception, of which one is related to the object known and the other to the object perceived. Knowledge would indeed have in relation to its object a single active substantial existence, and sense-perception in the same way in relation to its object, and so would the active to the passive, granted that they accomplish a single work, and the measure to the measured in respect of measuring it. But what product would like have in relation to like? It is not a question of a product, but of something which is there, of the sameness in the qualified. But there is nothing over and above the qualification in each of the like things. Nor is there in the case of equal things: for the sameness in the quantum is there before the state of being related. But what is this state of being related other than our judgement when we compare things which are what they are by themselves and say "this thing and this thing have the same size and the same quality", and "this man has produced this man, and this man controls this man"? And what would sitting and standing be over and above what sits and stands? But habitual state, when it refers to the possessor, would rather signify

σημαίνοι, ἡ δὲ κατὰ τὸ ἐχόμενον ποιὸν ἂν εἴη· καὶ ἐπὶ
διαθέσεως ὡσαύτως. τί ἂν οὖν εἴη παρὰ ταῦτα τὰ πρὸς
30 ἄλληλα ἢ ἡμῶν τὴν παράθεσιν νοούντων; τὸ δ᾽ ὑπερέχον
τὸ μὲν τοσόνδε μέγεθος, τὸ δὲ τοσόνδε· ἄλλο δὲ τόδε, τὸ
δὲ ἄλλο· ἡ δὲ παραβολὴ παρ᾽ ἡμῶν, οὐκ ἐν αὐτοῖς. ὁ δὲ
δεξιὸς πρὸς ἀριστερὸν καὶ ἔμπροσθεν καὶ ὄπισθεν
μᾶλλον ἂν ἴσως ἐν τῷ κεῖσθαι· ὁ μὲν ὡδί, ὁ δὲ ὡδί· ἡμεῖς
δὲ τὸ δεξιὸν καὶ τὸ ἀριστερὸν ἐνοήσαμεν, ἐν δὲ αὐτοῖς
35 οὐδέν. τό τε πρότερον καὶ ὕστερον χρόνοι δύο· τὸ δὲ
πρότερον καὶ ὕστερον ἡμεῖς ὡσαύτως.

7. Εἰ μὲν οὖν οὐδὲν λέγομεν, ἀλλὰ λέγοντες
ψευδόμεθα, οὐδὲν ἂν τούτων εἴη, ἀλλὰ κενὸν ἡ σχέσις·
εἰ δ᾽ ἀληθεύομεν λέγοντες ''πρότερος ὅδε τοῦδε, ὁ δ᾽
ὕστερος'', χρόνους δύο παραβάλλοντες ἕτερον παρὰ τὰ
5 ὑποκείμενα αὐτῶν λέγοντες τὸ πρότερον, καὶ ἐπὶ δεξιοῦ
καὶ ἐπὶ ἀριστεροῦ ὡσαύτως, καὶ ἐπὶ μεγεθῶν παρὰ τὸ
ποσὸν αὐτῶν τὴν σχέσιν, καθὸ τὸ μὲν ὑπερβάλλει, τὸ δ᾽
ὑπερβάλλεται, εἰ δὲ καὶ μὴ λεγόντων ἡμῶν μηδὲ
νοούντων ἔστιν οὕτως, ὥστε διπλάσιον εἶναι τόδε
τοῦδε, καὶ ἔχει, τὸ δ᾽ ἔχεται, καὶ πρὶν ἡμᾶς ἐπιστῆσαι,
10 καὶ ἴσα πρὸ ἡμῶν πρὸς ἄλληλα, καὶ ἐπὶ τοῦ ποιὰ εἶναι
ἔστιν ἐν ταυτότητι τῇ πρὸς ἄλληλα, καὶ ἐπὶ πάντων ὧν

possession, but when it refers to the possessed, would be a quale; and the same would be true of [changeable] disposition. What then would there be over and above these things which are related to each other except ourselves thinking their juxta-position? Exceeding is a matter of one thing of one definite size and another of another definite size; and this one and that one are two different things; the comparison comes from us, but is not in them. But right in relation to left, and before and behind perhaps rather belong in the category of position: one is here and the other there; but we thought the right and left; there is nothing of it in the things themselves. And the before and after are two times; but it is we who think the before and after in the same way.

7. If then we are not saying anything, but our statements are deceptive, none of these would exist and "the state of being related" would be an empty phrase; but if we speak the truth when we say "this time is before this one, and this one after", compar-ing two times and saying that the "before" is some-thing other than the underlying subjects, and it is the same with right and left, and if in the case of sizes [it is true to say] that their relationship is something over and above their quantitativeness, in that one exceeds and the other is exceeded; further, if, even when we do not speak or think, it is in fact so that this is the double of that, and one possesses and another is possessed, even before we notice it, and things are equal to one another prior to us, and, where being qualified is concerned, are in a relation of sameness to each other, and if in the case of all things which we say are related the state of being

λέγομεν πρός τι μετὰ τὰ ὑποκείμενα ἔστι πρὸς ἄλληλα
ἡ σχέσις, ἡμεῖς δὲ οὖσαν θεωροῦμεν καὶ ἡ γνῶσις πρὸς
τὸ γινωσκόμενον—οὗ δὴ καὶ φανερώτερον τὸ τῆς
15 ὑποστάσεως τὸ ἐκ τῆς σχέσεως—παυστέον μὲν τὸ
ζητεῖν, εἰ ἔστι σχέσις, ἐπισημηναμένους δὲ ὅτι τῶν
τοιούτων ἐπὶ μὲν ὤν, ἕως μένει τὰ ὑποκείμενα ὅπως
εἶχε, κἂν χωρὶς γένηται, ὑπάρχει ἡ σχέσις, ἐπὶ δὲ τῶν,
ὅταν συνέλθῃ, γίγνεται, ἐπὶ δὲ τῶν καὶ μενόντων
20 παύεται ἡ σχέσις ἢ ὅλως ἢ ἄλλη γίγνεται, οἷον ἐπὶ
δεξιοῦ καὶ πλησίον, ἐξ ὧν καὶ μάλιστα ἡ ὑπόνοια
τοῦ μηδὲν εἶναι ἐν τοῖς τοιούτοις· τοῦτ' οὖν ἐπισημηναμένους χρὴ ζητεῖν τί ταὐτὸν ἐν πᾶσι, καὶ εἰ ὡς
γένος, ἀλλὰ μὴ συμβεβηκός· εἶτα εὑρεθὲν τὸ ταὐτὸν
ποίαν ὑπόστασιν ἔχει. λεκτέον δὴ τὸ πρός τι οὐκ εἴ τι
25 ἁπλῶς ἑτέρου λέγεται, οἷον ἕξις ψυχῆς ἢ σώματος, οὐδ'
ὅτι ψυχὴ τοῦδέ ἐστιν ἢ ἐν ἑτέρῳ, ἀλλ' οἷς ἡ ὑπόστασις
οὐδαμόθεν ἢ ἐκ τῆς σχέσεως παραγίγνεται· ὑπόστασις
δὲ οὐχ ἡ τῶν ὑποκειμένων, ἀλλ' ἢ πρός τι λέγεται. οἷον
τὸ διπλάσιον πρὸς ἥμισυ τὴν ὑπόστασιν δίδωσιν οὔτε τῷ
30 διπήχει ἢ ὅλως δυσίν, οὔτε τῷ πηχυαίῳ ἢ ὅλως ἑνί,
ἀλλὰ τούτων ὄντων κατὰ τὴν σχέσιν αὐτῶν πρὸς τῷ
δύο,[1] τὸ δὲ ἓν εἶναι, ἔσχε τὸ μὲν διπλάσιον λέγεσθαί τε

---

[1] πρὸς τῷ δύο Kirchhoff (πρὸς τῷ τὸ μὲν δύο F³ᵐᵍ: *praeter id*
Ficinus): πρὸς (παρὰ R²ᵐᵍ) τὸ δύο Enn.

related to each other is subsequent to the subjects
related, but we observe it as presently existent, and
our knowledge is directed to the object being
known—at this point the substantiality arising out
of the state of relation is even more obvious—we
should stop enquiring whether the state of relation
exists; but we should also note that with some things
in this state, as long as the subjects remain as they
were, even if they become separated, the state of
relation persists, but with others it comes into
existence when they come together, and with others
again, even when they remain as they are, the state
of being related either comes to an end altogether or
becomes different, as in the case of right and near,
and it is from these particularly that our suspicion
arises that in things of this kind relation is nothing.
Having taken note of this, then, we must enquire
what is the same in all, and if it is so as a genus, but
not something incidental; then, when we have found
what is the same, we must enquire what kind of
existence it has. We must certainly speak of relation,
not if something is simply said to belong to another,
a state of soul or body for instance, nor because a
soul belongs to this man or is in something different
[from itself], but in things where the existence derives from nowhere else but the state of relation:
existence here does not mean that of the [related]
subjects, but that of the relation. For instance the
relation double to half gives existence neither to the
two-cubits-long nor in general to two things, nor to
the one-cubit-long nor in general to one thing, but
when these are in their state of being related, in
addition to being two and one respectively, the first
has the name and reality of double, and the one the

καὶ εἶναι, τὸ δὲ ἓν ἥμισυ ἔσχεν αὐτό. συνεγέννησεν οὖν
ἄμφω ἐξ αὐτῶν ἄλλο εἶναι διπλάσιον καὶ ἥμισυ, ἃ πρὸς
35 ἄλληλα ἐγεννήθη, καὶ τὸ εἶναι οὐκ ἄλλο τι ἢ τὸ ἀλλήλοις
εἶναι, τῷ μὲν διπλασίῳ παρὰ τοῦ ὑπερέχειν τὸ ἥμισυ,
τῷ δὲ ἡμίσει παρὰ τοῦ ὑπερέχεσθαι· ὥστε οὐκ ἔστι τὸ
μὲν αὐτῶν πρότερον, τὸ δὲ ὕστερον, ἀλλ᾽ ἅμα
ὑφίσταται. εἰ δὲ καὶ ἅμα μένει; ἢ ἐπὶ πατρὸς καὶ υἱοῦ
40 καὶ τῶν παραπλησίων πατρὸς ἀπελθόντος υἱός ἐστι, καὶ
ἀδελφοῦ ἀδελφός· ἐπεὶ καὶ τὸ "ὅμοιος οὗτος τῷ
τεθνηκότι" λέγομεν.

8. Ἀλλὰ ταῦτα μὲν παρεξέβημεν· ἐκεῖθεν δὲ
ζητητέον τὸ διὰ τί ἐπὶ τούτων οὐχ ὁμοίως. ἀλλὰ τὸ
εἶναι τοῦτο τὸ παρ᾽ ἀλλήλων τίνα ἔχει κοινὴν τὴν
ὑπόστασιν εἰπάτωσαν. σῶμα μὲν οὖν τι τοῦτο τὸ κοινὸν
5 οὐκ ἂν εἴη. λείπεται δέ, εἴπερ ἔστιν, ἀσώματον, καὶ ἢ ἐν
αὐτοῖς ἢ ἔξωθεν. καὶ εἰ μὲν ἡ αὐτὴ σχέσις, συνώνυμος, εἰ
δὲ μή, ἀλλ᾽ ἄλλη ἄλλων, ὁμώνυμος· οὐ γὰρ δή, ὅτι σχέσις
λέγεται, καὶ τὴν οὐσίαν τὴν αὐτὴν ἂν ἔχοι. ἆρ᾽ οὖν τὰς
σχέσεις ταύτῃ διαιρετέον, ᾗ τὰ μὲν ἔχει ἀργὸν τὴν σχέσιν,
10 οἷον κειμένην θεωρεῖν, καὶ ἅμα πάντῃ ἡ ὑπόστασις, τὰ δὲ
μετὰ δυνάμεως καὶ ἔργου ἢ ἀεὶ πρὸς τὴν σχέσιν καὶ εἶχε

name and reality of half. They both together, therefore, generated from themselves something else, the
existence of double and half, which came into
existence in relation to each other, and their being is
nothing else than being for each other; for the
double it comes from exceeding the half and for the
half from being exceeded; so that one of them is not
prior and the other posterior, but they come into
existence together. But do they remain in existence
together? Now in the case of father and son and
similar relations, when the father is gone the son is
[still] son, and a brother [is a brother] when his
brother is gone: for we say "he is like the dead man".

8. But we digressed here; and starting from this
point we must investigate the question why there is
dissimilarity in these relations. But let these philosophers[1] tell us what common substantiality this
being from each other has. Well now, this common
reality cannot be a body. So it remains that, suppos-
ing it exists, it is incorporeal, and is either in the
things related or comes from outside. And if the state
of being related is [always] the same, it is univocal,
but if not, but different in different cases, it is
equivocal: for it is certainly not just because it is
called a state of being related that it would have the
same essential character. Are then the states of
being related to be distinguished in this way, in that
some things have a relationship observable as inactive, just lying there, so to speak, and it only exists
when they are entirely simultaneous, but others,
along with their power and operation, are either
always disposed to relationship and had their

[1] The Peripatetics.

καὶ πρὸ τοῦ τὴν ἑτοιμότητα, ἐν δὲ τῇ συνόδῳ καὶ
ἐνεργείᾳ ὑπέστη, ἢ καὶ ὅλως τὰ μὲν πεποίηκε, τὰ δ᾽
ὑπέστη, καὶ τὸ ὑποστὰν ὄνομα μόνον παρέσχε τῷ
15 ἑτέρῳ, τὸ δὲ τὴν ὑπόστασιν; τοιοῦτον γὰρ καὶ ὁ πατὴρ
καὶ ὁ υἱός· καὶ τὸ ποιητικὸν δὲ καὶ παθητικὸν ἔχει τινὰ
οἷον ζωὴν καὶ ἐνέργειαν. ἆρ᾽ οὖν ταύτῃ διαιρετέον τὴν
σχέσιν καὶ διαιρετέον οὐχ ὡς ταὐτόν τι καὶ κοινὸν ἐν
διαφοραῖς, ἀλλ᾽ ὅλως ὡς ἑτέραν φύσιν τὴν σχέσιν ἐν
20 ἑκατέρῳ, καὶ λεκτέον ὁμώνυμον τὴν μὲν ποιοῦσαν
ποίησιν καὶ πάθησιν, ὡς μίαν ἄμφω, τὴν δὲ οὐ
ποιοῦσαν, ἀλλ᾽ ἐπ᾽ ἀμφοῖν τὸ ποιοῦν ἄλλο; οἷον ἰσότητα
τὴν τὰ ἴσα· ἰσότητι γὰρ ἴσα καὶ ὅλως ταυτότητί τινι
ταὐτά· τὸ δὲ μέγα καὶ μικρόν, τὸ μὲν μεγέθους
παρουσίᾳ, τὸ δὲ μικρότητος. ὅταν δὲ τὸ μὲν μεῖζον, τὸ
25 δὲ μικρότερον, οἱ μὲν μεταλαβόντες ὁ μὲν μείζων
ἐνεργείᾳ φανέντος τοῦ ἐν αὐτῷ μεγέθους, ὁ δὲ μικρὸς
τῆς μικρότητος.

9. Χρὴ οὖν ἐπὶ μὲν τῶν πρόσθεν εἰρημένων, οἷον
ποιοῦντος, ἐπιστήμης, ἐνεργῇ τὴν σχέσιν κατὰ τὴν
ἐνέργειαν καὶ τὸν ἐπὶ τῇ ἐνεργείᾳ λόγον τίθεσθαι, ἐπὶ δὲ
τῶν ἄλλων εἴδους καὶ λόγου μετάληψιν εἶναι. καὶ γάρ,

36

preparedness for it beforehand, and it comes into existence in their coming together and actualisation, or, in a quite general way, one set of them have produced and the others come to exist, and what has come to exist only gives a name to the other, but the producer gives the existence? For the father and the son are like this; and the active and the passive have a kind of life and actualisation. Are we then to divide the state of being related in this way, and divide it not as something identical and common in its differentiations, but on the general assumption that the state of relationship is a different nature in each of the two classes, and we are to speak of it equivocally when we say that one kind produces action and affection as a united pair, but the other does not produce, but what produces the relationship in both the related things is something other than them? For instance, equality is the state of relationship which produces equals: for they are equal by equality, and in general same things are the same by some kind of sameness; as for large and small, one is large by the presence of largeness and the other small by the presence of smallness. But when it is a question of larger and smaller, one of the participants is larger by the actualisation of the largeness apparent in him, and the other smaller by the actualisation of the smallness.

9. We must therefore in the cases mentioned earlier, of the producer and of knowledge for instance, posit that the state of being related is active by reason of the activity of the actual agent and the rational forming principle operative in the activity, and in the other cases that it is a participation in form and rational forming principle. For certainly, if

5 εἰ μὲν σώματα ἔδει τὰ ὄντα εἶναι, οὐδὲν ἔδει λέγειν εἶναι
ταύτας τὰς τοῦ πρός τι λεγομένας σχέσεις· εἰ δὲ καὶ
ἀσωμάτοις δίδομεν τὴν κυρίαν χώραν καὶ τοῖς λόγοις
λόγους λέγοντες τὰς σχέσεις καὶ εἰδῶν μεταλήψεις
αἰτίας—τοῦ γὰρ διπλάσιον εἶναι τὸ διπλάσιον αὐτὸ
10 αἴτιον, τῷ δὲ τὸ ἥμισυ. καὶ τὰ μὲν τῷ αὐτῷ εἴδει, τὰ δὲ
τοῖς ἀντικειμένοις εἶναι ἃ λέγεται· ἅμα οὖν τῷδε μὲν
προσῆλθε τὸ διπλάσιον, ἄλλῳ δὲ τὸ ἥμισυ, καὶ τῷδε μὲν
τὸ μέγεθος, τῷδε δὲ ἡ μικρότης. ἢ ἀμφότερά ἐστιν ἐν
ἑκάστῳ, καὶ ὁμοιότης καὶ ἀνομοιότης καὶ ὅλως ταὐτὸν
15 καὶ θάτερον· διὸ καὶ ὅμοιον καὶ ἀνόμοιον τὸ αὐτὸ καὶ
ταὐτὸν καὶ θάτερον. τί οὖν, εἰ ὁ μὲν αἰσχρός, ὁ δὲ
αἰσχίων εἴδους τοῦ αὐτοῦ μετουσίᾳ; ἢ, εἰ μὲν
παντάπασιν αἰσχροί, ἴσοι εἴδους ἀπουσίᾳ· εἰ δ' ἐν τῷ
μὲν τὸ μᾶλλον, τῷ δὲ τὸ ἧττον, μεταλήψει εἴδους οὐ
κρατοῦντος ὁ ἧττον αἰσχρός, ὁ δὲ μᾶλλον ἔτι μᾶλλον οὐ
20 κρατοῦντος· ἢ τῇ στερήσει, εἴ τις βούλοιτο τὴν
παραβολὴν ἔχειν, οἷον εἴδους αὐτοῖς ὄντος. αἴσθησις δὲ
εἶδός τι ἐξ ἀμφοῖν, καὶ γνῶσις ὡσαύτως ἐξ ἀμφοῖν τι
εἶδος· ἡ δὲ ἕξις πρὸς τὸ ἐχόμενον ἐνέργειά τις οἷον
συνέχουσα, ὥσπερ ποίησίς τις· ἡ δὲ μέτρησις τοῦ

realities had to be bodies, it would be necessary to say that the states which are said to belong to a relation were nothing; but if we give the principal place to incorporeal things and rational principles, saying that the states of relationship are rational principles and participations in forms their causes .....[1] for [it is necessary to say] that the double itself is cause of being double, and for the other [related] thing the half [is cause of its being half]. And some are what they are called by the same form, but others by opposed forms: for the double comes to one thing and the half to another simultaneously, and largeness comes to one thing at the same time as smallness to the other. Or both are in each thing, both likeness and unlikeness and, in a general sense, sameness and otherness. What then is going on if one man is ugly, but another uglier by participation in the same form? Now, if they are altogether ugly, they are equal by the absence of form; but if there is a greater degree of ugliness in one, and a lesser degree in the other, the less ugly is so by participation in a form which is not in control and the more ugly by participation in it when it is still more not in control; or, if one would like to get one's comparison [in this way, one could do it] by privation, which would be like a kind of form for them. But sense-perception is a kind of form coming from both [the related things] and knowledge in the same way a kind of form from both; but the habitual state in relation to what is possessed by it is a kind of activity which in a way holds it together, like a kind of making; and measuring is an activity of the

---

[1] The apodosis of this sentence is missing.

25 μετροῦντος ἐνέργεια πρὸς τὸ μετρούμενον λόγος τις. εἰ
μὲν οὖν [ὡς εἶδος]¹ γενικῶς τὴν τοῦ πρός τι σχέσιν ὡς
εἶδός τις θήσεται, γένος ἓν καὶ ὑπόστασις ὡς λόγος τις
πανταχοῦ· εἰ δὲ οἱ λόγοι καὶ ἀντικείμενοι καὶ διαφορὰς
ἔχοντες τὰς εἰρημένας, τάχα οὐκ ἂν ἓν γένος εἴη, ἀλλ᾽
30 εἰς ὁμοιότητά τινα πάντα ἀνάγεται καὶ κατηγορίαν
μίαν. ἀλλ᾽ εἰ καὶ εἰς ἓν δύναιτο ἀνάγεσθαι τὰ εἰρημένα,
ἀλλ᾽ εἰς γένος ἓν ἀδύνατον τὰ ὑπὸ τὴν αὐτὴν κατηγορίαν
αὐτοῖς τεθέντα. καὶ γὰρ τὰς ἀποφάσεις αὐτῶν εἰς ἓν
ἀνάγουσι, καὶ τὰ παρονομαζόμενα ἀπ᾽ αὐτῶν, οἷον καὶ
35 τὸ διπλάσιον καὶ ὁ διπλάσιος. πῶς ἂν οὖν ὑφ᾽ ἓν γένος
αὐτό τι καὶ ἡ ἀπόφασις, διπλάσιον καὶ οὐ διπλάσιον,
καὶ πρός τι καὶ οὐ πρός τι; ὥσπερ ἂν εἰ ζῷόν τις γένος
θεὶς καὶ τὸ οὐ ζῷον ἐκεῖ τιθείη. καὶ τὸ διπλάσιον καὶ ὁ
διπλάσιος ὥσπερ ἡ λευκότης καὶ ὁ λευκός, οὐχ ὅπερ
ταὐτόν.

10. Τὴν δὲ ποιότητα, ἀφ᾽ ἧς ὁ λεγόμενος ποιός, δεῖ
λαμβάνειν πρῶτον τίς οὖσα τοὺς λεγομένους ποιοὺς
παρέχεται, καὶ ⟨εἰ⟩² μία καὶ ἡ αὐτὴ κατὰ τὸ κοινὸν
ταῖς διαφοραῖς τὰ εἴδη παρέχεται ἤ, εἰ πολλαχῶς αἱ

¹ del. Theiler.
² Α³⁸ (*numquid* Ficinus), Perna.

measurer which is a rational principle in relation to the measured. If then one is going to consider the state belonging to relation generically as a form, it will be one genus and substantial reality, as there is a rational forming principle in all cases; but if the rational principles are both opposed and have the differences which have been stated, perhaps there would not be one genus, but all relatives are brought back to a certain likeness and a single category. But even if it was possible to bring back all the relatives we have mentioned into one, it would be impossible to bring into a single genus all the things which are grouped under the same category with them. For they bring back into one the denials of the relative terms and the things which derive their name from them, for instance the double and the double-sized man.[1] How then could one bring under one genus a thing itself and the denial of it, double and not double, and relative and not relative? It is just as if one made a genus "living being" and put the non-living being into it. And the double and the double-sized man are like whiteness and the white man, not at all identical.

10. And as for quality, from which what is called the qualified [or quale] derives, one must first grasp what is its real nature which enables it to produce what are called qualified beings, and whether, being one and the same according to what is common [to all kinds of quality], it produces its species by distinctive differences, or, if qualities are to be under-

[1] On ἀποφάσεις see Dexippus *In Categ.* 33. 8-13 (= Aristotle fr. 116 Rose[3], p. 106 Ross). παρονομαζόμενα are defined in Aristotle *Categories* 1. 1a12.

5 ποιότητες, οὐχ ἓν ἂν εἴη γένος. τί οὖν τὸ κοινὸν ἐπί τε
ἕξεως καὶ διαθέσεως καὶ παθητικῆς ποιότητος καὶ
σχήματος καὶ μορφῆς; καὶ λεπτόν, παχύ, ἰσχνόν; εἰ μὲν
γὰρ τὸ κοινὸν δύναμιν ἐροῦμεν, ἢ ἐφαρμόττει καὶ ταῖς
ἕξεσι καὶ ταῖς διαθέσεσι καὶ ταῖς φυσικαῖς δυνάμεσιν,
10 ἀφ’ ἧς τὸ ἔχον δύναται ἃ δύναται, οὐκέτι αἱ ἀδυναμίαι
ἁρμόσουσιν. ἔπειτα τὸ σχῆμα καὶ ἡ μορφὴ ἡ περὶ
ἕκαστον πῶς δύναμις; εἶτα καὶ τὸ ὂν ᾗ ὂν δύναμιν
οὐδεμίαν ἕξει, ἀλλ’ ὅταν αὐτῷ προσέλθῃ τὸ ποιόν. αἱ δὲ
ἐνέργειαι τῶν οὐσιῶν, ὅσαι μάλιστά εἰσιν ἐνέργειαι, τὸ
15 ποιοῦ καθ’ αὑτὰς ἐνεργοῦσαι καὶ τῶν οἰκείων δυνάμεων
ὅ εἰσιν. ἀλλ’ ἆρα κατὰ τὰς ἐπ’ αὐτὰς τὰς οὐσίας
δυνάμεις; οἷον ἡ πυκτικὴ δύναμις οὐ τοῦ ἀνθρώπου ᾗ
ἄνθρωπος, ἀλλὰ τὸ λογικόν· ὥστε οὐ ποιότης τὸ οὕτω
λογικόν, ἀλλὰ μᾶλλον ὃ ἐξ ἀρετῆς κτήσαιτο ἄν τις· ὥστε
ὁμώνυμον τὸ λογικόν· ὥστε εἴη ἂν ἡ ποιότης δύναμις
20 προστιθεῖσα ταῖς οὐσίαις μεθ’ αὑτὰς τὸ ποιαῖς εἶναι. αἱ
δὲ διαφοραὶ αἱ πρὸς ἀλλήλας τὰς οὐσίας διιστᾶσαι
ὁμωνύμως ποιότητες, ἐνέργειαι οὖσαι μᾶλλον καὶ λόγοι
ἢ μέρη λόγων, τὸ τὶ οὐδὲν ἧττον δηλοῦσαι, κἂν δοκῶσι
τὴν ποιὰν οὐσίαν λέγειν. αἱ δὲ ποιότητες αἱ κυρίως,
25 καθ’ ἃς ποιοί, ἃς δὴ λέγομεν δυνάμεις εἶναι, τὸ κοινὸν
εἶεν ἂν λόγοι τινὲς καὶ οἷον μορφαί, περί τε ψυχὴν κάλλη

---

[1] The passage of Aristotle under discussion in this
chapter is *Categories* 8. 8b25 ff.

stood in many different senses, there would not be one genus of quality. What, then, is the common element in state and disposition and passive quality and figure and shape [1]? And what about rarefied and solid and lean? For if we are going to say that the common quality is power, which fits states and dispositions and natural powers, from which that which has it has the powers which it has, the incapacities will not fit in any more. Then, how are individual figure and shape power? And further, being *qua* being will have no power except when the quale comes to it. And the activities of substances, which are activities in the strictest sense, activate what belongs to the quale by themselves, and what they are belongs to their own powers. But does this mean that qualities are according to the powers intrinsic to the essences themselves? For instance, the power of boxing does not belong to man *qua* man, but rationality does; so that rationality in this sense is not a quality, but rather the rationality which one might acquire from virtue; so "rationality" is equivocal; so that quality would be a power which adds to substances, posterior to their being themselves, the being qualified. But the specific differences which distinguish substances in relation to each other are qualities in an equivocal sense, being rather activities and rational forming principles, or parts of forming principles, making clear what the thing is none the less even if they seem to declare that the substance is of a specific quality. And the qualities in the strict and proper sense, according to which beings are qualified, which we say are powers, would in fact in their general character be a sort of forming principles and, in a sense, shapes, beauties

43

καὶ αἴσχη καὶ περὶ σῶμα ὡσαύτως. ἀλλὰ πῶς δυνάμεις
πᾶσαι; κάλλος μὲν γὰρ ἔστω καὶ ὑγίεια ἑκατέρα, αἶσχος
δὲ καὶ νόσος καὶ ἀσθένεια καὶ ἀδυναμία ὅλως; ἢ ὅτι καὶ
30 κατὰ ταύτας ποιοὶ λέγονται; ἀλλὰ τί κωλύει λεγομένους
ποιοὺς ὁμωνύμως λέγεσθαι καὶ μὴ καθ' ἕνα λόγον, καὶ
μὴ μόνον τετραχῶς, ἀλλὰ καὶ καθ' ἕκαστον τῶν
τεττάρων τοὐλάχιστον διχῶς; ἢ πρῶτον μὲν οὐ κατὰ τὸ
ποιῆσαι ἢ παθεῖν ἡ ποιότης, ὥστε ἄλλως μὲν τὸ
δυνάμενον ποιεῖν, ἄλλως δὲ τὸ πάσχον; ἀλλὰ καὶ τὴν
35 ὑγίειαν κατὰ[1] τὴν διάθεσιν καὶ τὴν ἕξιν ποιὸν καὶ τὴν
νόσον ὡσαύτως καὶ τὴν ἰσχὺν καὶ τὴν ἀσθένειαν. ἀλλ' εἰ
τοῦτο, οὐκέτι κοινὸν ἡ δύναμις, ἀλλὰ ἄλλο τι δεῖ τὸ
κοινὸν ζητεῖν. οὐδ' αὖ λόγους πάσας· πῶς γὰρ ἡ νόσος ἡ
ἐν ἕξει λόγος; ἀλλ' ἆρα τὰς μὲν ἐν εἴδεσι καὶ δυνάμεσι
40 ποιότητας, ταύτας δὲ στερήσεις; ὥστε μὴ ἓν γένος,
ἀλλὰ εἰς ἓν ὡς μίαν κατηγορίαν, οἷον ἐπιστήμην μὲν
εἶδος καὶ δύναμιν, ἀνεπιστημοσύνην δὲ στέρησιν καὶ
ἀδυναμίαν. ἢ μορφή τις καὶ ἡ ἀδυναμία· καὶ ἡ νόσος, καὶ
δύναται δὲ καὶ ποιεῖ πολλά, ἀλλὰ φαύλως, καὶ ἡ νόσος
45 καὶ ἡ κακία. ἢ ἔκπτωσις τοῦ σκοποῦ οὖσα πῶς δύναμις;
ἢ τὸ αὑτῆς ἑκάστη πράττει οὐ πρὸς τὸ ὀρθὸν βλέπουσα·
οὐ γὰρ ἂν ἐποίησέ τι, ὃ μὴ δύναται. καὶ τἀκαλλὲς[2] δὲ
δύναμιν ἔχει τινός. ἆρ' οὖν καὶ τὸ τρίγωνον; ἢ ὅλως οὐδὲ
πρὸς δύναμιν δεῖ βλέπειν, ἀλλὰ μᾶλλον πρὸς ὃ

[1] Igal, H–S²: καὶ Enn.
[2] Igal, H–S²: τὸ κάλλος Enn.

44

and uglinesses in the soul and in the body in the same way. But how can they all be powers? Let us grant that beauty and health are, of both kinds, but how can ugliness and illness and feebleness and in general incapacity be powers? Is it because beings are said to be qualified according to them? But what prevents the term "qualified" from being used equivocally and not according to one definition, and not only in four different senses, but in at least two in the case of each of the four? Now, first of all, is not quality [divided] according to active and passive, so that what is able to act is quality in one sense, and what is passive in another? And further, health determined by disposition and state is a quale, and illness in the same way, and strength and feebleness. But if this is so, power is no longer common [to all quality], but we must look for something else as the common element. Nor, again, are all qualities rational forming principles: for how can illness, a permanent state of illness, be a forming principle? But, then, are those which consist in forms and powers qualities, but these other ones privations? So there is not one genus, but they are brought into one as one category, as for instance knowledge is a form and power, but ignorance is a privation and incapacity. Now incapacity is a sort of shape, and so is illness, and both illness and vice are capable of and do many things, but badly. But when a quality is a missing of the mark, how is it a power? It does its own business, not having the correct end in view: for it would not have done anything which it could not do. And the unbeautiful has some sort of capacity. Well, then, does the triangle? Now in general we ought not even to look in the direction of power, but

50 διάκειται· ὥστε κατὰ τὰς οἷον μορφὰς καὶ χαρακτῆρας,
καὶ κοινὸν ἡ μορφὴ καὶ τὸ εἶδος τὸ ἐπὶ τῇ οὐσίᾳ μετὰ
τὴν οὐσίαν. ἀλλὰ πάλιν πῶς αἱ δυνάμεις; ἢ καὶ ὁ φύσει
πυκτικὸς τῷ διακεῖσθαί πως ἔχει τοῦτο, καὶ ὁ ἀδύνατος
πρός τι. καὶ ὅλως χαρακτήρ τις ἡ ποιότης οὐκ
55 οὐσιώδης, ὃ δ' ἂν τὸ αὐτὸ δοκῇ καὶ εἰς οὐσίαν
συμβάλλεσθαι καὶ εἰς μὴ οὐσίαν, οἷον θερμότης καὶ
λευκότης καὶ ὅλως χρόα· τὸ μὲν τῆς οὐσίας ἄλλο, οἷον
ἐνέργεια αὐτῆς, τὸ δὲ δευτέρως καὶ ἀπ' ἐκείνου καὶ
ἄλλο ἐν ἄλλῳ, εἴδωλον αὐτοῦ καὶ ὅμοιον. ἀλλ' εἰ κατὰ
60 τὴν μόρφωσιν καὶ χαρακτῆρα καὶ λόγον, πῶς τὰ κατὰ
ἀδυναμίαν καὶ αἴσχη; ἢ λόγους ἀτελεῖς λεκτέον, οἷον ἐν
τῷ αἰσχρῷ. καὶ ἐν τῇ νόσῳ πῶς ὁ λόγος; ἢ καὶ ἐνταῦθα
λόγον κινούμενον τὸν τῆς ὑγιείας. ἢ οὐκ ἐν λόγῳ πάντα,
ἀλλὰ ἀρκεῖ τὸ κοινὸν παρὰ τό πως διακεῖσθαι εἶναι

---

[1] Plotinus seems to be here concerned to exclude any
recourse to the "negative Forms" which undoubtedly
appear in Plato, but have generally been an embarrassment
to Platonists: he explicitly denies their existence in V. 9,10.
On negative Forms in Plato see W. D. Ross *Plato's Theory
of Ideas* (Oxford 1951) 167–9. Plotinus' "theory of ideas" is
of exactly the kind which Ross suggests on p. 169: "It *might*
be possible for a theory of Ideas to dispense with an Idea of
evil and with Ideas of its species, and to explain all evil in

rather to what [a quality] is disposed; so that quality is a matter of what one might call shapes and characteristics, and shape is the common element, and the form on the substance which is posterior to the substance. But again, how are there the powers? The natural boxer has this ability of his by being disposed in a certain way, and so does the man who is incapable of something. And in general quality is a kind of non-substantial characteristic; it is something which seems to be the same and to contribute both to substance and to non-substance, heat, for instance, and whiteness and in general colour: that which belongs to substance is one thing, a kind of activity of the substance, but that which does not has a secondary status and derives from that other and is one thing in another, an image of it and like it. But if quality corresponds to shaping and characteristic and rational forming principle, what about the cases of incapacity and ugliness? They must be said to be incomplete forming principles, as in the ugly. And how is the forming principle in illness? Here too we must speak about a disturbed forming principle, that of health.[1] Or perhaps all are not contained in rational forming principle, but the sufficient common element [of quality] is, besides being disposed in a particular way, being outside substance, and the

the sensible world as due to the fact that the relation of the phenomenal to the ideal is never one of perfect instantiation but always one of imitation which falls short of its pattern." Plotinus' close friend and colleague Amelius, however, took a different view, perhaps closer to Plato's own. He postulated Forms of Evils (Asclepius *In Nic. Arithm.* 44. 3–5 p. 32 Tarán; cp. Proclus *Platonic Theology* I. 21 p. 98 Saffrey-Westerink).

ἔξωθεν τῆς οὐσίας, καὶ τὸ ἐπιγιγνόμενον μετὰ τὴν
65 οὐσίαν ποιότης τοῦ ὑποκειμένου. τὸ δὲ τρίγωνον
ποιότης τοῦ ἐν ᾧ, οὐχ ἁπλῶς τρίγωνον, ἀλλὰ τὸ ἐν
τούτῳ καὶ καθόσον ἐμόρφωσεν. ἀλλὰ καὶ ἡ ἀνθρωπότης
ἐμόρφωσεν; ἢ οὐσίωσεν.

11. 'Αλλ' εἰ ταῦτα οὕτως, διὰ τί πλείω εἴδη
ποιότητος, καὶ ἕξεις καὶ διαθέσεις ἄλλο; οὐ γὰρ
διαφορὰ ποιότητος τὸ μόνιμον καὶ τὸ μή, ἀλλ' ἀρκεῖ ἡ
διάθεσις ὁπωσοῦν ἔχουσα πρὸς τὸ παρασχέσθαι ποιόν·
5 προσθήκη δ' ἔξωθεν τὸ μένειν· εἰ μή τις λέγοι τὰς μὲν
διαθέσεις μόνον ἀτελεῖς οἷον μορφάς, τὰς δὲ ἕξεις
τελείας. ἀλλ' εἰ ἀτελεῖς, οὔπω ποιότητες· εἰ δ' ἤδη
ποιότητες, προσθήκη τὸ μόνιμον. αἱ δὲ φυσικαὶ
δυνάμεις πῶς ἕτερον εἶδος; εἰ μὲν γὰρ κατὰ τὰς
δυνάμεις ποιότητες, οὐκ ἐφαρμόττει πάσαις τὸ τῆς
10 δυνάμεως, ὡς εἴρηται· εἰ δὲ τῷ διακεῖσθαι τὸν φύσει
πυκτικὸν ποιὸν λέγομεν, οὐδὲν ἡ δύναμις προστεθεῖσα
ποιεῖ, ἐπεὶ καὶ ἐν ταῖς ἕξεσι δύναμις. ἔπειτα διὰ τί ὁ
κατὰ δύναμιν τοῦ κατὰ ἐπιστήμην διοίσει; ἢ εἰ ποιοί,
οὐδὲ διαφοραὶ ποιότητος αὗται, εἰ ὁ μὲν μελετήσας
15 ἔχοι, ὁ δὲ φύσει, ἀλλ' ἔξωθεν ἡ διαφορά· κατ' αὐτὸ δὲ τὸ
εἶδος τῆς πυκτικῆς πῶς; καὶ εἰ αἱ μὲν ἐκ πάθους, αἱ δὲ
οὔ· οὐ γὰρ διαφέρει ὁπόθεν ἡ ποιότης· λέγω δὲ
48

quality of the substrate is what comes upon it posterior to the substance. But the triangle is a quality of that in which it is, not simply and solely a triangle, but the triangle which is in this thing and in so far as it has shaped this thing. But did manhood also shape? Rather, it gave substance.

11. But if all this is so, why are there several species of quality, and why is there a difference between state and disposition? For there is no specific difference of quality involved in persistence and non-persistence, but any kind of disposition is sufficient to make something a quale; and persisting is an external addition; unless someone says that dispositions are only incomplete sort of shapes, but states are complete ones. But if they are incomplete, they are not yet qualities; but if they are already qualities, persistence is an addition. But how are natural powers another species [of quality]? For if they are qualities because of the powers, the power-characteristic does not fit all of them, as has been said; but if we say that the natural boxer is qualified by being so disposed, then the addition of "power" does nothing, since there is power in states also. Then why will [the boxer] by natural power differ from the [boxer] by knowledge? If they are both [pugilistically] qualified, these differences are not specific differences of quality, if one is a boxer by practice and one by nature, but the difference is external. But how [are they to be differentiated] in relation to the very form of boxing? And [the difference is external again] if some qualities derive from being affected, but others not: for the source of the quality does not make a specific difference; but what I am talking about is differentiation by vari-

ποιότητος παραλλαγαῖς καὶ διαφοραῖς. ἔχοι δ' ἂν
ζήτησιν καί, εἰ ἐκ πάθους αἵδε, αἱ μὲν οὕτως, αἱ δὲ μὴ
20 τῶν αὐτῶν, πῶς ἐν εἴδει τῷ αὐτῷ· καὶ εἰ αἱ μὲν τῷ
γεγονέναι, αἱ δὲ τῷ ποιεῖν, ὁμωνύμως ἂν εἶεν. τί δὲ ἡ
περὶ ἕκαστον μορφή; εἰ μὲν γὰρ καθὸ εἶδός ἐστιν
ἕκαστον, οὐ ποιόν· εἰ δὲ καθὸ καλὸν μετὰ τὸ τοῦ
ὑποκειμένου εἶδος ἢ αἰσχρόν, λόγον ἂν ἔχοι. τὸ δὲ τραχὺ
25 καὶ τὸ λεῖον καὶ τὸ ἀραιὸν καὶ τὸ πυκνὸν οὐκ ὀρθῶς ἂν
λέγοιτο ποιά; οὐ γὰρ δὴ ταῖς διαστάσεσι ταῖς ἀπ'
ἀλλήλων καὶ ⟨τῷ⟩[1] ἐγγὺς τὸ μανὸν καὶ τὸ πυκνὸν καὶ
τραχύτης, καὶ οὐ πανταχοῦ ἐξ ἀνωμαλίας θέσεως καὶ
ὁμαλότητος· εἰ δὲ καὶ ἐκ τούτων, οὐδὲν κωλύει καὶ ὡς
ποιὰ εἶναι. τὸ δὲ κοῦφον καὶ βαρὺ γνωσθὲν δηλώσει,
30 ὅπου δεῖ αὐτὰ θεῖναι. εἴη δ' ἂν καὶ ὁμωνυμία περὶ τὸ
κοῦφον, εἰ μὴ τῷ σταθμῷ λέγοιτο τοῦ πλείονος καὶ
ἐλάττονος, ἐν ᾧ καὶ τὸ ἰσχνὸν καὶ λεπτόν, ὃ ἐν ἄλλῳ
εἴδει παρὰ τὰ τέτταρα.

12. Ἀλλ' εἰ μὴ οὕτω τις ἀξιώσειε τὸ ποιὸν διαιρεῖν,
τίνι ἂν διέλοι; ἐπισκεπτέον οὖν, εἰ δεῖ τὰς μὲν σώματος

---

[1] F³ˢ (= Ficinus), Sleeman, Bréhier, Theiler: τὸ Enn.

---

[1] A critical reference to the discussion of "passive"
qualities in Aristotle *Categories* 8. 9a35–b11.

ations and specific differences of quality. But there would also be room for enquiry how qualities are members of the same species if these particular ones derive from being affected, some in this way, but others not even belonging to the same things; and if some [derive from being affected] by coming into being, but others by producing [the affection], they would be called qualities equivocally.[1] And what about the shape of each individual thing? For if this is meant in the sense in which each thing is form, the thing is not [in this sense] a quale; but if it is meant in the sense in which a thing is beautiful or ugly in a way posterior to the form of its substrate, there would be some sense in it. And would not the rough and the smooth and the rare and the dense be correctly called qualia? For it is certainly not by the distances [of the parts] from each other or their nearness that something is subtle or dense or there is roughness, and it is not everywhere the result of the irregularity or regularity of the position [of the parts]; and even if these were their origins, nothing prevents them even so from being qualia. And knowledge of light and heavy will reveal where one ought to put them. But there might be an ambiguity about "light" if it is not used in the sense of more and less weight, since it has in it the idea of "lean" and "fine", which is in another species besides the four.[2]

12. But if one does not think it proper to divide the quale in this way, in what way could one divide it? We should consider, then, if we ought to say that some qualities belong to the body and some to the

[2] There seems to be a reference here to Andronicus, who according to Simplicius *In Categ.* 8, 263. 19–22 made a special genus for λέπτον, παχύ etc.

λέγοντα, τὰς δὲ ψυχῆς, τοῦ δὲ σώματος μερίζειν κατὰ
τὰς αἰσθήσεις, τὰς μὲν ὄψει νέμοντα,[1] τὰς δ' ἀκοῇ ἢ
5 γεύσει, ἄλλας ὀσφρήσει ἢ ἁφῇ. τὰς δὲ τῆς ψυχῆς πῶς;
ἐπιθυμητικοῦ, θυμοειδοῦς, λογιστικοῦ. ἢ ταῖς
διαφοραῖς τῶν ἐνεργειῶν, αἳ γίνονται κατ' αὐτάς, ὅτι
γεννητικαὶ αὗται τούτων. ἢ τῷ ὠφελίμῳ καὶ βλαβερῷ·
καὶ πάλιν διαιρετέον τὰς ὠφελείας καὶ τὰς βλάβας. τὰ
10 αὐτὰ δὲ καὶ ἐπὶ τῶν σωματικῶν τῷ ποιεῖν διάφορα ἢ τῷ
ὠφελίμῳ καὶ βλαβερῷ· οἰκεῖαι γὰρ διαφοραὶ
ποιότητος. ἢ γὰρ δοκεῖ ἡ ὠφέλεια καὶ τὸ βλάβος ἀπὸ
τῆς ποιότητος καὶ ποιοῦ ἢ ζητητέον τρόπον ἄλλον.
ἐπισκεπτέον δέ, πῶς καὶ ὁ ποιὸς ὁ κατὰ τὴν ποιότητα
15 ἐν τῇ αὐτῇ ἔσται· οὐ γὰρ δὴ ἓν γένος ἀμφοῖν. καὶ εἰ ὁ
πυκτικὸς ἐν ποιότητι, πῶς οὐ καὶ ὁ ποιητικός; καὶ εἰ
τοῦτο, καὶ τὸ ποιητικόν· ὥστε οὐδὲν δεῖ εἰς τὸ πρός τι
τὸ ποιητικὸν οὐδ' αὖ τὸ παθητικόν, εἰ ὁ παθητικὸς
ποιός. καὶ ἴσως βέλτιον ἐνταῦθα ὁ ποιητικός, εἰ κατὰ
δύναμιν λέγεται, ἡ δὲ δύναμις ποιότης. εἰ δὲ κατ' οὐσίαν
20 ἡ δύναμις ἤ τις δύναμις, οὐδ' οὕτω πρός τι οὐδὲ ποιὸν
ἔτι. οὐδὲ γὰρ ὡς τὸ μεῖζον τὸ ποιητικόν· τὸ γὰρ μεῖζον
τὴν ὑπόστασιν, καθὸ μεῖζον, πρὸς τὸ ἔλαττον, τὸ δὲ
ποιητικὸν τῷ τοιῶνδε εἶναι ἤδη. ἀλλ' ἴσως κατὰ μὲν τὸ
τοιόνδε ποιόν, ᾗ δὲ δύναται εἰς ἄλλο ποιητικὸν

---

[1] Igal, H–S[2]: λέγοντα Enn.: διδόντα Theiler, H–S[1].

soul, and classify the bodily ones according to the senses, allotting some to sight and some to hearing or taste, and others to smell or touch. But how are we to classify those of the soul? As belonging to the appetitive, emotional or rational part. Or by the differences of the activities which occur in accordance with them, because these qualities are such as to produce these activities. Or by helpfulness and harmfulness; and again one must divide the helps and the harms. But the same grounds of differentiation apply to bodily qualities, by doing different things or by helpfulness and harmfulness: for these are proper differences of quality. For one either thinks that help and harm come from quality and the quale or one must adopt a different method of investigation. But we must consider also how the qualified by the quality is in the same category [as the quality]: for there is certainly not one genus for both. And if the boxer is in the category of quality, why not also the doer and maker? And if this is so, then also the ability to do and make; so that there is no need to refer doing to the relative, nor again the ability to be affected [by the doing] if the one who is affected is qualified [by the doing]. And perhaps the doer and maker is better placed here, if he is called so in regard of power, and power is quality. But if power, or any power, appertains to substance, it is not in this way either a relative, and not, furthermore, a quale. For ability to do is not like more: for the more has its reality, in so far as it is more, in relation to the less, but ability to do by being such as it is already. But perhaps it is a quale by being such as it is, but in so far as it has power directed to something else it is called ability to do as a relative.

25 λεγόμενον πρός τι. διὰ τί οὖν οὐ καὶ ὁ πυκτικὸς πρός τι,
καὶ ἡ πυκτικὴ αὐτή; πρὸς ἄλλον γὰρ ὅλως ἡ πυκτική·
καὶ γὰρ οὐδὲν αὐτῆς θεώρημα, ὃ μὴ πρὸς ἄλλο. καὶ περὶ
τῶν ἄλλων δὲ τεχνῶν ἢ τῶν πλείστων ἐπισκεπτέον καὶ
λεκτέον ἴσως· ᾗ μὲν διατιθεῖσι τὴν ψυχήν, ποιότητες, ᾗ
30 δὲ ποιοῦσι, ποιητικαὶ καὶ κατὰ τοῦτο πρὸς ἄλλον καὶ
πρός τι· ἐπεὶ καὶ ἄλλον τρόπον πρός τι, καθὸ ἕξεις
λέγονται. ἆρ᾽ οὖν ἄλλη τις ὑπόστασις κατὰ τὸ
ποιητικὸν τοῦ "ποιητικὸν" οὐκ ἄλλου τινὸς ὄντος ἢ
καθόσον ποιόν; τάχα μὲν γὰρ ἄν τις ἐπὶ τῶν ἐμψύχων
35 καὶ ἔτι μᾶλλον ἐπὶ τῶν προαίρεσιν ἐχόντων τῷ
νενευκέναι πρὸς τὸ ποιεῖν [1] ὑπόστασιν εἶναι καὶ κατὰ τὸ
ποιητικόν· ἐπὶ δὲ τῶν ἀψύχων δυνάμεων, ἃς ποιότητας
εἴπομεν, τί τὸ ποιητικόν; ἢ ὅταν συντύχῃ αὐτῷ ἄλλο,
ἀπέλαυσε καὶ μετέλαβε [2] παρ᾽ ἐκείνου οὗ ἔχει. εἰ δὲ τὸ
αὐτὸ καὶ ποιεῖ εἰς ἄλλο καὶ πάσχει, πῶς ἔτι τὸ
40 ποιητικόν; ἐπεὶ καὶ τὸ μεῖζον τρίπηχυ ὂν καθ᾽ αὑτὸ καὶ
μεῖζον καὶ ἔλαττον ἐν τῇ συντυχίᾳ τῇ πρὸς ἄλλο. ἀλλ᾽
ἐρεῖ τις τὸ μεῖζον καὶ τὸ ἔλαττον μεταλήψει μεγέθους
καὶ μικρότητος· ἢ καὶ τοῦτο μεταλήψει ποιητικοῦ καὶ
παθητικοῦ. ζητητέον δὲ καὶ ἐνταῦθα καὶ εἰ αἱ τῇδε

---

[1] Kirchhoff (*ad faciendum* Ficinus): ποιὸν Enn.
[2] UF³ᵐᵍ (= Ficinus), Creuzer: μετέβαλε wBxC, H-S.

---

[1] This is common Platonic doctrine: cp. *Phaedo* 100E5–6.
But Plotinus is anxious, as appears in what follows, that it
should not be interpreted in a way which asserts that there

Why then is not the boxer relative, and boxing itself? For boxing is altogether directed to somebody else: for certainly there is no part of the art which is not other-directed. And perhaps we should consider and speak of the other arts, or most of them, like this: in so far as they dispose the soul, they are qualities, but in so far as they do or make they belong to the category of doing and making, and in this way are other-directed and relative; since they are also relative in another way, in that they are called states. Is there then another reality of the doer and maker, according to its ability to do and make, when it is not another thing than it is in so far as it is a quale? Perhaps in the case of living things, and still more those which have the power of choice, one might say that there is a reality in them also according to their capacity to do and make, because of their inclination to act so; but in the case of lifeless powers, which we call qualities, why bring in doing and making? Now, whenever a thing encounters another, it gets something from it and takes a share from that other of what it has. But if the same thing both acts on and is affected by something else, how is doing and making still there? Since the more also is three cubits long in itself and is more or less on the occasions when it meets something else. But someone will say that the greater and the less are so by participation in largeness and smallness[1]; so this [acting on and being affected] will also be by participation in activity and passivity. But one must

are Forms of qualities, and contradicts his own doctrine that there are no qualities in the intelligible world, but what we call qualities here below are activities of substances there. See II. 6 and VI. 2. 14.

45 ποιότητες καὶ αἱ ἐκεῖ ὑφ' ἕν· τοῦτο δὲ πρὸς τοὺς
τιθεμένους κἀκεῖ· ἢ κἂν μὴ εἴδη τις διδῷ, ἀλλὰ νοῦν
λέγων εἰ ἕξιν λέγοι, ἢ κοινόν τι ἐπ' ἐκείνης καὶ ταύτης
τῆς ἕξεως· καὶ σοφία δὲ συγχωρεῖται. ἢ εἰ ὁμώνυμος
πρὸς τὴν ἐνταῦθα, οὐκ ἠρίθμηται δηλονότι ἐν τούτοις·
50 εἰ δὲ συνωνύμως, ἔσται τὸ ποιὸν κοινὸν ἐνταῦθα κἀκεῖ,
εἰ μή τις τἀκεῖ λέγοι πάντα οὐσίας· καὶ τὸ νοεῖν τοίνυν.
ἀλλὰ τοῦτο κοινὸν καὶ πρὸς τὰς ἄλλας κατηγορίας, [ἢ]¹
εἰ τὸ διττὸν ὧδε κἀκεῖ, ἢ ὑφ' ἕν ἄμφω.

13. Περὶ δὲ τοῦ ποτὲ ὧδε ἐπισκεπτέον· εἰ τὸ χθὲς
καὶ αὔριον καὶ πέρυσι καὶ τὰ τοιαῦτα μέρη χρόνου, διὰ
τί οὐκ ἐν τῷ αὐτῷ ἔσται καὶ ταῦτα, ἐν ᾧπερ καὶ ὁ
χρόνος; ἐπεὶ καὶ τὸ ἦν καὶ τὸ ἔστι καὶ τὸ ἔσται, εἴδη
5 ὄντα χρόνου, δίκαιον δήπου ἐν ᾧ ὁ χρόνος τετάχθαι.
λέγεται δὲ τοῦ ποσοῦ ὁ χρόνος· ὥστε τί δεῖ κατηγορίας
ἄλλης; εἰ δὲ λέγοιεν ὡς οὐ μόνον χρόνος τὸ ἦν καὶ ἔσται,

¹ del. Kirchhoff.

---

¹ A Peripatetic would deny the Forms, but admit a
transcendent incorporeal Νοῦς and σοφία (which Plotinus,
as usual, interprets in his own way).
² In ch. 5 Plotinus makes it clear that time is not
quantity, though definite lengths of time are quanta; cp.
also VI. 3. 11. His doctrine of time in this treatise is by no
means as developed and carefully thought out as it is in the

enquire here also if the qualities here and those in the intelligible world come under one genus: this is directed to those who posit qualities in the intelligible world as well; or even if someone does not grant that there are Forms, all the same when he speaks of intelligence,[1] if he is speaking of a state, he certainly [implies that there is] something common to the state in the intelligible world and this one here; and it is agreed that there is wisdom. Now if the term "wisdom" is used of it equivocally in relation to the wisdom here below, it is clearly not counted among the things of this world; but if it is used univocally then the quale will be common to both worlds, unless someone says that all the things in the intelligible world belong to the category of substance; in which case being intelligent will be substance there too. But this is a general question about the other categories as well, whether there are two genera here and there, or whether both fall under one.

13. About the "when" we must enquire in this way: if the "yesterday" and "to-morrow" and "last year" and such are parts of time, why are not these also in the same genus in which time is too? Since it is surely right that the "was" and the "is" and the "will be", being parts of time, should be classed in the same genus in which time is. But time is said to belong to the quantum[2]: so what need is there of another category? But if they were to say that it is not only time that the "was" and the "will be"

treatise which follows *On The Kinds of Being* in Porphyry's chronological order, III. 7 (45) *On Eternity and Time*, perhaps written because Plotinus did not feel that he had dealt with time adequately in *On The Kinds of Being*.

καὶ τὸ χθὲς καὶ πέρυσι, τὰ ὑπὸ τὸ ἦν—ὑποβεβλῆσθαι
γὰρ δεῖ ταῦτα τῷ ἦν—ἀλλ' οὖν¹ οὐ μόνον χρόνος, ἀλλὰ
10 ποτὲ χρόνος, πρῶτον μὲν ἔσται, εἰ τὸ "ποτὲ χρόνος",
χρόνος· ἔπειτα, εἰ χρόνος παρεληλυθὼς τὸ χθές,
σύνθετόν τι ἔσται, εἰ ἕτερον τὸ παρεληλυθὸς καὶ ἕτερον
ὁ χρόνος· δύο οὖν κατηγορίαι καὶ οὐχ ἁπλοῦν. εἰ δὲ τὸ ἐν
χρόνῳ φήσουσι τὸ ποτὲ εἶναι, ἀλλ' οὐ χρόνον, τοῦτο
15 τὸ ἐν χρόνῳ εἰ μὲν τὸ πρᾶγμα λέγουσιν, οἷον Σωκράτης
ὅτι πέρυσιν ἦν, ὁ μὲν Σωκράτης ἔξωθεν ἂν εἴη, καὶ οὐχ
ἕν τι λέγουσιν. ἀλλὰ Σωκράτης ἢ ἡ πρᾶξις ἐν τούτῳ τῷ
χρόνῳ τί ἂν εἴη ἢ ἐν μέρει τοῦ χρόνου; εἰ δ' ὅτι μέρος
χρόνου λέγουσι, καὶ καθότι μέρος ἀξιοῦσι μὴ χρόνον
ἁπλῶς τι λέγειν, ἀλλὰ μέρος χρόνου παρεληλυθός,
20 πλείω ποιοῦσι, καὶ τὸ μέρος ᾗ μέρος πρός τι ὂν
προσλαμβάνουσι. καὶ τὸ παρεληλυθὸς ἐγκείμενον τί
αὐτοῖς ἔσται ἢ τὸ αὐτὸ τῷ ἦν, ὃ ἦν εἶδος χρόνου; ἀλλ' εἰ
τῷ ἀόριστον μὲν εἶναι τὸ ἦν, τὸ δὲ χθὲς καὶ τὸ πέρυσιν
ὡρίσθαι, πρῶτον μὲν τὸ ἦν ποῦ τάξομεν; ἔπειτα τὸ χθὲς
25 ἔσται "ἦν ὡρισμένον", ὥστε ἔσται ὡρισμένος χρόνος τὸ
χθές· τοῦτο δὲ ποσός τις χρόνος· ὥστε, εἰ χρόνος ποσόν,
ποσὸν ὡρισμένον ἕκαστον τούτων ἔσται. εἰ δέ, ὅταν
λέγωσι χθές, τοῦτο λέγομεν, ὡς ἐν χρόνῳ παρεληλυθότι
ὡρισμένῳ γέγονε τόδε, ἔτι πλείω καὶ μᾶλλον λέγουσιν·
30 ἔπειτα, εἰ δεῖ ἐπεισάγειν ἄλλας κατηγορίας τῷ ἕτερον
ἐν ἑτέρῳ ποιεῖν, ὡς ἐνταῦθα τὸ ἐν χρόνῳ, ἄλλας πολλὰς

---

¹ R²ᵐᵍ (inquam Ficinus): om. Enn.

are, and the "yesterday" and "last year"—for these must be classed under the "was"—but (as was just said) not only time but some time, then, first of all, if it is "some time" it will be time: then, if the "yesterday" is time past, it will be something composite, if past is one thing and time is another: two categories, then, and not something single and simple. But if they are going to assert that what is when is that which is in time, but not time, if they mean by this "in time" the state of affairs, for example that Socrates was last year, the "Socrates" would be brought in from outside, and they are not talking about one thing. But what would Socrates or the affair in this particular time be except in a part of time? But if because they say "a part of time", and in that it is a part claim that they are not saying that something is simply time, but a past part of time, they are making still more, and are adding on the part *qua* part, which is a relative. And will the past be for them either something included in or the same as the "was", which was a part of time? But if [they make their distinction] because the "was" is indefinite, but the "yesterday" and the "last year" are defined, first of all, where are we going to class the "was"? Since the "yesterday" will be a "definite was", so that the "yesterday" will be a definite time; but this is a time of a certain quantity: so that, if time is a quantum, each of these will be a definite quantum. But if, whenever they say "yesterday", we take this to mean that this particular thing happened in a past definite time, they are mentioning still more and more things; then, if one must introduce other categories by putting one thing in another, as in this case what is in time, we shall discover many others

ἀνευρήσομεν ἀπὸ τοῦ ποιεῖν ἄλλο ἐν ἄλλῳ. λεχθήσεται
δὲ σαφέστερον ἐν τοῖς ἑξῆς τοῖς περὶ τοῦ ποῦ.

14. Τὸ δὲ ποῦ, ἐν Λυκίῳ καὶ ἐν Ἀκαδημίᾳ. ἡ μὲν
οὖν Ἀκαδημία καὶ τὸ Λύκιον πάντως τόποι καὶ μέρη
τόπου, ὥσπερ τὸ ἄνω καὶ τὸ κάτω καὶ τὸ ὡδὶ εἴδη ἢ
μέρη· διαφέρει δέ, ὅτι ἀφωρισμένως μᾶλλον. εἰ οὖν τὸ
5 ἄνω καὶ τὸ κάτω καὶ τὸ μέσον τόποι, οἷον Δελφοὶ τὸ
μέσον, καὶ τὸ παρὰ τὸ μέσον, οἷον Ἀθῆναι καὶ Λύκιον
δὴ καὶ τὰ ἄλλα, τί δεῖ παρὰ τὸν τόπον ζητεῖν ἡμᾶς καὶ
ταῦτα λέγοντας τόπον ἐφ᾽ ἑκάστου τούτων σημαίνειν; εἰ
δὲ ἄλλο ἐν ἄλλῳ λέγομεν, οὐχ ἓν λέγομεν οὐδὲ ἁπλοῦν
10 λέγομεν. ἔπειτα, εἰ τοῦτον ἐνταῦθα λέγομεν, σχέσιν
τινὰ γεννῶμεν τοῦδε ἐν τῷδε καὶ τοῦ δεξαμένου πρὸς ὃ
ἐδέξατο· διὰ τί οὖν οὐ πρός τι, εἰ ἐκ τῆς ἑκατέρου πρὸς
ἑκάτερον σχέσεως ἀπεγεννήθη τι; εἶτα ⟨τί⟩[1] διαφέρει
τὸ ὧδε τοῦ Ἀθήνησιν; ἀλλὰ τὸ ὧδε τὸ δεικτικὸν τόπον
15 φήσουσι σημαίνειν· ὥστε καὶ τὸ Ἀθήνησιν· ὥστε τοῦ
τόπου τὸ Ἀθήνησιν. εἶτα, εἰ τὸ Ἀθήνησι τοῦτό ἐστι τὸ
"ἐν Ἀθήναις ἐστί", πρὸς τῷ τόπῳ καὶ τὸ ἔστι
προσκατηγορεῖται· δεῖ δὲ οὔ· ὥσπερ οὐδὲ τὸ "ποιότης
ἐστίν", ἀλλὰ τὸ "ποιότης" μόνον. πρὸς δὲ τούτοις, εἰ τὸ

[1] Creuzer.

from putting one thing in another. But this will be explained more clearly in the next discussion about the "where".

14. The "where", in the Lyceum and in the Academy. Now Academy and Lyceum are in every sense places, and parts of place, just as the "above" and the "here" are species or parts of place; the difference is only that Academy and Lyceum are more closely demarcated. If then the "above" and the "below" and the "middle" are places, Delphi, for instance, the middle,[1] and also the "to one side of middle", Athens and the Lyceum and the rest, for instance, why do we have to look for anything besides place, especially when we say that when we mention each and every one of them we are indicating a place? But if we are talking about one thing in another we are not talking about one thing and are not talking about anything simple either. Then further, when we say that this man is here, we are generating a relational state, of this man in this place and of the receptacle to what it receives: why then is there not a relation, if something was produced from the relatedness of one thing to the other? Then why is "here" different from "at Athens"? But they will assert that "here" signifies that which declares place; therefore so does "at Athens": so that "at Athens" belongs to place. Then, if this "in Athens" means "is in Athens", the "is" category is added to that of place; but it ought not to be added: just as one does not say "quality is", but only "quality". And, over and above all this, if what is in

---

[1] The ὀμφαλός, the navel-stone at Delphi, was in Greek tradition the central point of the earth.

20 ἐν χρόνῳ ἄλλο καὶ τὸ ἐν τόπῳ ἄλλο παρὰ χρόνον καὶ
τόπον, διὰ τί οὐ καὶ τὸ ἐν ἀγγείῳ ἄλλην κατηγορίαν
ποιήσει, καὶ τὸ ἐν ὕλῃ ἄλλο, καὶ τὸ ἐν ὑποκειμένῳ ἄλλο,
καὶ τὸ ἐν ὅλῳ μέρος καὶ τὸ ὅλον ἐν μέρεσι, καὶ γένος ἐν
εἴδεσι καὶ εἶδος ἐν γένει; καὶ οὕτως ἡμῖν πλείους αἱ
κατηγορίαι ἔσονται.

15. Ἐν δὲ τῷ ποιεῖν λεγομένῳ τάδ᾽ ἄν τις
ἐπισκέψαιτο. λέγεται γάρ· ὡς, ἐπεὶ μετὰ τὴν οὐσίαν τὰ
περὶ τὴν οὐσίαν ἦν ποσότης καὶ ἀριθμός, τὸ ποσὸν γένος
ἕτερον ἦν, καὶ ποιότητος οὔσης περὶ αὐτὴν ἄλλο γένος
5 τὸ ποιόν, οὕτω καὶ ποιήσεως οὔσης ἄλλο γένος τὸ
ποιεῖν. ἆρ᾽ οὖν τὸ ποιεῖν ἢ ἡ ποίησις, ἀφ᾽ ἧς τὸ ποιεῖν,
ὥσπερ καὶ ποιότης, ἀφ᾽ ἧς τὸ ποιόν; ἢ ἐνταῦθα ποίησις,
ποιεῖν, ποιῶν, ἢ ποιεῖν καὶ ποίησις εἰς ἓν ληπτέα;
ἐμφαίνει δὲ μᾶλλον τὸ ποιεῖν καὶ τὸν ποιοῦντα, ἡ δὲ
10 ποίησις οὔ· καὶ τὸ ποιεῖν ἐν ποιήσει εἶναί τινι, τοῦτο δὲ
ἐνεργείᾳ. ὥστε ἐνέργειαν μᾶλλον εἶναι τὴν κατηγορίαν,
ἢ περὶ τὴν οὐσίαν[1] λέγεται θεωρεῖσθαι, ὡς ἐκεῖ
ποιότης. καὶ ⟨εἰ⟩[2] αὐτὴ περὶ τὴν οὐσίαν ὥσπερ

---

[1] περὶ τὴν οὐσίαν del. Theiler, H–S[1].
[2] Igal, H–S[2].

time is something else besides time and what is in place is something else besides place, why will not what is in a pot make another category, and why is not what is in matter something else, and what is in a substrate something else, and the part in the whole and the whole in the parts, and the genus in the species and the species in the genus? And so we shall have more categories.

15. But in what is called "acting" [or doing and making][1] these are the points which one would enquire into. For it is said that, since after substance there were the accompaniments of substance, quantity and number, the quantum was another genus, and because quality accompanies substance the quale was another genus; so, since there is activity, acting is another genus. Is the genus then the acting or the activity from which the acting comes, just like the quality from which the quale comes? Or in this case are activity, acting and the agent, or acting and activity, to be included in one genus? But acting indicates more clearly that there is also the agent, but activity does not; and acting is in some kind of activity, that is, of active actuality. So would active actuality rather be the category, which is said to be observed as an accompaniment of substance, like quality in the other case? And [is there a question] whether active actuality is an accompaniment of substance just like movement? And the movement of

---

[1] ποιεῖν and ἐνέργεια present considerable difficulties to the translator. "Doing and making" and "active actuality" go some way towards bringing out the full range of meaning of the two words, but are too cumbersome to use continually and not always necessary. Various more or less unsatisfactory compromises will be detected in what follows.

κίνησις, καὶ ἓν γένος ἡ κίνησις τῶν ὄντων. διὰ τί γὰρ
ποιότης μὲν ἔν τι περὶ τὴν οὐσίαν, καὶ ποσότης ἔν τι,
15 καὶ πρός τι διὰ τὴν σχέσιν ἄλλου πρὸς ἄλλο, κινήσεως
δὲ περὶ τὴν οὐσίαν οὔσης οὐκ ἔσται τι καὶ κίνησις ἓν
γένος;

16. Εἰ δέ τις λέγοι τὴν κίνησιν ἀτελῆ
ἐνέργειαν εἶναι, οὐδὲν ἐκώλυε τὴν μὲν ἐνέργειαν
προτάττειν, εἶδος δὲ τὴν κίνησιν ὡς ἀτελῆ οὖσαν
ὑποβάλλειν, κατηγορούντά γε αὐτῆς τὴν ἐνέργειαν,
5 προστιθέντα δὲ τὸ ἀτελές. τὸ γὰρ ἀτελὲς λέγεται περὶ
αὐτῆς, οὐχ ὅτι οὐδὲ ἐνέργεια, ἀλλὰ ἐνέργεια μὲν
πάντως, ἔχει δὲ καὶ τὸ πάλιν καὶ πάλιν, οὐχ ἵνα
ἀφίκηται εἰς ἐνέργειαν—ἔστι γὰρ ἤδη—ἀλλ᾽ ἵνα
ἐργάσηταί τι, ὃ ἕτερόν ἐστι μετ᾽ αὐτήν. καὶ οὐκ αὐτὴ
τελειοῦται τότε, ἀλλὰ τὸ πρᾶγμα οὗ ἐστοχάζετο· οἷον
10 βάδισις ἐξ ἀρχῆς βάδισις ἦν. εἰ δ᾽ ἔδει στάδιον διανύσαι,
οὔπω δὲ ἦν διανύσας, τὸ ἐλλεῖπον οὐ τῆς βαδίσεως οὐδὲ
τῆς κινήσεως ἦν, ἀλλὰ τῆς ποσῆς βαδίσεως· βάδισις δὲ
ἦν καὶ ὁποσηοῦν καὶ κίνησις ἤδη· ὁ γοῦν κινούμενος καὶ
ἤδη κεκίνηται, καὶ ὁ τέμνων ἤδη ἔτεμε. καὶ ὡς ἡ
15 λεγομένη ἐνέργεια οὐ δεῖται χρόνου, οὕτως οὐδ᾽ ἡ
κίνησις, ἀλλ᾽ ἡ εἰς τοσοῦτον κίνησις· καὶ εἰ ἐν ἀχρόνῳ ἡ
ἐνέργεια, καὶ ἡ κίνησις ᾗ ὅλως κίνησις. εἰ δ᾽ ὅτι τὸ

[1] The reference here is to the "Platonic Category" of the intelligible world κίνησις (Plato Sophist 254D); see VI. 2. 7–8.

real beings is one genus.[1] For why is quality one single accompaniment of substance, and quality one, and the relative one because of the state of relatedness of one thing to another, but, when movement is an accompaniment of substance, will movement also not be a single genus?

16. But if someone were to say that movement was an incomplete active actuality,[2] nothing would prevent us from giving active actuality the priority and subordinating movement to it as a species as being incomplete, making its category active actuality, but adding the "incomplete". For the "incomplete" is said about it, not because it is not also active actuality, but it is altogether active actuality, but has also the "over and over again", not that it may arrive at active actuality—it is that already, but that it may do something, which is another thing subsequent to itself. And then [when it does do it] it is not itself brought to completion, but the business which was its object: walking, for instance, was walking from the beginning. But if one had to complete a lap, and had not yet arrived at the point of having completed it, what was lacking would not belong to walking or movement, but to walking a certain distance; but it was already walking, however short the walk was, and movement: for certainly the man who is in motion has already moved, and the man who is cutting, cut already. And just as what is called active actuality does not need time, so neither does movement, but [only] movement to a certain extent; and if active actuality is in timelessness, so is movement in that it is in a general way

[2] This is Aristotle's doctrine. See *Physics* Γ 2. 201b31–32; *Metaphysics* K 9. 1066a20–21.

συνεχὲς προσλαβοῦσα πάντως ἐν χρόνῳ, καὶ ἡ ὅρασις
μὴ διαλείπουσα τὸ ὁρᾶν ἐν συνεχείᾳ ἂν εἴη καὶ ἐν χρόνῳ.
20 μαρτυρεῖ δὲ τούτῳ καὶ ἡ ἀλογία[1] ἡ λέγουσα ἀεὶ οἷόν τε
εἶναι λαμβάνειν ἡστινοσοῦν κινήσεως καὶ μὴ εἶναι μήτε
τοῦ χρόνου ἀρχὴν ἐν ᾧ καὶ ἀφ' οὗ ἤρξατο μήτε αὐτῆς
ἀρχὴν τῆς κινήσεως, ἀλλ' εἶναι αὐτὴν διαιρεῖν ἐπὶ τὸ
ἄνω· ὥστε ἐξ ἀπείρου συμβαίνοι ἂν τοῦ χρόνου
25 κεκινῆσθαι τὴν ἄρτι ἀρξαμένην καὶ αὐτὴν ἄπειρον εἰς τὸ
ἀρξάμενον εἶναι. τοῦτο γὰρ συμβαίνει διὰ τὸ χωρίζειν
ἐνέργειαν κινήσεως καὶ τὴν μὲν ἐν ἀχρόνῳ φάσκειν
γενέσθαι, τὴν δὲ χρόνου δεῖσθαι λέγειν μὴ τὴν τόσην
μόνον, ἀλλ' ὅλως τὴν φύσιν αὐτῆς ἀναγκάζεσθαι ποσὴν
λέγειν καίτοι ὁμολογοῦντας καὶ αὐτοὺς κατὰ
30 συμβεβηκὸς τὸ ποσὸν αὐτῇ παρεῖναι, εἰ ἡμερησία εἴη ἢ
ὁποσουοῦν χρόνου. ὥσπερ οὖν ἐνέργεια ἐν ἀχρόνῳ,
οὕτως οὐδὲν κωλύει καὶ κίνησιν ἦρχθαι ἐν ἀχρόνῳ, ὁ δὲ
χρόνος τῷ τοσῷδε γεγονέναι. ἐπεὶ καὶ μεταβολαὶ ἐν
ἀχρόνῳ ὁμολογοῦνται γίγνεσθαι ἐν τῷ λέγεσθαι
35 ὥσπερ   οὐ   καὶ   ἀθρόας   γιγνομένης
μεταβολῆς. εἰ οὖν μεταβολή, διὰ τί οὐχὶ καὶ
κίνησις; εἴληπται δὲ μεταβολὴ οὐκ ἐν τῷ
μεταβεβληκέναι· οὐ γὰρ τῆς ἐν τῷ μεταβεβληκέναι
ἐδεῖτο.

17. Εἰ δέ τις λέγοι μήτε τὴν ἐνέργειαν μήτε τὴν
κίνησιν γένους δεῖσθαι καθ' αὑτά, ἀλλ' εἰς τὸ πρός τι

---

[1] Theiler, Harder, Cilento: ἀναλογία Enn.

movement. But if it must be in every way in time because it has acquired the character of continuity, then sight which does not interrupt its seeing would be in continuity and in time. There is evidence for this in the stupid statement which says that it is always possible to take a piece of any movement whatever, and there is not a beginning of the time in which and from which it began, nor a beginning of the movement itself, but it is always possible to divide it up and back: so that it would result that the movement which has just begun has been in motion from infinite time, and that movement is infinite in respect of its beginning. This results because of separating of active actuality from movement and asserting that active actuality occurs in timelessness, but saying that movement needs time, not movement of a certain length only; but they are compelled to say that its nature is quantitative; and yet even they admit that the quantum is incidentally present to it, if it is a day long or of any time you like. Therefore, just as active actuality is in timelessness, so nothing prevents movement from originating in timelessness, but time has come by its becoming of a certain length. Since changes also are admitted to take place in timelessness, in the remark "as if there was not a change which takes place all at once".[1] If then change, why not also motion? But change has here been taken, not in the sense of completed change: for there was no need of change in completion of the process of change.

17. But if someone were to say that neither active actuality nor movement need a genus in and by

[1] Aristotle *Physics* A 3. 186a15–16.

ἀνάγειν τῷ τὴν μὲν ἐνέργειαν τοῦ δυνάμει εἶναι
ἐνεργητικοῦ, τὴν δὲ τοῦ δυνάμει κινητικοῦ ἢ κινητοῦ,
5 λεκτέον ὡς τὰ μὲν πρός τι αὐτὴ ἡ σχέσις ἐγέννα, ἀλλ᾽ οὐ
τῷ πρὸς ἕτερον μόνον λέγεσθαι. ὅταν δὲ ᾖ τις
ὑπόστασις, κἂν ἑτέρου ᾖ κἂν πρὸς ἕτερον, τήν γε πρὸ
τοῦ πρός τι εἴληχε φύσιν. αὕτη τοίνυν ἡ ἐνέργεια καὶ ἡ
κίνησις καὶ ἡ ἕξις δὲ ἑτέρου οὖσα οὐκ ἀφῄρηται τὸ πρὸ
10 τοῦ πρός τι εἶναί τε καὶ νοεῖσθαι καθ᾽ αὑτά· ἢ οὕτω
πάντα ἔσται πρός τι· πάντως γὰρ ἔχει ὁτιοῦν σχέσιν
πρὸς ὁτιοῦν, ὡς καὶ ἐπὶ τῆς ψυχῆς. αὐτή τε ἡ ποίησις
καὶ τὸ ποιεῖν διὰ τί εἰς τὸ πρός τι οὐκ ἀναχθήσεται; ἢ
γὰρ κίνησις ἢ ἐνέργεια πάντως ἔσται. εἰ δὲ τὴν μὲν
15 ποίησιν εἰς τὸ πρός τι ἀνάξουσι, τὸ δὲ ποιεῖν ἓν γένος
θήσονται, διὰ τί οὐ καὶ τὴν μὲν κίνησιν εἰς τὸ πρός τι, τὸ
δὲ κινεῖσθαι ἕν τι γένος θήσονται, καὶ διαιρήσονται τὸ
κινεῖσθαι ὡς ἐν διχῇ ἐν εἴδεσι τοῦ ποιεῖν καὶ τοῦ
πάσχειν, ἀλλ᾽ οὐχ ὡς νῦν τὸ μὲν ποιεῖν λέγουσι, τὸ δὲ
πάσχειν;

18. Ἐπισκεπτέον δέ, εἰ ἐν τῷ ποιεῖν τὰς μὲν
ἐνεργείας φήσουσι, τὰς δὲ κινήσεις, τὰς μὲν ἐνεργείας
λέγοντες εἶναι τὰς ἀθρόας, τὰς δὲ κινήσεις, οἷον τὸ
τέμνειν—ἐν χρόνῳ γὰρ τὸ τέμνειν—ἢ πάσας κινήσεις ἢ
5 μετὰ κινήσεως, καὶ εἰ πάσας πρὸς τὸ πάσχειν τὰς

themselves, but they are to be referred to the relative in that active actuality belongs to that which is potentially active and actual, and movement to that which is potentially moving or moved, one must answer that it is the very state of relatedness which produces relatives, and they are not produced by the mere statement that a thing is related to another. But when there is some substantial reality, even if it belongs to something else or is related to something else, it certainly possesses its nature prior to the relativity. This active actuality, then, and movement and state, though belonging to another, do not lose their priority to the relative and being thought in and by themselves; otherwise in this way everything will be relative: for absolutely everything has a relation to something, as in the case of the soul. And why are not activity and acting to be referred to the relative? For movement and active actuality will be altogether so. But if they are going to refer activity to the relative, but make one genus of acting, why will they not refer movement to the relative, but posit being in motion as one genus, and divide being in motion, as one genus, into two, into the species of acting and being acted upon, instead of, as they do now, saying that acting is one genus and being acted upon another?

18. But we must investigate whether they are going to assert that in acting some activities are active actualities and some are movements, saying that those which occur all at once are active actualities and the others are movements, cutting for instance—for cutting goes on in time—or whether they are all movements or accompanied by movement; and whether all activities are related to passi-

ποιήσεις ἤ τινας καὶ ἀπολύτους, οἷον τὸ βαδίζειν καὶ τὸ
λέγειν, καὶ εἰ τὰς πρὸς τὸ πάσχειν πάσας κινήσεις, τὰς
δ' ἀπολύτους ἐνεργείας, ἢ ἐν ἑκατέροις ἑκάτερον. τὸ
γοῦν βαδίζειν ἀπολελυμένον ὂν κίνησιν ἂν εἴποιεν, τὸ δὲ
10 νοεῖν οὐκ ἔχον τὸ πάσχον καὶ αὐτὸ ἐνέργειαν, οἶμαι. ἢ
οὐδὲ ποιεῖν φατέον τὸ νοεῖν καὶ τὸ βαδίζειν. ἀλλ' εἰ μὴ
ἐν τῷ ποιεῖν ταῦτα, ποῦ λεκτέον· τάχα δὲ τὸ νοεῖν πρὸς
τὸ νοητόν, ὥσπερ τὴν νόησιν. καὶ γὰρ τὴν αἴσθησιν
πρὸς τὸ αἰσθητόν· ἀλλ' εἰ κἀκεῖ τὴν αἴσθησιν πρὸς τὸ
15 αἰσθητόν, διὰ τί αὐτὸ τὸ αἰσθάνεσθαι οὐκέτι πρὸς τὸ
αἰσθητόν; καὶ ἡ αἴσθησις δέ, εἰ πρὸς ἕτερον, σχέσιν μὲν
ἔχει πρὸς ἐκεῖνο, ἔχει δέ τι παρὰ τὴν σχέσιν, τὸ ἢ
ἐνέργεια ἢ πάθος εἶναι. εἰ οὖν τὸ πάθος παρὰ τό τινος
εἶναι καὶ ὑπό τινος ἔστι τι ἕτερον, καὶ ἡ ἐνέργεια. ἡ δὲ
20 δὴ βάδισις ἔχουσα καὶ αὐτὴ τό τινος εἶναι καὶ ποδῶν
εἶναι καὶ ὑπό τινος ἔχει τὸ κίνησις εἶναι. ἔχοι ἂν οὖν καὶ
ἡ νόησις παρὰ τὸ πρός τι τὸ ἢ κίνησις εἶναι ἢ ἐνέργεια.

19. Ἐπισκεπτέον δέ, εἰ καί τινες ἐνέργειαι δόξουσιν
ἀτελεῖς εἶναι μὴ προσλαβοῦσαι χρόνον, ὥστε εἰς ταὐτὸν

vity, or there are also some which are independent, walking and talking for instance, and whether all the activities which are related to passivity are movements, but the independent ones are active actualities, or whether there are some of each in each class. Walking at any rate, which is independent, they would say was a movement, but thinking, though it also has no passivity, an active actuality, I suppose. Or else it must be asserted that thinking and walking are not included in acting at all. But if they are not in acting, it must be said where they are; but perhaps the act of thinking is related to the object of thought just as thought [in general] is. For certainly sense perception is related to the sense-object; but if in that case sense-perception is related to the sense-object, why is not the actual [particular] act of sense-perception any longer related to the sense-object? And sense-perception, even if it is related to something else, has indeed a relatedness to that something, but has something over and above the relatedness, the being either an active actuality or a passive experience. If then the passive experience, over and above belonging to something and being caused by some agent, is something different so also is the active actuality. Certainly walking, which itself also has the characteristics of belonging to something, and in fact belonging to the feet, and of being caused by an agent, has the being a movement. Therefore thought also, over and above its relation, has the being either a movement or an active actuality.

19. But we must investigate whether some active actualities are going to appear as incomplete without acquiring an addition of time, so that they will

ταῖς κινήσεσιν ἐλθεῖν, οἷον τὸ ζῆν καὶ ἡ ζωή. ἐν χρόνῳ
γὰρ τελείῳ τὸ ζῆν ἑκάστου καὶ ἡ εὐδαιμονία ἐνέργεια
5 οὐκ ἐν ἀμερεῖ, ἀλλὰ οἷον ἀξιοῦσι καὶ τὴν κίνησιν εἶναι.
ὥστε κινήσεις ἄμφω λεκτέον, καὶ ἕν τι τὴν κίνησιν καὶ
γένος ἕν, θεωροῦντας παρὰ τὸ ποσὸν τὸ ἐν τῇ οὐσίᾳ καὶ
τὸ ποιὸν καὶ κίνησιν οὖσαν περὶ αὐτήν. καί, εἰ βούλει,
τὰς μὲν σωματικάς, τὰς δὲ ψυχικάς, ἢ τὰς μὲν παρ᾽
10 αὐτῶν, τὰς δὲ ὑπ᾽ ἄλλων εἰς αὐτά, ἢ τὰς μέν ἐξ αὐτῶν,
τὰς δὲ ἐξ ἄλλων, καὶ τὰς μὲν ἐξ αὐτῶν ποιήσεις εἴτε εἰς
ἄλλα εἴτε ἀπολελυμένας, τὰς δὲ ἐξ ἄλλων πείσεις.
καίτοι καὶ αἱ εἰς ἄλλα κινήσεις αἱ αὐταὶ ταῖς ἐξ ἄλλων·
ἡ γὰρ τμῆσις, ἥ τε παρὰ τοῦ τέμνοντος ἥ τε ἐν τῷ
15 τεμνομένῳ, μία, ἀλλὰ τὸ τέμνειν ἕτερον καὶ τὸ
τέμνεσθαι. τάχα δὲ οὐδὲ μία ἡ τμῆσις ἡ ἀπὸ τοῦ
τέμνοντος καὶ ἡ ἐν τῷ τεμνομένῳ, ἀλλ᾽ ἔστι τὸ τέμνειν
τὸ ἐκ τῆς τοιᾶσδε ἐνεργείας καὶ κινήσεως ἑτέραν ἐν τῷ
τεμνομένῳ διάδοχον κίνησιν γίγνεσθαι. ἢ ἴσως οὐ κατ᾽
20 αὐτὸ τὸ τέμνεσθαι τὸ διάφορον, ἀλλὰ κατ᾽ ἄλλο τὸ
ἐπιγιγνόμενον κίνημα, οἷον τὸ ἀλγεῖν· καὶ γὰρ τὸ
πάσχειν ἐν τούτῳ. τί οὖν, εἰ μή τι ἀλγοῖ; τί ἄλλο ἢ ἡ
ἐνέργεια τοῦ ποιοῦντος ἐν τῷδε οὖσα; οὕτω γὰρ καὶ τὸ
οὕτω λεγόμενον ποιεῖν. καὶ διττὸν οὕτως εἶναι τὸ
72

come into the same genus as movements, life and living for instance. For the life of every man is in a complete time, and his well-being is not in partlessness, but is like they maintain that movement also is. So that both are to be called movements, and movement is one thing and one genus, as we observe besides the quantum in the substance the quale as well, and a movement which appertains to the substance. And, if you like, some movements are of body and some of soul, or some are self-originated and others are produced in the moving things by the agency of others, or some come from themselves and some from others, and the ones which come from themselves are activities, whether they are directed to other things or independent, but those which come from others are passivities. And yet the movements to other things are the same as the movements from other things: for cutting, the cutting which comes from the cutter and the cutting which takes place in what is being cut, is one, but cutting and being cut are different. But perhaps even the cutting originating from the cutter and the cutting going on in the cut are not one, but what cutting is is the process in which, from an active actuality and movement of this particular kind, another successive movement comes to be in what is being cut. Or perhaps the difference does not lie in the actual being cut, but in something else, the subsequent movement, feeling pain for instance: for there is certainly passivity in this. Well then, what is the case if there is not any pain? What else is there than the active actuality of the agent existing in this particular thing? For in this way this description also fits acting. And in this way acting is double, one

ποιεῖν, τὸ μὲν μὴ ἐν ἄλλῳ, τὸ δ' ἐν ἄλλῳ συνιστάμενον·
25 καὶ οὐκέτι τὸ μὲν ποιεῖν, τὸ δὲ πάσχειν, ἀλλὰ τὸ ποιεῖν
ἐν ἄλλῳ πεποίηκε δύο νομίζειν εἶναι, τὸ μὲν ποιεῖν, τὸ
δὲ πάσχειν. οἷον καὶ τὸ γράφειν, καίτοι ὂν ἐν ἄλλῳ, οὐκ
ἐπιζητεῖ τὸ πάσχειν, ὅτι μὴ ἄλλο τι ἐν τῷ γραμματείῳ
ποιεῖ παρὰ τὴν ἐνέργειαν τοῦ γράφοντος οἷον τὸ ἀλγεῖν·
εἰ δέ τις λέγοι γεγράφθαι, οὐ τὸ πάσχειν λέγει. καὶ ἐπὶ
30 τοῦ βαδίζειν, καίτοι οὔσης γῆς ἐφ' ἧς, οὐ προσποιεῖται
τὸ πεπονθέναι. ἀλλ' ὅταν ἐπὶ σώματος ζῴου βαίνῃ, τὸ
πάσχειν ἐπινοεῖ, ὃ ἐπιγίγνεται ἄλγημα συλλογιζόμενος,
οὐ τὸ βαδίζειν· ἢ ἐπενόησεν ἂν καὶ πρότερον. οὕτω καὶ
ἐπὶ πάντων κατὰ μὲν τὸ ποιεῖν ἓν λεκτέον μετὰ τοῦ
35 λεγομένου πάσχειν, τοῦ ἀντιθέτου. ὃ δὲ πάσχειν
λέγεται, τὸ γενόμενον ὕστερον, οὐ τὸ ἀντίθετον οἷον τῷ
καίειν τὸ καίεσθαι, ἀλλὰ τὸ ἐκ τοῦ καίειν καὶ καίεσθαι
ἑνὸς ὄντος, τὸ ἐπ' αὐτῷ γιγνόμενον ἢ ἄλγημα ἤ τι ἄλλο,
οἷον μαραίνεσθαι. τί οὖν, εἴ τις αὐτὸ τοῦτο ἐργάζοιτο,
40 ὥστε λυπεῖν, οὐχ ὁ μέν ποιεῖ, ὁ δὲ πάσχει, κἂν ἐκ μιᾶς
ἐνεργείας τὰ δύο; [καὶ ὁ μὲν ποιεῖ, ὁ δὲ πάσχει][1] ἢ ἐν τῇ
ἐνεργείᾳ οὐκέτι τὸ τῆς βουλήσεως τοῦ λυπεῖν, ἀλλὰ
ποιεῖ τι ἕτερον, δι' οὗ λυπεῖ, ὃ ἐν τῷ λυπησομένῳ
γενόμενον ἓν ὂν καὶ ταὐτὸν πεποίηκεν ἄλλο, τὸ
λυπεῖσθαι. τί οὖν αὐτὸ τὸ ἓν γενόμενον, πρὶν καὶ λύπην

---

[1] del. Kirchhoff: defendit Cilento.

kind which does and one kind which does not occur
in another; and it is no longer a distinction of acting
and being passive, but acting in another has produced the supposition that there are two, acting and
being passive. Writing, for instance, although it is in
something else, does not require [the concept of]
passivity, because it does not produce anything else,
feeling pain for instance, in the writing-tablet
beyond the actual activity of the writer; but if
someone says that the tablet has been written on, he
is not referring to passive suffering. And in the case
of walking, though there is ground on which one
walks, [the concept of] its passive suffering is not
included. But when one steps on the body of a living
being, one does have passive suffering in mind, since
one reasons about the pain which occurs, not the
walking; otherwise one would have thought of it
before also. In this way too in all cases, where action
is concerned one genus must be mentioned together
with passive suffering, that of the opposite of action.
But what is called passive suffering is what occurs
subsequently, not the opposite like being burnt to
burning, but what results from burning and being
burnt which are one, either the pain which occurs in
the burnt object or something else, like shrivelling.
Well then, if someone does this very thing in order to
cause pain, does not one act and the other suffer,
even if the two come from one actual activity? Now,
in the actual activity what belongs to the will to
hurt is no longer contained, but the agent does
something else, by which he causes pain, which
something else, being one and the same when it
occurs in what is going to be hurt, produces another
effect, that of being hurt. Why then is not the one

45 ποιῆσαι, ἢ ὅλως λύπην οὐκ ἐμποιοῦν, οὐ πάθος ἐστὶ τοῦ
εἰς ὄν, οἷον τὸ ἀκοῦσαι; ἢ οὐ πάθος τὸ ἀκοῦσαι οὐδ'
ὅλως τὸ αἰσθάνεσθαι, ἀλλὰ τὸ λυπηθῆναί ἐστι γενέσθαι
ἐν πάθει, ὃ μὴ ἀντίθετον τῷ ποιῆσαι.

20. Ἀλλ' ἔστω μὴ ἀντίθετον· ὅμως δὲ ἕτερον ὂν τοῦ
ποιεῖν οὐκ ἐν τῷ αὐτῷ γένει τῇ ποιήσει. ἢ, εἰ κινήσεις
ἄμφω, ἐν τῷ αὐτῷ, οἷον ἀ λ λ ο ί ω σ ι ς   κ ί ν η σ ι ς
κ α τ ὰ   τ ὸ   π ο ι ό ν . ἆρ' οὖν, ὅταν μὲν ἀπὸ τοῦ ποι-
5 οῦν⟨τος ἡ κίνησις ἡ κατὰ τὸ ποιὸν⟩[1] ἴῃ, ἡ ἀλλοίωσις
ποίησις καὶ τὸ ποιεῖν ἀπαθοῦς αὐτοῦ ὄντος; ἢ ἐὰν μὲν
ἀπαθὴς ᾖ, ἐν τῷ ποιεῖν ἔσται, ἐὰν δὲ ἐνεργῶν εἰς ἄλλον,
οἷον τύπτων, καὶ πάσχῃ, οὐκέτι ποιεῖ. ἢ οὐδὲν κωλύει
ποιοῦντα καὶ πάσχειν. εἰ οὖν κατὰ ταὐτὸ[2] τὸ πάσχειν,
οἷον τὸ τρίβειν, διὰ τί ποιεῖν μᾶλλον ἢ πάσχειν; ἤ, ὅτι
10 ἀντιτρίβεται, καὶ πάσχει. ἆρ' οὖν, ὅτι ἀντικινεῖται, καὶ
δύο κινήσεις φήσομεν περὶ αὐτόν; καὶ πῶς δύο; ἀλλὰ
μία. καὶ πῶς ἡ αὐτὴ καὶ ποίησις καὶ πεῖσις; ἢ[3] οὕτω
μὲν ποίησις τῷ ἀπ' ἄλλου, εἰς ἄλλον δὲ πεῖσις ἡ αὐτὴ
οὖσα. ἀλλὰ ἄλλην φήσομεν; καὶ πῶς ἄλλο τι διατίθησι
15 τὸν πάσχοντα ἀλλοιοῦσα καὶ ὁ ποιῶν ἀπαθὴς ἐκείνου;
πῶς γὰρ ἂν πάθοι ὃ ποιεῖ ἐν ἄλλῳ; ἆρ' οὖν τὸ ἐν ἄλλῳ

[1] Igal, H–S².
[2] Igal, H–S²: κατ' αὐτὸ Enn.
[3] Kirchhoff: καὶ Enn., H–S¹.

---

[1] Aristotle *Physics* E 3. 226a26.

thing which occurs, before it also causes pain, or if it does not cause pain in its object at all, not a passive affection of that object, like hearing? Now hearing is not a passive affection, nor is sense-perception in general, but being hurt is coming into a passive state, which is not opposite to action.

20. But granted that it is not opposite, yet all the same it is different from action and not in the same genus as doing and making. Now if both are movements, it is in the same genus, as, for instance, "qualitative change is movement in respect of quality".[1] Whenever, therefore, the movement in respect of quality, the qualitative change, proceeds from the agent is it an action and is it doing, if the maker is unaffected? If the agent is unaffected, it is in the category of doing, but if the agent is acting on someone else, hitting him for instance, and is affected, the agent is no longer doing. Now nothing prevents the doer from also being affected. If then the affection is in respect of the same thing, for instance rubbing, why is it doing rather than being affected? It is because it is reciprocally rubbed that it is also affected. Are we then to say that there are two movements in it because it is reciprocally moved? How can there be two? But there must be one. And how can the same movement be both a doing and a being affected? It is a doing in that it comes from one thing and a being affected because it acts on another, being the same movement. But are we to say that it is another? And how does the movement in producing qualitative change dispose what is affected in a different way and the agent remain unaffected by that change in disposition? For how could it be affected by what it does in another?

τὴν κίνησιν εἶναι ποιεῖ τὸ πάσχειν, ὃ ἦν οὐ πάσχειν κατὰ
τὸν ποιοῦντα; ἀλλ' εἰ τὸ μὲν λευκαίνει ὁ λόγος ὁ τοῦ
κύκνου, ὁ δὲ λευκαίνεται ὁ γιγνόμενος κύκνος, πάσχειν
20 φήσομεν ἰόντα εἰς οὐσίαν; εἰ δὲ καὶ ὕστερον λευκαίνοιτο
γενόμενος; καὶ εἰ τὸ μὲν αὔξοι, τὸ δὲ αὔξοιτο, τὸ
αὐξόμενον πάσχειν; ἢ μόνον ἐν τῷ ποιῷ τὴν πεῖσιν; ἀλλ'
εἰ τὸ μὲν καλὸν ποιοῖ, τὸ δὲ καλλύνοιτο, τὸ
καλλυνόμενον πάσχειν; εἰ οὖν τὸ καλλῦνον χεῖρον
γίγνοιτο ἢ καὶ ἀφανίζοιτο, οἷον ὁ καττίτερος, τὸ δὲ
25 βέλτιον γίγνοιτο, ὁ χαλκός, πάσχειν τὸν χαλκὸν
φήσομεν, τὸν δὲ ποιεῖν; τὸν δὲ μανθάνοντα πῶς πάσχειν
τῆς τοῦ ποιοῦντος ἐνεργείας εἰς αὐτὸν ἰούσης; ἢ
πάθησις πῶς ἂν εἴη μία γε οὖσα; ἀλλ' αὕτη μὲν οὐ
πάθησις, ὁ δὲ ἔχων πάσχων ἔσται τοῦ πάσχειν τίνος
30 λαμβανομένου; οὐδὲ γὰρ τῷ μὴ ἐνηργηκέναι αὐτόν· οὐ
γὰρ τὸ μανθάνειν ὥσπερ τὸ πληγῆναι ἐν ἀντιλήψει ὂν
καὶ γνωρίσει, ὥσπερ οὐδὲ τὸ ὁρᾶν.

21. Τίνι οὖν γνωριοῦμεν τὸ πάσχειν; οὐ γὰρ δὴ τῇ
ἐνεργείᾳ τῇ παρ' ἄλλου, εἰ ὁ τὴν ἐνέργειαν
παραδεξάμενος αὐτοῦ ἐποιήσατο διαδεξάμενος. ἀλλ'
ἆρα ὅπου μὴ ἐνέργεια, πεῖσις δὲ μόνον; τί οὖν, εἰ
5 κάλλιον γίγνοιτο, ἡ δὲ ἐνέργεια τὸ χεῖρον ἔχοι; ἢ εἰ
78

Is it then the fact that the movement is in something else which produces being affected, which was not being affected in the case of the agent? But if on the one hand the rational form of the swan produces whiteness and [on the other] the swan coming into being is made white, are we going to say that the swan is affected as it proceeds to substantiality? But is it if it is made white afterwards when it has come into being? And if one thing is going to make something larger and the other is going to be made large, is that which is going to be made large affected? Or is being affected only in quality? But if one thing makes something beautiful and the other is made beautiful is that which is being made beautiful affected? If, then, that which makes beautiful becomes worse or even disappears, like the tin, and the other, the copper, becomes better, are we to say that the copper is affected and the tin acts? And how is the learner affected when the activity of the agent comes to him? How could the activity be a passivity when it is certainly one? But is this activity not a passivity, but will [the learner] who has it be passively affected, being affected being taken as somebody being affected? For it is not because the learner has not been active: for learning is not like being hit, since it consists in grasping and getting to know, and neither is seeing.

21. By what indication, then, are we to recognise being affected? Not, certainly, by the fact that the activity [affecting it] comes from another, if the one who received the activity took it over and made it his own. But is it when there is no activity and only passive affection? What then if it becomes more beautiful, and the activity has the worst of it? Or if

κατὰ κακίαν ἐνεργοῖ τις καὶ ἄρχοι εἰς ἄλλον
ἀκολάστως; ἢ οὐδέν κωλύει ἐνέργειαν εἶναι φαύλην καὶ
πεῖσιν καλήν. τίνι οὖν διοριοῦμεν; ἆρα τῷ τὸ μὲν εἰς
ἄλλον παρ' αὐτοῦ, τὸ δὲ ἀφ' ἑτέρου ἐν ἄλλῳ τὸ πάσχειν;
τί οὖν, εἰ ἐξ αὐτοῦ μέν, μὴ εἰς ἄλλον δέ, οἷον τὸ νοεῖν, τὸ
10 δοξάζειν; τὸ δὲ θερμανθῆναι παρ' αὐτοῦ διανοηθέντος ἢ
θυμωθέντος ἐκ δόξης μηδενὸς ἔξωθεν προσελθόντος; ἢ
τὸ μὲν ποιεῖν εἴτε ἐν αὐτῷ εἴτε εἰς ἄλλον ἰὸν κίνημα ἐξ
αὐτοῦ[1]; ἡ οὖν ἐπιθυμία τί καὶ πᾶσα ὄρεξις, εἰ ἡ ὄρεξις
κινεῖται ἀπὸ τοῦ ὀρεκτοῦ; εἰ μή τις μὴ προσποιοῖτο ἀφ'
15 οὗ κεκίνηται, ὅτι δὲ μετ' ἐκεῖνο ἐγήγερται. τί οὖν
διαφέρει τοῦ πεπλῆχθαι ἢ ὠσθέντα κατενεχθῆναι; ἀλλ'
ἆρα διαιρετέον τὰς ὀρέξεις λέγοντα τὰς μὲν ποιήσεις,
ὅσαι νῷ ἑπόμεναι, τὰς δὲ ὁλκὰς οὔσας πείσεις, τὸ δὲ
πάσχειν οὐ τῷ παρ' ἑτέρου ἢ παρ' ἑαυτοῦ—σαπείη γὰρ
20 ἄν τι ἐν ἑαυτῷ—ἀλλ' ὅταν μηδὲν συμβαλλόμενον αὐτὸ
ὑπομείνῃ ἀλλοίωσιν τὴν μὴ εἰς οὐσίαν ἄγουσαν, ἥτις
ἐξίστησι πρὸς τὸ χεῖρον ἢ μὴ πρὸς τὸ βέλτιον, τὴν
τοιαύτην ἀλλοίωσιν πεῖσιν καὶ τὸ πάσχειν ἔχειν; ἀλλ' εἰ
τὸ θερμαίνεσθαι θερμότητά ἐστιν ἴσχειν, εἴη δὲ τῷ μὲν
25 εἰς οὐσίαν συντελοῦν, τῷ δὲ μή, τὸ αὐτὸ πάσχειν καὶ οὐ

---

[1] ἰὸν κίνημα ἐξ αὐτοῦ Igal: τι ὄν, κίνημα ἐξ αὐτοῦ Enn., H–S[1].

someone is viciously active and starts an unscrupulous attack on another? Now, there is nothing to prevent activity from being bad and passive affection good. So by what shall we distinguish them? Perhaps by the fact that the one is directed from the agent to another, and the other, passive affection, is in another but comes from a different source? What then if it comes from oneself but is not directed to another, thinking or opining for instance? And what about getting heated as a result of one's own thought or of being put into a passion by an opinion, when nothing comes to one from outside? Is action, whether in oneself or going on to another, a self-caused movement? Then what is concupiscence and every sort of desire, if desire derives its movement from the desired object? Unless of course one does not make the assumption that it has derived its movement from the object, but only that it has been awakened after [the appearance of] the object. How then does desire differ from being hit, or pushed and knocked down? But perhaps we should divide desires, saying that some of them are actions, all that follow intellect, but those which drag one are passive affections, and that passive affection is not a matter of deriving from another or from oneself—for a thing can rot in itself—but that when without any contribution of its own a thing undergoes an alteration which does not bring it to substantiality and changes it for the worse, or not for the better, an alteration of this kind has the characteristic of passivity and being passively affected? But if being heated is acquiring heat, and this contributes to one thing's substantiality but not to another's, being affected and not being affected will be the same

πάσχειν ἔσται. καὶ πῶς οὐ τὸ θερμαίνεσθαι διττόν; ἢ τὸ
θερμαίνεσθαι, ὅταν εἰς οὐσίαν συντελῇ, καὶ τότε ἄλλου
πάσχοντος εἰς οὐσίαν συντελέσει, οἷον θερμαινομένου
τοῦ χαλκοῦ καὶ πάσχοντος, ἡ δὲ οὐσία ὁ ἀνδριάς, ὃς οὐκ
αὐτὸς ἐθερμαίνετο, ἀλλ᾽ ἢ κατὰ συμβεβηκός. εἰ οὖν
30 καλλίων ὁ χαλκὸς ἀπὸ τοῦ θερμαίνεσθαι ἢ κατὰ τὸ
θερμαίνεσθαι, οὐδὲν κωλύει πάσχειν λέγειν· διττὸν γὰρ
εἶναι τὸ πάσχειν, τὸ μὲν ἐν τῷ χεῖρον γίγνεσθαι, τὸ δ᾽ ἐν
τῷ βέλτιον, ἢ οὐδέτερον.

22. Οὐκοῦν γίγνεται τὸ πάσχειν τῷ ἔχειν ἐν αὐτῷ
κίνησιν [τὴν ἀλλοίωσιν][1] τὴν κατὰ τὸ ἀλλοιοῦσθαι
ὁπωσοῦν· καὶ τὸ ποιεῖν ἢ ἔχειν ἐν αὐτῷ κίνησιν τὴν
ἀπόλυτον παρ᾽ αὐτοῦ ἢ τὴν τελευτῶσαν εἰς ἄλλο ἀπ᾽
5 αὐτοῦ, ὁρμωμένην ἀπὸ τοῦ λεγομένου ποιεῖν. καὶ
κίνησις μὲν ἐπ᾽ ἀμφοῖν, ἡ δὲ διαφορὰ ἡ διαιροῦσα τὸ
ποιεῖν καὶ τὸ πάσχειν τὸ μὲν ποιεῖν, καθόσον ποιεῖν,
ἀπαθὲς τηροῦσα, τὸ δὲ πάσχειν ἐν τῷ διατίθεσθαι
ἑτέρως ἢ πρότερον εἶχε, τῆς τοῦ πάσχοντος οὐσίας οὐδὲν
εἰς οὐσίαν προσλαμβανούσης, ἀλλὰ ἄλλου ὄντος τοῦ
10 πάσχοντος, ὅταν τις οὐσία γίνηται. γίνεται τοίνυν τὸ
αὐτὸ ἐν σχέσει τινὶ ποιεῖν, ἐν ἄλλῃ δὲ πάσχειν· παρὰ μὲν
γὰρ τῷδε θεωρούμενον ποιεῖν ἔσται, κίνησις οὖσα ἡ
αὐτή, παρὰ δὲ τῷδε πάσχειν, ὅτι τάδε οὗτος διατίθεται·
ὥστε κινδυνεύειν ἄμφω πρός τι εἶναι, ὅσα τοῦ ποιεῖν
15 πρὸς τὸ πάσχειν, εἰ μὲν παρὰ τούτῳ τὸ αὐτό, ποιεῖν, εἰ
δὲ παρὰ τῷδε, πάσχειν. καὶ θεωρούμενον ἑκάτερον οὐ

[1] del. Kirchhoff.

thing. And, surely, being heated is double. Now being heated, when it contributes to substantiality, will then also contribute to substantiality by something else being affected; for instance when the bronze is heated and affected, but the substance is the statue, which was not heated itself except incidentally. If then the bronze is more beautiful as a result of being heated or according to the degree of heat, there is nothing against saying it is passively affected: for being passively affected is double, one kind consisting in becoming worse, the other in becoming better, or neither.

22. Passive affection, then, occurs by having in oneself an alterative motion of any kind; and action is either having in oneself an independent self-derived motion or one which starts from oneself and ends in another, [a motion, that is,] starting from that which is said to act. There is motion in both cases, but the difference which separates action and passive affection keeps action, in so far as it is action, unaffected, but makes passive affection consist in being disposed otherwise than it was before; the substance of what is affected gains nothing which contributes to its substantiality, but what is affected is different, when a substance comes to be. So the same is action in one relationship and passive affection in another. It is the same motion, but looked at on one side it will be action, but on the other passive affection, because this is disposed in this way; so it seems likely that both are relation, in all cases where action is related to passive affection; if one looks at the same on one side it is action, but if on the other, it is affection. And each of the two is looked at not by itself, but [one] along with that

καθ᾽ αὑτό, ἀλλὰ μετὰ τοῦ ποιοῦντος καὶ πάσχοντος·
οὗτος κινεῖ καὶ οὗτος κινεῖται, καὶ δύο κατηγορίαι
ἑκάτερον· καὶ οὗτος δίδωσι τῷδε κίνησιν, οὗτος δὲ
20 λαμβάνει, ὥστε λῆψις καὶ δόσις καὶ πρός τι. ἢ εἰ ἔχει ὁ
λαβών, ὥσπερ λέγεται ἔχειν χρῶμα, διὰ τί οὐ καὶ ἔχει
κίνησιν; καὶ ἡ ἀπόλυτος κίνησις, οἷον ἡ τοῦ βαδίζειν,
ἔχει βάδισιν, καὶ ἔχει δὲ νόησιν. ἐπισκεπτέον δέ, εἰ τὸ
προνοεῖν ποιεῖ, εἰ καὶ τὸ προνοίας τυγχάνειν πάσχειν·
εἰς ἄλλο γὰρ καὶ περὶ ἄλλου ἡ πρόνοια. ἢ οὐδὲ τὸ
25 προνοεῖν ποιεῖ, καὶ εἰ περὶ ἄλλου τὸ νοεῖν, ἢ ἐκεῖνο
πάσχειν. ἢ οὐδὲ τὸ νοεῖν ποιεῖν—οὐ γὰρ εἰς αὑτὸ τὸ
νοούμενον, ἀλλὰ περὶ αὑτοῦ—οὐδὲ ποίησις ὅλως. οὐδὲ
δεῖ πάσας ἐνεργείας ποιήσεις λέγειν οὐδὲ ποιεῖν τι·
κατὰ συμβεβηκὸς δὲ ἡ ποίησις. τί οὖν; εἰ βαδίζων ἴχνη
30 εἰργάσατο, οὐ λέγομεν πεποιηκέναι; ἀλλ᾽ ἐκ τοῦ εἶναι
αὐτὸν ἄλλο τι. ἢ ποιεῖν κατὰ συμβεβηκὸς καὶ τὴν
ἐνέργειαν κατὰ συμβεβηκός, ὅτι μὴ πρὸς τοῦτο ἑώρα·
ἐπεὶ καὶ ἐπὶ τῶν ἀψύχων ποιεῖν λέγομεν οἷον τὸ πῦρ
θερμαίνειν καὶ "ἐνήργησε τὸ φάρμακον". ἀλλὰ περὶ μὲν
τούτων ἅλις.

23. Περὶ δὲ τοῦ ἔχειν, εἰ τὸ ἔχειν πολλαχῶς, διὰ τί
οὐ πάντες οἱ τρόποι τοῦ ἔχειν εἰς ταύτην τὴν
κατηγορίαν ἀναχθήσονται; ὥστε καὶ τὸ ποσόν, ὅτι ἔχει
μέγεθος, καὶ τὸ ποιόν, ὅτι ἔχει χρῶμα, καὶ ὁ πατὴρ καὶ
5 τὰ τοιαῦτα, ὅτι ἔχει υἱόν, καὶ ὁ υἱός, ὅτι ἔχει πατέρα,
καὶ ὅλως κτήματα. εἰ δὲ τὰ μὲν ἄλλα ἐν ἐκείναις, ὅπλα

----

[1] The Peripatetics.

which acts, and [the other] with that which is affected: this one moves and this one is moved, and
each is two categories; and this one gives motion to
this, and this one receives it, so that there is taking
and giving and this is relation. Or, if the recipient
has, as in the phrase "have colour", why does it not
also "have movement"? And independent movement,
that of walking for instance, has walking, and also
has thinking. But one must consider whether forethought is action, if being the object of forethought
is being affected; since forethought is directed to
something else and is about something else. Now
forethought is not action, even if the thought is
about something else, nor is being its object being
affected. And thought is not action either—[it does
not operate] in the object of thought itself, but is
about it: it is not any kind of doing or making. And
one should not call all activities doings or makings,
or say that they do something. Doing is incidental.
Well then, if someone walking produces footprints,
do we not say he made them? But [he did so] because
he was something else. Or [we may say that] the
making is incidental and the activity [of footprint-
making] is incidental, because he did not have this
in view: since we speak of action in the case of
lifeless beings, that fire heats, for instance, or "the
drug acted". But that is enough of that.

23. But about having, if "having" is used in many
different senses, why will they[1] not refer all the
ways of having to this category? So the quantum,
because it has size, and the quale, because it has
colour, and the father and such, because he has a
son, and the son because he has a father, and, in
general, possessions. But if the other things are in

δὲ καὶ ὑποδήματα καὶ τὰ περὶ τὸ σῶμα, πρῶτον μὲν
ζητήσειεν ἄν τις, διὰ τί, καὶ διὰ τί ἔχων μὲν αὐτὰ μίαν
ἄλλην κατηγορίαν ποιεῖ, καίων δὲ ἢ τέμνων ἢ
κατορύττων ἢ ἀποβάλλων οὐκ ἄλλην ἢ ἄλλας; εἰ δ' ὅτι
10 περίκειται, κἂν ἱμάτιον κέηται ἐπὶ κλίνης, ἄλλη
κατηγορία ἔσται, κἂν κεκαλυμμένος ᾖ τις. εἰ δὲ κατὰ
τὴν κάθεξιν αὐτὴν καὶ τὴν ἕξιν, δηλονότι καὶ τὰ ἄλλα
πάντα ⟨αὖ τὰ⟩[1] κατὰ τὸ ἔχειν λεγόμενα καὶ εἰς ἕξιν
[αὐτά],[1] ὅπου ποτὲ ἡ ἕξις, ἀνακτέον· οὐ γὰρ διοίσει
15 κατὰ τὸ ἐχόμενον. εἰ μέντοι ποιότητα ἔχειν οὐ δεῖ λέγειν,
ὅτι ἤδη ποιότης εἴρηται, οὐδὲ ποσότητα ἔχειν, ὅτι
ποσότης, οὐδὲ μέρη ἔχειν, ὅτι οὐσία εἴρηται, διὰ τί δὲ
ὅπλα ἔχειν εἰρημένης οὐσίας, ἐν ᾗ ταῦτα; οὐσία γὰρ
ὑπόδημα καὶ ὅπλα. πῶς δ' ὅλως ἁπλοῦν καὶ μιᾶς
20 κατηγορίας "ὅδε ὅπλα ἔχει"; τοῦτο γὰρ σημαίνει τὸ
ὡπλίσθαι. ἔπειτα πότερον ἐπὶ ζῶντος μόνον ἢ κἂν
ἀνδριὰς ᾖ, ὅτῳ ταῦτα; ἄλλως γὰρ ἑκάτερον ἔχειν δοκεῖ
καὶ ἴσως ὁμωνύμως· ἐπεὶ καὶ τὸ "ἕστηκεν" ἐπ' ἀμφοῖν
οὐ ταὐτόν. ἔτι καὶ τὸ ἐν ὀλίγοις πῶς εὔλογον ἔχειν
κατηγορίαν γενικὴν ἄλλην;

24. Ἐπὶ δὲ τοῦ κεῖσθαι—ἐν ὀλίγοις καὶ αὐτὸ ὄν—
ἀνακεῖσθαι, καθῆσθαι, καίτοι οὐ κεῖσθαι ἁπλῶς

---

[1] transposuit Schwyzer (*Gnomon* 42, 1970, 654): ⟨τὰ⟩
Kirchhoff.

those categories [of quantity, quality and relation] but weapons and shoes and things around the body [are in this one], first of all one might enquire why, and why the person who *has* these things makes another category, but, if he burns them or cuts them or buries them or throws them out, does not make another or others. But if it is because they are around the body, if a cloak lies on a bed there will be one category and if someone has wrapped himself in it another. But if it is in accordance with possession and the state of possessing, obviously again all the other things spoken of in connection with having are also to be referred to the state of possessing, wherever one puts it: for there will be no differentiation according to what is possessed. If then one must not say that one has a quality, because quality has been mentioned already, or that one has quantity, because quantity has been mentioned, or that one has parts, because substance has been mentioned, then why should one say one has weapons, when substance has been mentioned, and they are in this category? For a shoe and weapons are substance. And how, altogether, is "this man here has weapons" a simple statement belonging to one category? For this means being armed. Then, can one say this only about a living man, or also if it is a statue which has the weapons? For each of the two appears to "have" them in a different way, and perhaps "have" is equivocal: since "stand" is not the same in both cases. And again, how is it reasonable that something which occurs in a few cases should have another general category?

24. About position—which also only occurs in a few cases—lying on, sitting: though these terms do

λεγομένων, ἀλλὰ "πῶς κεῖται" καὶ "κεῖται ἐν σχήματι
τοιῷδε". καὶ τὸ μὲν σχῆμα ἄλλο· τοῦ δὲ κεῖσθαι τί
5 ἄλλο σημαίνοντος ἢ "ἐν τόπῳ ἐστίν", εἰρημένου τοῦ
σχήματος καὶ τοῦ τόπου, τί δεῖ εἰς ἓν δύο κατηγορίας
συνάπτειν; ἔπειτα, εἰ μὲν τὸ "κάθηται" ἐνέργειαν
σημαίνει, ἐν ταῖς ἐνεργείαις τακτέον, εἰ δὲ πάθος, ἐν τῷ
πεπονθέναι ἢ πάσχειν. τὸ δὲ "ἀνάκειται" τί ἄλλο ἢ
"ἄνω κεῖται", ὥσπερ καὶ τὸ "κάτω κεῖται" ἢ "μεταξὺ
10 κεῖται"; διὰ τί δὲ ἀνακλίσεως οὔσης ἐν τῷ πρός τι οὐχὶ
καὶ ὁ ἀνακείμενος ἐκεῖ; ἐπεὶ καὶ τοῦ δεξιοῦ ὄντος ἐκεῖ
καὶ ὁ δεξιὸς ἐκεῖ καὶ ὁ ἀριστερός. ταῦτα μὲν οὖν ἐπὶ
τούτων.

25. Πρὸς δὲ τοὺς τέτταρα τιθέντας καὶ τετραχῶς
διαιροῦντας εἰς "ὑποκείμενα" καὶ "ποιὰ" καὶ "πῶς
ἔχοντα" καὶ "πρός τί πως ἔχοντα", καὶ κοινόν τι ἐπ'
αὐτῶν τιθέντας καὶ ἑνὶ γένει περιλαμβάνοντας τὰ
5 πάντα, ὅτι μὲν κοινόν τι καὶ ἐπὶ πάντων ἓν γένος
λαμβάνουσι, πολλὰ ἄν τις λέγοι. καὶ γὰρ ὡς ἀσύνετον
αὐτοῖς καὶ ἄλογον τὸ τὶ τοῦτο καὶ οὐκ ἐφαρμόττον
ἀσωμάτοις καὶ σώμασι. καὶ διαφορὰς οὐ
καταλελοίπασιν, αἷς τὸ τὶ διαιρήσουσι. καὶ τὸ τὶ τοῦτο
ἢ ὂν ἢ μὴ ὄν ἐστιν· εἰ μὲν οὖν ὄν, ἕν τι τῶν εἰδῶν ἐστιν·

---

[1] Again the Stoic τι; see ch. 2, n. 1, p. 16.
[2] For a good account of the Stoic Categories and of the
misunderstandings about them which may have arisen

not simply express position, but "they are in a certain position" or "he is posed in such and such an attitude". And the attitude is something else; but what else does position signify but "is in place" and, when place and attitude have been mentioned, what need is there to join up two categories into one? Then further, if "sits" signifies an activity, it must be ranked among activities, but if a passive affection, it must be placed in the class of having been or being affected. But what does "he lies on" mean except "he lies above", like "he lies under", or "he lies between"? And why, when lying on is in the category of relation, is not the man who is lying on something there too? Since being on the right is there too, and the one on the right and the left. So much for that.

25. But as for those who posit the four genera and make a fourfold division into subjects and qualia and things in a certain state and things in a certain state in relation to others, and posit over them a common something[1] and include all things in one genus, there is much that one could say against them because they assume a common something and one genus over all. For, really, how incomprehensible and irrational this something of theirs is, and how unadapted to bodiless things and bodies.[2] And they have not left any room for differences with which they will be able to differentiate the something. And this something is either existent or non-existent; if, then, it is existent, it is one of its species; but if it is

from the hostile character of most of our sources of evidence, of which these chapters are an important part, see J. M. Rist *Stoic Philosophy* (Cambridge 1969) ch. 9, "Categories and their Uses", 152–72.

10 εἰ δὲ μὴ ὄν, ἔστι τὸ ὂν μὴ ὄν. καὶ μυρία ἕτερα. ταῦτα μὲν
οὖν ἐν τῷ παρόντι ἐατέον, αὐτὴν δὲ τὴν διαίρεσιν
ἐπισκεπτέον. ὑποκείμενα μὲν γὰρ πρῶτα τάξαντες καὶ
τὴν ὕλην ἐνταῦθα τῶν ἄλλων προτάξαντες τὴν πρώτην
αὐτοῖς δοκοῦσαν ἀρχὴν συντάττουσι τοῖς μετὰ τὴν
15 ἀρχὴν αὐτῶν. καὶ πρῶτον μὲν τὰ πρότερα τοῖς ὕστερον
εἰς ἓν ἄγουσιν, οὐχ οἷόν τε ὂν ἐν γένει τῷ αὐτῷ τὸ μὲν
πρότερον, τὸ δὲ ὕστερον εἶναι. ἐν μὲν γὰρ τοῖς ἐν οἷς τὸ
πρότερον καὶ τὸ ὕστερον, τὸ ὕστερον παρὰ τοῦ
προτέρου λαμβάνει τὸ εἶναι, ἐν δὲ τοῖς ὑπὸ τὸ αὐτὸ
20 γένος τὸ ἴσον εἰς τὸ εἶναι ἕκαστον ἔχει παρὰ τοῦ γένους,
εἴπερ τοῦτο δεῖ γένος εἶναι τὸ ἐν τῷ τί ἐστι τῶν εἰδῶν
κατηγορούμενον· ἐπεὶ καὶ αὐτοὶ φήσουσι παρὰ τῆς
ὕλης, οἶμαι, τοῖς ἄλλοις τὸ εἶναι ὑπάρχειν. ἔπειτα τὸ
ὑποκείμενον ἓν ἀριθμοῦντες οὐ τὰ ὄντα ἐξαριθμοῦνται,
ἀλλ' ἀρχὰς τῶν ὄντων ζητοῦσι· διαφέρει δὲ ἀρχὰς
25 λέγειν καὶ αὐτά. εἰ δὲ ὂν μὲν μόνον τὴν ὕλην φήσουσι, τὰ
δ' ἄλλα πάθη τῆς ὕλης, οὐκ ἐχρῆν τοῦ ὄντος καὶ τῶν
ἄλλων ἕν τι γένος προτάττειν· μᾶλλον δ' ἂν βέλτιον
αὐτοῖς ἐλέγετο, εἰ τὸ μὲν οὐσίαν, τὰ δ' ἄλλα πάθη, καὶ
διῃροῦντο ταῦτα. τὸ δὲ καὶ λέγειν τὰ μὲν ὑποκείμενα,
30 τὰ δὲ τὰ ἄλλα, ἑνὸς ὄντος τοῦ ὑποκειμένου καὶ διαφορὰν
οὐκ ἔχοντος, ἀλλ' ἢ τῷ μεμερίσθαι, ὥσπερ ὄγκον εἰς
μέρη—καίτοι οὐδὲ μεμερίσθαι τῷ συνεχῆ λέγειν τὴν

non-existent, the existent is non-existent. And there are innumerable other objections. Well, we should leave these for the present and consider the division itself. They rank subjects first and at this point rank matter before the others, and so rank what they think is the first principle along with the things which come after their first principle. And first of all they bring prior things into one [genus] with posterior things, when it is not possible for that which is prior and that which is posterior to be in one genus. For in things in which there is prior and posterior, the posterior takes its being from the prior, but in things which come under the same genus each receives an equal contribution to its being from the genus, if the genus is what is predicated in speaking of the essential nature of the species: since they, I think, will agree that existence comes to the other things from matter. Then, when they count the subject as one, they do not enumerate existing things, but are looking for the principles of existing things. But it makes a difference whether one speaks of the principles or the things themselves. But if they are going to say that only matter exists, and that the other things are affections of matter, they ought not to place a single genus before being and the others: rather, it would have been better put if they had distinguished one thing as substance and the rest as affections and then divided these. And [it is unreasonable] to call some things subjects and [put] others in [categories], when the subject is one and has no differentiation except by being divided, like a mass, into parts—yet it cannot even be divided because they say that its substance is continuous—it would

οὐσίαν—βέλτιον λέγειν ἦν "τὸ μὲν ὑποκείμενον".

26. Ὅλως δὲ τὸ προτάττειν ἀπάντων τὴν ὕλην, ὃ
δυνάμει ἐστίν, ἀλλὰ μὴ ἐνέργειαν πρὸ δυνάμεως
τάττειν, παντάπασιν ἀτοπώτατον. οὐδὲ γὰρ ἔστι τὸ
δυνάμει εἰς ἐνέργειαν ἐλθεῖν ποτε τάξεως ἀρχὴν ἔχοντος
5 ἐν τοῖς οὖσι τοῦ δυνάμει· οὐ γὰρ δὴ αὐτὸ ἑαυτὸ ἄξει,
ἀλλὰ δεῖ ἢ πρὸ αὐτοῦ εἶναι τὸ ἐνεργείᾳ καὶ οὐκέτι τοῦτο
ἀρχή, ἤ, εἰ ἅμα λέγοιεν, ἐν τύχαις θήσονται τὰς ἀρχάς.
ἔπειτα, εἰ ἅμα, διὰ τί οὐκ ἐκεῖνο προτάττουσι; καὶ διὰ τί
τοῦτο μᾶλλον ὄν, ἢ ὕλη, ἀλλ' οὐκ ἐκεῖνο; εἰ δὲ ὕστερον
10 ἐκεῖνο, πῶς; οὐ γὰρ δὴ ἡ ὕλη τὸ εἶδος γεννᾷ, ἢ ἄποιος τὸ
ποιόν, οὐδ' ἐκ τοῦ δυνάμει ἐνέργεια· ἐνυπῆρχε γὰρ ἂν τὸ
ἐνεργείᾳ, καὶ οὐχ ἁπλοῦν ἔτι. καὶ ὁ θεὸς δεύτερος αὐτοῖς
τῆς ὕλης· καὶ γὰρ σῶμα ἐξ ὕλης ὢν καὶ εἴδους. καὶ
πόθεν αὐτῷ τὸ εἶδος; εἰ δὲ καὶ ἄνευ τοῦ ὕλην ἔχειν
ἀρχοειδὴς ὢν καὶ λόγος, ἀσώματος ἂν εἴη ὁ θεός, καὶ τὸ
15 ποιητικὸν ἀσώματον. εἰ δὲ καὶ ἄνευ τῆς ὕλης ἐστὶ τὴν
οὐσίαν σύνθετος, ἅτε σῶμα ὤν, ἄλλην ὕλην τὴν τοῦ θεοῦ
εἰσάξουσιν. ἔπειτα πῶς ἀρχὴ ἡ ὕλη σῶμα οὖσα; οὐ γάρ
ἐστι σῶμα μὴ οὐ πολλὰ εἶναι· καὶ πᾶν σῶμα ἐξ ὕλης καὶ
ποιότητος. εἰ δὲ ἄλλως τοῦτο σῶμα, ὁμωνύμως λέγουσι

have been better to say "the subject" [in the singular].

26. But, speaking generally, it is in every way superlatively absurd to rank matter, something which is potential, before all things, but not to put actuality before potency. For it is not even possible for what is in potency ever to come to actuality if the potential holds the rank of principle among beings: for it certainly will not bring itself to actuality, but the actual must be before it, and then this potential will no longer be a principle; or, if they say that [potential and actual] are simultaneous, they will put the principles in the realm of chance. And then, if they are simultaneous, why do they not give the actual the first rank? And why is this one, matter, the more existent, and not that one? But if the actual is later, how [did it come into being]? For, certainly, matter does not generate form, that which is without quality the qualified, nor does actuality come from the potential: for [if it did] the actual would exist in the potential, and it would no longer be simple. And God for them comes second after matter: for he is a body, and composed of matter and form. And where did he get his form from? But if [he had it] without having matter, having the nature of a principle and being a rational formative power, God would be bodiless and the creative bodiless. But if even without matter God is composite in his essential nature, in that he is a body, they will be introducing another matter, that of God. Then how is matter a principle if it is body? For it is not possible for a body not to be many; and every body is composed of matter and quality. But if this one is body in a different way,

93

20 σῶμα τὴν ὕλην. εἰ δὲ κοινὸν ἐπὶ σώματος τὸ τριχῇ
διαστατόν, μαθηματικὸν λέγουσιν· εἰ δὲ μετὰ
ἀντιτυπίας τὸ τριχῇ, οὐχ ἓν λέγουσιν. ἔπειτα ἡ
ἀντιτυπία ποιὸν ἢ παρὰ ποιότητος. καὶ πόθεν ἡ
ἀντιτυπία; πόθεν δὲ τὸ τριχῇ διαστατὸν ἢ τίς διέστησεν;
25 οὐ γὰρ ἐν τῷ λόγῳ τοῦ τριχῇ διαστατοῦ ἡ ὕλη, οὐδ᾽ ἐν
τῷ τῆς ὕλης τὸ τριχῇ διαστατόν. μετασχοῦσα τοίνυν
μεγέθους οὐκέτ᾽ ἂν ἁπλοῦν εἴη. ἔπειτα πόθεν ἡ ἕνωσις;
οὐ γὰρ δὴ αὐτοένωσις,[1] ἀλλὰ μετοχῇ ἑνότητος. ἐχρῆν
δὴ λογίσασθαι ὡς οὐκ ἔστι δυνατὸν προτάττειν
ἁπάντων ὄγκον, ἀλλὰ τὸ ἄογκον καὶ τὸ ἕν, καὶ ἐκ τοῦ
30 ἑνὸς ἀρξαμένους εἰς τὰ πολλὰ τελευτᾶν, καὶ ἐξ
ἀμεγέθους εἰς μεγέθη, εἴ γε οὐκ ἔστι πολλὰ εἶναι μὴ
ἑνὸς ὄντος, οὐδὲ μέγεθος μὴ ἀμεγέθους· εἴ γε τὸ
μέγεθος ἓν οὐ τῷ αὐτὸ ἕν, ἀλλὰ τῷ μετέχειν τοῦ ἓν καὶ
κατὰ σύμβασιν. δεῖ τοίνυν εἶναι τὸ πρώτως καὶ κυρίως
35 πρὸ τοῦ κατὰ σύμβασιν· ἢ πῶς ἡ σύμβασις; καὶ ζητεῖν,
τίς ὁ τρόπος τῆς συμβάσεως· τάχα γὰρ ἂν εὗρον τὸ μὴ
κατὰ συμβεβηκὸς ἕν. λέγω δὲ κατὰ συμβεβηκός, ὃ τῷ
μὴ αὐτὸ ἕν, ἀλλὰ παρ᾽ ἄλλου.

[1] U, H–S²: αὐτὸ ἕνωσις wBxC, Perna: αὐτὸ ἓν Arnim (SVF II
n. 315), H–S¹.

---

[1] This is the nearest Plotinus ever comes to any
awareness that Stoic corporealism was not as gross and
absurd as Platonist and Peripatetic opponents supposed.
The Stoic conception of "body" was much subtler and more
interesting than Plotinus represents it, here and elsewhere.

they are calling matter body equivocally.[1] But if three-dimensionality is the common characteristic of body, they are speaking of mathematical body; but if resistance accompanies three-dimensionality, then they are talking about something which is not one. And then resistance is a quale or derives from quality. And where did the resistance come from? And where the three-dimensional extension, and who extended it? For matter is not contained in the definition of three-dimensionality, nor three-dimensionality in the definition of matter. If then matter participates in magnitude, it would no longer be simple. Then where does its unification come from? For it is certainly not absolute unification, but by participation in unity. They should certainly have worked out that it is not possible to put mass in the first place of all, but that which is without mass and the one, and starting with the one to conclude in the many and starting with the sizeless to conclude in magnitudes, if it is not possible for many to be unless one is, nor size unless the sizeless is: if, that is, size is one not by being itself one but by participation in the one and a coming together. There must therefore be the primarily and properly [existent] before that [which exists] by coming together or how does the coming together occur? And one must enquire what is the manner of the coming together: for [if the Stoics had done so] they might perhaps have found the one which is not incidentally one. By "incidentally one" I mean that which is one not by being the one itself, but from another.

See S. Sambursky *The Physics of the Stoics* (London 1959), 29–44 (with interesting parallels to modern physics); A. A. Long *Hellenistic Philosophy* (London 1974), 152–8.

27. Ἐχρῆν δὲ καὶ ἄλλως τηροῦντας τὴν ἀρχὴν τῶν
πάντων ἐν τῷ τιμίῳ μὴ τὸ ἄμορφον μηδὲ τὸ παθητὸν
μηδὲ τὸ ζωῆς ἄμοιρον καὶ ἀνόητον καὶ σκοτεινὸν καὶ τὸ
ἀόριστον τίθεσθαι ἀρχήν, καὶ τούτῳ ἀναφέρειν καὶ
5 τὴν οὐσίαν. ὁ γὰρ θεὸς αὐτοῖς εὐπρεπείας ἕνεκεν
ἐπεισάγεται παρά τε τῆς ὕλης ἔχων τὸ εἶναι καὶ
σύνθετος καὶ ὕστερος, μᾶλλον δὲ ὕλη πως ἔχουσα.
ἔπειτα εἰ ὑποκείμενον, ἀνάγκη ἄλλο εἶναι, ὃ ποιοῦν εἰς
αὐτὴν ἔξω ὂν αὐτῆς παρέχει αὐτὴν ὑποκεῖσθαι τοῖς παρ'
10 αὐτοῦ πεμπομένοις εἰς αὐτήν. εἰ δ' ἐν τῇ ὕλῃ καὶ αὐτὸς
εἴη ὑποκείμενος καὶ αὐτὸς σὺν αὐτῇ γενόμενος, οὐκέτι
ὑποκείμενον τὴν ὕλην παρέξεται οὐδὲ μετὰ τῆς ὕλης
αὐτὸς ὑποκείμενον· τίνι γὰρ ὑποκείμενα ἔσται οὐκέτι
ὄντος τοῦ παρέξοντος ὑποκείμενα αὐτὰ ἁπάντων
καταναλωθέντων εἰς τὸ λεγόμενον ὑποκείμενον; πρός τι
15 γὰρ τὸ ὑποκείμενον, οὐ πρὸς τὸ ἐν αὐτῷ, ἀλλὰ πρὸς τὸ
ποιοῦν εἰς αὐτὸ κείμενον. καὶ τὸ ὑποκείμενον ὑπόκειται
πρὸς τὸ οὐχ ὑποκείμενον· εἰ τοῦτο, πρὸς τὸ ἔξω, ὥστε
παραλελειμμένον ἂν εἴη τοῦτο. εἰ δὲ οὐδὲν δέονται
ἄλλου ἔξωθεν, αὐτὸ δὲ πάντα δύναται γίγνεσθαι
20 σχηματιζόμενον, ὥσπερ ὁ τῇ ὀρχήσει πάντα αὐτὸν
ποιῶν, οὐκέτ' ἂν ὑποκείμενον εἴη, ἀλλ' αὐτὸ τὰ πάντα.
ὡς γὰρ ὁ ὀρχηστὴς οὐχ ὑποκείμενον τοῖς σχήμασιν—
ἐνέργεια γὰρ αὐτοῦ τὰ ἄλλα—οὕτως οὐδὲ ἦν λέγουσιν
ἔσται τοῖς πᾶσιν ὑποκείμενον, εἰ τὰ ἄλλα παρ' αὐτῆς
25 εἴη· μᾶλλον δὲ οὐδὲ τὰ ἄλλα ὅλως ἔσται, εἴ γέ πως

---

[1] A brief allusion to one of Plotinus' favourite images,
that of the cosmic dancer: cp. III. 2.16. 24–27 and 17. 8–11;
IV. 4.33. 6–25.

27. And in other ways, also, they ought to keep the principle of all things in the place of honour, and not to posit as principle the shapeless nor that which is without share in life and unintelligent and dark and is the indefinite, and then to attribute substance to this. For they bring in God for the sake of appearances, [a God] who has his being from matter and is composite and posterior, or rather is matter in a certain state. Then if matter is the substrate [or subject] there must necessarily be something else which acts upon it, being external to it, and makes it to be subjected to the things which are sent into matter by it. But if God himself was subjected in matter and himself came into being along with it, he will no longer make matter a subject, nor will he be the subject [or substrate] along with matter: for to what will they be substrates, when there will be nothing to make them substrates since everything has been used up in the so-called substrate? For the substrate is substrate in relation to something, not to what is in itself but to what acts upon it as it lies subjected. And the substrate is subjected in relation to what is not substrate: that is, to what is external, so that this would just have been left out. But if they do not require anything from outside, but the substrate itself is capable of becoming everything by being figured, like the dancer who in his dance makes himself everything,[1] then it will no longer be the substrate, but itself everything. For as the dancer is not the substrate of the figures—for all the rest are his active actuality—so what they call matter will not be the subject of all things, if all the rest come from it; or rather, all the rest will not even exist, if matter in a certain state is all the rest, just

ἔχουσα ὕλη τὰ ἄλλα, ὥς πως ἔχων [ὁ]¹ ὀρχούμενος τὰ
σχήματα. εἰ δὲ τὰ ἄλλα οὐκ ἔσται, οὐδὲ ὅλως
ὑποκείμενον αὕτη, οὐδὲ τῶν ὄντων ἡ ὕλη, ἀλλὰ ὕλη
μόνον οὖσα τούτῳ αὐτῷ οὐδὲ ὕλη· πρός τι γὰρ ἡ ὕλη. τὸ
γὰρ πρός τι πρὸς ἄλλο καὶ ἐκ τοῦ αὐτοῦ γένους, οἷον
30 διπλάσιον πρὸς ἥμισυ, οὐκ οὐσία πρὸς διπλάσιον· ὂν δὲ
πρὸς μὴ ὂν πῶς πρός τι, εἰ μὴ κατὰ συμβεβηκός; τὸ δὲ
καθ' αὑτὸ ὂν καὶ ἡ ὕλη ὂν πρὸς ὄν. εἰ γὰρ δύναμίς ἐστιν,
ὃ μέλλει ἔσεσθαι, ἐκεῖνο δὲ μὴ οὐσία, οὐδ' ἂν αὐτὴ
οὐσία· ὥστε συμβαίνει αὐτοῖς αἰτιωμένοις τοὺς ἐκ μὴ
35 οὐσιῶν οὐσίας ποιοῦντας αὐτοὺς ποιεῖν ἐξ οὐσίας μὴ
οὐσίαν· ὁ γὰρ κόσμος καθόσον κόσμος οὐκ οὐσία.
ἄτοπον δὲ τὴν μὲν ὕλην τὸ ὑποκείμενον οὐσίαν, τὰ δὲ
σώματα μὴ μᾶλλον οὐσίας, καὶ τούτων μᾶλλον μὴ τὸν
κόσμον οὐσίαν, ἀλλ' ἢ μόνον, καθόσον μόριον αὐτοῦ,
40 οὐσίαν· καὶ τὸ ζῷον μὴ παρὰ τῆς ψυχῆς ἔχειν τὴν
οὐσίαν, παρὰ δὲ τῆς ὕλης μόνον, καὶ τὴν ψυχὴν πάθημα
ὕλης καὶ ὕστερον. παρὰ τίνος οὖν ἔσχεν ἡ ὕλη τὸ
ἐψυχῶσθαι, καὶ ὅλως τῆς ψυχῆς ἡ ὑπόστασις; πῶς δὲ ἡ
ὕλη ὁτὲ μὲν σώματα γίνεται, ἄλλο δὲ αὐτῆς ψυχή; καὶ
γὰρ εἰ ἄλλοθεν προσίοι τὸ εἶδος, οὐδαμῇ ψυχὴ ἂν
45 γένοιτο ποιότητος προσελθούσης τῇ ὕλῃ, ἀλλὰ σώματα
ἄψυχα. εἰ δέ τι αὐτὴν πλάττοι καὶ ψυχὴν ποιοῖ, πρὸ τῆς
γινομένης ψυχῆς ἔσται ἡ ποιοῦσα ψυχή.

¹ del. Igal, H–S².

as the dancer in a certain state is the figures. But if all the rest are not going to exist, this matter will not in any way be a substrate, and not the matter of existing things, but, since it is purely and simply matter, will by this very fact not be matter: for matter is relative. For the relative is in relation to something else, and something of the same genus, double to half for instance, not substance to double; but how is being to non-being a relation, except incidentally? But the relation of being in itself to matter is one of being. For if it is potentiality, which is going to be, and that is not substance, it will not be itself substance; so that this is what happens to the Stoics: they blame those who make substances out of non-substances, but themselves make non-substance out of substance; for their universe, in so far as it is universe, is not substance. But it is absurd that matter, the substrate, is substance, but bodies are not more substantial and the universe more substantial than bodies, [but the universe according to them] is only substance in so far as it is a part of the substrate; and that the Living Being does not have its substantiality from soul but only from matter, and that the soul is an affection of and posterior to matter. From what, then, did matter derive its ensoulment, and in general from what did the real existence of soul derive? And why does matter sometimes become bodies, but another part of it becomes soul? For, even if the form comes from somewhere else, soul would in no way come into being when quality comes to matter, but soulless bodies. But if something moulds matter and makes soul, the soul which makes will be prior to the soul which comes to be.

28. Ἀλλὰ γὰρ πολλῶν ὄντων τῶν λεγομένων πρὸς
τὴν ὑπόθεσιν ταύτην τούτων μὲν παυστέον, μὴ καὶ
ἄτοπον ᾖ τὸ πρὸς οὕτω φανερὰν ἀτοπίαν φιλονεικεῖν,
δεικνύντα, ὅτι τὸ μὴ ὂν ὡς τὸ μάλιστα ὂν προτάττουσι
5 καὶ τὸ ὕστατον πρῶτον. αἴτιον δὲ ἡ αἴσθησις αὐτοῖς
ἡγεμὼν γενομένη καὶ πιστὴ εἰς ἀρχῶν καὶ τῶν ἄλλων
θέσιν. τὰ γὰρ σώματα νομίσαντες εἶναι τὰ ὄντα, εἶτα
αὐτῶν τὴν μεταβολὴν εἰς ἄλληλα φοβηθέντες τὸ μένον
ὑπ' αὐτὰ τοῦτο ᾠήθησαν τὸ ὂν εἶναι, ὥσπερ ἂν εἴ τις
μᾶλλον τὸν τόπον ἢ τὰ σώματα νομίσειεν εἶναι τὸ ὄν,
10 ὅτι οὐ φθείρεται ὁ τόπος νομίσας. καίτοι καὶ οὗτος
αὐτοῖς μένει, ἔδει δὲ οὐ τὸ ὁπωσοῦν μένον νομίσαι τὸ ὄν,
ἀλλὰ ἰδεῖν πρότερον, τίνα δεῖ προσεῖναι τῷ ἀληθῶς ὄντι,
οἷς οὖσιν ὑπάρχειν καὶ τὸ ἀεὶ μένειν. οὐδὲ γάρ, εἰ σκιὰ
ἀεὶ μένοι παρακολουθοῦσα ἀλλοιουμένῳ ἄλλῳ, μᾶλλόν
15 ἐστιν ἢ ἐκεῖνο. τό τε αἰσθητὸν μετ' ἐκείνου καὶ ἄλλων
πολλῶν τῷ πλήθει μᾶλλον ἂν τὸ ὅλον ὂν εἴη ἢ ἕν τι τῶν
ἐν ἐκείνῳ· εἰ δὲ δὴ καὶ τὸ ὅλον [ὑποβάθρα ἐκεῖνο] [1]
μὴ ὄν, πῶς ἂν ⟨ὑποβάθρα⟩ [1] ἐκεῖνο; πάντων τε
θαυμαστότατον τὸ τῇ αἰσθήσει πιστουμένους ἕκαστα τὸ
20 μὴ τῇ αἰσθήσει ἁλωτὸν τίθεσθαι ὄν. οὐδὲ γὰρ ὀρθῶς τὸ
ἀντιτυπὲς αὐτῇ διδόασι· ποιότης γὰρ τοῦτο. εἰ δὲ τῷ νῷ
λέγυυυι λαβεῖν, ἄτοπος ὁ νοῦς οὗτος ὁ τὴν ὕλην αὐτοῦ
προτάξας καὶ τὸ ὂν αὐτῇ δεδωκώς, ἀλλ' οὐχ αὑτῷ. οὐκ

28. But, though there are many things which are said against this hypothesis, we must stop here for fear that it may be absurd to strive for victory with so manifest an absurdity by showing that they give non-being the first rank as that which is most of all being and so rank the last first. The cause of this is that sense-perception became their guide and they trusted it for the placing of principles and the rest. For they considered that bodies were the real beings, and, since they were afraid of their transformation into each other, they thought that what persisted under them was reality, as if someone thought that place rather than bodies was real being, considering that place does not perish. Yet place also does persist for them, but they ought not to have considered that what persists in any kind of way was real being, but to see first what characteristics must belong to what is truly real, on the existence of which persistence for ever depends. For if a shadow always persisted which accompanied a being in process of alteration, it would not exist more than that being. And the sense-world with that [persistent substrate] and many other things would by its multiplicity be more real, being the whole, than any one of the things in it; but if indeed the whole is not real, how could that [substrate] be its foundation? But the most extraordinary of all is that, though they are assured of the existence of each and every thing by sense-perception, they posit as real being what cannot be apprehended by sense. For they do not rightly attribute resistance to it: resistance is a quality. But if they say they grasp it by intellect, it is an odd sort of intellect which ranks matter before itself and attributes real being to matter but not to itself. So,

ὧν οὖν ὁ νοῦς αὐτοῖς πῶς ἂν πιστὸς εἴη περὶ τῶν
κυριωτέρων αὐτοῦ λέγων καὶ οὐδαμῇ αὐτοῖς συγγενὴς
25 ὤν; ἀλλὰ περὶ μὲν ταύτης τῆς φύσεως καὶ τῶν
ὑποκειμένων ἱκανῶς καὶ ἐν ἄλλοις.

29. Τὰ δὲ ποιὰ αὐτοῖς ἕτερα μὲν δεῖ εἶναι τῶν
ὑποκειμένων, καὶ λέγουσιν· οὐ γὰρ ἂν αὐτὰ δεύτερα
κατηρίθμουν. εἰ τοίνυν ἕτερα, δεῖ αὐτὰ καὶ ἁπλᾶ εἶναι·
εἰ τοῦτο, μὴ σύνθετα· εἰ τοῦτο, μηδ' ὕλην ἔχειν, ᾗ ποιά·
5 εἰ τοῦτο, ἀσώματα εἶναι καὶ δραστήρια· ἡ γὰρ ὕλη πρὸς
τὸ πάσχειν αὐτοῖς ὑπόκειται. εἰ δὲ σύνθετα, πρῶτον μὲν
ἄτοπος ἡ διαίρεσις ἁπλᾶ καὶ σύνθετα ἀντιδιαστέλλουσα
καὶ ταῦτα ὑφ' ἓν γένος, ἔπειτα ἐν θατέρῳ τῶν εἰδῶν τὸ
ἕτερον τιθεῖσα, ὥσπερ ἄν τις διαιρῶν τὴν ἐπιστήμην
10 τὴν μὲν γραμματικὴν λέγοι, τὴν δὲ γραμματικὴν καὶ
ἄλλο τι. εἰ δὲ τὰ ποιὰ ὕλην ποιὰν λέγοιεν, πρῶτον μὲν οἱ
λόγοι αὐτοῖς ἔνυλοι, ἀλλ' οὐκ ἐν ὕλῃ γενόμενοι σύνθετόν
τι ποιήσουσιν, ἀλλὰ πρὸ τοῦ συνθέτου ὃ ποιοῦσιν ἐξ
ὕλης καὶ εἴδους ἔσονται· οὐκ ἄρα αὐτοὶ εἴδη οὐδὲ λόγοι.
15 εἰ δὲ λέγοιεν μηδὲν εἶναι τοὺς λόγους ἢ ὕλην πως
ἔχουσαν, τὰ ποιὰ δηλονότι πως ἔχοντα ἐροῦσι καὶ ἐν τῷ
τρίτῳ γένει τακτέον. εἰ δὲ ἥδε ἡ σχέσις ἄλλη, τίς
ἡ διαφορά; ἢ δῆλον, ὅτι τό πως ἔχειν ἐνταῦθα
ὑπόστασις μᾶλλον· καίτοι εἰ μὴ κἀκεῖ ὑπόστασις, τί

since their intellect is not real for them, how could it be trustworthy when it speaks about things more authentic than itself and is in no way related to them? But about this nature and about substrates we have spoken sufficiently elsewhere.

29. Qualia for them must be different from the subject-substrates, and this is what they mean; otherwise they would not have counted them second. If then they are different, they must also be simple; if this is so, not composite; and if this is so, they must not have matter, in so far as they are qualia; and if this is so, they must be bodiless and active: for matter is subjected to them for passivity. But if they are composite, first of all the division is absurd which sets simples and composites over against one another, and that under one genus, and then puts the other one in each of the species, as if someone dividing knowledge said that one kind was literary knowledge and another literary knowledge plus something else. But if they were to say that qualia are qualified matter, first of all their rational forming principles will be immanent in matter; they will not make something composite when they have come to be in matter, but before the composite which they make they will be composed of matter and form; they will not, then, themselves be forms or forming principles. But if they were to say that the forming principles are nothing but matter in a certain state, they obviously will be saying that qualia are things in a certain state, and they ought to be classed in the third genus. But if this is a different kind of state, what is the difference? Now clearly in this case being in a certain state is more of an existence. But if it is not an existence there too, why do they count it

20 καταριθμοῦσιν ὡς ἓν γένος ἢ εἶδος; οὐ γὰρ δὴ ὑπὸ τὸ
αὐτὸ τὸ μὲν ὄν, τὸ δὲ οὐκ ὂν δύναται εἶναι. ἀλλὰ τί
τοῦτο τὸ ἐπὶ τῇ ὕλῃ πως ἔχον; ἢ γὰρ ὂν ἢ οὐκ ὄν· καὶ εἰ
ὄν, πάντως ἀσώματον· εἰ δὲ οὐκ ὄν, μάτην λέγεται, καὶ
ὕλη μόνον, τὸ δὲ ποιὸν οὐδέν. ἀλλ᾽ οὐδὲ τό πως ἔχον· ἔτι
25 γὰρ μᾶλλον οὐκ ὄν. τὸ δὲ τέταρτον λεχθὲν καὶ πολλῷ
μᾶλλον. μόνον ὂν ἄρα ὕλη. τίς οὖν τοῦτό φησιν; οὐ γὰρ
δὴ αὐτὴ ἡ ὕλη. εἰ μὴ ἄρα αὐτή· πῶς γὰρ ἔχουσα ὁ νοῦς·
καίτοι τὸ "πῶς ἔχουσα" προσθήκη κενή. ἡ ὕλη ἄρα
λέγει ταῦτα καὶ καταλαμβάνει. καὶ εἰ μὲν ἔλεγεν
ἔμφρονα, θαῦμα ἂν ἦν, πῶς καὶ νοεῖ καὶ ψυχῆς ἔργα
30 ποιεῖ οὔτε νοῦν οὔτε ψυχὴν ἔχουσα. εἰ δ᾽ ἀφρόνως λέγοι
αὐτὴν τιθεῖσα ὃ μὴ ἔστι μηδὲ δύναται, τίνι ταύτην δεῖ
ἀνατιθέναι τὴν ἀφροσύνην; ἤ, εἰ ἔλεγεν, αὐτῇ· νῦν δὲ
οὔτε λέγει ἐκείνη, ὅ τε λέγων πολὺ τὸ παρ᾽ ἐκείνης ἔχων
λέγει, ὅλος μὲν ὢν ἐκείνης, εἰ καὶ μόριον ψυχῆς[1] ἔχοι,
35 ἀγνοίᾳ δὲ αὐτοῦ καὶ δυνάμεως τῆς λέγειν τἀληθῆ περὶ
τῶν τοιούτων δυναμένης.

30. Ἐν δὲ τοῖς πως ἔχουσιν ἄτοπον μὲν ἴσως τά πως
ἔχοντα τρίτα τίθεσθαι ἢ ὁπωσοῦν τάξεως ἔχει, ἐπειδὴ
περὶ τὴν ὕλην πως ἔχοντα πάντα. ἀλλὰ διαφορὰν τῶν
πως ἐχόντων φήσουσιν εἶναι καὶ ἄλλως πως ἔχειν τὴν
5 ὕλην ὡδὶ καὶ οὕτως, ἄλλως δὲ ἐν τοῖς πως ἔχουσι, καὶ

[1] μόριον ψυχῆς Igal, H–S²: μόνον ψυχὴν Enn.: ψυχὴν Theiler, H–S¹.

as one genus or species? For certainly that which is and that which is not cannot be under the same genus. But what is this being in a certain state imposed upon matter? It is either existent or non-existent; and if it is existent, it is altogether bodiless; but if it is non-existent, it is an empty appellation and there is only matter, but the quale is nothing. But neither is the thing in a certain state anything: for it is still more non-existent. And the fourth class mentioned is even still more non-existent. So, then, only matter is existent. Who, then, asserts this? Not, presumably, matter. But perhaps matter does assert it: for matter in a certain state is intellect; though the "in a certain state" is a meaningless addition. Matter, then, says this and understands it. And if it talked sense, it would be surprising how it thinks and does the works of soul, when it has neither intellect nor soul. But if it was talking senselessly, making itself what it is not and cannot be, to whom should we attribute the senselessness? Well, if it did speak, to itself; but, as things are, matter does not speak, but the speaker speaks with a large contribution from matter, to which he entirely belongs; even if he has a bit of soul, he speaks in ignorance of himself and of the power which is able to speak the truth about such things.

30. In the case of things in a certain state, it is perhaps absurd to put things in a certain state third, or however they are placed in the order, since everything in a certain state is in relation to mätter. But they will say that things in a certain state have a distinctive difference and that it is one thing for matter to be in this or that particular state, but something else in the case of things in a certain

ἔτι τὰ μὲν ποιὰ περὶ τὴν ὕλην πως ἔχοντα, τὰ ἰδίως δέ
πως ἔχοντα περὶ τὰ ποιά. ἀλλὰ τῶν ποιῶν αὐτῶν οὐδὲν
ἢ ὕλης πως ἐχούσης ὄντων πάλιν τά πως ἔχοντα ἐπὶ τὴν
ὕλην αὐτοῖς ἀνατρέχει καὶ περὶ τὴν ὕλην ἔσται. πῶς δὲ
10 ἐν τό πως ἔχον πολλῆς διαφορᾶς ἐν αὐτοῖς οὔσης; πῶς
γὰρ τὸ τρίπηχυ καὶ τὸ λευκὸν εἰς ἕν, τοῦ μὲν ποσοῦ, τοῦ
δὲ ποιοῦ ὄντος; πῶς δὲ τὸ ποτὲ καὶ τὸ ποῦ; πῶς δὲ ὅλως
πως ἔχοντα τὸ χθὲς καὶ τὸ πέρυσι καὶ τὸ ἐν Λυκίῳ καὶ
Ἀκαδημία; καὶ ὅλως πῶς δὲ ὁ χρόνος πως ἔχων; οὔτε
15 γὰρ αὐτὸς οὔτε τὰ ἐν αὐτῷ τῷ χρόνῳ, οὔτε τὰ ἐν τῷ
τόπῳ οὔτε ὁ τόπος. τὸ δὲ ποιεῖν πῶς πως ἔχον; ἐπεὶ
οὐδ' ὁ ποιῶν πως ἔχων, ἀλλὰ μᾶλλόν πως ποιῶν ἢ ὅλως
οὔ πως,[1] ἀλλὰ ποιῶν μόνον· καὶ ὁ πάσχων οὔ πως ἔχων,
ἀλλὰ μᾶλλόν πως πάσχων ἢ ὅλως πάσχων οὕτως. ἴσως
20 δ' ἂν μόνον ἁρμόσει ἐπὶ τοῦ κεῖσθαι τὸ "πὼς ἔχων" καὶ
ἐπὶ τοῦ ἔχειν· ἐπὶ δὲ τοῦ ἔχειν οὐ "πὼς ἔχων", ἀλλὰ
"ἔχων". τὸ δὲ πρός τι, εἰ μὲν μὴ ὑφ' ἓν τοῖς ἄλλοις
ἐτίθεσαν, ἕτερος λόγος ἦν ἂν ζητούντων εἴ τινα διδόασιν
ὑπόστασιν ταῖς τοιαύταις σχέσεσι, πολλαχοῦ οὐ
διδόντων. ἔτι δ' ἐν γένει τῷ αὐτῷ ⟨τὸ⟩[2] ἐπιγινόμενον
25 πρᾶγμα τοῖς ἤδη οὖσιν ἄτοπον συντάττειν [τὸ ἐπιγι-
νόμενον][3] εἰς ταὐτὸν γένος τοῖς πρότερον οὖσι· δεῖ

---

[1] Gollwitzer: οὐκ ὤν BxUC, Creuzer: οὐκ ὄν w, Perna.
[2] H–S.
[3] del. Kirchhoff.

state, and, besides, that qualia are in a certain state in relation to matter, but the things which are specifically in a certain state are so in relation to qualia. But, if the qualia themselves are nothing but matter in a certain state, again the things in a certain state go back for the Stoics to matter and are so in relation to matter. But how is the class of things in a certain state one when there is a great deal of difference between them? For how can the "three-cubits-long" and the "white" [be got] into one class, when one of them is quantitative and the other qualitative? And how the when and the where? And how altogether are "yesterday" and "last year" and "in the Lyceum" and "in the Academy" in a certain state? And, generally speaking, how is time in a certain state? For time is not so, nor are the things in time itself, nor the things in place nor place. But how is doing being in a certain state? Since the doer is not existing in a certain state but doing in a certain way, or not at all in a certain way, but just doing; and the one who is affected is not existing in a certain state but rather being affected in a certain way or simply being affected like this. But perhaps "being in a certain state" will only fit position and possession; but in the case of possession one is not "in possession of a certain state" but "in possession". But as regards the relative, if they did not class it under one genus with the other [things in a certain state] it would take another discussion to enquire if they give any reality to such [relative] states, since they often do not do so. And again it is absurd to put a thing which is subsequent to things already existing into the same genus as the things

γὰρ πρότερον ἓν καὶ δύο εἶναι, ἵνα καὶ ἥμισυ καὶ διπλάσιον.

Περὶ δὲ τῶν ὅσοι ἄλλως τὰ ὄντα ἢ τὰς ἀρχὰς τῶν ὄντων ἔθεντο, εἴτε ἄπειρα εἴτε πεπερασμένα, εἴτε 30 σώματα εἴτε ἀσώματα, ἢ καὶ τὸ συναμφότερον, χωρὶς περὶ ἑκάστων ἔξεστι ζητεῖν λαμβάνουσι καὶ τὰ παρὰ τῶν ἀρχαίων πρὸς τὰς δόξας αὐτῶν εἰρημένα.

which were there before: for one and two must be there first for there to be half and double.

But as for all the others who have made other assumptions about beings or the principles of beings, whether they said they were infinite or limited, bodies or bodiless, or both, one is free to enquire about each and every one of them, taking into account as well what the ancients said against their opinions.

VI. 2. (43) ΠΕΡΙ ΤΩΝ ΓΕΝΩΝ ΤΟΥ ΟΝΤΟΣ ΔΕΥΤΕΡΟΝ

1. Ἐπεὶ δὲ περὶ τῶν λεγομένων δέκα γενῶν
ἐπέσκεπται, εἴρηται δὲ καὶ περὶ τῶν εἰς ἓν ἀγόντων
γένος τὰ πάντα τέτταρα ὑπὸ τὸ ἓν οἷον εἴδη τιθεμένων,
ἀκόλουθον ἂν εἴη εἰπεῖν, τί ποτε ἡμῖν περὶ τούτων
5 φαίνεται τὰ δοκοῦντα ἡμῖν πειρωμένοις εἰς τὴν
Πλάτωνος ἀνάγειν δόξαν. εἰ μὲν οὖν ἓν ἔδει τίθεσθαι τὸ
ὄν, οὐδὲν ἂν ἔδει ζητεῖν, οὔτ᾽ εἰ γένος ἓν ἐπὶ πᾶσιν, οὔτε
εἰ γένη μὴ ὑφ᾽ ἕν, οὔτ᾽ εἰ ἀρχάς, οὔτε εἰ τὰς ἀρχὰς καὶ
γένη τὰς αὐτὰς δεῖ τίθεσθαι, οὔτε εἰ τὰ γένη καὶ ἀρχὰς
10 τὰ αὐτά, ἢ τὰς μὲν ἀρχὰς ἁπάσας καὶ γένη, τὰ δὲ γένη
οὐκ ἀρχάς, ἢ ἀνάπαλιν, ἢ ἐφ᾽ ἑκατέρων τινὰς μὲν ἀρχὰς
καὶ γένη καί τινα γένη καὶ ἀρχάς, ἢ ἐπὶ μὲν τῶν ἑτέρων
πάντα καὶ θάτερα, ἐπὶ δὲ τῶν ἑτέρων τινὰ καὶ θάτερα.
ἐπεὶ δὲ οὐχ ἓν φαμεν τὸ ὄν—διότι δέ, εἴρηται καὶ τῷ
15 Πλάτωνι καὶ ἑτέροις—ἀναγκαῖον ἴσως γίγνεται καὶ

---

[1] The critical discussion of the ten Aristotelian
categories occupies the first 24 chapters of VI. 1, of the
Stoic categories the last 0. Note the importance which
Plotinus gives here to the highest Stoic genus, τι (cp. VI. 1.
25 and below lines 21–5), which he did not quite understand
and which annoyed him particularly, perhaps because
Severus the Middle Platonist, who was read in his school
(*Life* ch. 14, 11), had taken it seriously and used it in his
exegesis of the Timaeus: see below n. 1, p. 112.

VI. 2. ON THE KINDS
OF BEING II

1. Now that our enquiry about what are called the ten genera has been completed, and we have spoken about those who bring all things into one genus and posit four species of a sort under the one,[1] the next thing would be to say how these things look to us, trying to lead back our own thoughts to the thought of Plato. Now if it was necessary to assume that being is one, there would be no need to investigate whether there is one genus over all, or whether the genera cannot be classed under one, or whether the principles [can or cannot be], or whether one should assume that principles are the same as genera or genera as principles, or whether all the principles are also genera but the genera not [all] principles, or the other way round, or whether in both groups some principles are also genera and some genera also principles, or whether in one group all are the others, but in the other some are also the others.[2] But since we maintain that being is not one—Plato and others have explained why[3]—it becomes, per-

[2] On the difference between principles and genera see ch. 2, 15–19. It is of great importance for Plotinus' exegesis of the *Sophist*.

[3] The reference to Plato is to *Sophist* 244B–245C and *Parmenides* 141C9–10. "Others": Aristotle and the Stoics; cp. VI. 1. 1. 5–9.

PLOTINUS: ENNEAD VI. 2.

περὶ τούτων ἐπισκέψασθαι πρότερον εἰς μέσον θέντας,
τίνα ἀριθμὸν λέγομεν καὶ πῶς. ἐπεὶ οὖν περὶ τοῦ ὄντος ἢ
τῶν ὄντων ζητοῦμεν, ἀναγκαῖον πρῶτον παρ' αὐτοῖς
διελέσθαι τάδε, τί τε τὸ ὂν λέγομεν, περὶ οὗ ἡ σκέψις
ὀρθῶς γίνοιτο νυνί, καὶ τί δοκεῖ μὲν ἄλλοις εἶναι ὄν,
20 γινόμενον δὲ αὐτὸ λέγομεν εἶναι, ὄντως δὲ οὐδέποτε ὄν.
δεῖ δὲ νοεῖν ταῦτα ἀπ' ἀλλήλων διῃρημένα οὐχ ὡς
γένους τοῦ τὶ εἰς ταῦτα διῃρημένου, οὐδ' οὕτως οἴεσθαι
τὸν Πλάτωνα πεποιηκέναι. γελοῖον γὰρ ὑφ' ἓν θέσθαι
τὸ ὂν τῷ μὴ ὄντι, ὥσπερ ἂν εἴ τις Σωκράτη ὑπὸ τὸ αὐτὸ
25 θείτο καὶ τὴν τούτου εἰκόνα. τὸ γὰρ ''διελέσθαι''
ἐνταῦθά ἐστι τὸ ἀφορίσαι καὶ χωρὶς θεῖναι, καὶ τὸ δόξαν
ὂν εἶναι εἰπεῖν οὐκ εἶναι ὄν, ὑποδείξαντα αὐτοῖς ἄλλο τὸ
ὡς ἀληθῶς ὂν εἶναι. καὶ προστιθεὶς τῷ ὄντι τὸ ''ἀεὶ''
ὑπέδειξεν, ὡς δεῖ τὸ ὂν τοιοῦτον εἶναι, οἷον μηδέποτε
30 ψεύδεσθαι τὴν τοῦ ὄντος φύσιν. περὶ δὴ τούτου τοῦ
ὄντος λέγοντες καὶ περὶ τούτου ὡς οὐχ ἑνὸς ὄντος
σκεψόμεθα· ὕστερον δέ, εἰ δοκεῖ, καὶ περὶ γενέσεως καὶ
τοῦ γινομένου καὶ κόσμου αἰσθητοῦ τι ἐροῦμεν.

2. Ἐπεὶ οὖν οὐχ ἓν φαμεν, ἆρα ἀριθμόν τινα ἢ
ἄπειρον; πῶς γὰρ δὴ τὸ οὐχ ἕν; ἢ ἓν ἅμα καὶ πολλὰ
λέγομεν, καί τι ποικίλον ἓν τὰ πολλὰ εἰς ἓν ἔχον.
ἀνάγκη τοίνυν τοῦτο τὸ οὕτως ἓν ἢ τῷ γένει ἓν εἶναι,

---

[1] *Timaeus* 27D5. The attack here is clearly on a Stoicising Platonist exegesis of this passage, probably that of Severus (Proclus *In Tim.* vol. I, p.227, 13–18 Diehl).

[2] In VI. 3.

haps, compulsory to enquire about these points, centring our discussion first on what number [of kinds of being] we intend and in what sense. Since, then, we are enquiring about being or beings, we must in our discussion first of all make a distinction between what we call being, about which at present our investigation would be correctly conducted, and what others think is being, but we call it becoming, and say that it is never really real. But in thinking of these two classes which are distinct from each other one must not think of them as if there was a genus of "something" divided into them, or suppose that Plato made this division. For it is absurd to put being under one genus with non-being, as if one were to put Socrates and his portrait under one genus. For "making a distinction" here [1] means marking off and setting apart, and saying that what seems to be being is not being, [and by this Plato] indicates to them that what is truly being is something else. And by prefixing "always" to being he indicated that being must be of such a kind as never to belie the nature of being. So we are speaking of this being, and this is the being about which we shall enquire on the assumption that it is not one; afterwards,[2] if it seems proper, we shall say something about becoming and what comes to be and the universe perceived by the senses.

2. Since, then, we maintain that being is not one, do we say that it is a number or infinite? What do we really mean by "not one"? Now we say that it is at the same time one and many, and that it is a richly variegated one keeping its many together in one. It is therefore necessary that this, which is one in this way, should either be generically one, and the

5 εἴδη δ' αὐτοῦ τὰ ὄντα, οἷς πολλὰ καὶ ἕν, ἢ πλείω ἑνὸς
γένη, ὑφ' ἓν δὲ τὰ πάντα, ἢ πλείω μὲν γένη, μηδὲν δὲ
ἄλλο ὑπ' ἄλλο, ἀλλ' ἕκαστον περιεκτικὸν τῶν ὑπ' αὐτό,
εἴτε καὶ αὐτῶν γενῶν ἐλαττόνων ὄντων ἢ εἰδῶν καὶ ὑπὸ
τούτοις ἀτόμων, συντελεῖν ἅπαντα εἰς μίαν φύσιν καὶ ἐκ
10 πάντων τῷ νοητῷ κόσμῳ, ὃν δὴ λέγομεν τὸ ὄν, τὴν
σύστασιν εἶναι. εἰ δὴ τοῦτο, οὐ μόνον γένη ταῦτα εἶναι,
ἀλλὰ καὶ ἀρχὰς τοῦ ὄντος ἅμα ὑπάρχειν· γένη μέν, ὅτι
ὑπ' αὐτὰ ἄλλα γένη ἐλάττω καὶ εἴδη μετὰ τοῦτο καὶ
ἄτομα· ἀρχὰς δέ, εἰ τὸ ὂν οὕτως ἐκ πολλῶν καὶ ἐκ
τούτων τὸ ὅλον ὑπάρχει. εἰ μέντοι πλείω μὲν ἦν ἐξ ὧν
15 συνελθόντα δὲ τὰ ὅλα ἐποίει τὸ πᾶν ἄλλο[1] οὐκ ἔχοντα
ὑπ' αὐτά, ἀρχαὶ μὲν ἂν ἦσαν, γένη δὲ οὐκ ἄν· οἷον εἴ τις
ἐκ τῶν τεσσάρων ἐποίει τὸ αἰσθητόν, πυρὸς καὶ τῶν
τοιούτων· ταῦτα γὰρ ἀρχαὶ ἂν ἦσαν, γένη δὲ οὔ· εἰ μὴ
ὁμωνύμως τὸ γένος. λέγοντες τοίνυν καὶ γένη τινὰ
20 εἶναι, τὰ δ' αὐτὰ καὶ ἀρχάς, ἆρα τὰ μὲν γένη, ἕκαστον
μετὰ τῶν ὑπ' αὐτά, ὁμοῦ μιγνύντες ἀλλήλοις τὰ πάντα,
τὸ ὅλον ἀποτελοῦμεν καὶ σύγκρασιν ποιοῦμεν ἁπάντων;
ἀλλὰ δυνάμει, οὐκ ἐνεργείᾳ ἕκαστον οὐδὲ καθαρὸν αὐτὸ
ἕκαστον ἔσται. ἀλλὰ τὰ μὲν γένη ἐάσομεν, τὰ δὲ
25 καθέκαστον μίξομεν; τίνα οὖν ἔσται ἐφ' αὐτῶν τὰ γένη;
ἢ ἔσται κἀκεῖνα ἐφ' αὐτῶν καὶ καθαρά, καὶ τὰ μιχθέντα

---

[1] coniecimus: ἀλλ' wBxC: ἀλλ' Creuzer (alia Ficinus):
om. U.

beings its species, by which it is many and one; or
that it should be more genera than one, but all
[grouped] under one; or that there should be more
genera, but none of them subordinated to any other,
but each including those below it (whether they
themselves are lesser genera or species with individuals [grouped] under them) and all contributing
to one nature; the intelligible universe, which is
certainly what we call being, would be constructed
from all of them. If this is so, these must certainly
not only be genera but at the same time also principles of being: genera, because there are other
lesser genera under them and subsequently species
and individuals; principles, if being is thus composed
of many and the whole derives its existence from
these. If then there were a number of originative
constituents and they came together as wholes and
made the all while having nothing else subordinated
to them, they would be principles, but not genera; as
if someone made the sense-world out of the four
elements, fire and such: for these would be principles, but not genera; unless "genus" is used
equivocally. If we say, then, that they are a kind of
genera, but that these same genera are also principles, then shall we achieve the completion of the
whole by mixing the genera, all of them, together
with each other, each with the things which come
under it, and make a blend of everything? But then
each and every thing will be potential and not
actual, and each will not be itself in a pure state. But
shall we let the genera go and mix up the individuals? What then will the genera by themselves
be? They will be by themselves and pure and their
mixed-up members will not abolish them. And how

οὐκ ἀπολεῖ αὐτά. καὶ πῶς; ἢ ταῦτα μὲν εἰς ὕστερον· νῦν
δ' ἐπεὶ συγκεχωρήκαμεν καὶ γένη εἶναι καὶ προσέτι καὶ
τῆς οὐσίας ἀρχὰς καὶ τρόπον ἕτερον ἀρχὰς καὶ
σύνθεσιν, πρῶτον λεκτέον πόσα λέγομεν γένη καὶ πῶς
30 διίσταμεν ἀπ' ἀλλήλων αὐτὰ καὶ οὐχ ὑφ' ἓν ἄγομεν,
ὥσπερ ἐκ τύχης συνελθόντα καὶ ἕν τι πεποιηκότα·
καίτοι πολλῷ εὐλογώτερον ὑφ' ἕν. ἤ, εἰ μὲν εἴδη οἷόν τε
ἦν τοῦ ὄντος ἅπαντα εἶναι καὶ ἐφεξῆς τούτοις τὰ ἄτομα
καὶ μηδὲν τούτων ἔξω, ἦν ἂν ἴσως ποιεῖν οὕτως. ἐπειδὴ
35 δὲ ἡ τοιαύτη θέσις ἀναίρεσίς ἐστιν αὐτῆς—οὐδὲ γὰρ τὰ
εἴδη εἴδη ἔσται, οὐδ' ὅλως πολλὰ ὑφ' ἕν, ἀλλὰ πάντα ἕν,
μὴ ἑτέρου ἢ ἑτέρων[1] ἔξω ἐκείνου τοῦ ἑνὸς ὄντων· πῶς
γὰρ ἂν πολλὰ ἐγένετο τὸ ἕν, ὥστε καὶ εἴδη γεννῆσαι, εἰ
μή τι ἦν παρ' αὐτὸ ἄλλο; οὐ γὰρ ἑαυτῷ πολλά, εἰ μή τις
40 ὡς μέγεθος κερματίζει[2]· ἀλλὰ καὶ οὕτως ἕτερον τὸ
κερματίζον. εἰ δ' αὐτὸ κερματιεῖ ἢ ὅλως διαιρήσει, πρὸ
τοῦ διαιρεθῆναι ἔσται διῃρημένον. ταύτῃ μὲν οὖν καὶ δι'
ἄλλα πολλὰ ἀποστατέον τοῦ "γένος ἕν", καὶ ὅτι οὐχ
οἷόν τε ἕκαστον ὁτιοῦν ληφθὲν ἢ ὂν ἢ οὐσίαν λέγειν. εἰ δέ
45 τις λέγοι ὄν, τῷ συμβεβηκέναι φήσει, οἷον εἰ λευκὸν
λέγοι τὴν οὐσίαν· οὐ γὰρ ὅπερ λευκὸν λέγει.

---

[1] Kirchhoff: ἕτερον Enn.
[2] coniecimus: -σει wU (vix recte, sed cf. μερίσεις VI.
4. 8. 20): -ση BxC: -εῖ Volkmann.

can this be? We will discuss this later [1]; but now, since we have agreed that there are genera, and further that they are principles of substance and principles and a composition in another way, first it must be stated how many genera we say there are and how we distinguish them from each other and do not bring them under one, as if they came together by chance and made some one thing; yet it would be much more reasonable if they did come under one. Now, if it was possible for them all to be species of being, with the individuals immediately subsequent to them, and nothing outside these, it might perhaps be possible to proceed like this. But since such an arrangement would be the abolition of substance— for the species would not be species, nor altogether would there be many under one, but all would be one, and there would be no other or others outside that one: for how could the one become many, so as to generate species, unless there was something else besides itself? For it could not by its own means become many, unless somebody cuts it up like a magnitude; but even so the cutter would be another. But if it is going to do the cutting up, or in general the dividing, itself, it will be divided before the division. Thus, and for many other reasons, we must abandon the "one genus", also because it is not possible to take any and every individual thing and call it being or substance. But if one does call it substance, one will do so by incidental predication, as if one called substance white: for one is not speaking of what is [essentially] white.

[1] Ch. 19, 12–17.

3. Πλείω μὲν δὴ λέγομεν εἶναι καὶ οὐ κατὰ τύχην
πλείω. οὐκοῦν ἀφ' ἑνός. ἤ, εἰ καὶ ἀφ' ἑνός, οὐ
κατηγορουμένου δὲ κατ' αὐτῶν ἐν τῷ εἶναι, οὐδὲν
κωλύει ἕκαστον οὐχ ὁμοειδὲς ὂν ἄλλῳ χωρὶς αὐτὸ εἶναι
5 γένος. ἆρ' οὖν ἔξωθεν τοῦτο τῶν γενομένων γενῶν τὸ
αἴτιον μέν, μὴ κατηγορούμενον δὲ τῶν ἄλλων ἐν τῷ τί
ἐστιν; ἢ τὸ μὲν ἔξω· ἐπέκεινα γὰρ τὸ ἕν, ὡς ἂν μὴ
συναριθμούμενον τοῖς γένεσιν, εἰ δι' αὐτὸ τὰ ἄλλα, ἃ
ἐπίσης ἀλλήλοις εἰς τὸ γένη εἶναι. καὶ πῶς ἐκεῖνο οὐ
10 συνηρίθμηται; ἢ τὰ ὄντα ζητοῦμεν, οὐ τὸ ἐπέκεινα.
τοῦτο μὲν οὖν οὕτως· τί δὲ τὸ συναριθμούμενον; ἐφ' οὗ
καὶ θαυμάσειεν ἄν τις, πῶς συναριθμούμενον τοῖς
αἰτιατοῖς. ἤ, εἰ μὲν ὑφ' ἓν γένος αὐτὸ καὶ τὰ ἄλλα,
ἄτοπον· εἰ δὲ οἷς αἴτιον συναριθμεῖται, ὡς αὐτὸ τὸ γένος
15 καὶ τὰ ἄλλα ἐφεξῆς—καὶ ἔστι διάφορα τὰ ἐφεξῆς πρὸς
αὐτό, καὶ οὐ κατηγορεῖται αὐτῶν ὡς γένος οὐδ' ἄλλο τι
κατ' αὐτῶν—ἀνάγκη καὶ αὐτὰ γένη εἶναι ἔχοντα ὑφ'
αὑτά. οὐδὲ γάρ, εἰ σὺ τὸ βαδίζειν ἐγέννας, ὑπὸ σὲ ὡς
γένος τὸ βαδίζειν ἦν ἄν· καὶ εἰ μηδὲν ἦν πρὸ αὐτοῦ ἄλλο
20 ὡς γένος αὐτοῦ, ἦν δὲ τι μετ' αὐτό, γένος ἂν ἦν τὸ

---

[1] This is the One-Being, the Second Hypostasis, sharply
distinguished as usual from the Absolute One, the First
Hypostasis; the subject of the One-Being and its relation to

ON THE KINDS OF BEING II

3. We certainly say that there are several genera, and that it is not by accident that there are several. They derive therefore from one. Now, even if they do derive from one, but a one which is not included in the definition of their being, nothing prevents each one of them, since it has not the same specific form as another, from being itself a separate genus. Is then this one which is outside the genera which have come into being [from it] their cause, but not predicated in the definitions of what each of the others are? Yes, it is outside, for the One is transcendent, so as not to be numbered with the genera, if the others exist through it, which are on equal terms with each other as far as being genera goes. And how does it come about that it is not numbered with them? We are looking for beings, not what transcends being. So much, then, for this One; but what about the one which is numbered with the others [1]? One might wonder about this, how it is numbered with those caused by it. Now if it and the others were under one genus, it would be absurd; but if it is numbered with those of which it is the cause, as if it was the absolute genus and the others were subsequent— and the subsequents are different from it, and it is not predicated of them as their genus or anything else with reference to them—then they too must be genera, if they have things classed under them. For if you generated walking, walking would not be classed under you as its genus; and if there was nothing else before it as its genus, but there were things after it, walking would be a genus in the

beings, and why "one" is not a genus like "being", is taken up again in ch. 9.

βαδίζειν ἐν τοῖς οὖσιν. ὅλως δὲ ἴσως οὐδὲ τὸ ἓν φατέον
αἴτιον τοῖς ἄλλοις εἶναι, ἀλλ᾽ οἷον μέρη αὐτοῦ καὶ οἷον
στοιχεῖα αὐτοῦ καὶ πάντα μίαν φύσιν μεριζομένην ταῖς
ἡμῶν ἐπινοίαις, αὐτὸ δὲ εἶναι ὑπὸ δυνάμεως θαυμαστῆς
ἓν εἰς πάντα, καὶ φαινόμενον πολλὰ καὶ γινόμενον
25 πολλά, οἷον ὅταν κινηθῇ κατὰ¹ τὸ πολύνουν² τῆς
φύσεως, ποιεῖν τὸ ἓν μὴ ἓν εἶναι, ἡμᾶς τε οἷον μοίρας
αὐτοῦ προφέροντας ταύτας ἓν ἕκαστον τίθεσθαι καὶ
γένος λέγειν ἀγνοοῦντας ὅτι μὴ ὅλον ἅμα εἴδομεν, ἀλλὰ
κατὰ μέρος προφέροντες πάλιν αὐτὰ συνάπτομεν οὐ
30 δυνάμενοι ἐπὶ πολὺν χρόνον αὐτὰ κατέχειν σπεύδοντα
πρὸς αὐτά. διὸ πάλιν μεθίεμεν εἰς τὸ ὅλον καὶ ἐῶμεν ἓν
γενέσθαι, μᾶλλον δὲ ἓν εἶναι. ἀλλὰ ἴσως σαφέστερα
ταῦτα ἔσται κἀκείνων ἐγνωσμένων, ἢν τὰ γένη
λάβωμεν ὁπόσα· οὕτω γὰρ καὶ τὸ πῶς. ἀλλ᾽ ἐπεὶ δεῖ
35 λέγοντα μὴ ἀποφάσεις λέγειν, ἀλλὰ καὶ εἰς ἔννοιαν καὶ
νόησιν ἰέναι τῶν λεγομένων, ὡδὶ ποιητέον.

4. Εἰ τὴν σώματος φύσιν ἰδεῖν ἐβουλόμεθα, οἷόν τί
ἐστιν ἐν τῷδε τῷ ὅλῳ ἡ τοῦ σώματος αὐτοῦ φύσις, ἆρ᾽
οὐ καταμαθόντες ἐπί τινος τῶν μερῶν αὐτοῦ, ὡς ἔστι τὸ

---

¹ Igal, H–S²: καὶ Enn.
² Igal, H–S²: πολύνουν EBUC, H–S¹: πολύχουν A (duo
puncta supra χ) x, Perna.

---

¹ We thankfully accept here Igal's excellent emendation
πολύνουν (cp. ch. 21, 4). The reading with most MSS
authority πολύχνουν ("downiness" or "furriness"), printed
in H-S¹, can surely on reflection only commend itself to
cats, and the πολύχουν of other MSS, generally adopted by
editors, is not used elsewhere by Plotinus and does not give
as exactly appropriate a sense.

realm of real beings. But in general, perhaps not even the one should be asserted to be the cause of the others, but they are something like parts of it, and something like elements of it, and all one nature divided into parts by our conceptions, but [this one] itself is by a wonderful power one into all, both appearing all and becoming all, as if when it is in motion, and, by its nature's fullness of intelligence,[1] it makes the one be not one, and we bring forward as it were parts of it and posit these, each of them as one and call it a genus, being unaware that we do not know the whole all at once, but bring forward piece by piece and join them up again, being unable to hold them back for long as they hasten to themselves.[2] Therefore we let them go into the whole, and allow them to become one, or rather to be one. But perhaps all this will be clearer when we know what is coming next, if we grasp how many genera there are: for this will tell us how they are. But since in our discourse we should not just make statements,[3] but form some idea and come to some understanding of what is being said, we must proceed as follows.

4. If we wanted to see the nature of body, [and asked ourselves] something like what the nature of body itself was in this [perceptible] universe, when we had got to know thoroughly in the case of one of

[2] A good example of Plotinus' continual insistence on the inadequacy of discursive reason to give an adequate account of the One-Being: cp. V. 8 (31). 5–6; VI. 7 (38). 35. 28–30; III. 5 (50). 9. 26–29 and Klaus Wurm *Substanz und Qualität* (Berlin & New York 1973).

[3] For Plotinus' use of ἀπόφασις in the sense of "declaration", "assertion", cp. III. 7.1.9.

μὲν ὡς ὑποκείμενον αὐτοῦ, οἷον ἐπὶ λίθου, τὸ δὲ ὁπόσον
5 αὐτοῦ, τὸ μέγεθος, τὸ δὲ ὁποῖον, οἷον τὸ χρῶμα, καὶ ἐπὶ
παντὸς ἄλλου σώματος εἴποιμεν ἄν, ὡς ἐν τῇ σώματος
φύσει τὸ μέν ἐστιν οἷον οὐσία, τὸ δέ ἐστι ποσόν, τὸ
δὲ ποιόν, ὁμοῦ μὲν πάντα, τῷ δὲ λόγῳ διαιρεθέντα
εἰς τρία, καὶ σῶμα ἂν ἦν ἓν τὰ τρία; εἰ δὲ
10 καὶ κίνησις αὐτοῦ παρῆν σύμφυτος τῇ συστάσει, καὶ
τοῦτο ἂν συνηριθμήσαμεν, καὶ τὰ τέτταρα ἦν ἂν ἕν, καὶ
τὸ σῶμα τὸ ἓν ἀπήρτιστο πρὸς τὸ ἓν καὶ τὴν αὐτοῦ
φύσιν τοῖς ἅπασι. τὸν αὐτὸν δὴ τρόπον, ἐπειδὴ περὶ
οὐσίας νοητῆς καὶ τῶν ἐκεῖ γενῶν καὶ ἀρχῶν ὁ λόγος
ἐστίν, ἀφελόντας χρὴ τὴν ἐν τοῖς σώμασι γένεσιν καὶ
15 τὴν δι᾽ αἰσθήσεως κατανόησιν καὶ τὰ μεγέθη—οὕτω
γὰρ καὶ τὸ χωρὶς καὶ τὸ διεστηκότα ἀπ᾽ ἀλλήλων
εἶναι—λαβεῖν τινα νοητὴν ὑπόστασιν καὶ ὡς ἀληθῶς ὂν
καὶ μᾶλλον ἕν. ἐν ᾧ καὶ τὸ θαῦμα πῶς πολλὰ καὶ ἓν τὸ
οὕτως ἕν. ἐπὶ μὲν γὰρ τῶν σωμάτων συγκεχώρηται τὸ
20 αὐτὸ ἓν καὶ πολλὰ εἶναι· καὶ γὰρ εἰς ἄπειρα τὸ αὐτό, καὶ
ἕτερον τὸ χρῶμα καὶ τὸ σχῆμα ἕτερον· καὶ γὰρ
χωρίζεται. εἰ δέ τις λάβοι ψυχὴν μίαν ἀδιάστατον
ἀμεγέθη ἁπλούστατον, ὡς δόξει τῇ πρώτῃ τῆς διανοίας
ἐπιβολῇ, πῶς ἄν τις ἐλπίσειε πολλὰ εὑρήσειν πάλιν αὖ;
25 καίτοι νομίσας εἰς τοῦτο τελευτᾶν, ὅτε διῃρεῖτο τὸ ζῷον
εἰς σῶμα καὶ ψυχήν, καὶ σῶμα μὲν πολυειδὲς καὶ

its parts—a stone for instance—that there was what
functioned as its substrate, and its quantity, the
magnitude, and its quality, colour for instance,
should we not say in the case of every other body
that there was what might be called substance, and
quantity, and quality, all together, but divided by
our reasoning into three, and that body was the
three as one? But if it also had movement as a
natural part of its constitution, and we counted this
in as well, then the four also would be one, and the
one body would be brought to completion by them
all in respect of its unity and its own nature. In the
same way, certainly, when the discussion is about
intelligible substance and the genera and principles
there, one must remove the coming into being in the
sphere of bodies and the understanding through
sense-perception and the magnitudes—for it is
[because bodies have size in] this way that there is
separation and they stand apart from each other—
and grasp an intelligible existence and that which
really and truly is and is more one. In this it is also
remarkable how that which is one in this way is
many and one. For in the case of bodies it has been
agreed that the same body is one and many; for the
same one [can be divided] to infinity, and its colour
is different from its shape; for they are in fact
separated. But if someone takes one soul, without
spatial separation of parts, without magnitude, su-
premely simple, as it will seem at the first appli-
cation of the mind to it, how would one expect to find
that it was after all many? For one would have
thought that one could stop at this, when one had
divided the living being into soul and body, and
found the body multiform and composite and vari-

σύνθετον καὶ ποικίλον, τὴν δὲ ψυχὴν ἐθάρρει ὡς ἁπλοῦν
εὑρὼν καὶ ἀναπαύσασθαι τῆς πορείας ἐλθὼν ἐπ' ἀρχήν.
ταύτην τοίνυν τὴν ψυχήν, ἐπειδήπερ ἐκ τοῦ νοητοῦ
τόπου προεχειρίσθη ἡμῖν, ὡς ἐκεῖ τὸ σῶμα ἐκ
30 τοῦ αἰσθητοῦ, λάβωμεν, πῶς τὸ ἓν τοῦτο πολλά ἐστι,
καὶ πῶς τὰ πολλὰ ἕν ἐστιν, οὐ σύνθετον ἓν ἐκ πολλῶν,
ἀλλὰ μία φύσις πολλά· διὰ γὰρ τούτου ληφθέντος καὶ
φανεροῦ γενομένου καὶ τὴν περὶ τῶν γενῶν τῶν ἐν τῷ
ὄντι ἔφαμεν ἀλήθειαν φανερὰν ἔσεσθαι.

5. Πρῶτον δὲ τοῦτο ἐνθυμητέον ὡς, ἐπειδὴ τὰ
σώματα, οἷον τῶν ζῴων καὶ τῶν φυτῶν, ἕκαστον αὐτῶν
πολλά ἐστι καὶ χρώμασι καὶ σχήμασι καὶ μεγέθεσι καὶ
εἴδεσι μερῶν καὶ ἄλλο ἄλλοθι, ἔρχεται δὲ τὰ πάντα ἐξ
5 ἑνός, ἢ [παντάπασιν]¹ ἐξ ἑνὸς ἥξει² πάντη πάντως ἑνὸς
ἢ μᾶλλον μὲν ἑνὸς ἢ οἷον τὸ ἐξ αὐτοῦ, ὥστε καὶ μᾶλλον
ὄντος ἢ τὸ γενόμενον—ὅσῳ γὰρ πρὸς ἓν ἡ ἀπόστασις,
τόσῳ καὶ πρὸς ὄν—ἐπεὶ οὖν ἐξ ἑνὸς μέν, οὐχ οὕτω δὲ
ἑνός, ὡς πάντη ἓν ἢ αὐτοέν—οὐ γὰρ ἂν διεστηκὸς
πλῆθος ἐποίει—λείπεται εἶναι ἐκ πλήθους ἑνός. τὸ δὲ
10 ποιοῦν ἦν ψυχή· τοῦτο ἄρα πλῆθος ἕν. τί οὖν; τὸ πλῆθος

¹ del. Igal.
² Igal: ἢ ἕξει Enn.: ἢ ἐξ ἔτι suspic. Theiler, scr. H–S.

¹ The phrase occurs in Plato *Republic* 508C1 and 517B5.
Plotinus' use of it here, and the presentation of soul as the
handiest example of a being " from the intelligible place",
show clearly that the distinction between ψυχή and νοῦς was

ous, but was confident that one had found that the soul was simple and could rest from one's journey since one had come to the principle. Since, then, this soul has come ready to hand for us from the "intelligible place",[1] as in the former discussion the body did from the perceptible, let us apprehend how this one is many, and how the many are one, not a one compounded from many, but one nature which is many; for through this, when it has been apprehended and has become clear, we maintained that the truth about the genera in real being would become clear.

5. But first we should think about this: that since bodies, of animals and plants for instance, are, each and every one of them, many in virtue of the colours and shapes and sizes and specific forms of their parts, and the fact that one is in one place and one in another, but all come from one, they will come either from a one which is in every way and altogether one or from a one which is more one than is that which comes from it,[2] so that it is also more real than that which has come into being—for the extent of the departure from being is as great as that of the departure from unity—since, then, they are from a one, but not a one such as to be in every way one or the absolute One—for this would not have made a discrete plurality—it remains that they must be from a plurality which is one. But what made them is soul: this then is a plurality which is one. What then? Is the plurality the rational forming principles

not always for him very clear-cut (Plato, of course, makes no such distinction).

[2] I adopt Igal's emendations here (see critical notes): they seem to me to be required to give a tolerable sense.

οἱ λόγοι τῶν γινομένων; ἆρ᾽ οὖν αὐτὸ μὲν ἄλλο, οἱ λόγοι
δὲ ἄλλοι; ἢ καὶ αὐτὴ λόγος καὶ κεφάλαιον τῶν λόγων,
καὶ ἐνέργεια αὐτῆς κατ᾽ οὐσίαν ἐνεργούσης οἱ λόγοι· ἡ
δὲ οὐσία δύναμις τῶν λόγων. πολλὰ μὲν δὴ οὕτω τοῦτο
15 τὸ ἓν ἐξ ὧν εἰς ἄλλα ποιεῖ δεδειγμένον. τί δ᾽ εἰ μὴ ποιοῖ,
ἀλλά τις αὐτὴν μὴ ποιοῦσαν λαμβάνοι ἀναβαίνων αὐτῆς
εἰς τὸ μὴ ποιοῦν; οὐ πολλὰς καὶ ἐνταῦθα εὑρήσει
δυνάμεις; εἶναι μὲν γὰρ αὐτὴν πᾶς ἄν τις συγχωρήσειεν·
ἆρα δὲ ταὐτὸν ὡς εἰ καὶ λίθον ἔλεγεν εἶναι; ἢ οὐ ταὐτόν.
20 ἀλλ᾽ ὅμως κἀκεῖ ἐπὶ τοῦ λίθου τὸ εἶναι τῷ λίθῳ ἦν οὐ τὸ
εἶναι, ἀλλὰ τὸ λίθῳ εἶναι· οὕτω καὶ ἐνταῦθα τὸ εἶναι
ψυχῇ μετὰ τοῦ εἶναι ἔχει τὸ ψυχῇ εἶναι. ἆρ᾽ οὖν ἄλλο τὸ
εἶναι, ἄλλο δὲ τὸ λοιπόν, ὃ συμπληροῖ τὴν τῆς ψυχῆς
οὐσίαν, καὶ τὸ μὲν ὄν, διαφορὰ δὲ ποιεῖ τὴν ψυχήν; ἤ τι
25 ὂν μὲν ἡ ψυχή, οὐ μέντοι οὕτως, ὡς ἄνθρωπος λευκός,
ἀλλ᾽ ὥς τις οὐσία μόνον· τοῦτο δὲ ταὐτὸν τῷ μὴ ἔξωθεν
τῆς οὐσίας ἔχειν ὃ ἔχει.

6. Ἀλλ᾽ ἆρα οὐκ ἔξωθεν μὲν ἔχει τῆς ἑαυτοῦ οὐσίας,
ἵνα ἡ μὲν κατὰ τὸ εἶναι ᾖ, ἡ δὲ κατὰ τὸ τοιόνδε εἶναι;
ἀλλ᾽ εἰ κατὰ τὸ τοιόνδε εἶναι καὶ ἔξωθεν τὸ τοιόνδε, οὐ
τὸ ὅλον καθὸ ψυχὴ ἔσται οὐσία, ἀλλὰ κατά τι, καὶ μέρος
5 αὐτῆς οὐσία, ἀλλ᾽ οὐ τὸ ὅλον οὐσία. ἔπειτα τὸ εἶναι

of the things which have come into being? Or is it rather itself one thing and the forming principles different from it? On the contrary, it is a forming principle itself and the sum of the forming principles, and the principles are its activity when it is active according to its substance; but the substance is the potentiality of the principles. It has then been demonstrated from what it does to other things that this one is indeed many. But what if it was not doing anything, but one was to consider it not doing by ascending to that of it which does not do? Will one not find many powers here too? For everyone would agree that the soul exists: but is this really the same thing as saying that a stone exists? Certainly not. But all the same there in the case of the stone also, existing for the stone is not [just] being but being a stone; so here, existing for soul has being soul along with being. Is then being one thing, and the rest something else, which contributes to the completion of the substance of the soul, and is there being [as such] and an essential difference makes the soul? No, the soul is a particular being but not in the way that a man is white, but only and simply like a particular substance; and this is the same as saying that it does not have what it has from outside its substance.

6. But, surely, does it not have [something] from outside its substance to make it in one respect existent but in another existent in a particular way? But if it is existent in a particular way, and the particularity comes from outside, it will not be substance as a whole and in so far as it is soul, but in a particular respect, and a part of it will be substance, but not the whole of it substance. Then what

αὐτῇ τί ἔσται ἄνευ τῶν ἄλλων ἢ λίθος; ἢ δεῖ τοῦτο τὸ
εἶναι αὐτῆς ἐντὸς εἶναι οἷον π η γ ὴ ν κ α ὶ ἀ ρ χ ή ν,
μᾶλλον δὲ πάντα, ὅσα αὐτή· καὶ ζωὴν τοίνυν· καὶ
συνάμφω ἓν τὸ εἶναι καὶ τὴν ζωήν. ἆρ' οὖν οὕτως ἕν, ὡς
10 ἕνα λόγον; ἢ τὸ ὑποκείμενον ἕν, οὕτω δὲ ἕν, ὡς αὖ δύο ἢ
καὶ πλείω, ὅσα ἐστὶν ἡ ψυχὴ τὰ πρῶτα. ἢ οὖν οὐσία καὶ
ζωή, ἢ ἔχει ζωήν. ἀλλ' εἰ ἔχει, τὸ ἔχον καθ' αὑτὸ οὐκ ἐν
ζωῇ, ἥ τε ζωὴ οὐκ ἐν οὐσίᾳ· ἀλλ' εἰ μὴ ἔχει θάτερον τὸ
ἕτερον, λεκτέον ἓν ἄμφω. ἢ ἓν καὶ πολλὰ καὶ τοσαῦτα,
15 ὅσα ἐμφαίνεται ἐν τῷ ἑνί· καὶ ἓν ἑαυτῷ, πρὸς δὲ τὰ ἄλλα
πολλά· καὶ ἓν μὲν ὄν, ποιοῦν δὲ ἑαυτὸ αὐτὰ ἐν τῇ οἷον
κινήσει πολλά· καὶ ὅλον ἕν, οἷον δὲ θεωρεῖν ἐπιχειροῦν
ἑαυτὸ πολλά· ὥσπερ γὰρ οὐκ ἀνέχεται ἑαυτοῦ τὸ ὂν ἓν
εἶναι πάντα δυνάμενον, ὅσα ἐστίν. ἡ δὲ θεωρία αἰτία τοῦ
20 φανῆναι αὐτὸ πολλά, ἵνα νοήσῃ· ἐὰν γὰρ ἓν φανῇ, οὐκ
ἐνόησεν, ἀλλ' ἔστιν ἤδη ἐκεῖνο.

7. Τίνα οὖν ἐστι καὶ πόσα τὰ ἐνορώμενα; ἐπειδὴ ἐν
ψυχῇ εὕρομεν οὐσίαν ἅμα καὶ ζωήν—καὶ τοῦτο κοινὸν ἡ
οὐσία ἐπὶ πάσης ψυχῆς, κοινὸν δὲ καὶ ἡ ζωή, ζωὴ δὲ καὶ
ἐν νῷ—ἐπεισαγαγόντες καὶ τὸν νοῦν καὶ τὴν τούτου
5 ζωήν, κοινὸν τὸ ἐπὶ πάσῃ ζωῇ τὴν κίνησιν ἕν τι γένος
θησόμεθα. οὐσίαν δὲ καὶ κίνησιν τὴν πρώτην ζωὴν
οὖσαν δύο γένη θησόμεθα. καὶ γὰρ εἰ ἕν, χωρίζει αὐτὰ
τῇ νοήσει ὁ ἓν οὐχ ἓν εὑρών· ἢ οὐκ ἂν ἠδυνήθη [1]

---

[1] Igal, H–S²: δυνηθῇ Enn.: δυνηθείη Kirchhoff: δυνηθείης
Theiler.

---

[1] "The stone" as an image of lifelessness occurs several
times in Plotinus: cp. VI. 5 (23). 11. 5–14 and possibly III. 2

will existence be to it, without all the rest, different from a stone [1]? Now this being of soul must be within, like a "source and principle",[2] or rather must be all that it is; so it must be life; and both must be one, being and life. Is it then one like a single forming principle? No, the underlying reality is one, but so one that it is also two or even more, all that soul primarily is. It is therefore substance and life, or it has life. But if it has it, that which has is, in itself, not in life, and the life not in substance; but if one does not have the other, one must say that both are one. Or rather one and many, and as many as appear in the one; and one for itself, but many in relation to the others; and it is one being, but makes itself many by what we may call its movement; and it is one whole, but when it undertakes, one might say, to contemplate itself, it is many: as if it cannot bear its being to be one when it is capable of being all the things that it is. And its contemplation is the cause of its appearing many, that it may think: for if it appears as one, it did not think, but is that One.

7. What, then, are the constituents seen in soul, and how many are there? Since we find in soul substance and life together, and substance is common to all soul, and life also common, and life is also in Intellect, if we bring in also Intellect and its life, we shall posit as common to all life a single genus, movement. And we shall posit substance and movement, which is the primary life, as two genera. For even if they are one, [the observer] separates them in thought, finding the one not one; otherwise it would (47). 17. 67 (see my note ad loc.). For further examples see *Lexicon Plotinianum* s. v. λίθος.

[2] Plato *Phaedrus* 245C9.

PLOTINUS: ENNEAD VI. 2.

χωρίσαι. ὅρα δὲ καὶ ἐν ἄλλοις σαφῶς τοῦ εἶναι τὴν
10 κίνησιν ἢ τὴν ζωὴν χωριζομένην, εἰ καὶ μὴ ἐν τῷ
ἀληθινῷ εἶναι, ἀλλὰ τῇ σκιᾷ καὶ τῷ ὁμωνύμῳ τοῦ εἶναι.
ὡς γὰρ ἐν τῇ εἰκόνι τοῦ ἀνθρώπου πολλὰ ἐλλείπει καὶ
μάλιστα τὸ κύριον, ἡ ζωή, οὕτω καὶ ἐν τοῖς αἰσθητοῖς
τὸ εἶναι σκιὰ τοῦ εἶναι ἀφηρημένον τοῦ μάλιστα εἶναι, ὃ
ἐν τῷ ἀρχετύπῳ ἦν ζωή. ἀλλ᾽ οὖν ἔσχομεν ἐντεῦθεν
15 χωρίσαι τοῦ ζῆν τὸ εἶναι καὶ τοῦ εἶναι τὸ ζῆν. ὄντος μὲν
δὴ εἴδη πολλὰ καὶ γένος· κίνησις δὲ οὔτε ὑπὸ τὸ ὂν
τακτέα οὔτ᾽ ἐπὶ τῷ ὄντι, ἀλλὰ μετὰ τοῦ ὄντος,
εὑρεθεῖσα ἐν αὐτῷ οὐχ ὡς ἐν ὑποκειμένῳ· ἐνέργεια γὰρ
αὐτοῦ καὶ οὐδέτερον ἄνευ τοῦ ἑτέρου ἢ ἐπινοίᾳ, καὶ αἱ
20 δύο φύσεις μία· καὶ γὰρ ἐνεργείᾳ τὸ ὄν, οὐ δυνάμει. καὶ
εἰ χωρὶς μέντοι ἑκάτερον λάβοις, καὶ ἐν τῷ ὄντι κίνησις
φανήσεται καὶ ἐν τῇ κινήσει τὸ ὄν, οἷον καὶ ἐπὶ τοῦ
ἑ ν ὸ ς ὄ ν τ ο ς ἑκάτερον χωρὶς εἶχε θάτερον, ἀλλ᾽ ὅμως
ἡ διάνοια δύο φησὶ καὶ εἶδος ἑκάτερον διπλοῦν ἕν.
25 κινήσεως δὲ περὶ τὸ ὂν φανείσης οὐκ ἐξιστάσης τὴν
ἐκείνου φύσιν, μᾶλλον δ᾽ ἐν τῷ εἶναι οἷον τέλειον
ποιούσης, ἀεί τε τῆς τοιαύτης φύσεως ἐν τῷ οὕτω
κινεῖσθαι μενούσης, εἴ τις μὴ στάσιν ἐπεισάγοι,
ἀτοπώτερος ἂν εἴη τοῦ μὴ κίνησιν διδόντος·
προχειροτέρα γὰρ ἡ τῆς στάσεως περὶ τὸ ὂν ἔννοια καὶ
30 νόησις τῆς περὶ τὴν κίνησιν οὔσης· τὸ γὰρ κ α τ ὰ
τ α ὐ τ ὰ κ α ὶ ὡ σ α ύ τ ω ς καὶ ἕνα λόγον ἔχον ἐκεῖ. ἔστω
δὴ καὶ στάσις ἓν γένος ἕτερον ὂν κινήσεως, ὅπου καὶ

---

[1] Plato *Sophist* 248A12.

not have been possible to separate them. But observe in other things also how movement and life are clearly separated from being, even if not in the true being, yet in the shadow and that which has the same name as being. For as in the portrait of a man many things are wanting, and especially the decisively important thing, life, so in the things perceived by sense being is a shadow of being, separated from that which is most fully being, which was life in the archetype. But then, this gives us grounds for separating living from being and being from living. Now there are many species of being and there is a genus of being; but movement is not to be classed under being nor yet over being, but with being; it is found in being not as inhering in a subject; for it is its active actuality and neither of them is without the other except in our conception of them, and the two natures are one nature: for being is actual, not potential. And if, none the less, you take either of them separately, movement will appear in being and being in movement, as if in the "one-being" each taken separately had the other, but all the same discursive thought says that they are separate and that each form is a double one. But since movement appears in the sphere of being, not as changing the nature of being, but rather in being as if making it perfect, if one does not introduce rest as well one would be even more perverse than one who did not grant that there was movement; for the notion, and intellectual perception, of rest comes readier to hand where being is concerned than that of movement; for "existing in the same state and in the same way"[1] and having a single definition are there in being. So let rest be one genus, different from move-

ἐναντίον ἂν φανείη. τοῦ δὲ ὄντος ὡς ἕτερον, πολλαχῇ
δῆλον ἂν εἴη καὶ διότι, εἰ τῷ ὄντι ταὐτὸν εἴη, οὐ μᾶλλον
τῆς κινήσεως ταὐτὸ τῷ ὄντι. διὰ τί γὰρ ἡ μὲν στάσις τῷ
35 ὄντι ταὐτόν, ἡ δὲ κίνησις οὔ, ζωή τις αὐτοῦ καὶ ἐνέργεια καὶ τῆς οὐσίας καὶ αὐτοῦ τοῦ εἶναι; ἀλλ' ὥσπερ
ἐχωρίζομεν τὴν κίνησιν αὐτοῦ ὡς ταὐτόν τε καὶ οὐ
ταὐτὸν αὐτῷ καὶ ὡς δύο ἄμφω ἐλέγομεν καὶ αὖ ἕν, τὸν
αὐτὸν τρόπον καὶ τὴν στάσιν χωριοῦμεν αὐτοῦ καὶ αὖ
40 οὐ χωριοῦμεν τοσοῦτον χωρίζοντες τῷ νῷ, ὅσον ἄλλο
γένος θέσθαι ἐν τοῖς οὖσιν. ἢ εἰ συνάγοιμεν πάντη εἰς ἓν
τὴν στάσιν καὶ τὸ ὂν μηδὲν μηδαμῇ διαφέρειν λέγοντες,
τό τε ὂν τῇ κινήσει ὡσαύτως, τὴν στάσιν καὶ τὴν
κίνησιν διὰ μέσου τοῦ ὄντος εἰς ταὐτὸν συνάξομεν, καὶ
45 ἔσται ἡμῖν ἡ κίνησις καὶ ἡ στάσις ἕν.

8. Ἀλλὰ χρὴ τρία ταῦτα τίθεσθαι, εἴπερ ὁ νοῦς χωρὶς
ἕκαστον νοεῖ· ἅμα δὲ νοεῖ καὶ τίθησιν, εἴπερ νοεῖ, καὶ
ἔστιν, εἴπερ νενόηται. οἷς μὲν γὰρ τὸ εἶναι μετὰ ὕλης
ἐστί, τούτων οὐκ ἐν τῷ νῷ τὸ εἶναι· [ἀλλ' ἔστιν ἄυλα]¹
5 ἃ δ' ἔστιν ἄυλα, εἰ νενόηται, τοῦτ' ἔστιν αὐτοῖς τὸ εἶναι.
ἴδε δὲ νοῦν καὶ καθαρὸν καὶ βλέψον εἰς αὐτὸν ἀτενίσας,
μὴ ὄμμασι τούτοις δεδορκώς. ὁρᾷς δὴ οὐσίας ἑστίαν καὶ
φῶς ἐν αὐτῷ ἄυπνον καὶ ὡς ἕστηκεν ἐν αὐτῷ καὶ ὡς
διέστηκεν, ὁμοῦ ὄντα καὶ ζωὴν μένουσαν καὶ νόησιν οὐκ
10 ἐνεργοῦσαν εἰς τὸ μέλλον, ἀλλ' εἰς τὸ ἤδη, μᾶλλον δὲ
"ἤδη καὶ ἀεὶ ἤδη", καὶ τὸ παρὸν ἀεί, καὶ ὡς νοῶν ἐν

¹ del. H–S.

ment, in that it would seem to be its opposite. But that it is different from being could be made clear in many ways, especially because, if it was the same as being, it could not be any more the same as being than motion. For why is rest the same as being, but motion not, when motion is its life and the active actuality of its substance and its very being? But, just as we separated movement from it as being the same and not the same as it, and spoke of them as two and yet again one, in the same way we shall also separate rest from it and yet again not separate it, separating it so far in the mind as to posit it as another genus among real beings. Otherwise, if we were to bring rest and being into one, saying that there was not in any way any difference between them, and bring being into one with movement in the same way, we shall bring rest and movement into identity through the medium of being, and movement and rest will be one for us.

8. But one must posit these three, if Intellect thinks each of them separately; but it does at once know and posit them, if it thinks, and they exist, if they have been thought. For the being of things whose being involves matter is not in the intellect; but if things which are without matter have been thought, this is their being. But behold Intellect, pure Intellect, and look upon it with concentrated gaze, not seeing it with these bodily eyes of ours. You see the hearth of substance and a sleepless light on it, and how they stand on it and how they stand apart, existing all together, abiding life and a thought whose activity is not directed towards what is coming but what is here already, or rather "here already and always here already", and the always

ἑαυτῷ καὶ οὐκ ἔξω. ἐν μὲν οὖν τῷ νοεῖν ἡ ἐνέργεια καὶ ἡ
κίνησις, ἐν δὲ τῷ "ἑαυτόν" ἡ οὐσία καὶ τὸ ὄν· ὢν γὰρ
νοεῖ καὶ ὄντα ἑαυτόν, καὶ εἰς ὃ οἷον ἐπερείδετο, ὄν. ἡ μὲν
γὰρ ἐνέργεια ἡ εἰς αὐτὸν οὐκ οὐσία, εἰς ὃ δὲ καὶ ἀφ' οὗ,
15 τὸ ὄν· τὸ γὰρ βλεπόμενον τὸ ὄν, οὐχ ἡ βλέψις· ἔχει δὲ
καὶ αὕτη τὸ εἶναι, ὅτι ἀφ' οὗ καὶ εἰς ὄν, ὄν. ἐνεργείᾳ δὲ
ὄν, οὐ δυνάμει, συνάπτει πάλιν αὖ τὰ δύο καὶ οὐ
χωρίζει, ἀλλὰ ποιεῖ ἑαυτὸν ἐκεῖνο κἀκεῖνο ἑαυτόν. ὂν δὲ
τὸ πάντων ἑδραιότατον καὶ περὶ ὃ τὰ ἄλλα, τὴν στάσιν
20 ὑπεστήσατο καὶ ἔχει οὐκ ἐπακτόν, ἀλλ' ἐξ αὑτοῦ καὶ ἐν
αὑτῷ. ἔστι δὲ καὶ εἰς ὃ λήγει ἡ νόησις οὐκ ἀρξαμένη
στάσις, καὶ ἀφ' οὗ ὥρμηται οὐχ ὁρμήσασα στάσις· οὐ
γὰρ ἐκ κινήσεως κίνησις οὐδ' εἰς κίνησιν. ἔτι δὲ ἡ μὲν
ἰδέα ἐν στάσει πέρας οὖσα νοῦ, ὁ δὲ νοῦς αὐτῆς ἡ
κίνησις.

25   Ὥστε ὂν πάντα καὶ κίνησις καὶ στάσις, καὶ δι' ὅλων
ὄντα γένη, καὶ ἕκαστον τῶν ὕστερόν τι ὂν καί τις στάσις
καί τις κίνησις. τρία δὴ ταῦτα ἰδών τις, ἐν προσβολῇ
τῆς τοῦ ὄντος φύσεως γεγενημένος, καὶ τῷ παρ' αὐτῷ
ὄντι τὸ ὂν καὶ τοῖς ἄλλοις ἰδὼν τὰ ἄλλα, τὴν κίνησιν τὴν
30 ἐν αὐτῷ τῇ ἐν ἑαυτῷ κινήσει, καὶ τῇ στάσει τὴν στάσιν,
καὶ ταῦτα ἐκείνοις ἐφαρμόσας, ὁμοῦ μὲν γενομένοις καὶ
οἷον συγκεχυμένοις συμμίξας οὐ διακρίνων, οἷον δ'

134

present, and it is a thought thinking in itself and not outside. In its thinking, then, there is activity and motion, and in its thinking itself, substance and being: for, existing, it thinks itself as existent, and the being on which it is, so to speak, founded. For its self-directed activity is not substance, but being is that to which the activity is directed and from which it comes: for that which is looked at is being, not the look; but the look, too, possesses being, because it comes from and is directed to being. And since it is in act, not in potency, it gathers the two together and does not separate them, but makes itself being and being itself. And since being is the most firmly set of all things and that about which the other things [are set], it has made rest exist and possesses it not as brought in from outside but from itself and in itself. It is that in which thought comes to a stop, though thought is a rest which has no beginning, and from which it starts, though thought is a rest which never started: for movement does not begin from or end in movement. And again the Form at rest is the defining limit of Intellect, and Intellect is the movement of the Form.

So all things are being, rest and motion; these are all-pervading genera, and each subsequent thing is a particular being, a particular rest, and a particular motion. Now when anyone sees these three, having come into intuitive contact with the nature of being, he sees being by the being in himself and the others, motion and rest, by the motion and rest in himself, and fits his own being, motion and rest to those in Intellect: they come to him together in a sort of confusion and he mingles them without distinguishing them; then as it were separating them a little and

PLOTINUS: ENNEAD VI. 2.

ὀλίγον διαστήσας καὶ ἐπισχὼν καὶ διακρίνας εἰσιδὼν ὂν
καὶ στάσιν καὶ κίνησιν, τρία ταῦτα καὶ ἕκαστον ἕν, ἆρ᾽
35 οὐχ ἕτερα ἀλλήλων εἴρηκε καὶ διέστησεν ἐν ἑτερότητι
καὶ εἶδε τὴν ἐν τῷ ὄντι ἑτερότητα τρία τιθεὶς καὶ ἓν
ἕκαστον, πάλιν δὲ ταῦτα εἰς ἓν καὶ ἓν ἑνὶ καὶ πάντα ἕν,
εἰς ταὐτὸν αὖ συνάγων καὶ βλέπων ταυτότητα εἶδε
γενομένην καὶ οὖσαν; οὐκοῦν πρὸς τρισὶν ἐκείνοις
ἀνάγκη δύο ταῦτα προστιθέναι, ταὐτόν, θάτερον, ὥστε
40 τὰ πάντα γένη γίγνεσθαι πέντε πᾶσι, καὶ ταῦτα διδόντα
τοῖς μετὰ ταῦτα τὸ ἑτέροις καὶ ταυτοῖς εἶναι· καί τι γὰρ
ταὐτὸν καί τι ἕτερον ἕκαστον· ἁπλῶς γὰρ ταὐτὸν καὶ
ἕτερον ἄνευ τοῦ "τι" ἐν γένει ἂν εἴη· καὶ πρῶτα δὲ γένη,
ὅτι μηδὲν αὐτῶν κατηγορήσεις ἐν τῷ τί ἐστι. τὸ γὰρ ὂν
45 κατηγορήσεις αὐτῶν· ὄντα γάρ· ἀλλ᾽ οὐχ ὡς γένος· οὐ
γὰρ ὅπερ ὄν τι. οὐδ᾽ αὖ τῆς κινήσεως οὐδὲ τῆς στάσεως·
οὐ γὰρ εἴδη τοῦ ὄντος· ὄντα γὰρ τὰ μὲν ὡς εἴδη αὐτοῦ,
τὰ δὲ μετέχοντα αὐτοῦ. οὐδ᾽ αὖ τὸ ὂν μετέχον τούτων
ὡς γενῶν αὐτοῦ· οὐδὲ γὰρ ἐπαναβέβηκεν αὐτῷ οὐδὲ
πρότερα τοῦ ὄντος.

9. Ἀλλ᾽ ὅτι μὲν ταῦτα γένη πρῶτα, ἐκ τούτων ἄν
τις, ἴσως δὲ καὶ ἄλλων, βεβαιώσαιτο· ὅτι δὲ μόνα ταῦτα
καὶ οὐκ ἄλλα πρὸς τούτοις, πῶς ἄν τις πιστεύσειε; διὰ
τί γὰρ οὐ καὶ τὸ ἕν; διὰ τί δ᾽ οὐ τὸ ποσὸν καὶ τὸ ποιὸν
5 δέ, τὸ δὲ πρός τι καὶ τὰ ἄλλα, ἅπερ ἤδη ἕτεροι

136

holding them away from him and distinguishing them he perceives being, motion and rest, three and each of them one. Does he not then say that they are different from each other and distinguish them in otherness, and see the otherness in being when he posits three, each of them one? And again, when he brings them back to unity and sees them in a unity, all one, does he not collect them into sameness and, as he looks at them, see that sameness has come to be and is? So we must add these two, the same and the other, to those first three, so that there will be in all five genera for all things, and the last two also will give to subsequent things the characters of being other and same; for each individual thing is a particular "same" and a particular "other"; for "same" and "other" without the "particular" would apply to genera. These are the primary kinds because you cannot apply any predicate to them which forms part of the definition of their essence. You will certainly predicate being of them, for they exist, but not as their genus, for they are not particular beings. Nor can you predicate being as the genus of motion and rest, for they are not specific forms of being; for some things exist as species of being, others as participating in being. Nor again does being participate in these others as if they were its genera: for they do not transcend being and are not prior to it.

9. But that these genera are primary one could confirm from these arguments, and perhaps also from others; but how could one be confident that there are only these [primary genera] and not others in addition to them? For why not also the one? And why not the quale and the quantum and the relative and the others, which other philosophers have al-

PLOTINUS: ENNEAD VI. 2.

κατηρίθμηνται; τὸ μὲν οὖν ἕν, εἰ μὲν τὸ πάντως ἕν, [ἕν] ¹
ᾧ μηδὲν ἄλλο πρόσεστι, μὴ ψυχή, μὴ νοῦς, μὴ ὁτιοῦν,
οὐδενὸς ἂν κατηγοροῖτο τοῦτο, ὥστε οὐδὲ γένος. εἰ δὲ
τὸ προσὸν τῷ ὄντι, ἐφ' οὗ τὸ ἓν ὂν λέγομεν, οὐ πρώτως
10 ἓν τοῦτο. ἔτι ἀδιάφορον ὂν αὐτοῦ πῶς ἂν ποιήσειεν εἴδη;
εἰ δὲ τοῦτο μή, οὐ γένος. πῶς γὰρ καὶ διαιρήσεις;
διαιρῶν γὰρ πολλὰ ποιήσεις· ὥστε αὐτὸ τὸ ἓν πολλὰ
ἔσται καὶ ἀπολεῖ ἑαυτό, εἰ ἐθέλοι γένος εἶναι. ἔπειτά τι
προσθήσεις διαιρῶν εἰς εἴδη· οὐ γὰρ ἂν εἶεν διαφοραὶ ἐν
15 τῷ ἕν, ὥσπερ εἰσὶ τῆς οὐσίας. ὄντος μὲν γὰρ δέχεται ὁ
νοῦς εἶναι διαφοράς, ἑνὸς δὲ πῶς; εἶτα ἑκάστοτε μετὰ
τῆς διαφορᾶς δύο τιθεὶς ἀναιρεῖς τὸ ἕν, ἐπείπερ
πανταχοῦ ἡ μονάδος προσθήκη τὸ πρότερον ποσὸν
ἀφανίζει. εἰ δέ τις λέγοι τὸ ἐπὶ τῷ ὄντι ἓν καὶ τὸ ἐπὶ
κινήσει ἓν καὶ τοῖς ἄλλοις κοινὸν εἶναι, εἰς μὲν ταὐτὸν
20 ἄγων τὸ ὂν καὶ τὸ ἕν, ἐν ᾧ λόγῳ τὸ ὂν οὐκ ἐποίει τῶν
ἄλλων γένος, ὅτι μὴ ὅπερ ⟨ὂν⟩ ὄντα,² ἀλλ' ἕτερον
τρόπον ὄντα, οὕτως οὐδὲ τὸ ἓν κοινὸν ἐπ' αὐτῶν ἔσται,
ἀλλὰ τὸ μὲν πρώτως, τὰ δὲ ἄλλως. εἰ δὲ μὴ πάντων
λέγοι ποιεῖν, ἀλλὰ ἕν τι ἐφ' αὑτοῦ, ὥσπερ τὰ ἄλλα, εἰ
μὲν ταὐτὸν αὑτῷ τὸ ὂν καὶ τὸ ἕν, ἤδη τοῦ ὄντος

¹ delendum suspic. Müller, del. Volkmann.
² ⟨ὂν⟩ ὄντα Müller: ὄντα Enn.: ὄν τι Igal, H–S².

138

ready counted up [1]? Well then, as for the one, if it is the absolutely One to which nothing else is added, not soul, not intellect, not anything at all, this could not be predicated of anything, so that it is not a genus. But if it is the one added to being, that of which we speak as one-being, this is not primarily one. Again, if it is undifferentiated in itself how could it make specific forms? But if it cannot do this, it is not a genus. For how could there be divisions? For in dividing you will make many: so that the one itself will be many and will destroy itself—if it wanted to be a genus. Then, you will add something to it in dividing it into specific forms. For there could be no differentiations in the one, as there are of substance. For the mind accepts that there are differentiations of being, but how could there be of one? Then, every time [you differentiate] you abolish the one by positing two with the differentiation, since everywhere the addition of a unit makes the previous quantum disappear. But if someone were to say that the one in being and the one in movement and the others is a common term, bringing being and one into identity, then, as in the argument that did not make being the genus of the others, because they are not beings as being is,[2] but beings in another way, so the one also will not be a common term over them, but it will be one primarily, and the others one in a different way. But if he were to say that he does not make the one the genus of all [genera] but one [genus] by itself, like the others, if being and the one are identical for him, since being has already been

---

[1] The reference is to the Aristotelian categories.
[2] I retain the ⟨ὄν⟩ ὄντα of Müller here.

25 ἠριθμημένου ἐν τοῖς γένεσιν ὄνομα εἰσάγει. εἰ δὲ ἓν
ἑκάτερον, τινὰ φύσιν λέγει, καὶ εἰ μὲν προστίθησί
⟨"τι"⟩,[1] τι ἓν λέγει, εἰ δὲ μηδέν, ἐκεῖνο, ὃ οὐδενὸς
κατηγορεῖται, πάλιν αὖ λέγει· εἰ δὲ τὸ τῷ ὄντι συνόν,
εἴπομεν μὲν ὅτι οὐ πρώτως ἓν λέγει. ἀλλὰ τί κωλύει
30 πρώτως εἶναι τοῦτο ἐξῃρημένου ἐκείνου τοῦ παντελῶς
ἕν; καὶ γὰρ τὸ ὂν μετ᾽ ἐκεῖνο λέγομεν ὂν καὶ ὂν πρώτως
ὄν. ἢ ὅτι οὐκ ἦν τὸ πρὸ αὐτοῦ ὂν ἤ, εἴπερ ἦν, οὐκ ἂν ἦν
πρώτως· τούτου δὲ τὸ πρὸ αὐτοῦ ἕν. ἔπειτα χωρισθὲν
τῇ νοήσει τοῦ ὄντος διαφορὰς οὐκ ἔχει· ἔπειτα ἐν τῷ
35 ὄντι, εἰ μὲν ἐπακολούθημα αὐτοῦ, καὶ πάντων καὶ
ὕστερον· πρότερον δὲ τὸ γένος. εἰ δὲ ἅμα, καὶ πάντων·
τὸ δὲ γένος οὐχ ἅμα. εἰ δὲ πρότερον, ἀρχή τις καὶ αὐτοῦ
μόνον· εἰ δὲ ἀρχὴ αὐτοῦ, οὐ γένος αὐτοῦ· εἰ δὲ μὴ αὐτοῦ,
οὐδὲ τῶν ἄλλων· ἢ δέοι ἂν καὶ τὸ ὂν καὶ τῶν ἄλλων
πάντων. ὅλως γὰρ ἔοικε τὸ ἓν ἐν τῷ ὄντι πλησιάζον τῷ
40 ἑνὶ καὶ οἷον συνεκπίπτον τῷ ὄντι, τοῦ ὄντος τὸ μὲν πρὸς
ἐκείνῳ ἓν ὄντος, τὸ δὲ μετ᾽ ἐκεῖνο ὄντος, ᾧ δύναται καὶ
πολλὰ εἶναι, μένον αὐτὸ ἓν καὶ οὐ θέλον μερίζευθαι οὐδὲ
γένος εἶναι βούλεσθαι.

[1] Bouillet, Harder, Theiler.

counted among the genera, he is introducing a [mere] name. But if each of them is one [different from the other], then he means [by the one] a nature, and if he adds "some" he means some particular one, but if he adds nothing, he means, yet again, the one which is predicated of nothing; but if he means the one which goes with being, we have said that he does not mean the primarily one. But what prevents this from being primarily one if that which is absolutely one is left out of account? For we do call the being which comes after it being and say that it is primarily being. Now we do so because that which is before it is not being, or, if what is before it was being, it would not be primarily being; but in this case what is before it is one. Then, when it is separated in thought from being it does not have differentiations; then, in being, if it is a consequence of being, it is a consequence of and posterior to all; but the genus is prior. But if it is simultaneous, it is simultaneous with all; but the genus is not simultaneous. But if it is prior, it is a principle, and a principle only of being; but if it is its principle, it is not its genus; but if it is not its genus, it is not the genus of the others either; or it would be necessary for being also to be the genus of all the other [genera]. For in general it appears likely that, since the one in being is near to the one and in a way coincides with being, and being in so far as it is close to that [absolute One] is one, but in so far as it is posterior to it, being, by which it is able also to be many, the one in being, remaining itself one and being unwilling to be divided into parts, does not want to be a genus either.

10. Πῶς οὖν ἕκαστον τοῦ ὄντος ἕν; ἢ τῷ τι ἓν οὐχ
ἕν—πολλὰ γὰρ ἤδη τῷ τι ἕν—ἀλλ' ὁμωνύμως ἓν
ἕκαστον τῶν εἰδῶν· τὸ γὰρ εἶδος πλῆθος, ὥστε ἓν
ἐνταῦθα ὡς στρατὸς ἢ χορός. οὐ τοίνυν τὸ ἐκεῖ ἓν ἐν
5 τούτοις, ὥστε οὐ κοινὸν τὸ ἓν οὐδ' ἐθεωρεῖτο ἐν τῷ ὄντι
καὶ τοῖς τι οὖσι τὸ αὐτό. ὥστε οὐ γένος τὸ ἕν· ἐπεὶ πᾶν
γένος καθ' οὗ ἀληθεύσεται ⟨τὸ ἓν ὡς γένος⟩,[1] οὐκέτι
καὶ τὰ ἀντικείμενα· καθ' οὗ δὲ παντὸς ὄντος ἀληθεύεται
τὸ ἓν καὶ τὰ ἀντικείμενα [καθ' οὗ ἀληθεύσεται τὸ ἓν ὡς
10 γένος],[2] κατὰ τούτου ἔσται οὐχ ὡς γένος. ὥστε οὔτε
τῶν πρώτων γενῶν ἀληθεύσεται ὡς γένος, ἐπείπερ καὶ
τὸ ἓν ὂν οὐ μᾶλλον ἓν ἢ πολλὰ οὐδέ τι τῶν ἄλλων γενῶν
οὕτως ἓν ὡς μὴ πολλά, οὔτε κατὰ τῶν ἄλλων τῶν
ὑστέρων ἃ πάντως πολλά. τὸ δ' ὅλον γένος οὐδὲν ἕν·
ὥστε, εἰ τὸ ἓν γένος, ἀπολεῖ τὸ εἶναι ἕν. οὐ γὰρ
15 ἀ ρ ι θ μ ὸ ς τ ὸ ἕ ν· ἀριθμὸς δ' ἔσται γενόμενον γένος.
ἔτι τὸ ἓν ἀριθμῷ ἕν· εἰ γὰρ γένει ἕν, οὐ κυρίως ἕν. ἔτι
ὥσπερ ἐν τοῖς ἀριθμοῖς τὸ ἓν οὐχ ὡς γένος κατ' αὐτῶν,
ἀλλ' ἐνυπάρχειν μὲν λέγεται, οὐ γένος δὲ λέγεται,
οὕτως οὐδ' εἰ ἐν τοῖς οὖσι τὸ ἕν, γένος ἂν εἴη οὔτε τοῦ

[1] transpos. H–S[2].
[2] del. Page, Harder

[1] Plotinus is here using the Stoic scale of degrees of
unification; it appears more clearly in ch. 11, 8–9 and VI.
9.4–8; cp. also V. 5.4. 31. For the scale in the Stoics see *SVF*

10. How then is each individual belonging to being one? Now by being a particular one it is not one—for it is already many by being a particular one—but each of the specific forms is equivocally one: for a specific form is a multiplicity, so that "one" here is [used as it is of] an army or a chorus.[1] So then the one there [in being] is not in these, so that the one is not a common term and it is not the same one which is observed in being and in particular beings. So that the one is not a genus; since every genus of which the one is truly predicated as genus can no longer have the opposites truly predicated of it; but in that the one and the opposites are truly predicated of every being, the one will not be predicated as their genus. So that it will not be truly predicated of the first genera either, since the one being also is not more one than many, nor is any one of the other genera one in such a way as not to be many, nor can [the one be truly predicated] of the others which come after, which are in every way many. But in general, no genus is one: so, if the one is a genus, it will destroy its unity. For "the one is not a number"[2]; but it will be a number if it has become a genus. Further, the one is one in number: for if it was one in genus, it would not be properly one. Further, just as in the numbers the one is not there as a genus predicated of them but is said to exist in them, but not said to be their genus, so, even if the one is in the beings, it would not be the genus either of being or of the other [genera] or of all of

II 366–8 and 1013; Philo *On The Eternity of the World* 79; Sextus Empiricus *Adv. Math.* VIII 102 (= *Against the Logicians* I 102 in Bury's Loeb edition).

[2] Aristotle *Metaphysics* N 1. 1088a6.

20 ὄντος οὔτε τῶν ἄλλων οὔτε τῶν πάντων. ἔτι ὥσπερ τὸ
ἁπλοῦν ἀρχὴ μὲν ἂν εἴη τοῦ οὐχ ἁπλοῦ, οὐ μὴν τούτου
καὶ γένος—ἁπλοῦν γὰρ ἂν εἴη καὶ τὸ μὴ ἁπλοῦν—οὕτω
καὶ ἐπὶ τοῦ ἑνός, εἰ τὸ ἓν ἀρχή, οὐκ ἔσται τῶν μετ' αὐτὸ
γένος. ἔσται οὖν οὔτε τοῦ ὄντος οὔτε τῶν ἄλλων. ἀλλ'
εἴπερ ἔσται, τῶν "ἓν" ἑκάστων, οἷον εἴ τις ἀξιώσειε
25 χωρίσαι ἀπὸ τῆς οὐσίας τὸ ἕν. τινῶν οὖν ἔσται. ὥσπερ
γὰρ τὸ ὂν οὐ πάντων γένος, ἀλλὰ τῶν "ὂν" εἰδῶν, οὕτω
καὶ τὸ ἓν τῶν "ἓν" ἑκάστων εἰδῶν. τίς οὖν διαφορὰ
ἄλλου πρὸς ἄλλο καθὸ ἕν, ὥσπερ ἄλλου πρὸς ἄλλο ὄντος
διαφορά; ἀλλ' εἰ συμμερίζεται τῷ ὄντι καὶ τῇ οὐσίᾳ, καὶ
30 τὸ ὂν τῷ μερισμῷ καὶ τῷ ἐν πολλοῖς θεωρεῖσθαι τὸ αὐτὸ
γένος, διὰ τί οὐ καὶ τὸ ἓν τοσαῦτα φαινόμενον ὅσα ἡ
οὐσία καὶ ἐπὶ τὰ ἴσα μεριζόμενον οὐκ ἂν εἴη γένος; ἢ
πρῶτον οὐκ ἀνάγκη, εἴ τι ἐνυπάρχει πολλοῖς, γένος
εἶναι οὔτε αὐτῶν, οἷς ἐνυπάρχει, οὔτε ἄλλων· οὐδ' ὅλως,
35 εἴ τι κοινόν, πάντως γένος. τὸ γοῦν σημεῖον ἐνυπάρχον
ταῖς γραμμαῖς οὐ γένος οὔτε αὐτῶν οὔτε ὅλως, οὐδέ γε,
ὥσπερ ἐλέγετο, τὸ ἐν τοῖς ἀριθμοῖς ἓν οὔτε τῶν ἀριθμῶν
οὔτε τῶν ἄλλων. δεῖ γὰρ τὸ κοινὸν καὶ ⟨ἓν⟩ ἐν[1] πολλοῖς
καὶ διαφοραῖς οἰκείαις χρῆσθαι καὶ εἴδη ποιεῖν καὶ ἐν
40 τῷ τί ἐστι. τοῦ δὲ ἑνὸς τίνες ἂν εἶεν διαφοραὶ ἢ ποῖα

[1] ⟨ἓν⟩ ἐν Ficinus, suspic. Creuzer, scr. Theiler: ἐν BxUC,
Kirchhoff: ἓν w, Perna, Creuzer.

them. Further, just as the simple might be principle of the non-simple, but could not also be its genus— for [if it were,] the non-simple would also be simple— so with the one, if the one is principle, it will not also be genus of the things posterior to it. It will not therefore be the genus either of being or of the other [genera]. But if it is going to be a genus, it will be the genus of the particular "ones", as if one were to think it right to separate the one from substance. It will be, then, a genus of particular things. For, just as being is not the genus of all things but of the specific forms which "are", so the one will be the genus of the particular specific forms which "are one". What then will be the difference of one from another in so far as they are one, as there is a difference of being of one from another? But if the one is divided along with being and substance, and being by the division and by being observed in many things as the same is a genus, why could not the one be a genus since it appears as many things as substance and is divided into an equal number of parts? Now, first of all it is not necessary, if something exists in many things, that it should be a genus, either of the things in which it exists or of other things; nor, in general, if something is common, is it at all necessary for it to be a genus. At any rate the point, which exists in the lines, is not a genus, either of them or generally speaking, nor, as was said, is the one in the numbers a genus either of the numbers or the other things. For that which is common and one in many things must employ differentiations which belong to itself and make specific forms and make them in its essential being. But what are the differentiations of the one or what

γεννᾷ εἴδη; εἰ δὲ τὰ αὐτὰ εἴδη ποιεῖ, ἃ περὶ τὸ ὄν, καὶ τὸ
αὐτὸ ἂν εἴη τῷ ὄντι, καὶ ὄνομα μόνον θάτερον, καὶ ἀρκεῖ
τὸ ὄν.

11. Ἐπισκεπτέον δέ, πῶς ἐν τῷ ὄντι τὸ ἕν, καὶ πῶς
ὁ λεγόμενος μερισμὸς καὶ ὅλως ὁ τῶν γενῶν, καὶ εἰ ὁ
αὐτὸς ἢ ἄλλος ἑκάτερος. πρῶτον οὖν, πῶς ὅλως ἓν
ἕκαστον ὁτιοῦν λέγεται καὶ ἔστιν, εἶτα εἰ ὁμοίως καὶ ἐν
5 τῷ ἑνὶ ὄντι λέγομεν καὶ ὡς ἐκεῖ λέγεται. τὸ μὲν οὖν ἐπὶ
πάντων ἓν οὐ ταὐτόν· οὔτε γὰρ ἐπὶ τῶν αἰσθητῶν
ὁμοίως καὶ τῶν νοητῶν—ἀλλὰ γὰρ οὐδὲ τὸ ὄν—οὔτ᾽
ἐπὶ τῶν αἰσθητῶν πρὸς ἄλληλα ὁμοίως· οὐ γὰρ ταὐτὸν
ἐν χορῷ καὶ στρατοπέδῳ καὶ νηὶ καὶ οἰκίᾳ οὐδ᾽ αὖ ἐν
τούτοις καὶ ἐν τῷ συνεχεῖ. ἀλλ᾽ ὅμως πάντα τὸ αὐτὸ
10 μιμεῖται, τυγχάνει δὲ τὰ μὲν πόρρωθεν, τὰ δὲ μᾶλλον,
ἤδη δὲ καὶ ἀληθέστερον ἐν τῷ νῷ· ψυχὴ γὰρ μία καὶ ἔτι
μᾶλλον νοῦς εἷς καὶ τὸ ὂν ἕν. ἆρ᾽ οὖν ἐν ἑκάστῳ τὸ ὂν
αὐτοῦ λέγοντες ἓν λέγομεν καὶ ὡς ἔχει ὄντος, οὕτω καὶ
τοῦ ἑνός; ἢ συμβέβηκε μὲν τοῦτο, οὐ μέντοι, καθὸ ὄν,
15 καὶ ἕν, ἀλλ᾽ ἔστι μὴ ἧττον ὂν ὑπάρχον ἧττον εἶναι ἕν. οὐ
γὰρ ἧττον ⟨ὂν⟩[1] στρατὸς ἢ χορὸς οἰκίας, ἀλλ᾽ ὅμως
ἧττον ἕν. ἔοικεν οὖν τὸ ἐν ἑκάστῳ ἓν πρὸς ἀγαθὸν
μᾶλλον βλέπειν, καὶ καθόσον τυγχάνει ἀγαθοῦ, κατὰ
τοσοῦτον καὶ ἕν, καὶ τὸ μᾶλλον καὶ ἧττον τοῦ ἓν ἐν

[1] Igal, H–S[2].

specific forms does it generate? But if it makes the same specific forms as occur in the sphere of being, it would be the same as being, and one of the two would be only a name, and being is sufficient.

11. But we must investigate how the one is in being, and how what we speak of as division [works], and in general the division of the genera, and if it is the same [as the division of being] or different in each of the two cases. First, then, how in general each and every thing is called one, and then if we mean the same [by "one" when we speak of it] in the one being and as transcendent. Now the one over all things is not the same; for [we do not mean] the same [by "one"] in the case of perceptible and of intelligible things—and certainly being is not [one in the same sense as the others]—[and it does not mean] the same in the case of perceptible things in comparison with each other; for it is not the same in a chorus and an army and a ship and a house, and not the same in these last and in what is continuous. But nevertheless all try to represent the same [One], but some attain only a remote resemblance, some come nearer, and attain it already more truly in Intellect: for soul is one and Intellect and being are still more one. So we then in each thing when we say its being also say its "one", and is it with its "one" as it is with its being? This happens incidentally, but a thing is not therefore one in proportion to its being, but it is possible to have no less real an existence but to be less one. For an army or a chorus has no less being than a house, but all the same it is less one. It seems then that the one in each thing looks more to good, and in so far as it attains to good it is also one, and being more or less one lies in this; for each thing

147

20 τούτῳ· εἶναι γὰρ θέλει ἕκαστον οὐχ ἁπλῶς, ἀλλὰ μετὰ
τοῦ ἀγαθοῦ. διὰ τοῦτο καὶ τὰ μὴ ἓν ὡς δύναται σπεύδει
ἓν γενέσθαι, τὰ μὲν φύσει αὐτῇ τῇ φύσει συνιόντα εἰς
ταὐτὸν ἑνοῦσθαι αὐτοῖς θέλοντα· οὐ γὰρ ἀπ᾿ ἀλλήλων
σπεύδει ἕκαστα, ἀλλ᾿ εἰς ἄλληλα καὶ εἰς αὐτά· καὶ
ψυχαὶ πᾶσαι εἰς ἓν ἂν βούλοιντο ἰέναι μετὰ τὴν αὐτῶν
25 οὐσίαν. καὶ ἀμφοτέρωθεν δὲ τὸ ἕν· καὶ γὰρ τὸ ἀφ᾿ οὗ καὶ
τὸ εἰς ὅ· καὶ γὰρ ἄρχεται ἀπὸ τοῦ ἓν καὶ σπεύδει εἰς τὸ
ἕν. οὕτω γὰρ καὶ τὸ ἀγαθόν· οὔτε γὰρ ὑπέστη ἐν τοῖς
οὖσιν ὁτιοῦν ὑποστάν τε οὐκ ἂν ἀνέχοιτο μὴ πρὸς τὸ ἓν
τὴν σπουδὴν ἔχον. τὰ μὲν δὴ φύσει οὕτω· τὰ δὲ ἐν ταῖς
30 τέχναις αὐτὴ ἑκάστη ἕκαστον πρὸς τοῦτο καθόσον
δύναται καὶ ὡς δύναται ἐκεῖνα οὕτως ἄγει.[1] τὸ δὲ ὂν
μάλιστα πάντων τούτου τυγχάνει· ἐγγὺς γάρ. ὅθεν τὰ
μὲν ἄλλα λέγεται ὃ λέγεται μόνον, οἷον ἄνθρωπος· καὶ
γάρ, εἴ ποτε λέγοιμεν εἷς, πρὸς δύο λέγομεν· εἰ δὲ καὶ
35 ἄλλως τὸ ἓν λέγομεν, ἀπ᾿ αὐτοῦ προστιθέντες λέγομεν.
ἐπὶ δὲ τοῦ ὄντος λέγομεν τὸ ὅλον τοῦτο ἓν ὂν καὶ
ἀξιοῦμεν ὡς ἓν ἐνδεικνύμενοι τὴν σφόδρα αὐτοῦ πρὸς τὸ
ἀγαθὸν συνουσίαν. γίγνεται οὖν τὸ ἓν καὶ ἐν αὐτῷ ὡς
ἀρχὴ καὶ τέλος, οὐχ ὡσαύτως δέ, ἀλλὰ ἄλλως, ὥστε καὶ
τὸ πρότερον καὶ τὸ ὕστερον καὶ ἐν τῷ ἕν. τί οὖν τὸ ἐν
40 αὐτῷ ἕν; οὐχὶ ὁμοίως ἐν ἅπασι τοῖς μέρεσι καὶ κοινὸν
θεωρούμενον; ἢ πρῶτον μὲν καὶ ἐν ταῖς γραμμαῖς κοινὸν
τὸ σημεῖον καὶ οὐ γένος τῶν γραμμῶν· καὶ ἐν τοῖς
ἀριθμοῖς κοινὸν τὸ ἓν δὴ ἴσως τοῦτο καὶ οὐ γένος· οὐδὲ

---

[1] Sleeman, Theiler: λέγει BxUC: λέγοι w: ποιεῖ Müller: τελεῖ
Seidel.

wishes not just for being, but for being together with the good. For this reason things which are not one strive as far as they can to become one, natural things by their very nature coming together, wishing to be united in identity with themselves; for all individual things do not strive to get away from each other, but towards each other and towards themselves; and all souls would like to come to unity, following their own nature. And the One is on both sides of them; for it is that from which they come and to which they go; for all things originate from the One and strive towards the One. For in this way they also strive towards the Good; for nothing whatever among the real beings could have come to exist or endure in existence if its striving was not directed towards the One. This is how it is with the things in nature. But as for the things of art, each art brings each of its products to this as far as it can and as far as their capacity allows. Being attains this most of all: for it is near. For this reason the other things are called only what they are called, man for instance; for even if we do sometimes say "one man", we say this in comparison with two; but if we do use the one in other contexts, we do so by adding, beginning from itself. But in the case of being we call this whole "one-being" and by indicating it as one claim its close communion with the Good. So the one in it also is principle and goal, but not in the same way, but otherwise, as there is prior and posterior also in that which is one. What then is the one in it? Is it not observed to be alike in all the parts and common? Now, first of all the point is common in lines and is not the genus of lines; there is something common in numbers, very likely this one, and it is not a genus:

γὰρ ταὐτὸν τὸ ἕν τὸ ἐπ' αὐτοῦ τοῦ ἕν τῷ[1] ἐπὶ μονάδος
45 καὶ δυάδος καὶ τῶν ἄλλων ἀριθμῶν. ἔπειτα καὶ ἐν τῷ
ὄντι οὐδὲν κωλύει τὰ μὲν πρῶτα, τὰ δ' ὕστερα εἶναι, καὶ
τὰ μὲν ἁπλᾶ, τὰ δὲ σύνθετα εἶναι. καὶ εἰ ταὐτὸν δὲ ἐν
πᾶσι τὸ ἕν τοῖς τοῦ ὄντος, διαφορὰ οὐκ οὖσα αὐτοῦ οὐδὲ
εἴδη ποιεῖ· εἰ δὲ μὴ εἴδη, οὐδὲ γένος αὐτὸ δύναται εἶναι.

12. Καὶ ταῦτα μὲν οὕτω. πῶς δὲ τοῖς ἀριθμοῖς τὸ
ἀγαθὸν ἐν τῷ ἓν εἶναι ἕκαστον ἀψύχοις οὖσιν; ἢ κοινὸν
τοῦτο καὶ ἐπὶ τῶν ἄλλων ἀψύχων. εἰ δέ τις λέγοι μὴ
εἶναι ὅλως αὐτούς, ἡμεῖς περὶ ὄντων εἴπομεν, καθὸ ἓν
5 ἕκαστον. εἰ δὲ τὸ σημεῖον ζητοῖεν πῶς ἀγαθοῦ μετέχει,
εἰ μὲν καθ' αὑτὸ φήσουσιν εἶναι, εἰ μὲν ἄψυχον φήσουσι,
τὸ αὐτὸ ὅπερ καὶ ἐπὶ τῶν ἄλλων τῶν τοιούτων
ζητοῦσιν· εἰ δ' ἐν ἄλλοις, οἷον ἐν κύκλῳ, τὸ ἀγαθὸν τὸ
ἐκείνου τοῦτο, καὶ ἡ ὄρεξις πρὸς τοῦτο καὶ σπεύδει ὡς
10 δύναται διὰ τούτου ἐκεῖ. ἀλλὰ πῶς τὰ γένη ταῦτα; ἆρα
κατακερματιζόμενα[2] ἕκαστα; ἢ ὅλον ἐν ἑκάστῳ ὢν
γένος. καὶ πῶς ἔτι ἕν; ἢ τὸ γένει ἓν ὡς ἐν πολλοῖς ὅλον.
ἆρ' οὖν μόνον ἐν τοῖς μετέχουσιν; ἢ οὔ, ἀλλὰ καὶ καθ'
αὑτὸ καὶ ἐν τοῖς μετέχουσιν. ἀλλ' ἴσως σαφέστερον
ἔσται ὕστερον.

13. Νῦν δέ, πῶς τὸ ποσὸν οὐκ ἐν τοῖς γένεσι τοῖς
πρώτοις, καὶ αὖ τὸ ποιόν; ἢ ποσὸν μὲν οὐ πρῶτον μετὰ
τῶν ἄλλων, ὅτι ἐκεῖνα μὲν ἅμα μετὰ τοῦ ὄντος. κίνησις

---

[1] Kirchhoff: τοῦ Enn.
[2] κατακ. U, Igal, H–S[2]: καὶ τὰ κ. wBxC.

for the one in the one itself is not the same as the one
in the unit and the two and the other numbers. And
then in being also nothing prevents some things
from being prior and others posterior, and some
simple and some composite. And if the one is the
same in all things which belong to being, as there is
no differentiation of it it does not make specific
forms; but if there are no specific forms, it cannot
itself be a genus.

12. And so much for this. But how does the good
for numbers lie in their being each of them one when
they are soulless? Now this is common also to other
soulless things. But if anyone were to say that
numbers do not exist at all, we for our part were
speaking of existing things, in so far as each of them
is one. But if they were to enquire how the point
partakes of the good, if they are going to assert that
it exists by itself, then, if they assert that it is
soulless, their enquiry is the same as in the case of
other things of the kind; but if in others, in the circle
for instance, this is the good of the point and its
desire is directed to this, and it will strive as far as it
can towards the transcendent through this circle.
But how can the genera be these things? Can they
really be particulars, all chopped up small? No, the
generic one is like a whole in many things. Does it
exist only in the things which participate in it? No,
but it exists both independently and in the things
which participate in it. But perhaps this will be
clearer later.

13. But now, why is the quantum not in the primary genera, and also the quale? Now, the quantum
is not primary with the others because they are
simultaneous with being. For movement is with

γὰρ μετὰ τοῦ ὄντος ἐνέργεια ὄντος ζωὴ αὐτοῦ οὖσα· καὶ
5 στάσις ἐν αὐτῇ τῇ οὐσίᾳ συνεισῄει· μᾶλλον δὲ συνῆν τὸ
εἶναι τούτοις ἑτέροις καὶ τοῖς αὐτοῖς, ὥστε συνορᾶσθαι
καὶ ταῦτα. ἀριθμὸς δὲ ὕστερός τε ἐκείνων καὶ ἑαυτοῦ,
καὶ τὸ "ὕστερος" παρὰ τοῦ προτέρου, καὶ ἐφεξῆς
ἀλλήλοις, καὶ ἐνυπάρχει τὰ ὕστερα ἐν προτέροις· ὥστε
10 ἐν μὲν τοῖς πρώτοις οὐκ ἂν καταριθμοῖτο· ζητητέον δέ,
εἰ ὅλως γένος. τὸ μέντοι μέγεθος ἔτι μᾶλλον ὕστερον καὶ
σύνθετον· ἀριθμὸς γὰρ ἐν τῷδε καὶ γραμμὴ δύο τινὰ καὶ
ἐπίπεδον τρία. εἰ μὲν οὖν παρὰ τοῦ ἀριθμοῦ ἔχει καὶ τὸ
συνεχὲς μέγεθος τὸ ποσόν, τοῦ ἀριθμοῦ οὐκ ὄντος
15 γένους πῶς ἂν τοῦτο ἔχοι; ἔνι δὲ καὶ ἐν τοῖς μεγέθεσι τὸ
πρότερον καὶ τὸ ὕστερον. εἰ δὲ κοινὸν ἐπ᾽ ἀμφοῖν τὸ
ποσοῖς, τί τοῦτό ἐστι ληπτέον, καὶ εὑρόντας θετέον
γένος ὕστερον, οὐκ ἐν τοῖς πρώτοις· καὶ εἰ γένος μὴ ἐν
τοῖς πρώτοις, εἴς τι ἀνακτέον τῶν πρώτων ἢ τῶν εἰς τὰ
20 πρῶτα. δῆλον τοίνυν ἴσως, ὅτι ὅσον τι δηλοῖ ἡ τοῦ
ποσοῦ φύσις καὶ μετρεῖ τὸ ὅσον ἑκάστου αὐτή τε ὅσον
τι. ἀλλ᾽ εἰ κοινὸν ἐπ᾽ ἀριθμοῦ καὶ μεγέθους τὸ ὅσον, ἢ ὁ
ἀριθμὸς πρῶτος, τὸ δὲ μέγεθος ἀπ᾽ ἐκείνου, ἢ ὅλως ὁ
μὲν ἀριθμὸς ἐν μίξει κινήσεως καὶ στάσεως, τὸ δὲ
25 μέγεθος κίνησίς τις ἢ ἐκ κινήσεως, τῆς μὲν κινήσεως εἰς
ἀόριστον προϊούσης, τῆς δὲ στάσεως ἐν τῇ ἐποχῇ τοῦ
προϊόντος μονάδα ποιούσης. ἀλλὰ περὶ γενέσεως

being as the activity of being, since it is its life; and rest came in as well in substance itself; and still more is being same and other associated with these three classes, so that sameness and otherness also are seen together with them. But number is posterior to these classes and posterior to itself, and the posterior comes from the prior and numbers come one after another in order, and the posterior exist in the prior; so number could not be counted among the first genera; and we should enquire whether it is a genus at all. But magnitude is still more subsequent and composite; for it is number in this particular thing—and a line is some sort of two and a surface three. If then the continuous magnitude has its quantitativeness from number, if number is not a genus how could this have [the status of a genus]? And there is prior and posterior also in magnitudes. But if it is common to both numbers and magnitudes to be quantitative, we must grasp what this [being quantitative] is and, when we have found it, posit it as a posterior genus, not among the primary genera; and if it is a genus not among the primary ones, it must be referred back to one of the primary genera or to one of those which go back to them. So it is perhaps clear that the nature of the quantum signifies a definite quantity and it measures how much each thing is and is itself a so much. But if definite quantity is common to number and magnitude, then either number is primary and magnitude comes from it, or number consists altogether in a mixture of movement and rest, but magnitude is a movement or derives from movement; movement goes forward into the indefinite, but rest in holding back what is going forward makes the unit. But we must consider later

ἀριθμοῦ καὶ μεγέθους, μᾶλλον δὲ ὑποστάσεως ὕστερον
καὶ ἐπινοίας θεωρητέον. τάχα γὰρ ὁ μὲν ἀριθμὸς ἐν τοῖς
πρώτοις γένεσι, τὸ δὲ μέγεθος ὕστερον ἐν συνθέσει· καὶ
30 ὁ μὲν ἀριθμὸς ἑστώτων, τὸ δὲ μέγεθος ἐν κινήσει. ἀλλὰ
ταῦτα μὲν ὕστερον, ὥς φαμεν.

14. Περὶ δὲ τοῦ ποιοῦ, διὰ τί οὐκ ἐν τοῖς πρώτοις; ἢ
ὅτι καὶ τοῦτο ὕστερον καὶ μετὰ τὴν οὐσίαν. [δεῖ δὲ τὴν
οὐσίαν παρακολουθοῦντα ταῦτα ἔχειν τὴν πρώτην, μὴ
ἐκ τούτων δὲ τὴν σύστασιν ἔχειν μηδὲ διὰ τούτων
5 συμπληροῦσθαι· ἢ εἴη ἂν ὑστέρα ποιότητος καὶ
ποσότητος.]¹ ἐν μὲν οὖν ταῖς συνθέταις οὐσίαις καὶ ἐκ
πολλῶν, ἐν αἷς καὶ ἀριθμοὶ καὶ ποσότητες² διαλλαγὴν
ἐποίησαν αὐτῶν, καὶ ποιότητες εἶεν ἂν καὶ κοινότης τις
ἐν αὐταῖς θεωρηθήσεται· ἐν δὲ τοῖς πρώτοις γένεσι τὴν
10 διαίρεσιν οὐχ ἁπλῶν καὶ συνθέτων δεῖ ποιεῖσθαι, ἀλλ'
ἁπλῶν καὶ τῶν τὴν οὐσίαν συμπληρούντων, οὐ τὴν τινὰ
οὐσίαν. [τὴν μὲν γὰρ τινὰ οὐσίαν συμπληροῦσθαι καὶ ἐκ
ποιότητος οὐδὲν ἴσως ἄτοπον, ἐχούσης ἤδη τὴν οὐσίαν
πρὸ τῆς ποιότητος, τὸ δὲ τοιόνδε ἔξωθεν, αὐτὴν δὲ τὴν
οὐσίαν ἃ ἔχει οὐσιώδη ἔχειν.]¹ καίτοι ἐν ἄλλοις
15 ἠξιοῦμεν τὰ μὲν τῆς οὐσίας συμπληρωτικὰ ὁμωνύμως
ποιὰ εἶναι, τὰ δ' ἔξωθεν μετὰ τὴν οὐσίαν ὑπάρχοντα
ποιά, καὶ τὰ μὲν ἐν ταῖς οὐσίαις ἐνεργείας αὐτῶν, τὰ δὲ
μετ' αὐτὰς ἤδη πάθη. νῦν δὲ λέγομεν οὐκ οὐσίας ὅλως
εἶναι συμπληρωτικὰ τὰ τῆς τινὸς οὐσίας· οὐ γὰρ οὐσίας
20 προσθήκη γίνεται τῷ ἀνθρώπῳ καθὸ ἄνθρωπος εἰς
οὐσίαν· ἀλλ' ἔστιν οὐσία ἄνωθεν, πρὶν ἐπὶ τὴν διαφορὰν
ἐλθεῖν, ὥσπερ καὶ ζῷον ἤδη, πρὶν ἐπὶ τὸ λογικὸν ἥκειν.

---

¹ del. H–S² ut e Simpl. huc insertum (cf. Schwyzer, *Mus.
Helv.* 26, 1969, 265).

the coming into being of number and magnitude, or rather their real or notional existence. For perhaps number is among the first genera, but magnitude comes later in a composition; and number is of static things, but magnitude is in movement. But, as we say, we will discuss these questions later.

14. But as for the quale, why is it not among the primary genera? It is because this also is posterior and comes after substance. In composite substances, then, which are made up of many elements, and in which numbers and quantities produce their differentiation, there might also be qualities, and a certain common element will be discerned in them; but in the primary genera the distinction which must be made is not between simples and composites but between simples and those which make an essential contribution to substance, not to a particular substance. All the same, we did think it right to say elsewhere that the elements which contributed to the essential completion of substance were qualities only in name, but those which came from outside subsequent to substance were qualities [in the proper sense], and that those which were in substances were their activities, but those which came after them were already passive affections. But now we are saying that the elements of particular substance make no contribution at all to the completion of substance as such; for there is no substantial addition to the substance of man by reason of his being man; but he is substance at a higher level, before coming to the differentiation, as is also the living being before coming to the "reasonable".

---

[2] Rieth: ποιότητες Enn.

15. Πῶς οὖν τὰ τέτταρα γένη συμπληροῖ τὴν οὐσίαν
οὔπω ποιὰν οὐσίαν ποιοῦντα; οὐδὲ γὰρ τινά. ὅτι μὲν οὖν
τὸ ὂν πρῶτον, εἴρηται, καὶ ὡς ἡ κίνησις οὐκ ἂν εἴη ἄλλο
οὐδ' ἡ στάσις οὐδὲ θάτερον οὐδὲ ταὐτόν, δῆλον· καὶ ὅτι
5 οὐ ποιότητα ἐνεργάζεται ἡ κίνησις αὕτη, ἴσως μὲν
φανερόν, λεχθὲν δὲ μᾶλλον ποιήσει σαφέστερον. εἰ γὰρ ἡ
κίνησις ἐνέργειά ἐστιν αὐτῆς, ἐνεργείᾳ δὲ τὸ ὂν καὶ
ὅλως τὰ πρῶτα, οὐκ ἂν συμβεβηκὸς εἴη ἡ κίνησις, ἀλλ'
ἐνέργεια οὖσα ἐνεργείᾳ ὄντος οὐδ' ἂν συμπληρωτικὸν
10 ἔτι λέγοιτο, ἀλλ' αὐτή· ὥστε οὐκ ἐμβέβηκεν εἰς ὕστερόν
τι οὐδ' εἰς ποιότητα, ἀλλ' εἰς τὸ ἅμα τέτακται. οὐ γὰρ
ἔστιν ὄν, εἶτα κεκίνηται, οὐδὲ ἔστιν ὄν, εἶτα ἔστη· οὐδὲ
πάθος ἡ στάσις· καὶ ταὐτὸν δὲ καὶ θάτερον οὐχ ὕστερα,
ὅτι μὴ ὕστερον ἐγένετο πολλά, ἀλλ' ἦν ὅπερ ἦν ἓν
15 πολλά· εἰ δὲ πολλά, καὶ ἑτερότης, καὶ εἰ ἓν πολλά, καὶ
ταὐτότης. καὶ ταῦτα εἰς τὴν οὐσίαν ἀρκεῖ· ὅταν δὲ
μέλλῃ πρὸς τὰ κάτω προϊέναι, τότε ἄλλα, ἃ οὐκέτι
οὐσίαν ποιεῖ, ἀλλὰ ποιὰν οὐσίαν καὶ ποσὴν οὐσίαν, καὶ
γιγνέσθω γένη οὐ πρῶτα.

16. Τὸ δὲ "πρός τι" παραφυάδι ἐοικὸς πῶς ἂν ἐν
πρώτοις; ἑτέρου γὰρ πρὸς ἕτερον καὶ οὐ πρὸς αὐτὸ ἡ
σχέσις [καὶ πρὸς ἄλλο].¹ "ποῦ" δὲ καὶ "πότε" ἔτι
πόρρω. τό τε γὰρ "ποῦ" ἄλλο ἐν ἄλλῳ, ὥστε δύο· τὸ δὲ

¹ del. Harder, Theiler.

15. How then do the four genera contribute to the completion of substance when they do not yet make it a kind of substance? For they do not make it a particular substance. It has been said that being is primary, and it is clear that movement cannot be other [than primary], nor rest, nor other, nor same; and it is perhaps also obvious that this movement does not produce quality, but if we say something about this, it will perhaps be clearer. For if movement is the activity of substance, and being and the primary genera altogether are actively actual, movement could not be something incidental, but, being the activity of what is actively actual, could not any longer be called something which contributes to the completion of substance, but is substance itself: so that it has not entered some subsequent genus, not even quality, but is ranked as simultaneous. For being is not first being and then in movement, nor is it first being and then at rest; nor is rest a passive affection of it; and same and other do not come after it, because it did not become many afterwards, but was what it was, one-many; but if it is many, it is also otherness, and if it is one-many, it is also sameness. And these are enough for its substance; but when it is going to proceed to the lower levels, then there are others, which no longer make substance, but qualified and quantified substance, and let us grant that these are non-primary genera.

16. But how could "relation", which is like a sideshoot, be among the first [genera]? For the state of being related is of one thing to another and not of a thing to itself. "Where" and "when" are still further away. For the "where" means one thing in another, so that there are two; but the genus must be one, and

PLOTINUS: ENNEAD VI. 2.

5 γένος ἓν δεῖ εἶναι, οὐ σύνθεσιν· καὶ οὐδὲ τόπος ἐκεῖ· νῦν
δὲ ὁ λόγος περὶ τῶν ὄντων κατ' ἀλήθειαν. ὅ τε χρόνος εἰ
ἐκεῖ, σκεπτέον· μᾶλλον δὲ ἴσως οὔ. εἰ δὲ καὶ μέτρον
καὶ οὐχ ἁπλῶς μέτρον, ἀλλὰ κινήσεως, δύο καὶ
σύνθετον τὸ ὅλον καὶ κινήσεως ὕστερον, ὥστε οὐχ ὅπου
10 κίνησις ἐν ἴσῃ διαιρέσει. τὸ δὲ "ποιεῖν" καὶ τὸ
"πάσχειν" ἐν κινήσει, εἰ ἄρα ἐκεῖ τὸ πάσχειν· καὶ τὸ
ποιεῖν δὲ δύο· ὁμοίως καὶ τὸ πάσχειν· οὐδέτερον οὖν
ἁπλοῦν. καὶ τὸ "ἔχειν" δύο καὶ τὸ "κεῖσθαι" ἄλλο ἐν
ἄλλῳ οὕτως, ὥστε τρία.

17. Ἀλλὰ τὸ καλὸν καὶ τὸ ἀγαθὸν καὶ αἱ ἀρεταὶ διὰ
τί οὐκ ἐν τοῖς πρώτοις, ἐπιστήμη, νοῦς; ἢ τὸ μὲν
ἀγαθόν, εἰ τὸ πρῶτον, ἣν δὴ λέγομεν τὴν τοῦ ἀγαθοῦ
φύσιν, καθ' ἧς οὐδὲν κατηγορεῖται, ἀλλ' ἡμεῖς μὴ
5 ἔχοντες ἄλλως σημῆναι οὕτω λέγομεν, γένος οὐδενὸς ἂν
εἴη. οὐ γὰρ κατ' ἄλλων λέγεται ἢ ἣν ἂν καθ' ὧν λέγεται
ἕκαστον ἐκεῖνο λεγόμενον. καὶ πρὸ οὐσίας δὲ ἐκεῖνο, οὐκ
ἐν οὐσίᾳ. εἰ δ' ὡς ποιὸν τὸ ἀγαθόν, ὅλως τὸ ποιὸν οὐκ ἐν
τοῖς πρώτοις. τί οὖν ἡ τοῦ ὄντος φύσις οὐκ ἀγαθόν; ἢ

---

[1] A very curious and paradoxical kind of intelligible
"place" does appear in V. 8.4. 15–19 (cp. VI. 7.31–33): but
the intelligible χώρα there is very different from the
Aristotelian τόπος here. Plotinus' unwillingness to dismiss
the question of time in the intelligible as summarily as he
dismisses that of place should be noted. Perhaps he was
already planning the work On Eternity and Time (III. 7
[45]), which follows VI, 1–3 immediately in Porphyry's
chronological order. There are passages in this and one or
two elsewhere in the Enneads which anticipate and may
have provided the starting-point for the doctrine of a
higher time on the intelligible level in Iamblichus and his
successors. See IV. 4 (28). 16. 13–16; VI. 7 (38). 1. 54–58; III.

not a compound; and there is not any place in the intelligible world; but now we are speaking of the things which truly exist. And we must consider whether time is there; but it is more likely that it is not.[1] But if it is a "measure", and not just a measure, but a "measure of movement", there are two [components] and the whole is composite and posterior to movement, so that it is not where movement is in a division on the same level. But "acting" and "being affected" are in movement—if being affected is really in the intelligible world at all; and "acting" involves two; and so likewise does "being affected"; neither, therefore, is simple. And "having" implies two, and "position" means one thing in another, so that there are three.

17. But why are not the beautiful and the good and the virtues among the primary genera—and knowledge and intellect? As for the good, if it is the first, the nature which we certainly do call that of the good, of which nothing is predicated, but we call it this because we cannot indicate it in any other way, it could not be the genus of anything. For it is not predicated of other things, or each of the other things of which it was predicated would be spoken of as the good. And that good is before substance, not in substance. But if it is the good as a quale, the qualified in general is not among the primary gen-

---

7 (45). 7. 7–10; on anticipations of the later doctrine in the much-discussed chapter 11 of III. 7 see Peter Manchester "Time and the Soul in Plotinus III 7 [45] 11" in *Dionysius* II, 1978; for the later doctrine itself see S. Sambursky and S. Pines *The Concept of Time in Late Neoplatonism* (a collection of passages with introduction and commentary), Jerusalem 1971.

10 πρῶτον μὲν ἄλλως καὶ οὐκ ἐκείνως ὡς τὸ πρῶτον· καὶ
ὡς ἐστιν ἀγαθὸν οὐχ ὡς ποιόν, ἀλλ' ἐν αὐτῷ. ἀλλὰ καὶ
τὰ ἄλλα ἔφαμεν γένη ἐν αὐτῷ, καὶ διότι κοινόν τι ἦν
ἕκαστον καὶ ἐν πολλοῖς ἑωρᾶτο, γένος. εἰ οὖν καὶ τὸ
ἀγαθὸν ὁρᾶται ἐφ' ἑκάστῳ μέρει τῆς οὐσίας ἢ τοῦ ὄντος
ἢ ἐπὶ τοῖς πλείστοις, διὰ τί οὐ γένος καὶ ἐν τοῖς
15 πρώτοις; ἢ ἐν ἅπασι τοῖς μέρεσιν οὐ ταὐτόν, ἀλλὰ
πρώτως καὶ δευτέρως καὶ ὑστέρως· ἢ γὰρ ὅτι θάτερον
παρὰ θατέρου, τὸ ὕστερον παρὰ τοῦ προτέρου, ἢ ὅτι
παρ' ἑνὸς πάντα τοῦ ἐπέκεινα, ἄλλα δ' ἄλλως κατὰ
φύσιν τὴν αὐτῶν μεταλαμβάνει. εἰ δὲ δὴ καὶ γένος
20 ἐθέλει τις θέσθαι, ὕστερον· ὕστερον γὰρ τῆς οὐσίας καὶ
τοῦ τί ἐστι τὸ εἶναι αὐτὸ ἀγαθόν, κἂν ἀεὶ συνῇ, ἐκεῖνα δὲ
ἦν τοῦ ὄντος ᾗ ὂν καὶ εἰς τὴν οὐσίαν. ἐντεῦθεν γὰρ καὶ τὸ
ἐ π έ κ ε ι ν α τ ο ῦ ὄ ν τ ο ς, ἐπειδὴ τὸ ὂν καὶ ἡ οὐσία
οὐ δύναται μὴ πολλὰ εἶναι, ἀλλὰ ἀνάγκη αὐτῷ ἔχειν
25 ταῦτα, ἠριθμημένα γένη, καὶ εἶναι ἐ ν π ο λ λ ά. εἰ
μέντοι τὸ ἀγαθὸν τὸ ἓν τὸ ἐν τῷ ὄντι—μὴ ὀκνοῖμεν
λέγειν τὴν ἐνέργειαν αὐτοῦ τὴν κατὰ φύσιν πρὸς τὸ ἓν
τοῦτο εἶναι τὸ ἀγαθὸν αὐτοῦ, ἵν' ἐκεῖθεν ἀγαθοειδὲς ᾖ—
ἔσται τὸ ἀγαθὸν τούτῳ ἐνέργεια πρὸς τὸ ἀγαθόν· τοῦτο
30 δὲ ἡ ζωὴ αὐτοῦ· τοῦτο δὲ ἡ κίνησις, ἢ ἤδη ἐστὶν ἕν τι
τῶν γενῶν.

18. Περὶ δὲ τοῦ καλοῦ, εἰ μὲν ἐκεῖνο ἡ πρώτη
καλλονή, τὰ αὐτὰ ἂν καὶ παραπλήσια λέγοιτο τοῖς ἐπὶ

era. Well then, is the nature of being not good? First, it is so otherwise, and not in that way in which the first is; and the way in which it is good is not as a quale, but in itself. But we said that the other genera also were in themselves, and it was because it was something common and was seen in many things that it was a genus. If then the good is seen in each part of substance or of being, or in most of them, why is it not a genus, and among the primary ones? Now it is not the same in all the parts, but is present primarily and secondarily and subsequently: either because one good comes from another, the posterior from the prior, or because all come from the one transcendent Good, but different ones partake of it in different ways according to their own nature. But if someone does want to posit it also as a genus, it will be posterior; for a thing's being good is posterior to its being and its being something, even if it always accompanies them, but those [primary genera] belong to being as being and enter into substance. For that is the reason for the "beyond being",[1] since being and substance cannot help being many, but it must contain these, the genera we have counted up, and be one-many. But if the good is the one in being—let us not shrink from saying that its natural activity towards the One is its good, that it may be by it in the form of good—the good for being is its activity towards the Good; but this is its life; but this is movement, which is already one of the genera.

18. As for the beautiful, if the primary beauty is that [transcendent First], what could be said about it

---

[1] This is one of the clearest indications in Plotinus of how he understood the ἐπέκεινα τῆς οὐσίας of Plato *Republic* 509B8; cp. V. 5.6. 5–13.

τοῦ ἀγαθοῦ λόγοις· καὶ εἰ τὸ ἐπὶ τῇ ἰδέᾳ οἷον
ἀποστίλβον, ὅτι μὴ τὸ αὐτὸ ἐν πᾶσι, καὶ ὅτι ὕστερον τὸ
5 ἐπιστίλβειν. εἰ δὲ οὐκ ἄλλο τι τὸ καλὸν ἢ ἡ οὐσία αὐτή,
ἐν τῇ οὐσίᾳ εἴρηται. εἰ δὲ πρὸς ἡμᾶς τοὺς ὁρῶντας τῷ
τοιόνδε πάθος ποιεῖν ἐστι, τοῦτο τὸ ἐνεργεῖν κίνησις,
καὶ εἰ πρὸς ἐκεῖνο ἡ ἐνέργεια, κίνησις. ἔστι δὲ καὶ ἡ
ἐπιστήμη αὐτοκίνησις ὄψις οὖσα τοῦ ὄντος καὶ
ἐνέργεια, ἀλλ᾽ οὐχ ἕξις· ὥστε καὶ αὐτὴ ὑπὸ τὴν κίνησιν,
10 εἰ δὲ βούλει, ὑπὸ τὴν στάσιν, ἢ καὶ ὑπ᾽ ἄμφω· εἰ δὲ ὑπ᾽
ἄμφω, ὡς μικτόν· εἰ τοῦτο, ὕστερον τὸ μικτόν. ὁ δὲ νοῦς
ὢν νοοῦν καὶ σύνθετον ἐκ πάντων, οὐχ ἕν τι τῶν γενῶν·
καὶ ἔστιν ὁ ἀληθινὸς νοῦς ὢν μετὰ πάντων καὶ ἤδη
πάντα τὰ ὄντα, τὸ δὲ ὂν [μόνον] [1] ψιλὸν εἰς γένος
15 λαμβανόμενον στοιχεῖον αὐτοῦ. δικαιοσύνη δὲ καὶ
σωφροσύνη καὶ ὅλως ἀρετὴ ἐνέργειαί τινες νοῦ πᾶσαι·
ὥστε οὐκ ἐν πρώτοις καὶ ὕστερα γένος [2] καὶ εἴδη.

19. Γένη δὴ ὄντα τὰ τέτταρα ταῦτα καὶ πρῶτα ἆρα
καθ᾽ αὑτὸ ἕκαστον εἴδη ποιεῖ; οἷον τὸ ὂν διαιροῖτο ἂν
ἤδη ἐφ᾽ ἑαυτοῦ ἄνευ τῶν ἄλλων; ἢ οὔ· ἐπειδὴ ἔξωθεν
τοῦ γένους λαβεῖν δεῖ τὰς διαφοράς, καὶ εἶναι μὲν τοῦ

---

[1] delevimus, ut glossam ad ψιλόν.
[2] A (γένου A[38]) EBxUC, Igal, H–S[2]: γένους A[pc], Kirchhoff.

---

[1] For the possibility of beauty being either the First or
the Second Hypostasis cp. I, 6.9. 40–43. In the great work
III, 8 (30)—V. 8 (31)—V. 5 (32)—II. 9 (33) beauty is
firmly identified as on the level of οὐσία, the Second Hypostasis.
V. 5. 12 brings out the difference between this and the First

would be the same and similar to what was said about the Good; and if it is that which, one might say, shines out upon the Idea, [we could say that it is not the same in all] the Forms and that the shining upon them is posterior. But if the beautiful is nothing else but substance itself, it has been included in what was said about substance.[1] But if it is the beautiful in relation to us who see it by affecting us in this kind of way, this active actuality is movement, and if the activity is directed towards the transcendent, it is [still] movement. And knowledge is self-movement, since it is a sight of being and an active actuality, not a state; so that it also comes under movement—but, if you like, under rest, or under both; but if under both, it is as something mixed; and if so, the mixed is posterior. But Intellect, since it is being as intelligent and a composite of all [the genera], is not one of the genera; and the true Intellect is being with all its contents and already all beings, but being in isolation, taken as a genus, is an element of it. But righteousness and self-control and virtues in general are all particular activities of Intellect; so that they are not among the primary [genera] and genus and species [of virtue] are posterior.

19. Granted that these four are genera, and primary genera, does each of them by itself make species? Does being, for instance, already divide by itself without the others? No: since it must take its differentiations from outside the genus, and they are

particularly sharply. For the "shining" of beauty on the Idea see VI. 7.21–22. Cp. my "Beauty and the Discovery of Divinity in the Thought of Plotinus" (*Plotinian and Christian Studies* XIX).

5 ὄντος διαφορὰς ᾗ ὄν, οὐ μέντοι τὰς διαφορὰς αὐτό.
πόθεν οὖν ἕξει; οὐ γὰρ δὴ ἐκ τῶν οὐκ ὄντων. εἰ δὴ ἐξ
ὄντων, ἦν δὲ τὰ γένη τὰ τρία τὰ λοιπά, δῆλον ὅτι ἐκ
τούτων καὶ μετὰ τούτων προστιθεμένων καὶ
συνδυαζομένων καὶ ἅμα γινομένων. ἀλλὰ ἅμα γινόμενα
10 τοῦτο δὴ ἐποίει τὸ ἐκ πάντων. πῶς οὖν τὰ ἄλλα ἐστὶ
μετὰ τὸ ἐκ πάντων; καὶ πῶς γένη πάντα ὄντα εἴδη
ποιεῖ; πῶς δὲ ἡ κίνησις εἴδη κινήσεως καὶ ἡ στάσις καὶ
τὰ ἄλλα; ἐπεὶ κἀκεῖνο δεῖ παραφυλάττειν, ὅπως μὴ
ἀφανίζοιτο ἕκαστον ἐν τοῖς εἴδεσι, μηθ’ αὖ τὸ γένος
κατηγορούμενον ᾖ μόνον ὡς ἐν ἐκείνοις θεωρούμενον,
15 ἀλλ’ ᾖ ἐκείνοις ἅμα καὶ ἐν αὐτῷ καὶ μιγνύμενον αὖ
καθαρὸν καὶ μὴ μιγνύμενον ὑπάρχῃ, μηδ’ ἄλλως
συντελοῦν εἰς οὐσίαν αὐτὸ ἀπολλύῃ. περὶ μὲν δὴ τούτων
σκεπτέον. ἐπεὶ δὲ ἔφαμεν τὸ ἐκ πάντων τῶν ὄντων νοῦν
εἶναι ἕκαστον, πρὸ δὲ πάντων ὡς εἰδῶν καὶ μερῶν τὸ ὂν
20 καὶ τὴν οὐσίαν τιθέμεθα νοῦν εἶναι, τὸν ἤδη νοῦν
ὕστερον λέγομεν εἶναι. καὶ δὴ ταύτην τὴν ἀπορίαν
χρήσιμον πρὸς τὸ ζητούμενον ποιησώμεθα καὶ οἷον
παραδείγματι χρησάμενοι εἰς γνῶσιν τῶν λεγομένων
αὑτοὺς ἐμβιβάζωμεν.

20. Λάβωμεν οὖν τὸν μὲν εἶναι νοῦν οὐδὲν
ἐφαπτόμενον τῶν ἐν μέρει οὐδ’ ἐνεργοῦντα περὶ ὁτιοῦν,
ἵνα μὴ τὶς νοῦς γίγνοιτο, ὥσπερ ἐπιστήμη πρὸ τῶν ἐν
μέρει εἰδῶν, καὶ ἡ ἐν εἴδει δὲ ἐπιστήμη πρὸ τῶν ἐν αὐτῇ
5 μερῶν· πᾶσα μὲν οὐδὲν τῶν ἐν μέρει δύναμις πάντων,

differentiations of being as being, but the differentiations are not being itself. Where will it get them from, then? Certainly not from non-beings. But if it got them from being and the three remaining genera existed, it is clear that the differentiations arose from them and with them, applied to being and coupled with it and coming to be simultaneous with it. But by coming to be simultaneous with it they made what is composed of all. How then do the others exist along with that which is from all? And how if they are all genera do they make species? How does movement make species of movement, and rest, and the other ones? For we must be careful about this, that each genus does not disappear in its species, and that the genus is not only predicated as observed in them, but that it is both in the species and in itself, and must be at once mingled and pure and unmingled, and must not contribute uselessly to substance by destroying itself. We shall have to consider these questions. But since we asserted that what is composed of all beings is each individual intelligence, but posited that the being and substance prior to all as species and parts was Intellect, we are saying that Intellect as it is is posterior. Well then, let us make this difficulty profitable for our enquiry and by using it as a kind of example embark upon getting to understand what we are saying.

20. Let us then apprehend one Intellect which in no way applies itself to partial things and is not active about anything in particular, so that it may not become a particular intellect, like the knowledge before the specific partial forms of knowledge and the knowledge in specific form before the parts in it; for every body of knowledge is none of its partial

ἕκαστον δὲ ἐνεργείᾳ ἐκεῖνο, καὶ δυνάμει δὲ πάντα, καὶ
ἐπὶ τῆς καθόλου ὡσαύτως· αἱ μὲν ἐν εἴδει, αἱ ἐν τῇ ὅλῃ
δυνάμει κεῖνται, αἱ δὴ τὸ ἐν εἴδει λαβοῦσαι, δυνάμει
εἰσὶν ἡ ὅλη· κατηγορεῖται γὰρ ἡ πᾶσα, οὐ μόριον τῆς
πάσης· αὐτήν γε μὴν δεῖ ἀκέραιον ἐφ' αὑτῆς εἶναι. οὕτω
10 δὴ ἄλλως μὲν νοῦν τὸν ξύμπαντα εἰπεῖν εἶναι, τὸν πρὸ
τῶν καθέκαστον ἐνεργείᾳ ὄντων, ἄλλως δὲ νοῦς
ἑκάστους,[1] τοὺς μὲν ἐν μέρει ἐκ πάντων πληρωθέντας,
τὸν δ' ἐπὶ πᾶσι νοῦν χορηγὸν μὲν τοῖς καθέκαστα,
δύναμιν δὲ αὐτῶν εἶναι καὶ ἔχειν ἐν τῷ καθόλου
15 ἐκείνους, ἐκείνους τε αὖ ἐν αὐτοῖς ἐν μέρει οὖσιν ἔχειν
τὸν καθόλου, ὡς ἡ τὶς ἐπιστήμη τὴν ἐπιστήμην. καὶ
εἶναι καὶ καθ' αὑτὸν τὸν μέγαν νοῦν καὶ ἑκάστους αὖ ἐν
αὐτοῖς ὄντας, καὶ ἐμπεριέχεσθαι αὖ τοὺς ἐν μέρει τῷ
ὅλῳ καὶ τὸν ὅλον τοῖς ἐν μέρει, ἑκάστους ἐφ' ἑαυτῶν καὶ
20 ἐν ἄλλῳ καὶ ἐφ' ἑαυτοῦ ἐκεῖνον καὶ ἐν ἐκείνοις, καὶ ἐν
ἐκείνῳ μὲν πάντας ἐφ' ἑαυτοῦ ὄντι δυνάμει, ἐνεργείᾳ
ὄντι τὰ πάντα ἅμα, δυνάμει δὲ ἕκαστον χωρίς, τοὺς δ'
αὖ ἐνεργείᾳ μὲν ὅ εἰσι, δυνάμει δὲ τὸ ὅλον. καθόσον μὲν
γὰρ τοῦτο ὅ λέγονταί εἰσιν, ἐνεργείᾳ εἰσὶν ἐκεῖνο ὅ
25 λέγονται· ᾗ δ' ἐν γένει ἐκεῖνο, δυνάμει ἐκεῖνο. ὅ δ' αὖ, ᾗ
μὲν γένος, δύναμις πάντων τῶν ὑπ' αὐτὸ εἰδῶν καὶ

<hr>

[1] νοῦς ἑκάστους Igal, H–S²: ἐκ δὲ ἑκάστους A (exp. et in mg.
scr. aliter ἑκάστου ἑκάστους δὲ A³) EBRᵃᶜCU (δε): ἐκδεεκάστους
J: ἑκάστους, ἑκάστους δὲ Creuzer: ἑκάστους Rᵖᶜ, Kirchhoff.

contents but the potentiality of all of them, but each part is actually that part which it is, and potentially all of them, and the same is true of universal knowledge: the specific bodies of knowledge, which lie potentially in the whole, those, that is, which grasp the specific contents, are potentially the whole; for the whole is predicated of them, not a part of the whole; yet it must certainly be pure and independent. Thus we can certainly say that universal Intellect exists in one way—that is the one before those which are actually the particular intellects— and particular intellects in another, those which are partial and fulfilled from all things; but the Intellect over all of them directs the particular intellects, but is their potentiality and contains them in its universality; and they on the other hand in their partial selves contain the universal Intellect, as a particular body of knowledge contains knowledge. And [we can say that] the great Intellect exists by itself, and so do the particular intellects which are in themselves, and again that the partial intellects are comprehended in the whole and the whole in the partial; the particular ones are on their own and in another, and that great Intellect is on its own and in those particular; and all are potentially in that Intellect which is on its own, which is actually all things at once, but potentially each particular separately, and the particular intellects are actually what they are, but potentially the whole. For in so far as they are this which they are called, they are actually that which they are called; but in that they are generically that whole, they are potentially that whole. And it again, in that it is the genus, is the potentiality of all the species under it and none of

οὐδὲν ἐνεργείᾳ ἐκείνων, ἀλλὰ πάντα ἐν αὐτῷ ἥσυχα· ᾗ
δὲ ὅ ἐστι πρὸ τῶν εἰδῶν ἐνεργείᾳ, τῶν οὐ καθέκαστα.
δεῖ δή, εἴπερ ἐνεργείᾳ ἔσονται οἱ ἐν εἴδει, τὴν ἀπ' αὐτοῦ
ἐνέργειαν αἰτίαν γίγνεσθαι.

21. Πῶς οὖν μένων αὐτὸς ἐν τῷ λόγῳ τὰ ἐν μέρει
ποιεῖ; τοῦτο δὲ ταὐτὸν πῶς ἐκ τῶν τεττάρων ἐκείνων τὰ
λεγόμενα ἐφεξῆς. ὅρα τοίνυν ἐν τούτῳ τῷ μεγάλῳ νῷ
καὶ ἀμηχάνῳ, οὐ πολυλάλῳ ἀλλὰ πολύνῳ νῷ τῷ πάντα
5 νῷ καὶ ὅλῳ καὶ οὐ μέρει οὐδὲ τινὶ νῷ, ὅπως ἔνι τὰ πάντα
ἐξ αὐτοῦ. ἀριθμὸν δὴ πάντως ἔχει ἐν τούτοις οἷς ὁρᾷ,
καὶ ἔστι δὲ ἓν καὶ πολλά, καὶ ταῦτα δὲ δυνάμεις καὶ
θαυμασταὶ δυνάμεις οὐκ ἀσθενεῖς, ἀλλ' ἅτε καθαραὶ
οὖσαι μέγισταί εἰσι καὶ οἷον σφριγῶσαι καὶ ἀληθῶς
10 δυνάμεις, οὐ τὸ μέχρι τινὸς ἔχουσαι· ἄπειροι τοίνυν καὶ
ἀπειρία καὶ τὸ μέγα. τοῦτο τοίνυν τὸ μέγα σὺν τῷ ἐν
αὐτῷ καλῷ τῆς οὐσίας καὶ τῇ περὶ αὐτὸ ἀγλαΐᾳ καὶ τῷ
φωτὶ ὡς ἐν νῷ ὄντα ἰδὼν ὁρᾷς καὶ τὸ ποιὸν ἤδη
ἐπανθοῦν, μετὰ δὲ τοῦ συνεχοῦς τῆς ἐνεργείας μέγεθος
15 προφαινόμενον τῇ σῇ προσβολῇ ἐν ἡσύχῳ κείμενον,
ἑνὸς δὲ καὶ δύο ὄντων καὶ τριῶν καὶ τὸ μέγεθος τριττὸν
ὂν καὶ τὸ ποσὸν πᾶν. τοῦ δὲ ποσοῦ ἐνορωμένου καὶ τοῦ
ποιοῦ καὶ ἄμφω εἰς ἓν ἰόντων καὶ οἷον γινομένων
καὶ σχῆμα ὅρα. εἰσπίπτοντος δὲ τοῦ θατέρου καὶ
διαιροῦντος καὶ τὸ ποσὸν καὶ τὸ ποιὸν σχημάτων τε
20 διαφοραὶ καὶ ποιότητος ἄλλαι. καὶ ταυτότης μὲν

them in actuality, but all rest quietly in it; but in that it is actually what it is before the species, it belongs to the non-particulars. But certainly, if the intellects in specific form are going to exist, the activity proceeding from universal Intellect must be the cause.

21. How then does Intellect itself, remaining one in its essential structure, produce the partial beings? This is the same [as asking] how from those four primary genera the things which we call subsequent proceed. Well then, see how in this great, this overwhelming Intellect, not full of talk but full of intelligence, this Intellect which is all things and a whole, not a partial or particular intellect, all things which come from it are present. It certainly has number in the things which it sees, and it is one and many, and the many are its powers, wonderful powers, not weak but because they are pure the greatest of powers, fresh and full of life, we may say, and truly powers, without any limit to their action: so they are infinite, and infinity [is there] and greatness. Then when you see existing in it in the way proper to Intellect this greatness, along with the beauty that there is in it of its substance and the glory and the light around it, you see quality also, already in flower on it; and with the continuity of its activity you see magnitude, quietly at rest, appearing to your gaze; there are one and two and three, magnitude and all that is quantitative being the third. And when you see quantity and quality in it, both tending to one and in a way becoming one, then observe figure also appearing. Then otherness tumbles in and separates quantity and quality, and there are differences of figures and other qualities. And

συνοῦσα ἰσότητα ποιεῖ εἶναι, ἑτερότης δὲ ἀνισότητα ἐν
ποσῷ ἕν τε ἀριθμῷ ἕν τε μεγέθει, ἐξ ὧν καὶ κύκλους καὶ
τετράγωνα καὶ τὰ ἐξ ἀνίσων σχήματα, ἀριθμούς τε
ὁμοίους καὶ ἀνομοίους, περιττούς τε καὶ ἀρτίους. οὖσα
25 γὰρ ἔννους ζωὴ καὶ ἐνέργεια οὐκ ἀτελὴς οὐδὲν
παραλείπει ὧν εὑρίσκομεν νῦν νοερὸν ἔργον ὄν, ἀλλὰ
πάντα ἔχει ἐν τῇ αὑτῆς δυνάμει ὄντα αὐτὰ ἔχουσα ὡς ἂν
νοῦς ἔχοι. ἔχει δὲ νοῦς ὡς ἐν νοήσει, νοήσει δὲ οὐ τῇ ἐν
διεξόδῳ· παραλέλειπται δὲ οὐδὲν τῶν ὅσα λόγοι, ἀλλ'
30 ἔστιν εἷς οἷον λόγος, μέγας, τέλειος, πάντας περιέχων,
ἀπὸ τῶν πρώτων αὐτοῦ ἐπεξιών, μᾶλλον δὲ ἀεὶ
ἐπεξελθών, ὥστε μηδέποτε τὸ ἐπεξιέναι ἀληθὲς εἶναι.
ὅλως γὰρ πανταχοῦ, ὅσα ἄν τις ἐκ λογισμοῦ λάβοι ἐν τῇ
φύσει ὄντα, ταῦτα εὑρήσει ἐν νῷ ἄνευ λογισμοῦ ὄντα,
ὥστε νομίζειν τὸ ὂν νοῦν λελογισμένον οὕτω ποιῆσαι,
35 οἷον καὶ ἐπὶ τῶν λόγων τῶν τὰ ζῷα ποιούντων· ὡς γὰρ
ἂν ὁ ἀκριβέστατος λογισμὸς λογίσαιτο ὡς ἄριστα,
οὕτως ἔχει πάντα ἐν τοῖς λόγοις πρὸ λογισμοῦ οὖσι. τί
χρὴ προσδοκᾶν ἐν τοῖς ⟨ἀνωτέρω⟩[1] πρὸ φύσεως καὶ
τῶν λόγων τῶν ἐν αὐτῇ [ἐν τοῖς ἀνωτέρω][2] εἶναι; ἐν οἷς
40 γὰρ ἡ οὐσία οὐκ ἄλλο τι ἢ νοῦς, καὶ οὐκ ἐπακτὸν οὔτε τὸ
ὂν αὐτοῖς οὔτε ὁ νοῦς, ἀμογητὶ ⟨πᾶν⟩[1] ἂν εἴη ἄριστα
ἔχον, εἴπερ κατὰ νοῦν κείσεται, καὶ τοῦτο ὄν, ὃ θέλει
νοῦς καὶ ἔστι· διὸ καὶ ἀληθινὸν καὶ πρῶτον· εἰ γὰρ παρ'
ἄλλου, ἐκεῖνο νοῦς. σχημάτων δὴ πάντων ὀφθέντων ἐν

[1] Igal, H–S[2].
[2] del. H–S· ἐν τοῖς del. Müller.

sameness, which is there as well, makes equality exist, and otherness, inequality, in quantity, number and magnitude, and from these derive circles and squares and figures with unequal sides, and like and unlike numbers, and odd and even. For since its life is intelligent and its activity without imperfection, it leaves out none of the things which we now find to be works of intelligence, possessing them as realities and in the manner proper to Intellect. Intellect possesses them as in thought, but not the discursive kind of thought; but nothing is left out of all the things of which there are intelligible forming principles, but Intellect is like one great complete intelligible principle embracing them all, and it goes through them starting from its own first principles, or rather it has always gone through them, so that it is never true that it is going through them. For in general everywhere, whatever one might apprehend by reasoning as being in nature one will find existing without reasoning in Intellect, so as to think that Intellect has made being as it is after reasoning—it is like the rational forming principles which make living beings: for as the most accurate reasoning would calculate was best, so are all things in the rational principles before reasoning. What, then, should one expect in the higher principles before nature and the principles in it? For in those of which the substance is nothing else than Intellect, and neither being nor intellect is brought to them from outside, there would be no trouble about everything being for the best, if it is disposed according to Intellect and is what Intellect wills and is; therefore it is true and primary: for if it came from another, that other would be Intellect. Now all figures have

45 τῷ ὄντι καὶ ποιότητος ἁπάσης—ἦν γὰρ οὔ τις· οὐδὲ γὰρ
ἦν εἶναι μίαν τῆς θατέρου φύσεως ἐνούσης, ἀλλὰ μία καὶ
πολλαί· καὶ γὰρ ταυτότης ἦν· ἓν δὲ καὶ πολλά, καὶ ἐξ
ἀρχῆς τὸ τοιοῦτον ὄν, ὥστε ἐν πᾶσιν εἴδεσι τὸ ἓν καὶ
πολλά· μεγέθη δὴ διάφορα καὶ σχήματα διάφορα καὶ
ποιότητες διάφοροι· οὐ γὰρ ἦν οὐδέ θεμιτὸν ἦν
50 παραλελεῖφθαι οὐδέν· τέλειον γάρ ἐκεῖ τὸ πᾶν ἢ οὐκ ἂν
ἦν πᾶν—καὶ ζωῆς ἐπιθεούσης, μᾶλλον δὲ συνούσης
πανταχοῦ, πάντα ἐξ ἀνάγκης ζῷα ἐγίνετο, καὶ ἦν καὶ
σώματα ὕλης καὶ ποιότητος ὄντων. γενομένων δὲ
πάντων ἀεὶ καὶ μενόντων καὶ ἐν τῷ εἶναι αἰῶνι
55 περιληφθέντων, χωρὶς μὲν ἕκαστον ὅ ἐστιν ὄντων, ὁμοῦ
δ᾽ αὖ ἐν ἑνὶ ὄντων, ἡ πάντων ἐν ἑνὶ ὄντων οἷον συμπλοκὴ
καὶ σύνθεσις νοῦς ἐστι. καὶ ἔχων μὲν τὰ ὄντα ἐν αὑτῷ
ζ ῷ ό ν ἐστι π α ν τ ε λ ὲ ς καὶ ὅ ἐ σ τ ι ζ ῷ ο ν, τῷ
δ᾽ ἐξ αὑτοῦ ὄντι παρέχων ἑαυτὸν ὁρᾶσθαι νοητὸν
γενόμενος ἐκεῖ νῷ[1] δίδωσιν ὀρθῶς λέγεσθαι.

22. Καὶ ᾐνιγμένως Πλάτωνι τὸ ᾗ π ε ρ ο ὖ ν ν ο ῦ ς
ἐ ν ο ύ σ α ς ἰ δ έ α ς ἐν τῷ π α ν τ ε λ ε ῖ ζ ῴ ῳ ο ἷ α ί
τ ε ἔ ν ε ι σ ι κ α ὶ ὅ σ α ι κ α θ ο ρ ᾷ. ἐπεὶ καὶ ψυχὴ
μετὰ νοῦν, καθόσον ψυχὴ ἔχουσα ἐν αὐτῇ, ἐν τῷ πρὸ
5 αὑτῆς βέλτιον καθορᾷ· καὶ ὁ νοῦς ἡμῶν ἔχων ἐν τῷ πρὸ
αὑτοῦ βέλτιον καθορᾷ· ἐν μὲν γὰρ αὐτῷ καθορᾷ μόνον, ἐν

---

[1] Igal: ἐκείνῳ BxUC, H–S: ἐκείνων w.

been seen in being and all quality—not a particular quality; for it could not be one since the nature of the other is there, but one and many; for sameness is there also: one and many, and being is like this from the beginning, so that the one and many is in all its specific forms; magnitudes are various and figures various and qualities various; for it was not possible or lawful for anything to be left out; for the intelligible All is complete, or it would not be the All—and since life is running over it, or rather everywhere accompanying it, all things necessarily become living beings, and there are bodies there also since there is matter and quality. Since all things eternally come into being and eternally abide, and are in eternity comprehended in being, each of them being what it is and all again being in one, the complex and construction, as we may put it, of all in one is Intellect. And since it has the real beings in itself it is a "complete" living being and "the absolute living being"[1]; but by giving itself to that which comes from it to behold, by becoming intelligible, it allows the transcendent Intellect to be rightly so called.[2]

22. And Plato speaks riddlingly of "the way in which Intellect sees the Ideas in the complete living creature [observing] of what kind they are and how many they are". For Soul too, which comes after Intellect, though in so far as it is Soul it has [the Forms] in itself, sees them better in that which is before it; and our intellect, though it has them, sees them better in that which is before it; for in itself it

[1] Plato *Timaeus* 31B1 and 39E7–9.

[2] I adopt here Igal's ἐκεῖ νῷ for ἐκείνῳ, a very small change which gives a clearer sense.

δὲ τῷ πρὸ αὐτοῦ καὶ καθορᾷ ὅτι καθορᾷ. ὁ δὴ νοῦς οὗτος,
ὃν φαμεν καθορᾶν, οὐκ ἀπαλλαγεὶς τοῦ πρὸ αὐτοῦ ἐξ
αὐτοῦ ὤν, ἅτε ὢν ἐξ ἑνὸς πολλὰ καὶ τὴν τοῦ θατέρου
10 φύσιν συνοῦσαν ἔχων, εἰς πολλὰ γίνεται. εἷς δὲ νοῦς καὶ
πολλὰ ὢν καὶ τοὺς πολλοὺς νοῦς ποιεῖ ἐξ ἀνάγκης τῆς
τοιαύτης. ὅλως δὲ οὐκ ἔστι τὸ ἓν ἀριθμῷ λαβεῖν καὶ
ἄτομον· ὅ τι γὰρ ἂν λάβῃς, εἶδος· ἄνευ γὰρ ὕλης. διὸ καὶ
τοῦτο αἰνιττόμενος ὁ Πλάτων εἰς ἄ π ε ι ρ ά φησι
κ α τ α κ ε ρ μ α τ ί ζ ε σ θ α ι τ ὴ ν ο ὐ σ ί α ν. ἕως μὲν
15 γὰρ εἰς ἄλλο εἶδος, οἷον ἐκ γένους, οὔπω ἄπειρον·
περατοῦται γὰρ τοῖς γεννηθεῖσιν εἴδεσι· τὸ δ' ἔσχατον
εἶδος ὃ μὴ διαιρεῖται εἰς εἴδη, μᾶλλον ἄπειρον. καὶ
τοῦτό ἐστι τὸ τ ό τ ε δ ὲ ἤ δ η ε ἰ ς τ ὸ ἄ π ε ι ρ ο ν
μ ε θ έ ν τ α ἐ ᾶ ν χ α ί ρ ε ι ν. ἀλλ' ὅσον μὲν ἐπ' αὐτοῖς,
20 ἄπειρα· τῷ δὲ ἑνὶ περιληφθέντα εἰς ἀριθμὸν ἔρχεται
ἤδη. νοῦς μὲν οὖν ἔχει τὸ μεθ' ἑαυτὸν ψυχήν, ὥστε ἐν
ἀριθμῷ εἶναι καὶ ψυχὴν μέχρι τοῦ ἐσχάτου αὐτῆς, τὸ δὲ
ἔσχατον αὐτῆς ἤδη ἄπειρον παντάπασι. καὶ ἔστι νοῦς
μὲν ὁ τοιοῦτος μέρος, καίπερ τὰ πάντα ἔχων καὶ ὁ πᾶς,
25 †καὶ οἱ αὐτοῦ μέρη ἐνεργείᾳ ὄντος αὐτοῦ ὄντες μέρος,†
ψυχὴ δὲ μέρος μέρους, ἀλλ' ὡς ἐνέργεια ἐξ αὐτοῦ. ὅτε
μὲν γὰρ ἐν αὐτῷ ἐνεργεῖ, τὰ ἐνεργούμενα οἱ ἄλλοι νοῖ,
ὅτε δὲ ἐξ αὐτοῦ, ψυχή. ψυχῆς δὲ ἐνεργούσης ὡς γένους ἢ
εἴδους αἱ ἄλλαι ψυχαὶ ὡς εἴδη. καὶ τούτων αἱ ἐνέργειαι
30 διτταί· ἡ μὲν πρὸς τὸ ἄνω νοῦς, ἡ δὲ πρὸς τὸ κάτω αἱ

---

[1] Plato *Parmenides* 144B4-C1.
[2] Plato *Philebus* 16E1-2.
[3] No satisfactory sense can be extracted either from

only sees, but in what is before it it also sees that it sees. Now this intellect of ours, which, we maintain, sees, is not separated from that before it, as it derives from it, and because it is many from one and has the nature of the other accompanying it, it becomes one-many. But the one Intellect, since it is also many, makes the many intellects as well by a necessity of this kind. But in general it is not possible to apprehend the numerical one and the individual; for whatever you apprehend is specific form; for it is without matter. So Plato makes this cryptic remark also, that "substance is cut up to infinity".[1] For as long as the division, of a genus for instance, arrives at another form, it is not yet infinite; for it is limited by the forms which have been generated; but the ultimate form which is not divided into forms is more infinite. This is the meaning of "at this point to let them go into the infinite and say goodbye to them".[2] But as far as they are on their own, they are infinite; but as soon as they are comprehended by the one they arrive at number. So then Intellect holds the soul which comes after it so that it is in number, and holds soul down to its last part, but its last part is altogether infinite. And an intellect of this kind is a part, although it contains all things, and the whole intellect ... but soul is a part of a part, but like an activity proceeding from it.[3] For when it is active in itself, the products of its activity are the other intellects, but when it acts outside itself, the product is Soul. And since Soul acts as genus or specific form, the other souls act as specific forms. And the activities of these are double: that which is directed above Kirchhoff's text or that printed by Henry and Schwyzer in their first edition.

ἄλλαι δυνάμεις κατὰ λόγον, ἡ δὲ ἐσχάτη ὕλης ἤδη
ἐφαπτομένη καὶ μορφοῦσα. καὶ τὸ κάτω αὐτῆς τὸ ἄλλο
πᾶν οὐ κωλύει εἶναι ἄνω. ἢ καὶ τὸ κάτω λεγόμενον
αὐτῆς ἴνδαλμά ἐστιν αὐτῆς, οὐκ ἀποτετμημένον δέ, ἀλλ'

35 ὡς τὰ ἐν τοῖς κατόπτροις, ἕως ἂν τὸ ἀρχέτυπον παρῇ
ἔξω. δεῖ δὲ λαβεῖν, πῶς τὸ ἔξω. καὶ μέχρι τοῦ πρὸ τοῦ
εἰδώλου ὁ νοητὸς κόσμος ἅπας τέλεος ἐκ πάντων
νοητῶν, ὥσπερ ὅδε μίμημα ὢν ἐκείνου, καθόσον οἷόν τε
ἀποσώζειν εἰκόνα ζῴου ζῷον αὐτό, ὡς τὸ γεγραμμένον

40 ἢ τὸ ἐν ὕδατι φάντασμα τοῦ πρὸ ὕδατος καὶ γραφῆς
δοκοῦντος εἶναι. τὸ δὲ μίμημα τὸ ἐν γραφῇ καὶ ὕδατι οὐ
τοῦ συναμφοτέρου, ἀλλὰ τοῦ ἑτέρου τοῦ μορφωθέντος
ὑπὸ θατέρου. νοητοῦ τοίνυν εἰκὼν ἔχουσα ἰνδάλματα
οὐ τοῦ πεποιηκότος, ἀλλὰ τῶν περιεχομένων ἐν τῷ

45 πεποιηκότι, ὧν καὶ ἄνθρωπος καὶ ἄλλο πᾶν ζῷον· ζῷον
δὲ καὶ τοῦτο καὶ τὸ πεποιηκός, ἄλλως ἑκάτερον καὶ
ἄμφω ἐν νοητῷ.

is intellect, that which is directed below is the other powers in proportion and order; the last of them is already grasping and shaping matter. And its underpart does not prevent all the rest from being above. Or rather, what we call its underpart is an image of it, but not cut off, but like images in mirrors, [which last] while the archetype is present outside. But one must understand what "outside" means. And as far as that which is before the image [extends] the total intelligible universe, completed from all intelligibles, like this universe here below, which is an image of that one, as far as it is possible for an image of the Living Being to preserve the Living Being itself, as a drawing or a reflection in water is the ghostly image of that which appears to be there before the water and the drawing. But the image in the drawing and the water is not of the composite, but of the one formed by the other. So then the image of the intelligible is not of its maker but of the things contained in the maker, which include man and every other living being: this here is a living being and so is that which made it, each in a different sense and both in the intelligible.

VI. 3. (44) ΠΕΡΙ ΤΩΝ ΓΕΝΩΝ ΤΟΥ ΟΝΤΟΣ ΤΡΙΤΟΝ

1. Περὶ μὲν τῆς οὐσίας ὅπη δοκεῖ, καὶ ὡς συμφώνως
ἂν ἔχοι πρὸς τὴν τοῦ Πλάτωνος δόξαν, εἴρηται. δεῖ δὲ
καὶ περὶ τῆς ἑτέρας φύσεως ἐπισκέψασθαι, πότερα τὰ
αὐτὰ γένη θετέον, ἅπερ κἀκεῖ ἐθέμεθα, ἢ πλείω ἐνταῦθα
5 πρὸς ἐκείνοις ἄλλα τιθέντας ἢ ὅλως ἕτερα, ἢ τὰ μὲν ὡς
ἐκεῖ, τὰ δ᾽ ἄλλως. δεῖ μέντοι τὸ "ταὐτὰ" ἀναλογίᾳ καὶ
ὁμωνυμίᾳ λαμβάνειν· τοῦτο δὲ φανήσεται γνωσθέντων.
ἀρχὴ δὲ ἡμῖν ἥδε· ἐπειδὴ περὶ τῶν αἰσθητῶν ὁ λόγος
ἡμῖν, πᾶν δὲ τὸ αἰσθητὸν τῷδε τῷ κόσμῳ περιείληπται,
10 περὶ τοῦ κόσμου ἀναγκαῖον ἂν εἴη [ζητεῖν διαιροῦντας][1]
τὴν φύσιν αὐτοῦ καὶ ἐξ ὧν ἐστι ⟨ζητεῖν⟩[1] διαιροῦντας
κατὰ γένη θεῖναι, ὥσπερ ἂν εἰ τὴν φ ω ν ὴ ν διῃρούμεθα
ἄ π ε ι ρ ο ν οὖσαν εἰς ὡρισμένα ἀνάγοντες τὸ ἐν πολλοῖς
ταὐτὸν εἰς ἕν, εἶτα πάλιν ἄλλο καὶ ἕτερον αὖ, ἕως
15 εἰς ἀριθμόν τινα θέντες ἕκαστον αὐτῶν, τὸ μὲν ἐπὶ τοῖς
ἀτόμοις εἶδος λέγοντες, τὸ δ᾽ ἐπὶ τοῖς εἴδεσι γένος. τὸ
μὲν οὖν ἐπὶ τῆς φωνῆς ἕκαστον εἶδος καὶ ὁμοῦ πάντα

[1] H–S[2].

178

VI. 3. ON THE KINDS
OF BEING III

1. We have explained the way in which we think about substance and how it might accord with the thought of Plato. But we must also enquire about the other nature, whether we should posit the same genera which we posited in the intelligible, or more here below, adding others to those, or altogether different ones, or some as they were there but others otherwise. We must of course understand "the same" [genera] analogously and ambiguously: this will become obvious when we have got to know them. Our starting-point is this: since our discussion is about sense-objects and every sense-object is included in this universe of ours, it will be necessary in considering the universe to seek to divide its nature and distinguish its elements and arrange them by genera: as if we were to divide articulate sound,[1] which is unlimited, into limited sections by bringing back to one what is the same in many, and then to another one and again a different one, until we have brought each and every one of them into a definite number, calling the one under which individuals are classed a species, and the one under which species are classed a genus. Now in the case of articulate sound each and every species and all of them which

[1] This passage on the collection and division of sounds corresponds closely to Plato *Philebus* 17B-18C.

τὰ φανέντα εἰς ἓν ἦν ἀνάγειν, καὶ κατηγορεῖν πάντων
σ τ ο ι χ ε ῖ ο ν ἢ φωνήν· ἐπὶ δὲ ὧν ζητοῦμεν οὐχ οἷόν
τε, ὡς δέδεικται. διὸ δεῖ πλείω γένη ζητεῖν, καὶ ἐν
20 τῷδε τῷ παντὶ ἕτερα ἐκείνων, ἐπειδὴ καὶ ἕτερον τοῦτο
ἐκείνου καὶ οὐ συνώνυμον, ὁμώνυμον δὲ καὶ εἰκών.
ἀλλ' ἐπεὶ καὶ ἐνταῦθα ἐν τῷ μίγματι καὶ ἐν τῇ
συνθέσει τὸ μέν ἐστι σῶμα, τὸ δὲ ψυχή—ζῷον γὰρ τὸ
πᾶν—ἡ δὲ ψυχῆς φύσις ἐν ἐκείνῳ τῷ νοητῷ καὶ
οὐδ' ἁρμόσει οὐδ' εἰς οὐσίας τῆς ἐνταῦθα λεγομένης
25 σύνταξιν, ἀφοριστέον, εἰ καὶ χαλεπῶς, ὅμως μὴν τῆς
ἐνταῦθα πραγματείας, ὥσπερ ἂν εἴ τις βουλόμενος τοὺς
πολίτας συντάξαι πόλεώς τινος, οἷον κατὰ τιμήσεις ἢ
τέχνας, τοὺς ἐπιδημοῦντας ξένους παραλίποι χωρίς.
περὶ δὲ τῶν παθημάτων, ὅσα μετὰ τοῦ σώματος ἢ
30 διὰ τὸ σῶμα περὶ ψυχὴν συμβαίνει, περὶ τούτων
ἐπισκεπτέον ὕστερον, ὅπως τακτέον, ὅταν περὶ τῶν
ἐνταῦθα ζητῶμεν.

2. Καὶ πρῶτον περὶ τῆς λεγομένης οὐσίας
θεωρητέον συγχωροῦντας τὴν περὶ τὰ σώματα φύσιν
ὁμωνύμως ἢ οὐδὲ ὅλως οὐσίαν διὰ τὸ ἐφαρμόττειν τὴν
ἔννοιαν ῥεόντων, ἀλλὰ γένεσιν οἰκείως λέγεσθαι. εἶτα
5 τῆς γενέσεως τὰ μὲν τοιά, τὰ δὲ τοιά· καὶ τὰ μὲν
σώματα εἰς ἕν, τά τε ἁπλᾶ τά τε σύνθετα, τὰ δὲ
συμβεβηκότα ἢ παρακολουθοῦντα, διαιροῦντας ἀπ'

---

[1] In VI. 1. 6 and 25.

have been discovered can be brought back to one, and we can predicate "letter" or "sound" of all; but in the case of the things we are investigating this is not possible, as has been shown.[1] Therefore we must look for more genera, and different ones in this All from those in the intelligible, since this All is different from that and it is not called the All in the same sense but in a different one, and is an image. But since here below also in the mixture and composition one element is body and the other soul—for the All is a living thing—and the nature of soul is in that intelligible All and will not fit into the classification of what is called substance here below, we must, even if it is difficult to do so, all the same leave soul out of the investigation in which we are at present occupied; just as if someone wishing to classify the citizens of a city, by their property assessments or skills for instance, left the resident foreigners out of account. But as regards the affections, which occur in soul with the body or because of the body, we must consider later how they are to be classed, when we are enquiring about things here below.

2. And first of all we should consider what is called substance, agreeing that the nature in the sphere of bodies can only be called substance ambiguously, or should not properly be called substance at all but coming into being, because it is adapted to the idea of things in flux. Then some of the things which belong to coming into being are of this kind, and some of that: there are bodies; these, both simple and composite, we put into one class; and then there are incidentals and consequentials, and these we should also distinguish from each

ἀλλήλων καὶ ταῦτα. ἢ τὸ μὲν ὕλην, τὸ δὲ εἶδος ἐπ' αὐτῇ,
καὶ χωρὶς ἑκάτερον ὡς γένος ἢ ὑφ' ἓν ἄμφω, ὡς οὐσίαν
10 ἑκάτερον ὁμωνύμως ἢ γένεσιν. ἀλλὰ τί τὸ κοινὸν ἐπὶ
ὕλης καὶ εἴδους; πῶς δὲ γένος ἢ ὕλη καὶ τίνων; τίς γὰρ
διαφορὰ ὕλης; ἐν τίνι δὲ τὸ ἐξ ἀμφοῖν τακτέον; εἰ δὲ τὸ
ἐξ ἀμφοῖν εἴη αὐτὸ ἡ σωματικὴ οὐσία, ἐκείνων δὲ
ἑκάτερον οὐ σῶμα, πῶς ἂν ἐν ἑνὶ τάττοιτο καὶ τῷ αὐτῷ
μετὰ τοῦ συνθέτου; πῶς δ' ἂν τὰ στοιχεῖά τινος μετ'
15 αὐτοῦ; εἰ δ' ἀπὸ τῶν σωμάτων ἀρχοίμεθα, ἀρχοίμεθ' ἂν
ἀπὸ συλλαβῶν. διὰ τί δὲ οὐκ ἀνάλογον, εἰ καὶ μὴ κατὰ
ταὐτὰ ἡ διαίρεσις, λέγοιμεν ἂν ἀντὶ μὲν τοῦ ἐκεῖ ὄντος
ἐνταῦθα τὴν ὕλην, ἀντὶ δὲ τῆς ἐκεῖ κινήσεως ἐνταῦθα τὸ
εἶδος, οἷον ζωήν τινα καὶ τελείωσιν τῆς ὕλης, τῆς δὲ
20 ὕλης τὴν οὐκ ἔκστασιν κατὰ τὴν στάσιν, καὶ τὸ ταὐτὸν
καὶ θάτερον οὔσης καὶ ἐνταῦθα ἑτερότητος πολλῆς καὶ
ἀνομοιότητος μᾶλλον; ἢ πρῶτον μὲν ἡ ὕλη οὐχ οὕτως
ἔχει καὶ λαμβάνει τὸ εἶδος ὡς ζωὴν αὐτῆς οὐδὲ
ἐνέργειαν αὐτῆς, ἀλλ' ἔπεισιν ἀλλαχόθεν οὐκ ὄν τι
25 ἐκείνης. εἶτα ἐκεῖ τὸ εἶδος ἐνέργεια καὶ κίνησις, ἐνταῦθα
δὲ ἡ κίνησις ἄλλο καὶ συμβεβηκός· τὸ δὲ εἶδος στάσις
αὐτῆς μᾶλλον καὶ οἷον ἡσυχία· ὁρίζει γὰρ ἀόριστον
οὖσαν. τό τε ταὐτὸν ἐκεῖ καὶ τὸ ἕτερον ἑνὸς τοῦ αὐτοῦ

other. Or there is one thing which is matter, and another which is the form upon it, and either each as a genus is separate or both fall under one genus, being each of them substance in the ambiguous sense or coming into being. But what is the common factor of matter and form? And how can matter be a genus, and a genus of what? For what essential differentiation is there belonging to matter? But in what genus is the product of both to be ranked? If the product of both is itself bodily substance, and each of them is not body, how could they be ranked in one and the same genus with the composite? And how could the elements[1] of a thing be ranked with the thing itself? But if we were to start with bodies, we should be starting with syllables. But why should we not say analogously, even if the division is not on the same lines, that instead of being in the intelligible there is matter here below, and instead of the intelligible movement there is form here below, a kind of life and perfection of matter, and that matter's not going out of itself corresponds to rest, and that there are sameness and otherness, since there is plenty of otherness, or rather unlikeness, here below? Now, first of all, matter does not hold or grasp form as its life or its activity, but form comes upon it from elsewhere and is not one of matter's possessions. Then, in the intelligible the form is activity and motion, but here below motion is something else and an incidental; but form is rather matter's rest and a kind of quietness: for it limits matter which is unlimited. And in the intelligible sameness and otherness belong to one thing, which

[1] Or "letters": cp. ch. 1, 18.

καὶ ἑτέρου ὄντος, ἐνταῦθα δὲ ἕτερον μεταλήψει, καὶ
30 πρὸς ἄλλο, καί τι ταὐτὸν καὶ ἕτερον, οὐδ' ὡς ἐκεῖ εἴη ἄν
τι ἐν τοῖς ὑστέροις τι ταὐτὸν καί τι ἕτερον. στάσις δὲ
τῆς ὕλης πῶς ἐπὶ πάντα ἑλκομένης μεγέθη καὶ ἔξωθεν
τὰς μορφὰς καὶ οὐκ αὐτάρκους ἑαυτῇ μετὰ τούτων τὰ
ἄλλα γεννᾶν; ταύτην μὲν οὖν τὴν διαίρεσιν ἀφετέον.

3. Πῶς δέ, λέγωμεν· ἔστι δὴ πρῶτον οὕτως, τὸ μὲν
ὕλην εἶναι, τὸ δὲ εἶδος, τὸ δὲ μικτὸν ἐξ ἀμφοῖν, τὰ δὲ περὶ
ταῦτα· τῶν δὲ περὶ ταῦτα τὰ μὲν κατηγορούμενα μόνον,
τὰ δὲ καὶ συμβεβηκότα· τῶν δὲ συμβεβηκότων τὰ μὲν
5 ἐν αὐτοῖς, τὰ δὲ αὐτὰ ἐν ἐκείνοις, τὰ δὲ ἐνεργήματα
αὐτῶν, τὰ δὲ πάθη, τὰ δὲ παρακολουθήματα. καὶ τὴν
μὲν ὕλην κοινὸν μὲν καὶ ἐν πάσαις ταῖς οὐσίαις, οὐ μὴν
γένος, ὅτι μηδὲ διαφορὰς ἔχει, εἰ μή τις τὰς διαφορὰς
κατὰ τὸ τὴν μὲν πυρίνην, τὴν δὲ τὴν ἀέρος μορφὴν
10 ἔχειν. εἰ δέ τις ἀρκοῖτο τῷ κοινῷ τῷ ἐν πᾶσιν οἷς ἐστιν
ὕλην εἶναι, ἢ ὡς ὅλον πρὸς μέρη, ἄλλως γένος ἂν εἴη·
καὶ στοιχεῖον δὲ ἓν τοῦτο δυναμένου καὶ τοῦ στοιχείου
γένους εἶναι. τὸ δὲ εἶδος προσκειμένου τοῦ "περὶ ὕλην"
ἢ "ἐν ὕλῃ" τῶν μὲν ἄλλων εἰδῶν χωρίζει, οὐ μὴν
15 περιλαμβάνει πᾶν εἶδος οὐσιωδῶς. εἰ δὲ εἶδος λέγομεν τὸ
184

is both same and other, but here below a thing is other by participation and in relation to something else, and the same and other is some particular same and other, not as it might be in the intelligible but a particular same and a particular other which is something among the things which come later. But how can there be a rest of matter when it is being pulled into all sizes and gets its shapes from outside and is not sufficient in itself to generate the other things with these shapes? We must therefore reject this division.

3. But let us explain how we should divide; this is the way to begin with: it is one thing to be matter, another to be form, another to be the composite of both, and another to be the peripheral characteristics; and of these peripheral characteristics, some are only predicated, some are also incidental; and of the incidentals some are in these three [, matter, form and composite], but in other cases these three are in the incidentals; others are their activities, others their passive affections, and others consequences. And matter is common and in all the substances, but is certainly not a genus, because it has no essential differences, unless one understood the differences as one part having a fiery shape and one the shape of air. But if one was satisfied with what is common, that there is matter in all existing things, or that it is like a whole in relation to parts, it would be a genus in another sense; and this would be one element, and an element can be a genus. But the form, with the addition "about matter" or "in matter", separates from the other forms, but does not include all substantial form. But if we mean by form that which makes substance, and by rational forma-

185

ποιητικὸν οὐσίας καὶ λόγον τὸν οὐσιώδη κατὰ τὸ εἶδος,
οὔπω τὴν οὐσίαν εἴπομεν πῶς δεῖ λαμβάνειν. τὸ δὲ ἐξ
ἀμφοῖν εἰ τοῦτο μόνον οὐσίαν, ἐκεῖνα οὐκ οὐσίας· εἰ δὲ
κἀκεῖνα καὶ τοῦτο, τί τὸ κοινὸν σκεπτέον. τὰ δὲ
20 κατηγορούμενα μόνον ἐν τῷ πρός τι ἂν εἴη, οἷον αἴτιον
εἶναι, στοιχεῖον εἶναι. τῶν δὲ ἐν αὐτοῖς συμβεβηκότων
τὸ μὲν ποσὸν εἶναι, τὸ δὲ ποιὸν εἶναι, ἃ ἐν αὐτοῖς· τὰ δ'
αὐτὰ ἐν ἐκείνοις ὡς τόπος καὶ χρόνος, τὰ δὲ ἐνεργήματα
αὐτῶν καὶ πάθη ὡς κινήσεις, τὰ δὲ παρακολουθήματα
ὡς τόπος καὶ χρόνος, ὁ μὲν τῶν συνθέτων, ὁ δὲ τῆς
25 κινήσεως ὁ χρόνος. καὶ τὰ μὲν τρία εἰς ἕν, ⟨εἰ⟩[1]
εὕροιμεν κοινόν τι τὴν ἐνταῦθα ὁμώνυμον οὐσίαν· εἶτα
τὰ ἄλλα ἐφεξῆς, πρός τι, ποσόν, ποιόν, ἐν τόπῳ, ἐν
χρόνῳ, κίνησις, τόπος, χρόνος. ἢ λειφθέντος[2] τόπου καὶ
χρόνου περιττὸν τὸ ἐν χρόνῳ καὶ τόπῳ, ὥστε εἶναι
30 πέντε, ὡς ἓν τῶν πρώτων τριῶν· εἰ δὲ μὴ εἰς ἓν τὰ τρία,
ἔσται ὕλη, εἶδος, συναμφότερον, πρός τι, ποσόν, ποιόν,
κίνησις. ἢ καὶ ταῦτα εἰς τὰ πρός τι· περιεκτικὸν γὰρ
μᾶλλον.

4. Τί οὖν ταὐτὸν ἐν τοῖς τρισί, καὶ τί ἔσται, ὃ ταῦτα
ποιεῖ οὐσίαν τὴν ἐν τούτοις; ἆρα ὑποβάθραν τινὰ τοῖς
ἄλλοις; ἀλλ' ἡ μὲν ὕλη ὑποβάθρα καὶ ἕδρα δοκεῖ τῷ

[1] Igal, H–S[2].
[2] coniecimus: ληφθέντος Enn.

tive principle that which is substantial according to
the form, we have not yet said how substance is to be
understood. But, as for that composed of both [mat-
ter and form], if this alone is substance, matter and
form are not substances; but if they are also this, we
must investigate what they have in common. But the
characteristics which are only predicated would
come under relation, being a cause or being an
element for instance. And the incidental characteristics in the three would be quantitative or qualitative, in so far as they are in them; as for the cases
where the three are in the incidentals, this would be
like place and time; their activities and passive
affections would be like movements; their consequences like place and time, the place a consequence
of the composites, the time, the time of the movement. But the three will go into one, if we can find
something common, the ambiguous substance here
below; then the others will follow in order, relation,
quantity, quality, in place, in time, movement, place,
time. Or, if one leaves out place and time, "in place"
and "in time" are superfluous, so that there are five,
on the assumption that the first three are one; but if
the first three do not go into one, there will be
matter, form, composite, relation, quantity, quality,
movement. Or these last also could go into relation:
for it is more inclusive.

4. What is it, then, which is the same in the three,
and what will it be which makes them substance, the
substance in things here below? Is it a kind of base
for everything else? But matter is thought to be a
base and "seat"[1] for form, so that the form will not

[1] Plato *Timaeus* 52B1.

εἴδει εἶναι, ὥστε τὸ εἶδος οὐκ ἔσται ἐν οὐσίᾳ. τό τε
5 σύνθετον ἄλλοις ὑποβάθρα καὶ ἕδρα, ὥστε καὶ τὸ εἶδος
μετὰ τῆς ὕλης ὑποβεβλήσεται τοῖς συνθέτοις ἢ πᾶσί γε
τοῖς μετὰ τὸ σύνθετον, οἷον ποσῷ, ποιῷ, κινήσει. ἀλλ᾽
ἆρα τὸ "μὴ ἑτέρου" ὃ λέγεται; λευκὸν μὲν γὰρ καὶ
μέλαν ἄλλου τοῦ λελευκωμένου, καὶ τὸ διπλάσιον δὲ
10 ἑτέρου—λέγω δὲ οὐ τοῦ ἡμίσεος εἶναι, ἀλλὰ ξύλον
διπλάσιον—καὶ πατὴρ ἄλλου ᾗ πατήρ ἐστι, καὶ ἡ
ἐπιστήμη δὲ ἄλλου τοῦ ἐν ᾧ, καὶ τόπος δὲ πέρας ἄλλου,
καὶ χρόνος μέτρον ἄλλου. πῦρ δὲ οὐκ ἄλλου, οὐδὲ ξύλον
καθὸ ξύλον ἄλλου, οὐδ᾽ ἄνθρωπος ἄλλου, οὐδὲ
Σωκράτης, οὐδ᾽ ὅλως ἡ σύνθετος οὐσία οὐδὲ τὸ
15 κατὰ τὴν οὐσίαν εἶδος ἄλλον, ὅτι οὐκ ἄλλου πάθος ἦν.
οὐ γὰρ τῆς ὕλης εἶδος, τοῦ δὲ συναμφοτέρου μέρος· τὸ
δὲ τοῦ ἀνθρώπου εἶδος καὶ ὁ ἄνθρωπος ταὐτόν· καὶ ἡ
ὕλη μέρος ὅλου καὶ ἄλλου ὡς τοῦ ὅλου, οὐχ ὡς ἑτέρου
ὄντος ἐκείνου, οὗ λέγεται· λευκὸν δὲ ὃ λέγεται εἶναι,
20 ἑτέρου ἐστίν. ὃ οὖν ἄλλου ὂν ἐκείνου λέγεται, οὐκ οὐσία·
οὐσία τοίνυν, ὃ ὅπερ ἐστὶν αὐτοῦ ἐστιν, ἢ μέρος ὂν
τοιούτου συμπληρωτικόν ἐστι συνθέτου· ὄντος μὲν
αὐτοῦ ἕκαστον μὲν ἢ ἑκάτερον αὐτοῦ, πρὸς δὲ τὸ

be included in substance. And the composite is a base and seat for other things, so that the form with the matter will be a base for the composites, or at least for all that come after the composites, quantity, quality, movement for instance. But then, is the same in the three what is called "not belonging to another"? For white and black belong to something else, that which has become white, and the double belongs to something else—I do not mean that it belongs to the half but I am speaking of a double-sized piece of wood—and a father is someone else's, in so far as he is a father; and knowledge belongs to another, in whom it is, and place is the boundary of another, and time the measure of another. But fire does not belong to something else, nor does a piece of wood in so far as it is a piece of wood, nor does man belong to something else, nor does Socrates, or "composite substance"[1] in general, or the substantive form belong to something else, because it is not an affection of something else. For form does not belong to matter, but is a part of the composite; and the form of man and man are the same thing; and matter is part of a whole, and belongs to another as belonging to the whole, and not in the sense that that of which it is said to be is another thing; but what is said to be white is the white of something else. That then which belongs to another and is said to be of that other is not substance: substance, that is, is what belongs to that which it is, or, if it is a part, is an essential completion of a composite of its own kind; for the composite is either or both parts of itself, but in relation to the composite each part is

[1] Aristotle *Metaphysics* H 3. 1043a30.

σύνθετον ἄλλον τρόπον ἐκείνου λεγόμενον· ἢ εἰ μὲν
25 μέρος, πρὸς ἄλλο λεγόμενον, καθ' αὑτὸ δὲ φύσει ἐν τῷ
εἶναι ὅ ἐστιν, οὐχ ἑτέρου λεγόμενον. κοινὸν δὲ καὶ τὸ
ὑποκείμενον ἐπί τε τῆς ὕλης καὶ τοῦ εἴδους καὶ τοῦ
συναμφοτέρου· ἀλλὰ ἄλλως μὲν ἡ ὕλη τῷ εἴδει, ἄλλως
δὲ τὸ εἶδος τοῖς πάθεσι καὶ τὸ συναμφότερον. ἢ οὔτε ἡ
30 ὕλη ὑποκείμενον τῷ εἴδει—τελείωσις γὰρ τὸ εἶδος
αὐτῆς καθόσον ὕλη καὶ καθόσον δυνάμει—οὐδ' αὖ τὸ
εἶδος ἐν ταύτῃ· μεθ' οὗ γάρ τι ἀπαρτίζει ἔν τι, οὐκ ἔσται
θάτερον ἐν θατέρῳ, ἀλλ' ἄμφω ἡ ὕλη καὶ τὸ εἶδος ὁμοῦ
ὑποκείμενα ἄλλῳ—οἷον ἄνθρωπος καὶ τὶς ἄνθρωπος
ὑπόκεινται τοῖς πάθεσι καὶ προϋπάρχουσι τῶν
35 ἐνεργειῶν καὶ τῶν παρακολουθούντων—καὶ ἀφ' ἧς δὲ
τὰ ἄλλα καὶ δι' ἢν τὰ ἄλλα καὶ περὶ ἢν[1] τὸ πάσχειν καὶ
ἀφ' ἧς τὸ ποιεῖν.

5. Ἀκουστέον δὲ ταῦτα περὶ τῆς ἐνθάδε οὐσίας
λεγομένης· εἰ δέ πῃ ταῦτα καὶ ἐπ' ἐκείνης συμβαίνει,
ἴσως μὲν κατ' ἀναλογίαν καὶ ὁμωνύμως. καὶ γὰρ τὸ
πρῶτον ὡς πρὸς τὰ μετ' αὐτὸ λέγεται. οὐ γὰρ ἁπλῶς
5 πρῶτον, ἀλλ' ἔστιν ὡς πρὸς ἐκεῖνα ἔσχατα ἄλλα πρῶτα
μετ' ἐκεῖνα. καὶ τὸ ὑποκείμενον ἄλλως, καὶ τὸ πάσχειν εἰ
ἐκεῖ ἀμφισβητεῖται, καὶ εἰ κἀκεῖ, ἄλλο τὸ ἐκεῖ πάσχειν.
καὶ τὸ μὴ ἐν ὑποκειμένῳ εἶναι κατὰ
πάσης οὐσίας, εἰ τὸ ἐν ὑποκειμένῳ εἶναι δεῖ μὴ
ὡς μέρος ὑπάρχειν τοῦ ἐν ᾧ ἐστι, μηδ'

---

[1] Simplicius, Theiler: ὃ Enn., H–S.

---

[1] I adopt the περὶ ἢν of Simplicius and Theiler here rather
than the reading of the MSS, περὶ ὅ.
[2] Aristotle *Categories* 5. 3a7–8.
[3] Ibid. 2. 1a24–25.

said to belong to it in another sense; or if it is a part, it is called so in relation to something else, but by itself its natural existence is said to be in being what it is, not in belonging to another. The substrate is also common to matter, form, and the composite; but the matter is substrate to the form in one sense, and the form [and the composite] to the affections in another. Or, alternatively, the matter is not substrate to the form—for the form is its perfection in so far as it is matter and in so far as it is potential—nor, again, is the form in it: for when something completes some one thing with something else, neither of them is in the other, but both the matter and the form together are substrates to something else—man and a particular man are substrates to the affections, and precede the activities and consequences—and [substance is] that from which the others come and through which the others exist and the subject which is affected [1] and the origin of doing and making.

5. This is to be understood as being said about what is called substance here below: if it applies in any way to that intelligible substance, it is perhaps analogously and ambiguously. Thus it is said to be the first in relation to what comes after it. For it is not the first in any unqualified sense, but substantial sensibles are last in relation to intelligibles but first after them. And "substrate" is used in a different sense, and it is disputed whether there is passive affection in the intelligible, and, if it is there, passivity there is something different. And the statement "not being in a substrate applies to all substance" [2] [is true] if that which is in a substrate must "not be there as a part of that in which it is", [3] nor in such a

10 οὕτως, ὥστε μηδὲ συντελεῖν μετ᾽ ἐκείνου εἰς ἕν τι· μεθ᾽
οὗ γὰρ συντελεῖ εἰς σύνθετον οὐσίαν, ἐν ἐκείνῳ ὡς ἐν
ὑποκειμένῳ οὐκ ἂν εἴη· ὥστε μήτε τὸ εἶδος ἐν τῇ ὕλῃ
εἶναι ὡς ἐν ὑποκειμένῳ μήτε τὸν ἄνθρωπον ἐν τῷ
Σωκράτει μέρος ὄντα Σωκράτους. ὃ οὖν μὴ ἐν
ὑποκειμένῳ, οὐσία· εἰ δὲ λέγομεν μ ή τ ε   ἐ ν
15 ὑ π ο κ ε ι μ έ ν ῳ   μ ή τ ε   κ α θ᾽   ὑ π ο κ ε ι μ έ ν ο υ,
προσθετέον "ὡς ἄλλου", ἵνα καὶ ὁ ἄνθρωπος λεγόμενος
κατὰ τοῦ τινὸς ἀνθρώπου περιλαμβάνηται τῷ λόγῳ ἐν
τῇ προσθήκῃ τῇ "μὴ κατ᾽ ἄλλου". ὅταν γὰρ τὸν
ἄνθρωπον κατηγορῶ τοῦ Σωκράτους, οὕτως λέγω, οὐχ
20 ὡς τὸ ξύλον λευκόν, ἀλλ᾽ ὡς τὸ λευκὸν λευκόν· τὸν γὰρ
Σωκράτη λέγων ἄνθρωπον τὸν τινὰ ἄνθρωπον λέγω
ἄνθρωπον, κατὰ τοῦ ἐν τῷ Σωκράτει ἀνθρώπου τὸν
ἄνθρωπον· τοῦτο δὲ ταὐτὸν τῷ τὸν Σωκράτη Σωκράτη
λέγειν, καὶ ἔτι τῷ κατὰ ζῴου λογικοῦ τοιοῦδε τὸ ζῷον
κατηγορεῖν. εἰ δέ τις λέγοι μ ὴ   ἴ δ ι ο ν   εἶναι τῆς
25 ο ὐ σ ί α ς   τὸ μὴ ἐν ὑποκειμένῳ εἶναι, τὴν γὰρ
δ ι α φ ο ρ ὰ ν   μ η δ᾽   α ὐ τ ὴ ν   εἶναι   τ ῶ ν   ἐ ν   ὑ π ο-
κ ε ι μ έ ν ῳ, μέρος οὐσίας λαμβάνων τὸ δίπουν
τοῦτο ο ὐ κ   ἐ ν   ὑ π ο κ ε ι μ έ ν ῳ   φησὶν εἶναι· ἐπεί, εἰ μὴ
τὸ δίπουν λαμβάνοι, ὅ ἐστι τοιόδε οὐσία, ἀλλὰ διποδίαν,
μὴ οὐσίαν λέγων, ἀλλὰ ποιότητα, ἐν ὑποκειμένῳ ἔσται
30 τὸ δίπουν. ἀλλ᾽ οὐδὲ ὁ χρόνος ἐν ὑποκειμένῳ, οὐδ᾽ ὁ
τόπος. ἀλλ᾽ εἰ μὲν τ ὸ   μ έ τ ρ ο ν   λαμβάνεται

way as to contribute with it to the completeness of some one thing; for it could not be as in a substrate in that with which it contributes to a composite substance; so the form is not in the matter as in a substrate, nor is humanity in Socrates [in this way], since it is a part of Socrates. What is not in a substrate, therefore, is substance; but if we say that it is "not in a substrate nor predicated of a substrate",[1] we must add "as of something else", that the human also, predicated of a particular human being, may be included by the statement in the addition "not of something else". For when I predicate humanity of Socrates, I mean it not in the sense in which the wood is white, but in the sense that the white thing is white: for in saying that Socrates is human, I am saying that a particular human being is human, predicating humanity of the human in Socrates; but this is the same as calling Socrates Socrates, and again as predicating "living being" of this particular rational living being. But if someone says[2] that not being in a substrate is not a peculiarity of substance, for the essential differentiation is not itself one of the things in a substrate, it is by understanding [the differentiation] as "the two-footed" that he makes this assertion that it is not in a substrate: since, if he did not understand "the two-footed", which is a particular kind of substance, but "two-footedness", not meaning a substance but a quality, then the two-footed will be in a substrate. But time is not in a substrate either, nor is place. But if "the measure of movement" is understood as

[1] Ibid. 5. 2a12–15.
[2] Aristotle, in *Categories* 5. 3a21–28.

κινήσεως κατὰ τὸ μεμετρημένον, τὸ μέτρον ἐν τῇ
κινήσει ὑπάρξει ὡς ἐν ὑποκειμένῳ, ἥ τε κίνησις ἐν τῷ
κινουμένῳ· εἰ δὲ κατὰ τὸ μετροῦν λαμβάνεται, ἐν τῷ
μετροῦντι ἔσται τὸ μέτρον. ὁ δὲ τόπος, πέρας τοῦ
35 περιέχοντος ὤν, ἐν ἐκείνῳ. καὶ τὸ περὶ ταύτην τὴν
οὐσίαν, περὶ ἧς ὁ λόγος; γίνεται ἐναντίως ἢ κατὰ ἓν
τούτων ἢ κατὰ πλείω ἢ κατὰ πάντα τὰ εἰρημένα
λαμβάνεσθαι τὴν οὐσίαν τὴν τοιαύτην ἐφαρμοττόντων
καὶ τῇ ὕλῃ καὶ τῷ εἴδει καὶ τῷ συναμφοτέρῳ τῶν
εἰρημένων.

6. Εἰ δέ τις λέγοι, ὡς ταῦτα μὲν ἔστω τεθεωρημένα
περὶ τὴν οὐσίαν, ὃ δ᾽ ἔστιν οὐκ εἴρηται, αἰτεῖ ἔτι ἴσως
αἰσθητὸν ἰδεῖν τοῦτο· τὸ δ᾽ "ἔστι" τοῦτο καὶ τὸ "εἶναι"
οὐκ ἂν ὁρῷτο. τί οὖν; τὸ πῦρ οὐκ οὐσία καὶ τὸ ὕδωρ;
5 οὐσία οὖν ἑκάτερον, ὅτι ὁρᾶται; οὔ. ἀλλὰ τῷ ὕλην ἔχειν;
οὔ. ἀλλὰ τῷ εἶδος; οὐδὲ τοῦτο. ἀλλ᾽ οὐδὲ τῷ
συναμφότερον. ἀλλὰ τίνι δή; τῷ εἶναι. ἀλλὰ καὶ τὸ
ποσὸν ἔστι, καὶ τὸ ποιὸν ἔστιν. ἡμεῖς δὴ φήσομεν ἄρα,
ὅτι ὁμωνύμως. ἀλλὰ τί τὸ ⟨ "ἔστιν" ⟩[1] ἐπὶ πυρὸς καὶ
γῆς καὶ τῶν τοιούτων [τὸ ἔστι][2] καὶ τίς ἡ διαφορὰ
10 τούτου τοῦ "ἔστι" καὶ τοῦ ἐπὶ τῶν ἄλλων; ἢ ὅτι τὸ μὲν
ἁπλῶς εἶναι λέγει καὶ ἁπλῶς ὄν, τὸ δὲ λευκὸν εἶναι. τί
οὖν; τὸ εἶναι τὸ προσκείμενον τῷ λευκῷ ταὐτὸν τῷ ἄνευ
προσθήκης; οὐχί, ἀλλὰ τὸ μὲν πρώτως ὄν, τὸ δὲ κατὰ
μετάληψιν καὶ δευτέρως. τό τε γὰρ λευκὸν προστεθὲν
15 πεποίηκε τὸ ὂν λευκόν, τό τε ὂν τῷ "λευκὸν" προστεθὲν
πεποίηκε ⟨τὸ⟩[3] λευκὸν ὄν, ὥστε ἑκατέρῳ, τῷ μὲν ὄντι

---

[1] Theiler.
[2] del. Kirchhoff, Müller, Theiler.
[3] Creuzer.

applying to what is measured, the measure will exist in the movement as in a substrate, and the movement in what is moved; but if it is taken as referring to the measurer, then the measure will be in the measurer. And place, being the "boundary of the surroundings", is in those surroundings. But what is to be said about this substance here which we are discussing? It comes about that this substance can be understood in contrary ways according to one or more or all of these statements, since the statements fit both matter and form and the composite as well.

6. But if anyone should say that, granted that these are observations about substance, what it is has not been said, he is perhaps still requiring to see this with his bodily eyes; but this "is" and this "being" could not be seen [in this way]. Well then, is not fire substance, and water? Is each of them substance because it is seen? No. But by having matter? No. But by having form? Not this either. And not by being a composite either. But by what, then? By being. But the quantum is, and the quale is. But, we shall insist, only in an ambiguous sense. But what is this "is" which applies to fire and earth and suchlike things, and what is the difference between this "is" and the "is" which applies to the others? It is that one means simply to be and simply existing, but the other means to be white. Well then, is the "is" which is added to the "white" the same as the "is" without addition? No, but one means primary being, the other being by participation and secondarily. For the "white" added to "being" makes the being white, and the "being" added to the "white" makes the white being, so that in both cases [there is something incidental], the "white" incidental to the

συμβεβηκὸς τὸ λευκόν, τῷ δὲ λευκῷ συμβεβηκὸς τὸ ὄν.
καὶ οὐχ οὕτως λέγομεν, ὡς ἂν εἴποι τις τὸν Σωκράτη
λευκὸν καὶ τὸ λευκὸν Σωκράτη· ἐν γὰρ ἀμφοτέροις ὁ
20 Σωκράτης ὁ αὐτός, ἀλλ' ἴσως τὸ λευκὸν οὐ ταὐτόν· ἐπὶ
γὰρ τοῦ "τὸ λευκὸν Σωκράτης" ἐμπεριείληπται ὁ
Σωκράτης τῷ λευκῷ, ἐν δὲ τῷ "Σωκράτης λευκὸς"
καθαρῶς συμβεβηκὸς τὸ λευκόν. καὶ ἐνταῦθα "τὸ ὂν
λευκὸν" συμβεβηκὸς ἔχει τὸ λευκόν, ἐν δὲ τῷ "τὸ
25 λευκὸν ὄν" τὸ λευκὸν συνειλημμένον τὸ ὄν. καὶ ὅλως τὸ
μὲν λευκὸν ἔχει τὸ εἶναι, ὅτι περὶ τὸ ὂν καὶ ἐν ὄντι· παρ'
ἐκείνου οὖν τὸ εἶναι· τὸ δὲ ὂν παρ' αὐτοῦ τὸ ὄν, παρὰ δὲ
τοῦ λευκοῦ τὸ λευκόν, οὐχ ὅτι αὐτὸ ἐν τῷ λευκῷ, ἀλλ'
ὅτι τὸ λευκὸν ἐν αὐτῷ. ἀλλ' ἐπεὶ καὶ τοῦτο τὸ ὂν τὸ ἐν
τῷ αἰσθητῷ οὐ παρ' αὐτοῦ ὄν, λεκτέον, ὅτι παρὰ τοῦ
30 ὄντως ὄντος ἔχει τὸ ὄν, παρὰ δὲ τοῦ ὄντος λευκοῦ ἔχει
τὸ λευκὸν εἶναι, κἀκείνου τὸ λευκὸν ἔχοντος κατὰ
μετάληψιν τοῦ ἐκεῖ ὄντος ἔχοντος τὸ εἶναι.

7. Εἰ δέ τις λέγοι παρὰ τῆς ὕλης ἔχειν τὰ τῇδε ὅσα
ἐπ' αὐτῆς τὸ εἶναι, πόθεν ἕξει ἡ ὕλη τὸ εἶναι καὶ τὸ ὂν
ἀπαιτήσομεν. ὅτι δὲ μὴ πρῶτον ἡ ὕλη, εἴρηται ἐν
ἄλλοις. εἰ δέ, ὅτι τὰ ἄλλα οὐκ ἂν συσταίη μὴ ἐπὶ τῆς
5 ὕλης, τὰ αἰσθητὰ φήσομεν. πρὸ τούτων δὲ οὖσαν
ὕστερον πολλῶν εἶναι καὶ τῶν ἐκεῖ πάντων οὐδὲν

"being" and the "being" incidental to the "white". And we do not mean this in the sense in which one might say that Socrates is white and the white thing is Socrates; for in both these cases Socrates is the same, but perhaps the white is not the same; for in the statement "the white thing is Socrates", Socrates is included in "the white", but in the statement "Socrates is white" the white is simply and solely incidental. And here [in the case we are discussing] "being is white" has "white" as incidental, but in the statement "the white is being", "the white" has being included in it. And in general the white has being because it is about being and in being; it derives its existence therefore from being; but being has being from itself and white from the white, not because it is in the white, but because the white is in it. But, since this being in the sense-world does not exist of itself, it must be said that it has its being from the real being and has its being white from the real white; that also which has the white has its being by participation in the being of that other intelligible world.

7. But if anyone should say that the things here which are based on matter have their being from it we shall demand where matter gets being and the existent from. We have explained elsewhere that matter is not primary.[1] But if one says that the other things could not come into existence except on the basis of matter, we shall agree as far as sense-objects are concerned. But even if matter is prior to these, nothing prevents it from being posterior to many things and to all the things there in the intelligible,

[1] In VI. 1. 25–28 (the critique of Stoic corporealism).

κωλύει ἀμυδρὸν τὸ εἶναι ἔχουσαν καὶ ἧττον ἢ τὰ ἐφ᾽
αὑτῆς, ὅσῳ τὰ μὲν λόγοι καὶ μᾶλλον ἐκ τοῦ ὄντος, ἡ δ᾽
ἄλογος παντελῶς, σκιὰ λόγου καὶ ἔκπτωσις λόγου· εἰ δέ
τις λέγοι, ὅτι τὸ εἶναι αὕτη δίδωσι τοῖς ἐπ᾽ αὐτῆς,
10 ὥσπερ ὁ Σωκράτης τῷ ἐπ᾽ αὐτοῦ λευκῷ, λεκτέον, ὅτι
τὸ μὲν μᾶλλον ὂν δοίη ἂν τῷ ἧττον ὄντι τὸ [ἧττον]¹
εἶναι, τὸ δὲ ἧττον ὂν οὐκ ἂν δοίη τῷ μᾶλλον ὄντι. ἀλλ᾽ εἰ
μᾶλλον ὂν τὸ εἶδος τῆς ὕλης, οὐκέτι κοινόν τι τὸ ὂν κατ᾽
ἀμφοῖν, οὐδ᾽ ἡ οὐσία γένος ἔχον τὴν ὕλην, τὸ εἶδος, τὸ
15 συναμφότερον, ἀλλὰ κοινὰ μὲν πολλὰ αὐτοῖς ἔσται,
ἅπερ λέγομεν, διάφορον δ᾽ ὅμως τὸ εἶναι. περὶ γὰρ
ἐλαττόνως ὂν μᾶλλον ὂν προσελθὸν τάξει μὲν πρῶτον ἂν
εἴη, οὐσίᾳ δὲ ὕστερον· ὥστε, εἰ μὴ ἐπίσης τὸ εἶναι τῇ
ὕλῃ καὶ τῷ εἴδει καὶ τῷ συναμφοτέρῳ, κοινὸν μὲν οὐκ
20 ἂν ἔτι εἴη ἡ οὐσία ὡς γένος. ἄλλως μέντοι ἕξει πρὸς τὰ
μετὰ ταῦτα, ὡς κοινόν τι πρὸς ἐκεῖνα ἔχουσα τῷ αὐτῶν
εἶναι, ὡς ζωῆς ἡ μέν τις ἀμυδρά, ἡ δὲ ἐναργεστέρα,² καὶ
εἰκόνων ἡ μέν τις ὑποτύπωσις, ἡ δὲ ἐξεργασία μᾶλλον.
εἰ δὲ τῷ ἀμυδρῷ τοῦ εἶναι μετροῖ τις τὸ εἶναι, τὸ δὲ ἐν
25 τοῖς ἄλλοις πλέον ἐῴη, τούτῳ πάλιν αὖ κοινὸν ἔσται τὸ
εἶναι. ἀλλὰ μήποτε οὐχ οὕτω δεῖ ποιεῖν. ἄλλο γὰρ
ἕκαστον ὅλον, ἀλλ᾽ οὐ κοινόν τι τὸ ἀμυδρόν, ὥσπερ ἐπὶ
τῆς ζωῆς οὐκ ἂν εἴη κοινόν τι ἐπὶ θρεπτικῆς καὶ
αἰσθητικῆς καὶ νοερᾶς. καὶ ἐνταῦθα τοίνυν τὸ εἶναι ἄλλο

---

¹ del. Kirchhoff.
² Perna^{mg}, Creuzer: ἐνεργ– Enn.

since the being it has is dim and less than the things based upon it, in so far as they are rational principles and derive more from the existent but matter is utterly irrational, a shadow of rational form and a falling away from rational form; but if one says that this matter gives being to the things based on it as Socrates does to the whiteness based upon him, we must say that what is more existent might give being to what is less existent, but the less existent could not give being to the more existent. But if the form is more existent than the matter, existence is no more something common to both, nor is substance a genus containing matter, form and the composite, but they have many things, those we are speaking of, in common, but their being is different. For when something which is more existent arrives about something which is less existent, [the latter] would be first in order, but posterior in substance; so that, if being is not equal for matter, form and the composite, substance would not still be common as a genus. It will, certainly, be otherwise disposed to the things which come after it, as having something common in relation to them by the fact of their being, as there is a dimmer and a clearer life, and one picture is a sketch and another a more finished work. But if one were to measure being by the dimness of being and let go what is more of it in the others, in this way again being will be common. But one should not perhaps proceed like this. For each [of the three, matter, form and composite] is different as a whole, and the dimness is not something common, just as in the case of life there would be nothing in common between nutritive, perceptive and intelligent life. So here also being is different in

τὸ ἐπὶ τῆς ὕλης καὶ εἴδους, καὶ συνάμφω ἀφ' ἑνὸς ἄλλως
30 καὶ ἄλλως ῥυέντος. οὐ γὰρ μόνον δεῖ, εἰ τὸ δεύτερον ἀπὸ
τοῦ πρώτου, τὸ δὲ τρίτον ἀπὸ τοῦ δευτέρου, τὸ μὲν
μᾶλλον, τὸ δὲ ἐφεξῆς χεῖρον καὶ ἔλαττον, ἀλλὰ κἂν ἀπὸ
τοῦ αὐτοῦ ἄμφω, ᾗ δὲ τὸ μὲν μᾶλλον μετασχὸν πυρός,
οἷον κέραμος, τὸ δὲ ἧττον, ὥστε μὴ κέραμος γενέσθαι.
35 τάχα δὲ οὐδ' ἀπὸ τοῦ αὐτοῦ ἡ ὕλη καὶ τὸ εἶδος·
διάφορα[1] γὰρ καὶ ἐν ἐκείνοις.

8. Ἀλλ' ἆρα τὸ μὲν διαιρεῖν εἰς στοιχεῖα ἐᾶν δεῖ, καὶ
μάλιστα περὶ τῆς αἰσθητῆς οὐσίας λέγοντα, ἣν δεῖ
αἰσθήσει μᾶλλον ἢ λόγῳ λαμβάνειν, καὶ τὸ ἐξ ὧν
σύγκειται μὴ προσποιεῖσθαι—οὐ γὰρ οὐσίαι ἐκεῖνα,
5 ἢ οὐκ ἂν αἰσθηταί γε οὐσίαι—ἑνὶ δὲ γένει περι-
λαμβάνοντα τὸ κοινὸν ἐπὶ λίθου καὶ γῆς καὶ ὕδατος
καὶ τῶν ἐκ τούτων φυτῶν, ᾗ αἰσθητά, καὶ ζῴων
ὡσαύτως; οὐ γὰρ παραλελείψεται ἡ ὕλη οὐδὲ τὸ εἶδος· ἡ
γὰρ αἰσθητὴ οὐσία ἔχει ταῦτα· ὕλη γὰρ καὶ εἶδος πῦρ
καὶ γῆ καὶ τὰ μεταξύ, τὰ δὲ σύνθετα ἤδη πολλαὶ οὐσίαι
εἰς ἕν. καὶ τὸ κοινὸν πᾶσι τούτοις, ᾗ τῶν ἄλλων
10 κεχώρισται· ὑποκείμενα γὰρ ταῦτα τοῖς ἄλλοις καὶ οὐκ
ἐν ὑποκειμένῳ οὐδὲ ἄλλου· καὶ ὅσα εἴρηται, ὑπάρχει
ταύτῃ. ἀλλ' εἰ ἡ αἰσθητὴ οὐσία οὐκ ἄνευ μεγέθους οὐδ'
ἄνευ ποιότητος, πῶς ἔτι τὰ συμβεβηκότα χωριοῦμεν;
χωρίζοντες γὰρ ταῦτα, τὸ μέγεθος, τὸ σχῆμα, τὸ
15 χρῶμα, ξηρότητα, ὑγρότητα, τί τὴν οὐσίαν αὐτὴν

---

[1] Igal, H–S²: διαφορὰ Enn.

matter and in form, and both together come from one
which flows in all sorts of different ways. For it is not
only necessary for one to exist more and the other
worse and less if the second comes from the first and
the third from the second, but even if both come from
the same, in that one has a larger share in fire, like a
pot, and the other less, so as not to become a pot. But
perhaps matter and form do not even come from the
same: for there are different things also in the intelligible world.

8. But ought one then to drop division into elements, especially when one is speaking about sensible substance, which one must grasp by sense
rather than reason, and not to take into consideration the parts of which they are composed—for
those parts are not substances, or at least not sensible substances—and include in one genus what is
common to stone and earth and water and the plants
which arise from these, in so far as they are sense-
objects, and the animals likewise? For [if one does
this] matter and form will not have been left out; for
sensible substance has these; for fire and earth and
the elements between are matter and form, and the
composites are already many substances coming
together into one. And what is common to all these
is how they are separated from the other things; for
these are substrates to the others and not in a
substrate nor belonging to another; and everything
else which has been said applies here. But if sensible
substance does not exist without size or without
quality, how shall we still be able to separate what is
incidental? For when we separate off this, size,
shape, colour, dryness, moistness, what are we going
to establish as substance itself? For these [sensible]

θησόμεθα; ποιαὶ γὰρ οὐσίαι αὗται. ἀλλὰ τί ἐστι, περὶ ὃ
συμβαίνει τὰ ποιοῦντα ἐκ τοῦ μόνον οὐσίαν εἶναι ποιὰν
οὐσίαν εἶναι; καὶ ἔσται τὸ πῦρ οὐχ ὅλον οὐσία, ἀλλά τι
αὐτοῦ, οἷον μέρος; τοῦτο δὲ τί ἂν εἴη; ἢ ὕλη. ἀλλὰ ἆρά
20 γε ἡ αἰσθητὴ οὐσία συμφόρησίς τις ποιοτήτων καὶ
ὕλης, καὶ ὁμοῦ μὲν πάντα ταῦτα συμπαγέντα ἐπὶ ὕλης
μιᾶς οὐσία, χωρὶς δὲ ἕκαστον λαμβανόμενον τὸ μὲν
ποιόν, τὸ δὲ ποσὸν ἔσται, ἢ ποιὰ πολλά; καὶ ὃ μὲν
ἂν ἐλλεῖπον μήπω ἀπηρτισμένην ἐᾷ γίνεσθαι τὴν
ὑπόστασιν, μέρος τῆσδε τῆς οὐσίας, ὃ δ᾽ ἂν γενομένῃ
25 τῇ οὐσίᾳ ἐπισυμβῇ, τὴν οἰκείαν ἔχει τάξιν οὐ
κρυπτόμενον ἐν τῷ μίγματι τῷ ποιοῦντι τὴν λεγομένην
οὐσίαν; καὶ οὐ τοῦτό φημι, ὡς ἐκεῖ μετὰ τῶν ἄλλων ὂν
ἐστιν οὐσία, συμπληροῦν ἕνα ὄγκον τοσόνδε καὶ
τοιόνδε, ἀλλαχοῦ δὲ μὴ συμπληροῦν ποιόν, ἀλλὰ μηδὲ
30 ἐκεῖ ἕκαστον οὐσίαν, τὸ δ᾽ ὅλον τὸ ἐκ πάντων οὐσίαν.
καὶ οὐ δυσχεραντέον, εἰ τὴν οὐσίαν τὴν αἰσθητὴν ἐξ οὐκ
οὐσιῶν ποιοῦμεν· οὐδὲ γὰρ τὸ ὅλον ἀληθὴς οὐσία, ἀλλὰ
μιμούμενον τὴν ἀληθῆ, ἥτις ἄνευ τῶν ἄλλων τῶν περὶ
αὐτὴν ἔχει τὸ ὂν καὶ τῶν ἄλλων ἐξ αὐτῆς γινομένων, ὅτι
35 ἀληθῶς ἦν· ὡδὶ δὲ καὶ τὸ ὑποβεβλημένον ἄγονον καὶ
οὐχ ἱκανὸν εἶναι ὄν, ὅτι μηδὲ ἐξ αὐτοῦ τὰ ἄλλα, σκιὰ δὲ
καὶ ἐπὶ σκιᾷ αὐτῇ οὔσῃ ζωγραφία καὶ τὸ φαίνεσθαι.

substances are qualified substances. But is there
something around which occur what make being
simply substance into being qualified substance?
And will fire be not as a whole substance, but
something belonging to it, like a part? And what
could this be? Just matter. But then, is sensible
substance a conglomeration of qualities and matter,
and are all these compounded together on one matter substance, but when each is taken separately will
one be a quale and one a quantum, or will they be
many qualia [1]? And will that which, if it is lacking,
does not allow a completed coming into existence to
take place be a part of this substance, but that
which, when a substance has come to be, comes to it
as an addition, have its own position and not be
hidden in the mixture which makes up what is called
substance? I do not mean this in the sense that when
it is there with the others it is substance, completing
one mass of a particular size and quality, but elsewhere when it is not contributing to completion it is
a quality, but that even in the former case each
particular one is not a substance, but the whole
made up from them all is substance. And there is no
need to object if we make sensible substance out of
non-substances; for even the whole is not true substance but imitates the true substance, which has its
being without the others which attend on it, and the
others come into being from it, because it truly is;
but here what underlies is sterile and inadequate to
be being, because the others do not come from it, but
it is a shadow, and upon what is itself a shadow, a
picture and a seeming.

[1] Cp. ch. 15, 24–38 and II. 7.3.

9. Καὶ περὶ μὲν τῆς λεγομένης οὐσίας αἰσθητῆς καὶ
γένους ἑνὸς ταύτῃ. εἴδη δ' αὐτοῦ τίνα ἄν τις θεῖτο καὶ
πῶς διέλοι; σῶμα μὲν οὖν τὸ σύμπαν θετέον εἶναι,
τούτων δὲ τὰ μὲν ὑλικώτερα, τὰ δὲ ὀργανικά·
5 ὑλικώτερα μὲν πῦρ, γῆ, ὕδωρ, ἀήρ· ὀργανικὰ δὲ τὰ τῶν
φυτῶν καὶ τὰ τῶν ζῴων σώματα κατὰ τὰς μορφὰς τὰς
παραλλαγὰς σχόντα. εἶτα εἴδη γῆς λαμβάνειν καὶ τῶν
ἄλλων στοιχείων, καὶ ἐπὶ τῶν σωμάτων τῶν ὀργανικῶν
τά τε φυτὰ κατὰ τὰς μορφὰς διαιροῦντα καὶ τὰ τῶν
10 ζῴων σώματα· ἢ τῷ τὰ μὲν ἐπίγεια καὶ ἔγγεια, καὶ καθ'
ἕκαστον στοιχεῖον τὰ ἐν αὐτῷ· ἢ τῶν σωμάτων τὰ μὲν
κοῦφα, τὰ δὲ βαρέα, τὰ δὲ μεταξύ, καὶ τὰ μὲν ἑστάναι ἐν
μέσῳ, τὰ δὲ περιέχειν ἄνωθεν, τὰ δὲ μεταξύ· καὶ ἐν
τούτων ἑκάστῳ σώματα ἤδη σχήμασι διειλημμένα, ὡς
εἶναι σώματα τὰ μὲν ζῴων οὐρανίων, τὰ δὲ κατὰ ἄλλα
15 στοιχεῖα· ἢ κατ' εἴδη διαστησάμενον τὰ τέσσαρα τὸ
μετὰ τοῦτο ἄλλον τρόπον ἤδη συμπλέκειν
καταμιγνύντα[1] τὰς διαφορὰς αὐτῶν κατὰ τοὺς τόπους
καὶ τὰς μορφὰς καὶ τὰς μίξεις, οἷον πύρινα ἢ γήϊνα τῷ
πλείονι καὶ ἐπικρατοῦντι λεγόμενα. τὸ δὲ π ρ ώ τ α ς καὶ
δ ε υ τ έ ρ α ς λέγειν—"τόδε τὸ πῦρ" καὶ "πῦρ"—
20 ἄλλως μὲν ἔχειν διαφοράν, ὅτι τὸ μὲν καθέκαστον, τὸ δὲ
καθόλου, οὐ μέντοι οὐσίας διαφοράν· καὶ γὰρ καὶ ἐν
ποιῷ "τὶ λευκὸν" καὶ "λευκὸν" καὶ "τὶς γραμματικὴ"

---

[1] Igal, H–S²: καὶ μιγνύντα Enn.

---

[1] The bodies of celestial living beings are, of course,
spherical.

9. So much for what is called sensible substance and the one genus. But what species of it should one posit, and how should one divide them? Now the whole must be classed as body, and of bodies some are matterish and some organic; the matterish are fire, earth, water, air; the organic the bodies of plants and animals, which have their differences according to their shapes. Then one should take the species of earth and of the other elements, and in the case of organic bodies one should divide the plants, and the bodies of animals, according to their shapes; or by the fact that some are on and in the earth, and, element by element, [one should class separately] the bodies in each; or [one could class them on the ground that] some are light, some are heavy, and some in between, and that some stand in the middle, some surround them above, and some are in between; and in each of these the bodies are already differentiated by their outlines, so as to be some of them bodies of celestial living beings[1] and others appropriate to the other elements; or one should divide the four according to their species and afterwards proceed in another way to weave them together by blending their differences according to places and shapes and mixtures, classing them as fiery or earthly, called so according to the largest and predominant element [in the mixture]. But as for calling them "first" and "second"[2]—"this fire" and "fire"—these have a difference in another way, because one is individual and one universal, but not a difference of substance; under quality, also, there is "something white" and "white" and "a particular

[2] Aristotle *Categories* 5. 2a11–19.

καὶ "γραμματική". ἔπειτα τί ἔλαττον ἔχει ἡ γραμματικὴ πρὸς τινὰ γραμματικὴν καὶ ὅλως ἐπιστήμη
25 πρὸς τινὰ ἐπιστήμην; οὐ γὰρ ἡ γραμματικὴ ὕστερον τῆς
τινὸς γραμματικῆς, ἀλλὰ μᾶλλον οὔσης γραμματικῆς
καὶ ἡ ἐν σοί· ἐπεὶ ἡ ἐν σοί τίς ἐστι τῷ ἐν σοί, αὐτὴ δὲ
ταὐτὸν τῇ καθόλου. καὶ ὁ Σωκράτης οὐκ αὐτὸς ἔδωκε
τῷ μὴ ἀνθρώπῳ τὸ εἶναι ἀνθρώπῳ, ἀλλ' ὁ ἄνθρωπος τῷ
30 Σωκράτει· μεταλήψει γὰρ ἀνθρώπου ὁ τὶς ἄνθρωπος.
ἔπειτα ὁ Σωκράτης τί ἂν εἴη ἢ ἄνθρωπος τοιόσδε, τὸ δὲ
"τοιόσδε" τί ἂν ἐργάζοιτο πρὸς τὸ μᾶλλον οὐσίαν εἶναι;
εἰ δ' ὅτι τὸ μὲν "εἶδος μόνον ὁ ἄνθρωπος", τὸ δὲ "εἶδος
ἐν ὕλῃ", ἧττον ἄνθρωπος κατὰ τοῦτο ἂν εἴη· ἐν ὕλῃ γὰρ
ὁ λόγος χείρων. εἰ δὲ καὶ ὁ ἄνθρωπος οὐ καθ' αὑτὸ
35 εἶδος, ἀλλ' ἐν ὕλῃ, τί ἔλαττον ἕξει τοῦ ἐν ὕλῃ, καὶ αὐτὸς
λόγος τοῦ ἔν τινι ὕλῃ; ἔτι πρότερον τῇ φύσει τὸ
γενικώτερον, ὥστε καὶ τὸ εἶδος τοῦ ἀτόμου· τὸ δὲ
πρότερον τῇ φύσει καὶ ἁπλῶς πρότερον· πῶς ἂν οὖν
ἧττον εἴη; ἀλλὰ τὸ καθέκαστον πρὸς ἡμᾶς
γνωριμώτερον ὂν πρότερον· τοῦτο δ' οὐκ ἐν τοῖς
40 πράγμασι τὴν διαφορὰν ἔχει. ἔπειτα οὕτως οὐχ εἷς
λόγος τῆς οὐσίας· οὐ γὰρ ὁ αὐτὸς τοῦ πρώτως καὶ
δευτέρως, οὐδ' ὑφ' ἓν γένος.

10. Ἔστι δὲ καὶ οὕτως διαιρεῖν, θερμῷ καὶ ξηρῷ,
καὶ ξηρῷ καὶ ψυχρῷ, καὶ ὑγρῷ καὶ ψυχρῷ, ἢ ὅπως
βούλεται τὸν συνδυασμὸν εἶναι, εἶτα ἐκ τούτων σύνθεσιν

---

[1] Aristotle. The reference is probably to *De Gen. et Corr.*
B 2–3. 330a24–35.

literary skill" and "literary skill". For what less does "literary skill" have in comparison with "a particular literary skill" and in general "body of knowledge" in comparison with "a particular body of knowledge"? For literary skill is not posterior to the particular literary skill but rather it is because literary skill exists that that in you exists; since that in you is particular by being in you, but in itself is the same as the universal. And Socrates did not in his own person give being human to the non-human but humanity gave being human to Socrates: the particular human is so by participation in humanity. Since what could Socrates be except "a man of a particular kind" and what could the "of a particular kind" do towards being more of a substance? But if it is because "humanity is only a form" but Socrates is "form in matter", he would be less human in this respect: for the rational form is worse in matter. But if humanity is not in itself form, but in matter, what less will it have than the particular human in matter, when it is itself the rational form of something in a kind of matter? Again, the more general is prior by nature, as the species is prior to the individual; but the prior by nature is also simply prior: how then could it be less? But the individual is prior in relation to us because it is more knowable; but this does not make a difference in actual fact. Then, if it were so, there would not be one definition of substance: for the definition of what is primarily and what is secondarily is not the same, nor do they come under one genus.

10. It is also possible to divide like this, by hot and dry, and dry and cold, and moist and cold, or whatever kind of coupling he[1] wants, and then a compo-

καὶ μίξιν· καὶ ἢ μένειν ἐνταῦθα στάντα ἐπὶ τοῦ
5 συνθέτου, ἢ κατὰ τὸ ἔγγειον καὶ ἐπίγειον, ἢ κατὰ τὰς
μορφὰς καὶ κατὰ τὰς τῶν ζῴων διαφοράς, οὐ τὰ ζῷα
διαιροῦντα, ἀλλὰ κατὰ τὰ σώματα αὐτῶν ὥσπερ
ὄργανα διαιροῦντα. οὐκ ἄτοπος δὲ ἡ κατὰ τὰς μορφὰς
διαφορά, εἴπερ οὐδ' ἡ κατὰ τὰς ποιότητας αὐτῶν
διαίρεσις, θερμότης, ψυχρότης καὶ τὰ τοιαῦτα. εἰ δέ τις
10 λέγοι "ἀλλὰ κατὰ ταύτας ποιεῖ τὰ σώματα", καὶ κατὰ
τὰς μίξεις φήσομεν ποιεῖν καὶ κατὰ τὰ χρώματα καὶ τὰ
σχήματα. ἐπεὶ γὰρ περὶ αἰσθητῆς οὐσίας ὁ λόγος, οὐκ
ἄτοπος ἂν εἴη, διαφοραῖς εἰ λαμβάνοιτο ταῖς πρὸς τὴν
αἴσθησιν· οὐδὲ γὰρ ὂν ἁπλῶς αὕτη, ἀλλ' αἰσθητὸν ὂν
15 τὸ ὅλον τοῦτο· ἐπεὶ καὶ τὴν δοκοῦσαν ὑπόστασιν αὐτῆς
σύνοδον τῶν πρὸς αἴσθησιν ἔφαμεν εἶναι καὶ ἡ πίστις
τοῦ εἶναι παρὰ τῆς αἰσθήσεως αὐτοῖς. εἰ δὲ ἄπειρος ἡ
σύνθεσις, κατ' εἴδη τῶν ζῴων διαιρεῖν, οἷον ἀνθρώπου
εἶδος τὸ ἐπὶ σώματι· ποιότης γὰρ αὕτη σώματος,
20 τὸ τοιοῦτον εἶδος, ποιότησι δ' οὐκ ἄτοπον διαιρεῖν.
εἰ δ' ὅτι τὰ μὲν ἁπλᾶ, τὰ δὲ σύνθετα εἴπομεν, ἀντι-
διαιροῦντες τὸ σύνθετον τῷ ἁπλῷ, ὑλικώτερα εἴπομεν
καὶ ὀργανικὰ οὐ προσποιούμενοι τὸ σύνθετον. ἔστι δ'
οὐκ ἀντιδιαίρεσις τὸ σύνθετον πρὸς τὸ ἁπλοῦν εἶναι,
ἀλλὰ κατὰ πρώτην διαίρεσιν τὰ ἁπλᾶ τῶν σωμάτων
25 θέντα μίξαντα αὐτὰ ἀπ' ἄλλης ἀρχῆς ὑποβεβηκυίας[1]

[1] Sleeman, H-S: -βεβλη- Enn.

sition and mixture of these; and either to stop there, coming to a halt at the composite, or [to go on dividing] according to whether things are in or on the earth, or according to the shapes and according to the differences of animals, not dividing the animals but dividing according to their bodies, which are like their tools. The division according to their shapes is not out of place, since the division according to their qualities is not either, hotness, coldness and such like. But if someone were to say "but bodies act by these", we shall reply that they also act according to the mixtures and the colours and the outlines. For since our discussion is about sensible substance the division would not be out of place if it was taken to be made by the differences which present themselves to sense-perception; for this sensible substance is not simply being, but is perceived by sense, being this whole world of ours; since we maintained that its apparent existence was a congress of perceptibles, and the guarantee of their being comes from sense-perception. But if the composition has no limits, one should divide according to the species-forms of living things, the bodily species of man, for instance. For this, a species-form of this kind, is a quality of body, and it is not out of place to divide by qualities. But if we said that some bodies are simple and some are composite, opposing the composite to the simple in our division, we were speaking of matterish and organic bodies, not taking the composite seriously into account. It is not a division by opposition which sets the composite against the simple, but, when one had placed the simple bodies by the first division, one mixed them and differentiated the composites starting from an-

διαφορὰν συνθέτων ἢ τόποις ἢ μορφαῖς ποιεῖσθαι, οἷον
τὰ μὲν οὐράνια, τὰ δὲ γήινα. καὶ περὶ μὲν τῆς ἐν τοῖς
αἰσθητοῖς οὐσίας ἢ γενέσεως ταῦτα.

11. Περὶ δὲ ποσοῦ καὶ ποσότητος, ὡς ἐν ἀριθμῷ δεῖ
τίθεσθαι καὶ μεγέθει, καθόσον τοσοῦτον ἕκαστον, ὃ
ἐστιν ἐν ἀριθμῷ τῶν ἐνύλων καὶ διαστήματι τοῦ
ὑποκειμένου—οὐ γὰρ περὶ χωριστοῦ ποσοῦ ὁ λόγος,
5 ἀλλ' ὃ ποιεῖ τρίπηχυ εἶναι τὸ ξύλον, καὶ ἡ πεμπὰς ἡ ἐπὶ
τοῖς ἵπποις—εἴρηται πολλάκις, ὅτι ταῦτα ποσὰ μόνον
λεκτέον, τόπον δὲ καὶ χρόνον μὴ κατὰ τὸ ποσὸν
νενοῆσθαι, ἀλλὰ τὸν μὲν χρόνον τῷ μ έ τ ρ ο ν
κ ι ν ή σ ε ω ς εἶναι καὶ τῷ πρός τι δοτέον αὐτόν, τὸν δὲ
τόπον σώματος περιεκτικόν, ὡς καὶ τοῦτον ἐν σχέσει
10 καὶ τῷ πρός τι κεῖσθαι· ἐπεὶ καὶ ἡ κίνησις συνεχὴς καὶ
οὐκ ἐν ποσῷ ἐτέθη. μέγα δὲ καὶ μικρὸν διὰ τί οὐκ ἐν
ποσῷ; ποσότητι γάρ τινι μέγα τὸ μέγα, καὶ τὸ μέγεθος
δὲ οὐ τῶν πρός τι, ἀλλὰ τὸ μεῖζον καὶ τὸ ἔλαττον τῶν
πρός τι· πρὸς γὰρ ἕτερον, ὥσπερ καὶ τὸ διπλάσιον. διὰ
15 τί οὖν ὅ ρ ο ς μ ι κ ρ ό ν, κ έ γ χ ρ ο ς δ ὲ μ ε γ ά λ η; ἢ
πρῶτον μὲν ἀντὶ τοῦ "μικρότερον" λέγεται. εἰ γὰρ πρὸς
τὰ ὁμογενῆ ὁμολογεῖται καὶ παρ' αὐτῶν εἰρῆσθαι,
ὁμολογεῖται, ὅτι ἀντὶ τοῦ "μικρότερον" λέγεται. καὶ
μεγάλη κέγχρος οὐχ ἁπλῶς λεγομένη "μεγάλη", ἀλλὰ
"κέγχρος μεγάλη"· τοῦτο δὲ ταὐτὸν "τῶν ὁμογενῶν",

other subordinate principle, either by positions or shapes, some celestial and others earthly, for instance. And so much for substance or coming-to-be in the things perceived by sense.

11. But about the quantum and quantity, it has often been said how one should locate it in number and size, in so far as each individual thing which is in the number of things in matter and the extension of the substrate is of a certain size—for the discussion is not about separate quantity but about the quantity which makes the wood three cubits long and the five which applies to the horses—and that only these things should be called quanta, but that place and time should not be considered under quantity, but that time because it is the "measure of motion" should in its own nature also be given to the relative, and that place is what surrounds body, so that this too is put in relation and the relative; further, movement is continuous and so was not put in the class of quantity. But why are large and small not in quantity? For the large is large by some kind of quantity and size is not something relative, but larger and smaller belong to the relative; for they are so in regard to another, like the double. Why then is "the mountain small, but the millet-seed large" [1]? Now, first of all, this is said instead of "smaller". For if it is agreed that it is called small in regard to and from [comparison with] things of the same kind, it is agreed that it is said instead of "smaller". And a large millet-seed is not simply called "large" but "large millet-seed" and this is the same as "of things of the same kind", and it can

---

[1] Aristotle *Categories* 6. 5b18–19.

20 τῶν δὲ ὁμογενῶν κατὰ φύσιν ἂν λέγοιτο μείζων. ἔπειτα
διὰ τί οὐ καὶ τὸ καλὸν λέγοιτο ἂν τῶν πρός τι; ἀλλά
φαμεν καλὸν μὲν καθ' ἑαυτὸ καὶ ποιόν, κάλλιον δὲ τῶν
πρός τι· καίτοι καὶ καλὸν λεγόμενον φανείη ἂν πρὸς
ἄλλο αἰσχρόν, οἷον ἀνθρώπου κάλλος πρὸς θεόν·
25 π ι θ ή κ ω ν, φησίν, ὁ κ ά λ λ ι σ τ ο ς α ἰ σ χ ρ ὸ ς
σ υ μ β ά λ λ ε ι ν ἑ τ έ ρ ῳ γ έ ν ε ι· ἀλλ' ἐφ' ἑαυτοῦ
μὲν καλόν, πρὸς ἄλλο δὲ ἢ κάλλιον ἢ τοὐναντίον. καὶ
ἐνταῦθα τοίνυν ἐφ' ἑαυτοῦ μὲν μέγα μετὰ μεγέθους,
πρὸς ἄλλο δὲ οὐ τοιοῦτον. ἢ ἀναιρετέον τὸ καλόν, ὅτι
ἄλλο κάλλιον αὐτοῦ· οὕτω τοίνυν οὐδ' ἀναιρετέον τὸ
30 μέγα, ὅτι ἔστι τι μεῖζον αὐτοῦ· ἐπεὶ οὐδὲ τὸ μεῖζον ὅλως
ἂν εἴη μὴ μεγάλου ὄντος, ὥσπερ οὐδὲ κάλλιον μὴ
καλοῦ.

12. Ἀπολειπτέον τοίνυν καὶ ἐναντιότητα εἶναι περὶ
τὸ ποσόν· αἱ γὰρ ἔννοιαι τὴν ἐναντιότητα συγχωροῦσιν,
ὅταν "μέγα" λέγωμεν καὶ ὅταν "μικρόν", ἐναντίας τὰς
φαντασίας ποιοῦσαι, ὥσπερ ὅταν "πολλὰ" καὶ
5 "ὀλίγα"· καὶ γὰρ τὰ παραπλήσια περὶ τοῦ "ὀλίγα" καὶ
"πολλὰ" λεκτέον. "πολλοὶ γὰρ οἱ ἐν τῇ οἰκίᾳ" ἀντὶ τοῦ
"πλείους"· τοῦτο δὲ πρὸς ἄλλο· καὶ "ὀλίγοι ἐν τῷ
θεάτρῳ" ἀντὶ τοῦ "ἐλάττους". καὶ δεῖ ὅλως τὰ πολλὰ
πολὺ λέγειν πλῆθος ἐν ἀριθμῷ—πλῆθος δὲ πῶς τῶν
10 πρός τι;—τοῦτο δὲ ταὐτὸν τῷ "ἐπέκτασις ἀριθμοῦ" τὸ

---

[1] Heraclitus fr. B 82 DK, as quoted by Plato *Hippias Major* 289A3–4.

naturally be called larger than things of the same kind. Next, why is "beautiful" not said to be one of the relatives? But we call something beautiful in itself; it has the quality of beauty, but "more beautiful" is one of the relative terms; and then what is called beautiful might appear ugly in relation to something else, like the beauty of a man compared to a god; "the most beautiful of monkeys", he[1] says, "is ugly in comparison with another kind"; but it is beautiful by itself, but in relation to something else it is more beautiful or the opposite. And in the case of size, then, a thing is large in itself by possession of size, but in relation to something else it is not so. Otherwise one would have to deny the "beautiful" because something else was more beautiful; so here one must not deny the "large" because there is something larger than it: since it could not be larger at all if it was not large, just as a thing could not be more beautiful if it was not beautiful.

12. We must allow then that there is opposition in the quantitative; for our notions admit the opposition, when we say "large" and when we say "small", and make our mental images opposite, just as when we say "many" and "few": for we ought to say much the same about "few" and "many". For "there are many people in the house" is instead of "more people"; but this is in relation to something else; and we say "few people in the theatre" instead of "fewer".[2] And one ought in general to call the many "many" as a multiplicity in number—and how can multiplicity be one of the relatives?—but this is the same as saying "an expansion of number" and

δὲ ἐναντίον "συστολή". τὸ δ' αὐτὸ καὶ ἐπὶ τοῦ συνεχοῦς
τῆς ἐννοίας τὸ συνεχὲς προαγούσης εἰς τὸ πόρρω. ποσὸν
μὲν οὖν, ὅταν τὸ ἓν προέλθῃ καὶ τὸ σημεῖον. ἀλλ' ἐὰν μὲν
ταχὺ στῇ ἑκάτερον, τὸ μὲν ὀλίγον, τὸ δὲ μικρόν· ἐὰν δ' ἡ
15 πρόοδος προϊοῦσα μὴ παύσηται ταχύ, τὸ μὲν πολύ, τὸ
δὲ μέγα. τίς οὖν ὅρος; τίς δὲ καλοῦ; θερμοῦ δέ; καὶ ἔνι
θερμότερον καὶ ἐνταῦθα. ἀλλὰ λέγεται τὸ μὲν
θερμότερον πρός τι, τὸ δὲ θερμὸν ἁπλῶς ποιόν. ὅλως δὲ
λόγον τινά, ὥσπερ καλοῦ, οὕτω καὶ μεγάλου εἶναι, ὃς
μεταληφθεὶς μέγα ποιεῖ, ὥσπερ καλὸν ὁ τοῦ καλοῦ.
20 ἐναντιότης τοίνυν κατὰ ταῦτα περὶ τὸ ποσόν· κατὰ γὰρ
τὸν τόπον οὐκέτι, ὅτι μὴ τοῦ ποσοῦ· ἐπεὶ καί, εἰ τοῦ
ποσοῦ ἦν ὁ τόπος, οὐκ ἦν ἐναντίον τὸ ἄνω τινὶ μὴ ὄντος
τοῦ κάτω ἐν τῷ παντί. ἐν δὲ τοῖς μέρεσι τὸ ἄνω καὶ
κάτω λεγόμενον ἄλλο οὐδὲν ἂν σημαίνοι ἢ ἀνωτέρω καὶ
25 κατωτέρω καὶ ὅμοιον τῷ "δεξιὸν" καὶ "ἀριστερόν"·
ταῦτα δὲ τῶν πρός τι. συλλαβῇ δὲ καὶ λόγῳ συμβαίνει
ποσοῖς εἶναι καὶ ὑποκεῖσθαι τῷ ποσῷ· φωνὴ γὰρ ποσή·
αὐτὴ[1] δὲ κίνησίς τις· εἰς κίνησιν οὖν ὅλως ἀνακτέον,
ὥσπερ καὶ τὴν πρᾶξιν.

13. Τὸ μὲν οὖν συνεχὲς ἀπὸ τοῦ διωρισμένου
κεχωρίσθαι καλῶς τῷ κοινῷ καὶ τῷ ἰδίῳ ὅρῳ εἴρηται·

---

[1] Ficinus (*ipsa*): αὔτη Enn., H–S[1].

the opposite "contraction". And the same applies to the continuous, in that our notion of it prolongs the continuous into the distance. So there is a quantum when the unit moves forward, and also when the point does. But if either of them comes to a stop quickly, one is few and the other small; but if the advance does not halt quickly in its progress, one is many and the other large. What then is the defining limit? What is it of the beautiful? Or the hot? And it is possible here also to be hotter. But "the hotter" is said in relation to something, but "the hot" is simply a quale. But in general there must be a rational form of the large just as there is of the beautiful, which when it is participated makes a thing large, as the form of the beautiful makes a thing beautiful. In these respects, then, there is an opposition in the quantitative; for there is no longer one in place, because place does not belong to the quantitative; since, even if place did belong to the quantitative, "up" would not be opposite to anything, since there is no "down" in the All. But when "up" and "down" are spoken of in the parts, they could not mean anything else but "higher up" and "lower down" and are like "right" and "left"; and these belong to the relatives. But "syllable" and "word" have a quantitative character and come under the quantitative; for they are a sound of a certain length [1]; but sound itself is a movement; so it must be generally referred to movement, as action is.

13. It has been well said [2] that the continuous is distinguished from the discrete by the common and

---

[1] On sound as quantitative cp. VI. 1. 5.
[2] By Aristotle: *Categories* 6. 4b.

τὸ δ' ἐντεῦθεν ἤδη ἐπὶ μὲν ἀριθμοῦ περιττῷ, ἀρτίῳ.
καὶ πάλιν, εἴ τινες διαφοραὶ τούτων ἑκατέρου, ἢ
5 παραλειπτέον τοῖς περὶ ἀριθμὸν ἔχουσιν ἤδη, ἢ δεῖ
ταύτας μὲν διαφορὰς τῶν μοναδικῶν ἀριθμῶν τίθεσθαι,
τῶν δ' ἐν τοῖς αἰσθητοῖς οὐκέτι. εἰ δὲ τοὺς ἐν τοῖς
αἰσθητοῖς ἀριθμοὺς χωρίζει ὁ λόγος, οὐδὲν κωλύει καὶ
τούτων τὰς αὐτὰς νοεῖν διαφοράς. τὸ δὲ συνεχὲς πῶς,
10 εἰ τὸ μὲν γραμμή, τὸ δ' ἐπίπεδον, τὸ δὲ στερεόν; ἢ τὸ
μὲν ἐφ' ἕν, τὸ δ' ἐπὶ δύο, τὸ δ' ἐπὶ τρία, οὐκ
εἰς εἴδη διαιρουμένου δόξει, ἀλλὰ καταρίθμησιν
μόνον ποιουμένου. εἰ¹ γὰρ ἐν τοῖς ἀριθμοῖς οὕτω
λαμβανομένοις κατὰ τὸ πρότερον καὶ τὸ ὕστερον κοινόν
τι ἐπ' αὐτῶν οὐκ ἔστι γένος, οὐδ' ἐπὶ πρώτης καὶ
15 δευτέρας καὶ τρίτης αὔξης κοινόν τι ἔσται. ἀλλὰ ἴσως
καθόσον ποσὸν τὸ ἴσον ἐπ' αὐτοῖς, καὶ οὐ τὰ μὲν μᾶλλον
ποσά, τὰ δὲ ἧττον, κἂν τὰ μὲν ἐπὶ πλείω τὰς διαστάσεις
ἔχῃ, τὰ δὲ ἐπ' ἔλαττον. καὶ ἐπὶ τῶν ἀριθμῶν τοίνυν,
καθόσον πάντες ἀριθμοί, τὸ κοινὸν ἂν εἴη· ἴσως γὰρ οὐχ
20 ἡ μονὰς τὴν δυάδα, οὐδ' ἡ δυὰς τὴν τριάδα, ἀλλὰ τὸ
αὐτὸ πάντα. εἰ δὲ μὴ γίνεται, ἀλλ' ἔστιν, ἡμεῖς δ'
ἐπινοοῦμεν γινόμενα, ἔστω ὁ μὲν ἐλάττων πρότερος, ὁ
δὲ ὕστερος ὁ μείζων· ἀλλὰ καθόσον ἀριθμοὶ πάντες, ὑφ'
ἕν. καὶ ἐπὶ μεγεθῶν τοίνυν τὸ ἐπ' ἀριθμῶν μετενεκτέον·
χωριοῦμεν δὲ ἀπ' ἀλλήλων γραμμήν, ἐπίπεδον,

---

¹ Westerink, H–S²: ἀεὶ Enn.: ἐπεὶ Theiler, H–S¹.

the particular limit; and further, in the case of number, that it is distinguished by odd and even. And again, if there are distinctions in each of these [divisions] they should be left to those whose business is number, or we should posit that these are distinctions of the monadic [ideal] numbers, but no longer of those in sense-objects. But if logic separates the numbers in sense-objects [from the objects], nothing prevents us from making in thought the same distinctions of these. But how do we make distinctions in the continuous, if one kind is line, one plane and one solid? Now the distinctions one-dimensional, two-dimensional and three-dimensional do not seem to be proper to one who is dividing into species, but rather to one who is simply making a count. For if in numbers also when they are taken like this according to the before and after, there is no genus common to them, there will be nothing common either to the first, second and third dimensions. But perhaps it is in so far as they are quantitative that they are one and the same, and some of them are not more quantitative and some less, even if some have wider extensions and some narrower. And numbers then would have what is in common to them in so far as they are all numbers; for perhaps the number one does not produce the number two or the number two the number three, but the same produces all. But if the number-series does not come into being, but is, but we think it as having come into being, let the lesser number be earlier and the greater later; but in so far as they are all numbers they are classed under one head. And now we must transfer what applied to numbers to magnitudes: we shall separate from each other line, sur-

25 στερεόν, ὃ δὴ κέκληκε σῶμα, τῷ διάφορα τῷ εἴδει
μεγέθη ὄντα εἶναι. εἰ δὲ δεῖ ἕκαστον τούτων διαιρεῖν,
γραμμὴν μὲν εἰς εὐθύ, περιφερές, ἑλικοειδές, ἐπίπεδον
δὲ ⟨εἰς⟩[1] εὐθύγραμμον καὶ περιφερὲς σχῆμα, στερεὸν
δὲ εἰς στερεὰ σχήματα, σφαῖραν, [εἰς][2] εὐθυγράμμους
30 πλευράς, καὶ ταῦτα πάλιν, οἷα οἱ γεωμέτραι ποιοῦσι
τρίγωνα, τετράπλευρα, καὶ πάλιν ταῦτα εἰς ἄλλα,
ἐπισκεπτέον.

14. Τί γὰρ ἂν φαῖμεν εὐθεῖαν; οὐ μέγεθος εἶναι; ἢ
ποιὸν μέγεθος τὸ εὐθὺ φαίη τις ἄν. τί οὖν κωλύει
διαφορὰν εἶναι ἢ γραμμή;—οὐ γὰρ ἄλλου τινὸς τὸ εὐθὺ
ἢ γραμμῆς—ἐπεὶ καὶ οὐσίας διαφορὰς κομίζομεν παρὰ
5 τοῦ ποιοῦ. εἰ οὖν γραμμὴ εὐθεῖα, ποσὸν μετὰ διαφορᾶς,
καὶ οὐ σύνθετον διὰ τοῦτο ἡ εὐθεῖα ἐξ εὐθύτητος καὶ
γραμμῆς· εἰ δὲ σύνθετον, ὡς μετὰ οἰκείας διαφορᾶς. τὸ
δ' ἐκ τριῶν γραμμῶν—τὸ τρίγωνον—διὰ τί οὐκ ἐν τῷ
ποσῷ; ἢ οὐχ ἁπλῶς τρεῖς γραμμαὶ τὸ τρίγωνον, ἀλλὰ
10 οὑτωσὶ ἐχουσῶν, καὶ τὸ τετράπλευρον τέσσαρες
οὑτωσί· καὶ γὰρ ἡ γραμμὴ ἡ εὐθεῖα οὑτωσὶ καὶ ποσόν.
εἰ γὰρ τὴν εὐθεῖαν οὐ ποσὸν μόνον, τί κωλύει καὶ τὴν
πεπερασμένην μὴ ποσὸν μόνον λέγειν; ἀλλὰ τὸ πέρας τῆς
γραμμῆς στιγμὴ καὶ οὐκ ἐν ἄλλῳ. καὶ τὸ πεπερασμένον
15 τοίνυν ἐπίπεδον ποσόν, ἐπείπερ γραμμαὶ περατοῦσιν, αἳ
πολὺ μᾶλλον ἐν τῷ ποσῷ. εἰ οὖν τὸ πεπερασμένον
ἐπίπεδον ἐν τῷ ποσῷ, τοῦτο δὲ ἢ τετράγωνον ἢ

---

[1] Kirchhoff.
[2] delevimus: καὶ F[3s] (= Ficinus), Müller.

face and solid (which Aristotle calls body) by their all being magnitudes specifically different. But we must investigate whether we should divide each of them, line into straight, circular and spiral, plane into rectangular and circular form, solid into solid forms, sphere and those bounded by straight-line sides, and these again, as the geometers do, into those with triangular and those with quadrilateral sides, and these again into others.

14. What, then, are we to say that a straight line is? Is it not that it is a magnitude? Now one could say that the straight is a magnitude of a certain quality. What then prevents it from being a specific differentiation of the line as line?—for the straight does not belong to anything else but a line—since we get our specific differentiations of substance also from the qualitative. If a line, then, is straight, it is a quantum with a specific difference, and the straight line is not for this reason a composite of straight and line; but if it is a composite, it is as with its specific difference. But the figure made of three lines—the triangle—why is it not in the quantitative? Now the triangle is not just three lines, but three lines in this particular disposition, and the quadrilateral four lines in this particular disposition; and indeed the straight line is both disposed in a particular way and quantitative. If then we say that the straight line is not only quantitative, what prevents us from saying that the limited straight line is not only quantitative? But the limit of the line is a point, and not in anything else. And so the limited surface is quantitative, since lines limit it, which are much more in the quantitative. If then the limited surface is in the quantitative, and this is either a quadrilateral or a

πολύπλευρον ἢ ἑξάπλευρον, καὶ τὰ σχήματα πάντα ἐν
τῷ ποσῷ. εἰ δ᾽ ὅτι τὸ τρίγωνον λέγομεν ποιὸν καὶ τὸ
τετράγωνον, ἐν ποιῷ θησόμεθα, οὐδὲν κωλύει ἐν
20 πλείοσι κατηγορίαις θέσθαι τὸ αὐτό· καθὸ μὲν μέγεθος
καὶ τοσόνδε[1] μέγεθος, ἐν τῷ ποσῷ, καθὸ δὲ τοιάνδε
μορφὴν παρέχεται, ἐν ποιῷ. ἢ καθ᾽ αὐτὸ[2] τοιάδε μορφὴ
τὸ τρίγωνον. τί οὖν κωλύει καὶ τὴν σφαῖραν ποιὸν
λέγειν; εἰ οὖν τις ὁμόσε χωροῖ, τὴν γεωμετρίαν τοίνυν
25 οὐ περὶ μεγέθη, ἀλλὰ περὶ ποιότητα καταγίνεσθαι.
ἀλλ᾽ οὐ δοκεῖ τοῦτο, ἀλλ᾽ ἡ πραγματεία αὕτη περὶ
μεγέθη. αἱ δὲ διαφοραὶ τῶν μεγεθῶν οὐκ ἀναιροῦσι τὸ
μεγέθη αὐτὰ εἶναι, ὥσπερ οὐδ᾽ αἱ τῶν οὐσιῶν οὐκ
οὐσίας τὰς οὐσίας εἶναι. ἔτι πᾶν ἐπίπεδον
πεπερασμένον, οὐ γὰρ οἷόν τε ἄπειρον εἶναί τι ἐπίπεδον.
30 ἔτι ὥσπερ, ὅταν περὶ οὐσίαν ποιότητα λαμβάνω,
οὐσιώδη ποιότητα λέγω, οὕτω καὶ πολὺ μᾶλλον, ὅταν τὰ
σχήματα λαμβάνω, ποσότητος διαφορὰς λαμβάνω.
ἔπειτα, εἰ μὴ ταύτας διαφορὰς μεγεθῶν ληψόμεθα,
τίνων θησόμεθα; εἰ δὲ μεγεθῶν εἰσι διαφοραί, τὰ
35 γενόμενα ἐκ τῶν διαφορῶν μεγέθη διάφορα ἐν εἴδεσιν
αὐτῶν τακτέον.

15. Ἀλλὰ πῶς ἴδιον τοῦ ποσοῦ τὸ ἴσον
καὶ ἄνισον; ὅμοια γὰρ τρίγωνα λέγεται. ἢ καὶ ὅμοια
λέγεται μεγέθη, καὶ ἡ ὁμοιότης λεγομένη οὐκ ἀναιρεῖ
τὸ ὅμοιον καὶ τὸ ἀνόμοιον εἶναι ἐν τῷ ποιῷ· ἴσως γὰρ

---

[1] Igal, H–S²: τοιόνδε Enn.
[2] ἢ καθ᾽ αὐτὸ Igal, H–S²: ἢ καὶ αὐτὸ BUC: ἢ καὶ αὐτὸ wx,
Perna.

polygon or a hexagon, then all figures are in the quantitative. But if, because we say that the triangle is a quale and the quadrilateral also, we are going to put them in the qualified, there is no objection to putting the same thing in several categories: in so far as it is a magnitude, and a magnitude of a certain size, it is in the quantitative, but in so far as it presents a shape of a certain quality, it is in the qualitative. Now the triangle is in itself a shape of a certain quality: what then prevents us from calling the sphere a quale? If then one comes to the real point at issue, geometry will not be concerned with magnitudes but with quality. But this does not appear to be so, but this activity is concerned with magnitudes. But the specific differences of magnitudes do not take away their being magnitudes, just as those of substances do not make them non-substances. Further, every surface is limited, for it is not possible for any surface to be unlimited. And further, just as when I grasp a quality of a substance, I call it a substantial quality, so, and much more, when I grasp figures, I grasp specific differences of quantity. Then, if we are not going to take these as specific differences of magnitudes, of what are we going to posit that they are differences? But if they are specific differences of magnitudes, the different magnitudes arising from the differences must be arranged in species of magnitudes.

15. But how do the "equal and unequal properly belong to the quantitative"? For triangles are spoken of as like. Now, magnitudes are also spoken of as "like" and the likeness which is spoken of does not abolish the fact that the like and the unlike are in the qualitative; for perhaps here in magnitudes

5 ἐνταῦθα ἐν τοῖς μεγέθεσι τὸ ὅμοιον ἄλλως καὶ οὐχ ὡς ἐν
τῷ ποιῷ. ἔπειτα οὐκ, εἰ ἴδιον εἶπε τὸ ἴσον καὶ
ἄνισον, ἀνεῖλε καὶ τὸ ὅμοιον κατηγορεῖν τινων· ἀλλ'
εἰ εἶπε τὸ ὅμοιον καὶ ἀνόμοιον τοῦ ποιοῦ,
ἄλλως λεκτέον, ὡς ἔφαμεν, τὸ ἐπὶ τοῦ ποσοῦ. εἰ δὲ
ταὐτὸν τὸ ὅμοιον καὶ ἐπὶ τούτων, ἐπισκέψασθαι δεῖ
10 ἰδιότητας ἄλλας ἑκατέρου τοῦ γένους, τοῦ τε ποσοῦ καὶ
τοῦ ποιοῦ. ἢ λεκτέον, τὸ ὅμοιον καὶ ἐπὶ τοῦ ποσοῦ
λέγεσθαι, καθόσον αἱ διαφοραὶ ἐν αὐτῷ, καθόλου δέ, ὅτι
συντάττειν δεῖ τὰς συμπληρούσας διαφορὰς τῷ[1] οὗ
διαφοραί, καὶ μάλιστα, ὅταν μόνου ἐκείνου ᾗ διαφορὰ ἡ
15 διαφορά. εἰ δ' ἐν ἄλλῳ μὲν συμπληροῖ τὴν οὐσίαν, ἐν
ἄλλῳ δὲ μή, οὗ μὲν συμπληροῖ, συντακτέον, οὗ δὲ μὴ
συμπληροῖ, μόνον ἐφ' ἑαυτοῦ ληπτέον· συμπληροῦν δὲ
λέγω τὴν οὐσίαν οὐ τὴν ἁπλῶς, ἀλλὰ τὴν τοιάνδε, τοῦ
"τοιάνδε" προσθήκην οὐκ οὐσιώδη δεχομένου. κἀκεῖνο
20 δὲ ἐπισημαντέον, ὅτι ἴσα μὲν λέγομεν καὶ τρίγωνα καὶ
τετράγωνα καὶ ἐπὶ πάντων σχημάτων, ἐπιπέδων τε
καὶ στερεῶν· ὥστε ἴσον τε καὶ ἄνισον κείσθω ἐπὶ
ποσοῦ ἴδιον. ὅμοιον δὲ καὶ ἀνόμοιον, εἰ ἐπὶ ποιοῦ,
ἐπισκεπτέον.

---

[1] F^{pc}, Kirchhoff: τοῦ Enn.

"like" is used differently, and not as in the qualitative. Then, if he[1] said that "equal and unequal
properly belong to the quantitative", he did not
abolish the possibility of predicating likeness of
some magnitudes; but if he said that "the like and
unlike belong to the qualitative", then, as we asserted, likeness in the quantitative must be understood in a different way. But if "the like" is understood in the same way also in magnitudes, we must
investigate other characteristics proper to each
genus, the quantitative and the qualitative. Now we
must say that the term "like" can be used also of the
quantitative, in so far as the specific differences are
present in it, and in general that one ought to class
the differences which help to complete the essence
under that of which they are the differences, and
especially when the specific difference as specific
difference belongs to that alone. But if in one it
contributes to the completion of the essence, but in
the other not, it must be classed where it contributes, but where it does not contribute, simply
taken by itself: I mean that it contributes to the
completion not simply of the essence, but of the
essence of such a kind, since "of such a kind" allows
a non-substantial addition. And we must note this as
well, that we call both triangles and quadrilaterals
"equal" and apply the term to all figures, plane and
solid. So let it be established that "equal" and
"unequal" properly belong to the quantitative. But
we must investigate whether "like" and "unlike"
belong to the qualitative.

[1] Aristotle. The statements about equality and inequality
and likeness and unlikeness discussed here are *Categories*
6. 6a26 and 8. 11a18–19.

Περὶ δὲ τοῦ ποιοῦ ἐλέχθη, ὡς σὺν ἄλλοις μὲν ὕλῃ καὶ
25 ποσῷ συμμιχθὲν συμπλήρωσιν ἐργάζεται αἰσθητῆς
οὐσίας, καὶ ὅτι κινδυνεύει ἡ λεγομένη αὕτη οὐσία εἶναι
τοῦτο τὸ ἐκ πολλῶν, οὐ τὶ ἀλλὰ ποιὸν μᾶλλον· καὶ ὁ μέν
λόγος εἶναι οἷον πυρὸς τὸ "τὶ" σημαίνων μᾶλλον, ἣν δὲ
μορφὴν ἐργάζεται, ποιὸν μᾶλλον· καὶ ὁ λόγος ὁ τοῦ
30 ἀνθρώπου τὸ "τὶ" εἶναι, τὸ δ᾽ ἀποτελεσθὲν ἐν σώματος
φύσει εἴδωλον ὂν τοῦ λόγου ποιόν τι μᾶλλον εἶναι. οἷον
εἰ ἀνθρώπου ὄντος τοῦ Σωκράτους τοῦ ὁρωμένου ἡ
εἰκὼν αὐτοῦ ἡ ἐν γραφῇ χρώματα καὶ φάρμακα ὄντα
Σωκράτης λέγοιτο· οὕτως οὖν καὶ λόγου ὄντος, καθ᾽ ὃν
35 Σωκράτης, τὸν αἰσθητὸν Σωκράτη ⟨ὀρθῶς λεκτέον οὐ
Σωκράτη⟩,[1] ἀλλὰ[2] χρώματα καὶ σχήματα ἐκείνων τῶν
ἐν τῷ λόγῳ μιμήματα εἶναι· καὶ τὸν λόγον δὲ τοῦτον
πρὸς τὸν ἀληθέστατον ἤδη λόγον τὸν ἀνθρώπου τὸ αὐτό
πεπονθότα εἶναι. ταῦτα μὲν οὖν οὕτως.

16. Ἕκαστον δὲ λαμβανόμενον χωρὶς τῶν ἄλλων τῶν
περὶ τὴν λεγομένην οὐσίαν ποιότητα τὴν ἐν τούτοις
εἶναι, οὐ τὸ "τὶ" οὐδὲ τὸ "ποσὸν" οὐδὲ "κίνησιν"
σημαίνοντα, χαρακτῆρα δὲ καὶ τὸ "τοιόνδε" [καὶ τὸ
5 οἷον][3] καὶ τὸ "ὁποῖον"[4] δηλοῦντα, ⟨οἷον⟩[3] καλὸν
αἰσχρὸν τὸ ἐπὶ σώματι· ὁμώνυμον γὰρ τὸ καλὸν τὸ τῇδε
κἀκεῖ, ὥστε καὶ τὸ ποιόν· ἐπεὶ καὶ τὸ μέλαν καὶ τὸ λευκόν
ἄλλα. ἀλλὰ τὸ ἐν τῷ σπέρματι καὶ τῷ τοιούτῳ λόγῳ
πότερα τὸ αὐτὸ ἢ ὁμώνυμον τῷ φαινομένῳ; καὶ τοῖς ἐκεῖ

---

[1] Igal, H–S²: ⟨λέγομεν⟩ Müller; ⟨λέγομεν Σωκράτη⟩ H–S¹.
[2] Enn.: lac. † ἀλλὰ Kirchhoff: ἄλλα Harder, Cilento,
Theiler.
[3] Müller.
[4] Enn.: ποιὸν Volkmann.

It was said about the qualitative that, mixed together with others, matter and the quantitative, it effects the completion of sensible substance, and that this so-called substance is this compound of many, and is not a "something" but a "something like"; and the rational form, of fire for instance, indicates rather the "something", but the shape it produces is rather a quale. And the rational form of man is the being a "something", but its product in the nature of body, being an image of the form, is rather a sort of "something like". It is as if, the visible Socrates being a man, his painted picture, being colours and painter's stuff, was called Socrates; in the same way, therefore, since there is a rational form according to which Socrates is, the perceptible Socrates should not rightly be said to be Socrates, but colours and shapes which are representations of those in the form; and this rational form in relation to the truest form of man is affected in the same way. And so much for that.

16. But when each of the categories which have to do with so-called substance is taken separately, quality [must be said] to be in sense-objects, not the terms signifying "something" or "how much" or "movement" but those indicating the distinctive characteristic and the "of such a kind" and "of what kind", for instance beautiful and ugly applied to the body; for there is only a verbal identity between the beautiful here and there in the intelligible, as there is also between the qualitative here and there; since black and white also are different here and there. But is the qualitative in the seed, that is in the rational principle of a particular kind, the same or only verbally identical with that which appears?

10 προσνεμητέον ἢ τοῖς τῇδε; καὶ τὸ αἰσχρὸν τὸ περὶ τὴν
ψυχήν; τὸ μὲν γὰρ καλὸν ὅτι ἄλλο, ἤδη δῆλον. ἀλλ᾽ εἰ ἐν
τούτῳ τῷ ποιῷ καὶ ἡ ἀρετή, εἰ ἐν τοῖς τῇδε ποιοῖς. ἢ
τὰς μὲν ἐν τοῖς τῇδε ποιοῖς, τὰς δὲ ἐν τοῖς ἐκεῖ. ἐπεὶ καὶ
τὰς τέχνας λόγους οὔσας ἀπορήσειεν ἄν τις εἰ ἐν τοῖς τῇδε·
καὶ γὰρ εἰ ἐν ὕλῃ λόγοι, ἀλλὰ ὕλη αὐτοῖς ἡ ψυχή. ἀλλ᾽
15 ὅταν καὶ μετὰ ὕλης, πῶς ἐνταῦθα; οἷον κιθαρῳδία· καὶ
γὰρ περὶ χορδὰς καὶ μέρος πως τῆς τέχνης ἡ ᾠδή, φωνὴ
αἰσθητή, εἰ μὴ ἄρα ἐνεργείας ταύτας τις, ἀλλ᾽ οὐ μέρη,
θεῖτο. ἀλλ᾽ οὖν ἐνέργειαι αἰσθηταί· ἐπεὶ καὶ τὸ καλὸν τὸ
ἐν σώματι ἀσώματον· ἀλλ᾽ ἀπέδομεν αὐτὸ αἰσθητὸν ὂν
20 τοῖς περὶ σῶμα καὶ σώματος. γεωμετρίαν δὲ καὶ
ἀριθμητικὴν διττὴν θεμένους τὰς μὲν ὡδὶ ἐν τῷδε τῷ
ποιῷ τακτέον, τὰς δὲ αὐτῆς τῆς ψυχῆς πραγματείας
πρὸς τὸ νοητὸν ἐκεῖ τακτέον. καὶ δὴ καὶ μουσικὴν φησιν
ὁ Πλάτων καὶ ἀστρονομίαν ὡσαύτως. τὰς τοίνυν τέχνας
25 περὶ σώματα ἐχούσας καὶ ὀργάνοις αἰσθητοῖς καὶ
αἰσθήσει χρωμένας, εἰ καὶ ψυχῆς εἰσι διαθέσεις, ἐπειδὴ
κάτω νευούσης εἰσίν, ἐν τῷδε τῷ ποιῷ τακτέον. καὶ δὴ
226

And is it to be assigned to the intelligibles there or the sense-objects here? And what about ugliness in the soul? For that beauty in the soul is something different [from bodily beauty] is already clear. But if [ugliness or vice in the soul] is in this qualitative here, the question arises if virtue is among the qualitatives here. Perhaps some virtues are among the qualitatives here, and some among those there. Since one might be in some difficulty whether the arts, which are rational forms, belong among those here [1]: for even if they are rational forms in matter, their matter is the soul. But when they are also with [bodily] matter, how are they here? Take lyre-playing for instance; for it has to do with the strings, and the tune, sensible sound, is in some way part of the art, unless perhaps one were to suppose that these are activities, not parts. But even so they are sense-perceived activities; since the beauty also which is in body is bodiless; but since it is perceived by the senses we allotted it to what has to do with body and belongs to body. But we suppose that geometry and arithmetic are double, and should rank one kind of them here in this qualitative, but the works of the soul itself directed to the intelligible should be ranked there. And indeed Plato says the same about music and astronomy. So then the arts which are concerned with body and use perceptible tools and sense-perception, even if they are dispositions of the soul, since they are dispositions of the soul inclining downwards are to be ranked in this qualitative here. And indeed there is nothing to

[1] On the status of the arts in the intelligible and sensible worlds see also V. 9.11–12.

καὶ τὰς πρακτικὰς ἀρετὰς οὐδὲν κωλύει ἐνταῦθα τὰς
οὕτω πραττούσας ὡς πολιτικῶς τὸ πράττειν ἔχειν,
30 ὅσαι μὴ χωρίζουσι τὴν ψυχὴν πρὸς τὰ ἐκεῖ ἄγουσαι,
ἀλλ' ἐνταῦθα τὸ καλῶς ἐνεργοῦσι προηγούμενον τοῦτο,
ἀλλ' οὐχ ὡς ἀναγκαῖον τιθέμεναι. καὶ τὸ ἐν τῷ
σπέρματι τοίνυν καλὸν καὶ πολὺ μᾶλλον τὸ μέλαν καὶ τὸ
λευκὸν ἐν τούτοις. τί οὖν; καὶ τὴν ψυχὴν τὴν τοιαύτην,
ἐν ᾗ οὗτοι οἱ λόγοι, ἐν οὐσίᾳ τῇ τῇδε τάξομεν; ἢ οὐδὲ
35 ταῦτα σώματα εἴπομεν, ἀλλ' ἐπεὶ περὶ σῶμα καὶ
σωμάτων ποιήσεις οἱ λόγοι, ἐν ποιότητι ἐθέμεθα τῇ
τῇδε· οὐσίαν δὲ αἰσθητὴν τὸ ἐκ πάντων τῶν εἰρημένων
θέμενοι οὐδαμῶς ἀσώματον οὐσίαν ἐν αὐτῇ τάξομεν.
ποιότητας δὲ ἀσωμάτους ἁπάσας λέγοντες ἐν αὐτῇ
40 πάθη ὄντα νενευκότα τῇδε ἐνηριθμήσαμεν καὶ λόγους
ψυχῆς τινος· τὸ γὰρ πάθος μεμερισμένον εἰς δύο, εἴς τε
τὸ περὶ ὅ ἐστι καὶ ἐν ᾧ ἐστι, τῇ ψυχῇ, ἐδίδομεν ποιότητι
οὐ σωματικῇ οὔσῃ, περὶ σῶμα δὲ οὔσῃ· οὐκέτι δὲ τὴν
ψυχὴν τῇδε τῇ οὐσίᾳ, ὅτι τὸ πρὸς σῶμα αὐτῆς πάθος
ἤδη δεδωκότες ἦμεν ποιῷ· ἄνευ δὲ τοῦ πάθους καὶ τοῦ
45 λόγου νοουμένην τῷ ὅθεν ἐστὶν ἀποδεδώκαμεν οὐδεμίαν
οὐσίαν ὁπωσοῦν νοητὴν ἐνταῦθα καταλιπόντες.

17. Εἰ μὲν οὖν οὕτω δοκεῖ, διαιρετέον τὰς μὲν
ψυχικάς, τὰς δὲ σωματικάς, ὡς σώματος οὔσας
ποιότητας. εἰ δὲ τὰς ψυχὰς ἁπάσας ἐκεῖ τις βούλεται,

---

[1] The terminology here is Stoic: cp. SVF III 280.

prevent us from ranking the practical virtues here below, those which act in such a way that their action is of a civic [or social] kind, all those which do not separate the soul and lead it to the things there above, but work the good life here below, regarding this as preferable but not as necessary.[1] Then the beautiful in the seed and still more the black and the white belong among these here below. Well then, shall we rank the soul of this particular kind, in which these rational forms are, with the substance here below? Now we did not say that these were bodies, but since the rational forms were concerned with bodies and bodies' doings, we put them in the quality here below; but when we take sensible substance to be that which is composed of all that we have mentioned, we shall certainly not rank an incorporeal substance in it. But, though we said that all the qualities were incorporeal, we counted them in the sensible since they are affections inclining to this world and forms belonging to a particular soul; for since the affection is divided into two, into that with which it is concerned and that in which it is, we allotted it to the quality which is not corporeal but in the sphere of body; but we do not go on to allot the soul to the substance here below because we had already allotted its body-directed affection to the qualitative; but when it was thought of without the affection and the rational form [we have been discussing] we have assigned it to the region from which it came and have left no substance in any way intelligible here below.

17. If we think this is so, we should divide qualities into soul-qualities and (as belonging to body) body-qualities. But if one wishes all souls to be in the

229

ταῖς αἰσθήσεσι τὰς τῇδε ποιότητας ἔστι διαιρεῖν, τὰς μὲν
5 δι' ὀμμάτων, τὰς δὲ δι' ὤτων, τὰς δὲ δι' ἁφῆς, γεύσεως,
ὀσφρήσεως· καὶ τούτων εἴ τινες διαφοραί, ὄψεσι μὲν
χρώματα, ἀκοαῖς δὲ φωνάς, καὶ ταῖς ἄλλαις αἰσθήσεσι·
φωνὰς δέ, ᾗ ποιαί, ἡδύ, τραχύ, λεῖον. ἐπεὶ δὲ τὰς
διαφορὰς τὰς περὶ τὴν οὐσίαν ποιότησι διαιρούμεθα καὶ
10 τὰς ἐνεργείας καὶ τὰς πράξεις καλὰς ἢ αἰσχρὰς καὶ
ὅλως τοιάσδε—τὸ γὰρ ποσὸν ἢ ὀλιγάκις εἰς τὰς
διαφορὰς τὰς εἴδη ποιούσας ἢ οὐδαμοῦ—καὶ τὸ ποσὸν
δὲ ποιότησι ταῖς αὐτῶν οἰκείαις, πῶς ἄν τις καὶ τὸ
ποιὸν διέλοι κατ' εἴδη, ἀπορήσειεν ἄν τις, ποίαις
χρώμενος διαφοραῖς καὶ ἐκ ποίου γένους. ἄτοπον γὰρ
15 ἑαυτῷ καὶ ὅμοιον, ὥσπερ ἂν εἴ τις διαφορὰς οὐσίας
οὐσίας πάλιν αὖ λέγοι. τίνι οὖν τὸ λευκὸν καὶ τὸ μέλαν;
τίνι δὲ τὰ χρώματα ὅλως; ἀπὸ χυμῶν καὶ τῶν ἁπτικῶν
ποιοτήτων; εἰ δὲ τοῖς διαφόροις αἰσθητηρίοις ταῦτα,
οὐκ ἐν τοῖς ὑποκειμένοις ἡ διαφορά. ἀλλὰ τὰ κατὰ τὴν
20 αὐτὴν αἴσθησιν πῶς; εἰ δ' ὅτι τὸ μὲν συγκριτικόν, τὸ δὲ
διακριτικὸν ὀμμάτων, τὸ δὲ διακριτικὸν γλώττης καὶ
συγκριτικόν, πρῶτον μὲν ἀμφισβητεῖται καὶ περὶ
αὐτῶν τῶν παθῶν, εἰ διακρίσεις τινὲς καὶ συγκρίσεις
ταῦτα· ἔπειτα οὐκ αὐτὰ οἷς διαφέρει εἴρηκεν. εἰ δέ τις
25 λέγοι οἷς δύνανται—καὶ οὐκ ἄλογον δὲ οἷς δύνανται—

---

[1] This way of explaining the differences of sense-
perceived qualities seems to go back to the Atomists: cp.
Democritus A 120 DK. It was adopted by Plato (*Timaeus*
67E5–6) and Aristotle (*Metaphysics* I 7. 1057b8–9, *Topica*
H 3. 153a38–b1), who is criticised here.

intelligible one can divide the qualities here below by the senses, some [perceived] through the eyes, some through the ears, some through touch, taste, smell; and if there are any differentiations of these, [they are to be distinguished,] colours by sight, sounds by hearing and [others] by the other senses: sounds, in so far as they are qualified, are sweet, harsh, soft. But, since we distinguish the differentiations of substances by qualities, and activities and actions as fine or ugly and in general of some kind— for the quantitative comes into the differentiations which make species seldom or nowhere—and the quantitative by the qualities peculiar to quanta, one might be in some difficulty about how one should divide the qualitative by species, what kind of differentiations one should use and from what kind of genus one should take them. For it is absurd to divide it by its identical self, as if one said that differentiations of substances were again substances. By what then does one differentiate white and black? And by what colours in general? From tastes and tangible qualities? But if these differentiations are by different sense-organs, the distinction is not in its subjects. But how does one distinguish qualia perceived by the same sense? If it is because one concentrates and one diffuses the eyes, and one diffuses and one concentrates the tongue, first there is a dispute about the experiences themselves, whether these are diffusions and concentrations; and then Aristotle has not stated by what the experiences themselves are differentiated.[1] But if one says "by their powers"[2]—and "by their powers" is

---

[2] Aristotle *Categories* 8. 9a14–16.

ἐκεῖνο ἴσως λεκτέον, ὡς οἷς δύνανται διαιρετέον τὰ μὴ
ὁρώμενα, οἷον τὰς ἐπιστήμας· αἰσθητὰ δὲ ταῦτα ὄντα
διὰ τί ἐξ ὧν ποιεῖ; καὶ ἐν ταῖς ἐπιστήμαις δὲ διαιροῦντες
οἷς δύνανται, καὶ ὅλως ταῖς τῆς ψυχῆς δυνάμεσι
30 διαστησάμενοι ὡς ἕτεραι ἐξ ὧν ποιοῦσιν, ἔχομεν λόγῳ
διαφορὰς αὐτῶν λαμβάνειν, οὐ μόνον περὶ ἅ, ἀλλὰ καὶ
λόγους αὐτῶν ὁρῶντες. ἢ τὰς μὲν τέχνας ἕξομεν τοῖς
λόγοις αὐτῶν καὶ τοῖς θεωρήμασι, τὰς δὲ ἐπὶ σώμασι
ποιότητας πῶς; ἢ κἀκεῖ ἐπὶ τῶν λόγων τῶν διαφόρων
πῶς ἕτεροι, ζητήσειεν ἄν τις. καὶ γὰρ φαίνεται τὸ
35 λευκὸν τοῦ μέλανος διαφέρειν· ἀλλὰ τίνι, ζητοῦμεν.

18. Ἀλλὰ γὰρ ταῦτα ἅπαντα τὰ ἀπορηθέντα
δεικνύει ὡς τῶν ἄλλων δεῖ διαφορὰς ζητεῖν, αἷς
χωριοῦμεν ἀπ᾽ ἀλλήλων ἕκαστα, τῶν δὲ διαφορῶν
διαφορὰς καὶ ἀδύνατον καὶ ἄλογον· οὔτε γὰρ οὐσίας
5 οὐσιῶν οὔτε ποσοῦ ποσότητας οὔτε ποιότητας
ποιοτήτων οὔτε διαφορὰς διαφορῶν οἷόν τε. ἀλλ᾽
ἀνάγκη, οὗ ἐγχωρεῖ, τοῖς ἔξωθεν ἢ τοῖς ποιητικοῖς ἢ
τοῖς τοιούτοις· οὗ δὲ μηδὲ ταῦτα, υἷον πράσιον ὠχροῦ,
ἐπειδὴ [1] λευκοῦ καὶ μέλανος λέγουσι, τί ἄν τις εἴποι;

---

[1] Vitringa: ἐπεὶ δὲ Enn.

not unreasonable—one should perhaps reply that
invisible things are to be distinguished by their
powers, branches of knowledge for instance; but why
should these, which are perceptible, be distinguished by what they do? And when in the case of
branches of knowledge we are distinguishing them
by their powers, and in general with the powers of
soul separating them as different by what they do,
we are able to grasp their differentiations rationally,
since we see not only what they are concerned with,
but their rational forms. We shall be able to divide
the arts by their rational forms and their theories,
but how shall we divide the qualities in bodies? Now
even in that case one might enquire how the differing rational forms are different. And white certainly
does appear to differ from black: but by what, we are
still enquiring.

18. But all these points of difficulty show that one
should look for differentiations of other things, by
which we separate them from each other, but to look
for differentiations of differentiations is impossible
and irrational: for it is not possible to look for
substances of substances or quantities of quantity or
qualities of qualities or differentiations of differentiations. But it is necessary, where the circum-
stances admit, [to distinguish them] by their powers
to make or something of the sort; but where even
these are not present, as [when distinguishing] leek-
green from greenish-yellow (since they say[1] that
these belong to white and black), what is one going
to say? But the truth is that it is either sense-

---

[1] The Peripatetics: cp. Aristotle *De Sensu* 4. 442a24–25;
Categories 10. 12a18.

ἀλλὰ γάρ, ὅτι ἕτερα, ἡ αἴσθησις ἢ ὁ νοῦς ἐρεῖ, καὶ οὐ
10 δώσουσι λόγον, ἡ μὲν αἴσθησις, ὅτι μηδ' αὑτῆς ὁ λόγος,
ἀλλὰ μόνον μηνύσεις διαφόρους ποιήσασθαι, ὁ δὲ νοῦς
ἐν ταῖς αὑτοῦ ἐπιβολαῖς ἁπλαῖς καὶ οὐ λόγοις χρῆται
πανταχοῦ, ὡς λέγειν ἕκαστον τόδε τόδε, τόδε τόδε· καὶ
ἔστιν ἑτερότης ἐν ταῖς κινήσεσιν αὐτοῦ διαιροῦσα
15 θάτερον ἀπὸ θατέρου οὐχ ἑτερότητος αὐτὴ δεομένη. αἱ
τοίνυν ποιότητες πότερα διαφοραὶ πᾶσαι γένοιντο ἂν ἢ
οὔ; λευκότης μὲν γὰρ καὶ ὅλως αἱ χρόαι καὶ ⟨αἱ⟩[1] περὶ
ἀφὴν καὶ χυμοὺς γένοιντο ἂν διαφοραὶ ἑτέρων καὶ εἴδη
ὄντα, γραμματικὴ δὲ καὶ μουσικὴ πῶς; ἢ τῷ τὴν μὲν
20 γραμματικὴν ψυχήν, τὴν δὲ μουσικήν, καὶ μάλιστα, εἰ
φύσει εἶεν, ὥστε καὶ εἰδοποιοὺς διαφορὰς γίνεσθαι. καὶ
εἰ εἴη τις οὖν διαφορά, ἐκ τούτου τοῦ γένους ἢ καὶ ἐξ
ἄλλου· καὶ εἰ ἐκ ταὐτοῦ γένους, τῶν ἐκ τοῦ αὐτοῦ
γένους, οἷον ποιοτήτων ποιότητας. ἀρετὴ γὰρ καὶ
κακία ἡ μὲν γὰρ ἕξις τοιάδε, ἡ δὲ τοιάδε· ὥστε
25 ποιοτήτων οὐσῶν τῶν ἕξεων αἱ διαφοραὶ ποιότητες· εἰ
μή τις φαίη τὴν μὲν ἕξιν ἄνευ τῆς διαφορᾶς μὴ ποιότητα
εἶναι, τὴν δὲ διαφορὰν τὴν ποιότητα ποιεῖν. ἀλλ' εἰ τὸ
γλυκὺ ὠφέλιμον, βλαβερὸν δὲ τὸ πικρόν, σχέσει, οὐ
ποιότητι, διαιρεῖ. τί δ' εἰ τὸ γλυκὺ παχύ, τὸ δὲ
30 αὐστηρὸν λεπτόν; οὐ τί ἦν γλυκὺ ἴσως λέγει παχύ, ἀλλ'

---

[1] Müller, Cilento, Theiler.

---

[1] This sentence is one of the clearest statements in
Plotinus of the close resemblance between αἴσθησις and
νόησις: cp. VI. 7. 7. 29–31; he seems here to be developing the

perception or intellect which says that they are different, and they will not give a reason, sense-perception because the reason does not belong to it, but only giving different indications, but the intellect everywhere uses its own simple acts of attention, not reasons, so that it says of each thing "this is this and that is that"; and there is an otherness in its movements which distinguishes one thing from another and does not itself need an otherness.[1] Then will all qualities be differentiations or not? Whiteness, indeed, and colours in general and touch- and taste-qualities would be differentiations of other things even if they are species, but how could literature and music be? By the fact that one soul is literary and another musical, especially when they are so by nature, so that these become species-forming differentiations. And if quality, then, was a differentiation, it would be either from this genus or also from another; and if from the same genus, it would be a differentiation of what is from the same genus, qualities of qualities for instance. For virtue and vice are states, one of this kind and one of that; so that since states are qualities the differentiations are qualities; unless one were to say that the state without the differentiation was not a quality, but the differentiation made the quality. But if [one says] that the sweet is beneficial but the bitter harmful, one is distinguishing them by relation, not quality. But suppose [one says] that the sweet is dense and the sour rare? One does not perhaps mean that what the sweet is is dense, but that in which the sweetness

thought of Aristotle: cp. *Nicomachean Ethics* VI 11. 1143a35–b5.

PLOTINUS: ENNEAD VI. 3.

ᾧ ἡ γλυκύτης· καὶ ἐπὶ τοῦ αὐστηροῦ ὁ αὐτὸς λόγος.
ὥστε εἰ πανταχοῦ μὴ ποιότητος ποιότης διαφορὰ
σκεπτέον, ὥσπερ οὐδὲ οὐσίας οὐσία, οὐδὲ ποσοῦ
ποσότης. ἢ τὰ πέντε τῶν τριῶν διαφέρει δυσίν. ἢ
ὑπερέχει δυσί, "διαφέρει" δ' οὐ λέγεται· πῶς γὰρ ἂν
35 καὶ διαφέροι δυσὶν ἐν τοῖς τρισίν; ἀλλ' οὐδὲ κίνησις
κινήσεως κινήσει διαφέροι ἄν, οὐδ' ἐπὶ τῶν ἄλλων ἄν
τις εὕροι. ἐπὶ δὲ τῆς ἀρετῆς καὶ κακίας τὸ ὅλον πρὸς τὸ
ὅλον ληπτέον, καὶ οὕτως αὐτοῖς διοίσει. τὸ δὲ ἐκ ταὐτοῦ
γένους, τοῦ ποιοῦ, καὶ μὴ ἐξ ἄλλου, εἴ τις διαιροῖ τῷ τὴν
40 μὲν περὶ ἡδονάς, τὴν δὲ περὶ ὀργάς, καὶ τὴν μὲν περὶ
καρποῦ κομιδήν, καὶ οὕτω παραδέξαιτο καλῶς
ὡρίσθαι, δῆλον ὅτι ἔστι διαφορὰς εἶναι καὶ μὴ
ποιότητας.

19. Τῇ δὲ ποιότητι συντακτέον, ὥσπερ ἐδόκει, καὶ
τοὺς κατ' αὐτὰς ποιούς, καθόσον ποιότης περὶ αὐτούς,
οὐ προσποιουμένους αὐτούς, ἵνα μὴ κατηγορίαι δύο,
ἀλλ' εἰς τοῦτο ἀνιόντας ἀπ' αὐτῶν, ἀφ' οὗ λέγονται. τὸ
5 δὲ οὐ λευκόν, εἰ μὲν σημαίνει ἄλλο χρῶμα, ποιότης· εἰ
δὲ ἀπόφασις μόνον εἴη, [πραγμάτων ἢ ἐξαρίθμησις]¹
οὐδὲν ἂν εἴη, εἰ μὴ φωνὴ ἢ ὄνομα ἢ λόγος γινομένου
κατ'² αὐτοῦ πράγματος· καὶ εἰ μὲν φωνή, κίνησίς τις, εἰ
δ' ὄνομα ἢ λόγος, πρός τι, καθὸ σημαντικά. εἰ δὲ μὴ
10 μόνον πραγμάτων ἡ ἐξαρίθμησις κατὰ γένος, ἀλλὰ δεῖ
καὶ τὰ λεγόμενα καὶ τὰ σημαίνοντα, τίνος ἕκαστον

¹ del. Theiler.
² coniecimus: καὶ Enn.

236

is; and the same applies to the sour. So one must investigate whether everywhere quality is a differentiation of what is not quality, as substance is not a differentiation of substance or quantity of quantity. Now five differs from three by two. No, it exceeds by two and "difference" is not the word used: for how could it differ by "two" which is in the "three"? But neither would movement differ by movement from movement, nor would one find this in the other genera. But with vice and virtue one must compare the whole with the whole, and so one will distinguish the wholes by themselves. But as for the differentiations being derived from the same genus, the qualitative, and not from another, if one distinguished by one [virtue or vice] being concerned with pleasures, and one with tempers, and one with the acquisition of produce, and accepted that this was a good distinction, it is clear that it is possible for non-qualities also to be differentiations.

19. We should rank with quality, as it appeared, the differentiated qualia, in so far as there is quality in them, not bringing them themselves into consideration, to avoid having two categories, but going up from them, to that after which they are called qualia. But the "not-white", if it indicates another colour, is a quality; but if it was only a negation it would be nothing but a sound or a name or a definition of the thing to which it is applicable; and if it is a sound, it is a movement, but if it is a name or definition, it is relative in that these are significant. But if there is not only a counting-out of things according to their genus, but one must also count out the words and the significations, saying what genus each of them signifies, we shall say that

γένους σημαντικόν, ἐροῦμεν τὰ μὲν τίθεσθαι αὐτὰ μόνον
δηλοῦντα, τὰ δὲ ἀναιρεῖν αὐτά. καίτοι βέλτιον ἴσως τὰς
ἀποφάσεις αὐτῶν μὴ συναριθμεῖν τάς γε καταφάσεις
15 διὰ τὸ σύνθετον μὴ συναριθμοῦντας. τὰς δὲ στερήσεις
πῶς; [τὰς δὲ στερήσεις]¹ εἰ ὧν αἱ στερήσεις ποιότητες,
καὶ αὐταὶ ποιότητες, οἷον νωδὸς ἢ τυφλός. ὁ δὲ γυμνὸς
καὶ ἠμφιεσμένος οὐδέτερος ποιός, ἀλλὰ μᾶλλόν πως
ἔχων· ἐν σχέσει οὖν τῇ πρὸς ἄλλο. πάθος δὲ τὸ μὲν ἐν τῷ
πάσχειν ἔτι οὐ ποιότης, ἀλλά τις κίνησις· τὸ δὲ ἐν τῷ
20 πεπονθέναι καὶ ἔχειν μένον ἤδη τὸ πάθος ποιότης· εἰ δὲ
μὴ ἔχοι ἔτι τὸ πάθος, λέγοιτο δὲ πεπονθέναι,
κεκινῆσθαι· τοῦτο δὲ ταὐτὸν τῷ "ἦν ἐν κινήσει". δεῖ δὲ
μόνον κίνησιν νοεῖν ἀφαιροῦντα τὸν χρόνον· οὐδὲ γὰρ
οὐδὲ τὸ "νῦν" προσλαμβάνειν προσήκει. τὸ δὲ "καλῶς"
25 καὶ τὰ τοιαῦτα εἰς μίαν νόησιν τὴν τοῦ γένους ἀνακτέον.
εἰ δὲ τὸ μὲν ἐρυθριᾶν εἰς τὸ ποιὸν ἀνακτέον, τὸν δὲ
ἐρυθρὸν μηκέτι, ἐπισκεπτέον. τὸ μὲν γὰρ ἐρυθαίνεσθαι
ὀρθῶς οὐκ ἀνακτέον· πάσχει γὰρ ἢ ὅλως κινεῖται· εἰ δὲ
μηκέτι ἐρυθαίνεται, ἀλλ' ἤδη ἔστι, διὰ τί οὐ ποιός; οὐ
30 γὰρ χρόνῳ ὁ ποιός —ἢ τίνι ὁριστέον;—ἀλλὰ τῷ τοιῷδε,
καὶ ἐρυθρὸν λέγοντες ποιὸν λέγομεν· ἢ οὕτως τὰς ἕξεις

¹ del. Creuzer.

positive terms posit things by simply indicating them, but negative terms take them away. Yet perhaps it is better not to count in the negations, at any rate if we do not count in the positive terms because they are composite. But what about privations? If what they are privations of are qualities, they themselves are qualities, "toothless" or "blind" for instance. But the "naked" and the "clothed" are neither of them qualified, but rather in a particular state: in a relation, therefore, to something else. An affection, as long as being affected continues, is not a quality but a kind of movement; but when affection means having been affected and having the affection still remaining, it is a quality, but if something does not still have the affection but is said to have been affected, this means to have been moved; and this is the same as "was in movement". But one must only think of the movement, taking away the time: for it is not even proper to bring in the "now". The "well done" and such-like are to be referred to the single notion of the genus. But we must enquire whether being of a red complexion is to be referred to the qualitative, but not as well the [temporarily] red-faced man. Now turning red in the face is correctly not so referred; for there is affection or in general movement; but if someone is not any more turning red, but is red in the face already, why is he not qualified? For being qualified does not depend on time—or by what interval of time would it be defined?—but by being of such a kind, and when we say "red-faced" we say "qualified"; or otherwise we shall only call [settled] states, and not any more

239

μόνας ποιότητας ἐροῦμεν, τὰς δὲ διαθέσεις οὐκέτι. καὶ
θερμὸς τοίνυν οὐχ ὁ θερμαινόμενος, καὶ νοσῶν οὐχ ὁ
ἀγόμενος εἰς νόσον.

20. Ὁρᾶν δὲ δεῖ, εἰ μὴ πάσῃ ποιότητί ἐστί τις ἄλλη
ἐναντία· ἐπεὶ καὶ τὸ μέσον τοῖς ἄκροις δοκεῖ ἐπ' ἀρετῆς
καὶ κακίας ἐναντίον εἶναι. ἀλλ' ἐπὶ τῶν χρωμάτων τὰ
μεταξὺ οὐχ οὕτως. εἰ μὲν οὖν, ὅτι μίξεις τῶν ἄκρων τὰ
5 μεταξύ, ἔδει μὴ ἀντιδιαιρεῖν, ἀλλὰ λευκῷ καὶ μέλανι, τὰ
δ' ἄλλα συνθέσεις. ἢ τῷ μίαν τινὰ ἄλλην ἐπὶ τῶν
μεταξύ, κἂν ἐκ συνθέσεως ᾖ, θεωρεῖσθαι ἀντιτίθεμεν. ἢ
ὅτι δὲ τὰ ἐναντία οὐ μόνον διαφέρει, ἀλλὰ καὶ πλεῖστον.
ἀλλὰ κινδυνεύει τὸ πλεῖστον διαφέρειν λαμβάνεσθαι ἐν
10 τῷ θέσθαι ἤδη ταῦτα τὰ μεταξύ· ἐπεί, εἴ τις ταύτην τὴν
διάταξιν ἀφέλοι, τίνι τὸ πλεῖστον ὁριεῖ; ἢ ὅτι τὸ φαιὸν
ἐγγυτέρω τοῦ λευκοῦ μᾶλλον ἢ τὸ μέλαν· καὶ τοῦτο
παρὰ τῆς ὄψεως μηνύεται, καὶ ἐπὶ τῶν χυμῶν ὡσαύτως
⟨καὶ τῶν ἁπτῶν πικρὸν γλυκύ⟩,[1] θερμὸν ψυχρόν, τὸ
15 μηδέτερον μεταξύ· ἀλλ' ὅτι μὲν οὕτως ὑπολαμβάνειν
εἰθίσμεθα, δῆλον, τάχα δ' ἄν τις ἡμῖν οὐ συγχωροῖ
ταῦτα· τὸ δὲ λευκὸν καὶ τὸ ξανθὸν καὶ ὁτιοῦν πρὸς
ὁτιοῦν ὁμοίως πάντῃ ἕτερα ἀλλήλων εἶναι καὶ ἕτερα

[1] H–S².

240

[temporary] dispositions, qualities. And then a warm man would not be a man who is getting warm, and a sick man not a man on the way to sickness.

20. But one must see if there is not to every quality another contrary one; since in the case of virtue and vice even the mean appears to be contrary to the extremes. But in the case of colours [he[1] says that] the intermediates are not so. Perhaps therefore, because the intermediate colours are mixtures of the extremes, we ought not to make a division of them by opposition, but [only] by white and black, [regarding] the others as compositions [of white and black]. Or else we divide them by opposition because one particular colour among the intermediates is different [from the others] even if they can be seen as resulting from composition. Or because the contraries do not only differ, but differ as much as possible. But it is likely that "differing as much as possible" is only apprehended in already positing these intermediates: since if one takes away this arrangement of intermediates, by what will one define "as much as possible"? Or because grey is nearer to white than black is; and we are informed of this by sight, and it is the same with tastes and touch-sensations, bitter, sweet, hot, cold, and what is neither in between; but that this is how we are accustomed to apprehend things is clear, but perhaps someone would not concede us this, that white and yellow and any colour in relation to any other are altogether different from each other, and since

___

[1] Aristotle. Plotinus is contrasting *Nicomachean Ethics* II 5. 1106b24–28 (on virtue and vice as mean and extremes) with e.g. *Categories* 8. 10b12–18 (on colours).

ὄντα ποιὰ ἐναντία εἶναι. οὐδὲ γὰρ τῷ εἶναι μεταξὺ
αὐτῶν, ἀλλὰ τούτῳ ἡ ἐναντιότης. ὑγιείᾳ γοῦν καὶ νόσῳ
20 οὐδὲν παρεμπέπτωκε μεταξύ, καὶ ἐναντία· ἢ ὅτι τὰ
γινόμενα ἐξ ἑκατέρου πλείστην παραλλαγὴν ἔχει. καὶ
πῶς πλείστην ἔστιν εἰπεῖν μὴ οὐσῶν ἐν τοῖς μέσοις
ἐλαττόνων; οὐκ ἔστιν οὖν ἐπὶ ὑγιείας καὶ νόσου
πλεῖστον εἰπεῖν. ἄλλῳ τοίνυν τὸ ἐναντίον, οὐ τῷ
πλεῖστον, ὁριστέον. εἰ δὲ τῷ πολλῷ, εἰ μὲν τὸ πολὺ ἀντὶ
25 τοῦ πλέον πρὸς ἔλαττον, πάλιν τὰ ἄμεσα ἐκφεύξεται·
εἰ δ' ἁπλῶς πολύ, ἑκάστῃ φύσει πολὺ ἀφεστάναι
συγχωρηθέντος, μὴ τῷ πλείονι μετρεῖν τὴν ἀπόστασιν.
ἀλλ' ἐπισκεπτέον, πῶς τὸ ἐναντίον. ἆρ' οὖν τὰ μὲν
ἔχοντά τινα ὁμοιότητα—λέγω δὲ οὐ κατὰ τὸ γένος οὐδὲ
30 πάντως τῷ μεμίχθαι ἄλλαις οἷον μορφαῖς αὐτῶν—ἢ
πλείονα ἢ ἐλάττονα οὐκ ἐναντία, ἀλλ' οἷς μηδὲν ταὐτὸν
κατὰ τὸ εἶδος, ἐναντία; καὶ προσθετέον δέ· ἐν γένει τῷ
ποιῷ. ἐντεῦθεν γὰρ καὶ τὰ μὲν ἄμεσα τῶν ἐναντίων, οἷς
μηδὲν εἰς ὁμοίωσιν, οὐκ ὄντων ἄλλων τῶν οἷον
ἐπαμφοτεριζόντων καὶ ὁμοιότητα πρὸς ἄλληλα
35 ἐχόντων, τῶν δέ τινων μόνον μὴ ἐχόντων. εἰ τοῦτο, οἷς
μέν ἐστι κοινότης ἐν τοῖς χρώμασιν, οὐκ ἂν εἴη ἐναντία.

they are different qualia are contrary. For their contrariety is not due to the fact that there are intermediates, but to this being different. At any rate, no intermediate intervenes between health and sickness, and they are contraries: perhaps because the results of each have the greatest possible difference. And how is it possible to say "the greatest possible" if there are not lesser differences in the intermediates? One cannot therefore say "the greatest possible" in the case of health and sickness. So contrariety is to be determined by something else, not by the "as much as possible". But if it is determined by the "much", if "much" is said instead of "more" compared with "less", again the contraries without intermediates will get away; but if it means simply "much", when it is agreed that there is much distance between each and every thing, one cannot measure the distance by the "more". But we must investigate how there is contrariety. Is it, then, that things which have some likeness—I do not mean likeness according to genus, nor at all that which results from the mixture of something like other forms of them—either greater or lesser, are not contraries, but those are contraries which have nothing the same in their specific form? And one must add: in the genus of quality. For then also the contraries which have no intermediates [will be contrary], those which have nothing tending to likeness, as there are no others which so to speak face both ways and have a likeness to each other—but of some of them only some intermediates do not have a likeness. If this is so those among colours which have something in common will not be contraries. But there will be nothing to prevent, not

ἀλλ' οὐδὲν κωλύσει μὴ πᾶν μὲν παντί, ἄλλο δὲ ἄλλῳ
οὕτως εἶναι ἐναντίον, καὶ ἐπὶ χυμῶν ὡσαύτως. ταῦτα
μὲν οὕτω διηπορήσθω. περὶ δὲ τοῦ μᾶλλον ἐν μὲν τοῖς
40 μετέχουσιν ὅτι ἐστίν, ἐδόκει, ὑγίεια δὲ αὐτὴ καὶ
δικαιοσύνη ἠπορεῖτο. εἰ δὴ πλάτος ἔχει τούτων ἑκάστη
αὐτῶν, καὶ τὰς ἕξεις αὐτὰς δοτέον· ἐκεῖ δ' ἕκαστον τὸ
ὅλον καὶ οὐκ ἔχει τὸ μᾶλλον.

21. Περὶ δὲ κινήσεως, εἰ δεῖ γένος θέσθαι, ὧδ' ἄν τις
θεωρήσειε· πρῶτον μέν, εἰ μὴ εἰς ἄλλο γένος ἀνάγειν
προσῆκεν, ἔπειτα, εἰ μηδὲν ἄνωθεν αὐτῆς ἐν τῷ τί ἐστι
κατηγοροῖτο, εἶτα, εἰ πολλὰς διαφορὰς λαβοῦσα εἴδη
5 ποιήσει. εἰς ποῖόν τις γένος αὐτὴν ἀνάξει; οὔτε γὰρ
οὐσία οὔτε ποιότης τῶν ἐχόντων αὐτήν· οὐ μὴν οὐδ' εἰς
τὸ ποιεῖν—καὶ γὰρ ἐν τῷ πάσχειν πολλαὶ κινήσεις—
οὐδ' αὖ εἰς τὸ πάσχειν, ὅτι πολλαὶ κινήσεις ποιήσεις·
ποιήσεις δὲ καὶ πείσεις εἰς ταύτην. οὐδ' αὖ εἰς τὸ πρός
10 τι ὀρθῶς, ὅτι τινὸς ἡ κίνησις καὶ οὐκ ἐφ' αὑτῆς· οὕτω
γὰρ ἂν καὶ τὸ ποιὸν ἐν τῷ πρός τι· τινὸς γὰρ ἡ ποιότης
καὶ ἔν τινι· καὶ τὸ ποσὸν ὡσαύτως. εἰ δ' ὅτι ὄντα ἐκεῖνά
τινα, κἂν τινος ᾖ καθό ἐστι, τὸ μὲν ποιότης, τὸ δὲ
ποσότης εἴρηται, τὸν αὐτὸν τρόπον, ἐπειδή, κἂν τινος ἡ
κίνησις ᾖ, ἔστι τι πρὸ τοῦ τινος εἶναι, ὅ ἐστιν ἐφ' αὑτοῦ

every colour being contrary to every colour, but one colour to another. And the same will apply to tastes. And let that be the end of this discussion. But as for the "more" it appeared that it is in the participants, but there was a difficulty about health and justice. Certainly if each of these has the breadth for it, the permanent states themselves must be granted to have it. But there in the intelligible each is the whole and does not have a "more".

21. About movement, whether one should posit it as a genus, one might look at it in this way: first, whether it would not be appropriate to refer it to another genus, and then whether nothing higher than it could be predicated of it in its essence, and then whether by receiving many differentiations it will make species. To what genus will one refer it? For it is neither substance or quality of the things which have it; one will certainly not refer it to active doing and making—for there are certainly many movements in passivity—nor to passivity because many movements are active doings and makings; but one should rather refer activities and passivities to this [genus of movement]. Nor again could it be correctly referred to relation, because movement is movement of something and not on its own; for in this way the qualitative would be in the category of relation; for quality is quality of something and in something; and the same will apply to the quantitative. But if it is because these are something particular, even if in so far as they exist they are of something else, that one is called quality and the other quantity, in the same way, since, even if movement is movement of something, it is something before it is of something, we should grasp what it is

15 ληπτέον ἂν εἴη. ὅλως γὰρ πρός τι δεῖ τίθεσθαι οὐχ ὅ
ἐστιν, εἶτ᾽ ἄλλου ἐστίν, ἀλλ᾽ ὃ ἡ σχέσις ἀπογεννᾷ
οὐδενὸς ὄντος ἄλλου παρὰ τὴν σχέσιν καθὸ λέγεται, οἷον
τὸ διπλάσιον καθὸ λέγεται διπλάσιον ἐν τῇ πρὸς τὸ
πηχυαῖον παραβολῇ τὴν γένεσιν λαβὸν καὶ τὴν
20 ὑπόστασιν οὐδὲν νοούμενον πρὸ τούτου ἐν τῷ πρὸς
ἕτερον παραβεβλῆσθαι ἔσχε τοῦτο λέγεσθαί τε καὶ
εἶναι. τί οὖν ἐστι τοῦτο, ὃ ἑτέρου ὄν ἐστί τι, ἵνα καὶ
ἑτέρου ᾖ, ὡς τὸ ποιὸν καὶ τὸ ποσὸν καὶ ἡ οὐσία; ἢ
πρότερον, ὅτι μηδὲν πρὸ αὐτοῦ ὡς γένος κατηγορεῖται,
25 ληπτέον. ἀλλ᾽ εἰ τὴν μεταβολήν τις λέγοι πρὸ κινήσεως
εἶναι, πρῶτον μὲν ἢ ταὐτὸν λέγει ἢ γένος λέγων ἐκεῖνο
ποιήσει ἕτερον παρὰ τὰ πρόσθεν εἰρημένα· εἶτα δῆλον,
ὅτι ἐν εἴδει τὴν κίνησιν θήσεται καί τι ἕτερον ἀντιθήσει
τῇ κινήσει, τὴν γένεσιν ἴσως, μεταβολήν τινα κἀκείνην
30 λέγων, κίνησιν δὲ οὔ. διὰ τί οὖν οὐ κίνησις ἡ γένεσις; εἰ
μὲν γάρ, ὅτι μήπω ἐστὶ τὸ γινόμενον, κίνησις δὲ οὐ περὶ
τὸ μὴ ὄν, υϐϐ᾽ ἂν μεταβολὴ δηλονότι ἂν εἴη ἡ γένεσις.
εἰ δ᾽ ὅτι ἡ γένεσίς ἐστιν οὐδὲν ἄλλο ἢ ἀλλοίωσίς τις
καὶ αὔξη τῷ ἀλλοιουμένων τινῶν καὶ αὐξομένων τὴν

on its own. In general, one should posit as relative
not what first is, and then is of something else, but
what the relationship generates without there being
anything else beside the relationship in virtue of
which it gets its name, for instance the double, in so
far as it is called double, has its origin and its
existence in the comparison with the single cubits-
length, and, without anything before this entering
the mind, is called and is double in being compared
with something else. What then [in the case of
movement] is this, which, though it is of something,
is something in order to be of something, like the
qualitative and the quantitative and substance?
Now first we must understand that nothing prior to
it is predicated of it as its genus. But if someone were
to say[1] that change is prior to motion, first of all he
is either speaking of the same thing, or, if he is
calling change a genus, he will be making another
genus besides those previously mentioned; then it is
clear that he will set movement among the species
[of change] and set some other kind [of change]
against movement, perhaps coming-to-be, saying
that it also is a change, but not a movement. Why
then is not coming-to-be a movement? If it is because
what is coming into being does not yet exist, but
movement has nothing to do with the non-existent,
coming-to-be obviously could not be change either.
But if it is because coming-to-be is nothing but a
change of quality and an increase of quantity,
because coming-to-be takes place when certain
things are changed and increased, he is thinking

[1] Aristotle, *Physics* E 1. 225a34–b3; the discussion of
Aristotle continues through the rest of the chapter.

γένεσιν εἶναι, τὰ πρὸ τῆς γενέσεως λαμβάνει. δεῖ δὲ τὴν
35 γένεσιν ἐν τούτοις ἕτερόν τι εἶδος λαβεῖν. οὐ γὰρ ἐν τῷ
ἀλλοιοῦσθαι παθητικῶς τὸ γίνεσθαι καὶ ἡ γένεσις,
οἷον θερμαίνεσθαι ἢ λευκαίνεσθαι—ἔστι γὰρ τούτων
γενομένων μήπω τὴν ἁπλῶς γένεσιν γεγενῆσθαι, ἀλλά
τι γίνεσθαι, αὐτὸ τοῦτο τὸ ἠλλοιῶσθαι—ἀλλ' ὅταν
40 ⟨εἶδός τι λαμβάνῃ⟩[1] ζῷον ἢ φυτόν [ὅταν εἶδός τι
λαμβάνῃ].[1] εἴποι δ' ἄν τις τὴν μεταβολὴν μᾶλλον
ἁρμόττειν ἐν εἴδει τίθεσθαι ἢ τὴν κίνησιν, ὅτι τὸ μὲν τῆς
μεταβολῆς ἄλλο ἀνθ' ἑτέρου ἐθέλει σημαίνειν, τὸ δὲ τῆς
κινήσεως ἔχει καὶ τὴν οὐκ ἐκ τοῦ οἰκείου μετάστασιν,
ὥσπερ ἡ τοπικὴ κίνησις. εἰ δὲ μὴ τοῦτο βούλεταί τις,
45 ἀλλ' ἡ μάθησις καὶ ἡ κιθάρισις, ἢ ὅλως ἡ ἀφ' ἕξεως
κίνησις. ὥστε εἶδός τι ἂν εἴη κινήσεως μᾶλλον ἢ
ἀλλοίωσις ἐκστατική τις οὖσα κίνησις.

22. Ἀλλ' ἔστω ταὐτὸν νοούμενον τὸ τῆς
ἀλλοιώσεως κατὰ τὸ παρακολουθεῖν τῇ κινήσει τὸ
ἄλλο. τί οὖν δεῖ λέγειν τὴν κίνησιν; ἔστω δὴ ἡ κίνησις,
ὡς τύπῳ εἰπεῖν, ἡ ἐκ δυνάμεως ὁδὸς εἰς ἐκεῖνο, ὃ
5 λέγεται δύνασθαι. ὄντος γὰρ τοῦ ⟨μὲν⟩[2] δυνάμει [τοῦ
μέν],[2] ὅτι ἥκοι ἂν εἰς εἶδός τι, οἷον δυνάμει ἀνδριάς, τοῦ
δέ, ὅτι ἥκοι ἂν εἰς ἐνέργειαν, οἷον τὸ βαδιστικόν, ὅταν
τὸ μέν προΐῃ[3] εἰς ἀνδριάντα, ἡ πρόοδος κίνησις, τὸ δ' ἐν
τῷ βαδίζειν ᾖ, τὸ βαδίζειν αὐτὸ κίνησις· καὶ ὄρχησις
ἐπὶ τοῦ δυναμένου ὀρχεῖσθαι, ὅταν ὀρχῆται. καὶ ἐπὶ μέν

[1] Theiler.
[2] H–S².
[3] Kirchhoff (procedit Ficinus): προσίῃ Enn.

about what is prior to coming-to-be. But one must consider coming-to-be in these things here to be a different species. For having come to be and becoming do not consist in being passively changed, like being heated or whitened—for it is possible when these changes occur that coming-to-be in the absolute sense has not yet occurred, but only coming to be something, that is, this very change we are talking about—but when an animal or a plant acquires a specific form. But someone might say that it is more appropriate to make change a species than movement, because change intends to signify one thing instead of another, but the range of meaning of movement includes transition which does not take a thing out of its proper nature, such as local movement. But if this is not what one intends, it must be learning and playing the lyre, or in general movement which comes from a state. So change would be rather a species of movement, being a movement which takes a thing out of itself.

22. But let us grant that the idea of change is the same [as that of movement] in that "different" is a consequence of movement. What, then, are we to say that movement is? Let us grant that movement, to describe it sketchily, is the passage from potentiality to that which it is said to be the potentiality of. For one thing is potential because it can arrive at a particular form, potentially a statue for instance, and another because it can arrive at an activity, the activity of walking for instance, and when one progresses to a statue, its progress is movement, and when the other is engaged in walking, the walking itself is movement; and, with someone who is a potential dancer, his dancing whenever he dances is

PLOTINUS: ENNEAD VI. 3.

10 τινι κινήσει τῇ εἰς ἀνδριάντα εἶδος ἄλλο ἐπιγίγνεται, ὃ
εἰργάσατο ἡ κίνησις, τὸ δὲ ὡς ἁπλοῦν εἶδος ὂν τῆς
δυνάμεως, ἡ ὄρχησις, οὐδὲν ἔχει μετ᾽ αὐτὴν παυσαμένης
τῆς κινήσεως. ὥστε, εἴ τις λέγοι τὴν κίνησιν εἶδος
ἐγρηγορὸς ἀντίθετον τοῖς ἄλλοις εἴδεσι τοῖς ἑστηκόσιν,
15 ᾗ τὰ μὲν μένει, τὸ¹ δὲ οὔ, καὶ αἴτιον τοῖς ἄλλοις εἴδεσιν,
ὅταν μετ᾽ αὐτήν τι γίνηται, οὐκ ἂν ἄτοπος εἴη. εἰ δὲ καὶ
ζωήν τις λέγοι σωμάτων ταύτην, περὶ ἧς ὁ λόγος νῦν,
τήν γε κίνησιν ταύτην ὁμώνυμον δεῖ λέγειν ταῖς νοῦ καὶ
ψυχῆς κινήσεσιν. ὅτι δὲ γένος ἐστίν, οὐχ ἧττον ἄν τις
20 καὶ ἐκ τοῦ μὴ ῥάδιον εἶναι ὁρισμῷ ἢ καὶ ἀδύνατον εἶναι
λαβεῖν πιστώσαιτο. ἀλλὰ πῶς εἶδός τι, ὅταν πρὸς τὸ
χεῖρον ἡ κίνησις ἢ ὅλως παθητικὴ ἡ κίνησις; ἢ ὅμοιον,
ὥσπερ ἂν ἡ θέρμανσις τὰ μὲν αὔξῃ ἡ παρὰ τοῦ ἡλίου, τὰ
δ᾽ εἰς τοὐναντίον ἄγῃ, καὶ ᾗ κοινόν τι ἡ κίνησις καὶ ἡ
25 αὐτὴ ἐπ᾽ ἀμφοῖν, τοῖς δὲ ὑποκειμένοις τὴν διαφορὰν τὴν
δοκοῦσαν ἔχῃ. ὑγίανσις οὖν καὶ νόσανσις ταὐτόν; ἢ
καθόσον μὲν κίνησις ταὐτόν· τίνι δὲ διοίσει; πότερα τοῖς
ὑποκειμένοις ἢ καὶ ἄλλῳ; ἀλλὰ τοῦτο ὕστερον, ὅταν
περὶ ἀλλοιώσεως ἐπισκοπῶμεν. νῦν δὲ τί ταὐτὸν ἐν
30 πάσῃ κινήσει σκεπτέον· οὕτω γὰρ ἂν καὶ γένος εἴη. ἢ
πολλαχῶς ἂν λέγοιτο καὶ οὕτως ἔσται, ὥσπερ ἂν εἰ τὸ
ὄν. πρὸς δὲ τὴν ἀπορίαν, ὅτι ἴσως δεῖ, ὅσαι μὲν εἰς τὸ
κατὰ φύσιν ἄγουσιν ἢ ἐνεργοῦσιν ἐν τοῖς κατὰ φύσιν,
ταύτας μὲν οἷον εἴδη εἶναι, ὡς εἴρηται, τὰς δὲ εἰς τὰ
παρὰ φύσιν ἀγωγὰς ἀνάλογον τίθεσθαι τοῖς ἐφ᾽ ἃ

¹ Harder, Theiler: τὰ Enn.

movement. And in one kind of movement, that to the statue, another form is acquired which the movement has made, but the other kind, dancing, as being a simple form of the potentiality, has nothing after it when the movement has stopped. So that it would not be inappropriate if one were to say that movement is a form awake, opposed to the other forms which are static, in that they abide but it does not, and is a cause to other forms, when something comes to be after it. But if someone were to say that this movement which we are now discussing is the life of bodies, one must give it the same name as the movements of Intellect and Soul. But one could be confident that movement is a genus no less because it is difficult, or even impossible, to comprehend it in a definition. But how can it be a form, in cases when the movement is to the worse, or in general passive? It is like when heating, the heating from the sun, makes some things grow and takes others the opposite way, and it is the same for both, but the apparent difference is in the subjects. Is it the same as becoming healthy or sick? Yes, in so far as they are movements it is the same; but in what will the difference lie? Will it be in the subjects, or in something else? But we will discuss this later, when we consider change. But now we must investigate what is the same in all movement: for in this way it could be a genus. Or perhaps it might be used in many senses, and be a genus in the way that being is. And [we must investigate] as well the difficulty that perhaps all the movements which lead to what is according to nature or are active in what is according to nature must be like species-forms, as has been said, but those which lead to what is against nature

35 ἄγουσιν. ἀλλὰ τί τὸ κοινὸν ἐπί τε ἀλλοιώσεως καὶ
αὐξήσεως καὶ γενέσεως καὶ τῶν ἐναντίων τούτοις ἐπί[1]
τε τῆς κατὰ τόπον μεταβολῆς, καθὸ κινήσεις αὗται
πᾶσαι; ἢ τὸ μὴ ἐν τῷ αὐτῷ ἕκαστον, ἐν ᾧ πρότερον ἦν,
εἶναι μηδ' ἠρεμεῖν μηδ' ἐν ἡσυχίᾳ παντελεῖ, ἀλλά,
40 καθόσον κίνησις πάρεστιν, ἀεὶ πρὸς ἄλλο τὴν ἀγωγὴν
ἔχειν, καὶ τὸ ἕτερον οὐκ ἐν τῷ αὐτῷ μένειν· ἀπόλλυσθαι
γὰρ τὴν κίνησιν, ὅταν μὴ ἄλλο· διὸ καὶ ἑτερότης οὐκ ἐν
τῷ γεγονέναι καὶ μεῖναι ἐν τῷ ἑτέρῳ, ἀλλ' ἀεὶ ἑτερότης.
ὅθεν καὶ ὁ χρόνος ἕτερον ἀεί, διότι κίνησις αὐτὸν ποιεῖ·
45 μεμετρημένη γὰρ κίνησις οὐ μένουσα· συνθεῖ οὖν αὐτῇ
ὡς ἐπὶ φερομένης ὀχούμενος. κοινὸν δὲ πᾶσι τὸ ἐκ
δυνάμεως καὶ τοῦ δυνατοῦ εἰς ἐνέργειαν πρόοδον καὶ
ἀγωγὴν εἶναι· πᾶν γὰρ τὸ κινούμενον καθ' ὁποιανοῦν
κίνησιν, προϋπάρχον δυνάμενον τοῦτο ποιεῖν ἢ πάσχειν,
ἐν τῷ κινεῖσθαι γίγνεται.

23. Καὶ ἔστιν ἡ κίνησις ἡ περὶ τὰ αἰσθητὰ παρ'
ἄλλου ἐνιεμένη σείουσα καὶ ἐλαύνουσα καὶ ἐγείρουσα
καὶ ὠθοῦσα τὰ μεταλαβόντα αὐτῆς, ὥστε μὴ εὕδειν
μηδ' ἐν ταὐτότητι εἶναι, ἵνα δὴ τῇ μὴ ἡσυχίᾳ καὶ οἷον
5 πολυπραγμονήσει ταύτῃ εἰδώλῳ συνέχηται ζωῆς. δεῖ
δὲ οὐ τὰ κινούμενα τὴν κίνησιν εἶναι νομίζειν· οὐ γὰρ οἱ
πόδες ἡ βάδισις, ἀλλ' ἡ περὶ τοὺς πόδας ἐνέργεια ἐκ
δυνάμεως. ἀοράτου δὲ τῆς δυνάμεως ὑπαρχούσης τοὺς

---

[1] Igal, H–S²: ἔτι Enn.

---

[1] In spite of the sharp contrast implied between the
sense-world and the intelligible world, the function of
κίνησις here below is described here in terms remarkably
like those in which the functions of ἑτερότης and κίνησις in
the intelligible world are described in VI. 7. 13. 11–16. And
for Plotinus the function of movement and time in this
world here below is positive. Such substantial existence

must be considered in the same way as what they lead to. But what is the common element in change of quality and quantity and coming-to-be and the opposites of these, and in change of place, in so far as these are all movements? It is that each thing is not in the same in which it formerly was, and is not at rest or in total quiet, but, in so far as movement is present, is always being led away to something else and its being other is not abiding in the same; for movement perishes when there is no other; for this reason otherness is not in the having come to be in and remaining in another [state], but perpetual otherness. So time is always another, because motion makes time; for it is measured movement which does not stay still; for it runs along with movement, as if riding on it as it goes. But common to all is being a progress and a leading from potentiality and the possible to active actuality; for everything that is moved according to any kind of movement has the pre-existing potentiality to do this when it comes into motion.

23. And the movement which is in sense-objects comes in from another and shakes and drives and wakes and pushes the things which have a share in it, so that they do not sleep and are not in sameness, in order that they may be held together by this inquietude and this sort of fussiness which is an image of life.[1] But one must not think that the things which are being moved are movement: for walking is not the feet but the activity in the feet which comes from their potentiality. But since the potentiality is

and coherence as the things here below have depend here on their being in motion and in III. 7.4. 19–29 on their being in time.

ἐνεργοῦντας πόδας ὁρᾶν μόνον ἀνάγκη, οὐ πόδας ἁπλῶς,
10 ὥσπερ ἂν εἰ ἡσύχαζον, ἀλλ᾽ ἤδη μετ᾽ ἄλλου, ἀοράτου
μὲν τούτου, ὅτι δὲ μετ᾽ ἄλλου, κατὰ συμβεβηκὸς
ὁρωμένου τῷ τοὺς πόδας ὁρᾶν ἄλλον τόπον ἔχοντας καὶ
ἄλλον καὶ μὴ ἠρεμεῖν· τὸ δ᾽ ἀλλοιοῦσθαι¹ παρὰ τοῦ
ἀλλοιουμένου, ὅτι μὴ ἡ αὐτὴ ποιότης. ἐν τίνι οὖν ἡ
κίνησις, ὅταν ἄλλο κινῇ, καὶ ὅταν δὲ ἐκ τῆς ἐνούσης
15 δυνάμεως εἰς ἐνέργειαν ἴῃ; ἆρα ἐν τῷ κινοῦντι; καὶ πῶς
τὸ κινούμενον καὶ πάσχον μεταλήψεται; ἀλλ᾽ ἐν τῷ
κινουμένῳ; διὰ τί οὖν ἐλθοῦσα οὐ μένει; ἢ δεῖ μήτε τοῦ
ποιοῦντος ἀπηλλάχθαι μήτε ἐν αὐτῷ εἶναι, ἀλλ᾽ ἐξ
αὐτοῦ μὲν καὶ εἰς ἐκεῖνο, οὐκ ἐν ἐκείνῳ δὲ ἀπο-
20 τετμημένην εἶναι, ἀλλ᾽ ἀπ᾽ ἐκείνου εἰς ἐκεῖνο, οἷον
πνοὴν εἰς ἄλλο. ὅταν μὲν οὖν ἡ δύναμις τοῦ κινεῖν
βαδιστικὴ ᾖ, οἷον ὦσε καὶ πεποίηκεν ἄλλον ἀλλάττειν
ἀεὶ τόπον, ὅταν δὲ θερμαντική, ἐθέρμανε· καὶ ὅταν ἡ
δύναμις ὕλην λαβοῦσα εἰς φύσιν οἰκοδομῇ, αὔξησις,
25 ὅταν δ᾽ ἄλλη δύναμις ἀφαιρῇ, μείωσις τοῦ δυναμένου
ἀφαίρεσιν παθεῖν μειουμένου· καὶ ὅταν ἡ γεννῶσα φύσις
ἐνεργῇ, γένεσις, ὅταν δὲ αὕτη ἀδυνατῇ, ἡ δὲ φθείρειν
δυναμένη ἐπικρατῇ, φθορά, οὐχ ἡ ἐν τῷ ἤδη γεγονότι,
ἀλλ᾽ ἡ ἐν τῷ πορευομένῳ· καὶ ὑγίανσις δὲ κατὰ τὰ
αὐτά, τῆς ποιεῖν δυναμένης ὑγίειαν ἐνεργούσης καὶ
30 κρατούσης [ὑγίανσις],² τῆς δ᾽ ἐναντίας δυνάμεως

---

¹ Theiler: ἀλλοιούμενον Enn.
² del. H–S¹.

invisible, it is necessary to look only at the active feet, not simply the feet, as if they were at rest, but the feet already with something else; this is invisible, but because it is with something else, it is seen incidentally by looking at the feet occupying one place and then another and not staying still; but one sees the alteration from that which is altered, because its quality is not the same. In what, then, is the movement, when it moves something else, and indeed when it passes to actuality from an immanent potentiality? Is it in the mover? Then how will that which is moved and affected participate in it? But is it in that which is moved? Why then does it not stay when it has come? Now, it must not be separated from its producer nor in it, but from it and to that which is moved, and not be in that as cut off, but it comes from that and goes to that other, as a breath of wind goes to another. When, therefore, the potentiality of moving is a walking potentiality, it pushes, so to speak, and produces a continual change of place, but when it is a heating potentiality, it heats; and when the potentiality takes matter and builds it into a nature, it is growth, but when another potentiality takes away, it is diminution when that which has the potentiality of experiencing taking away is diminished; and when the generative nature is active, there is coming-to-be, but when this is impotent and that which has the potentiality of making things pass away is dominant, there is passing-away, not that which occurs in what has already come to be, but in that which is on the way; and becoming healthy works the same way, when that which has the potentiality of producing health is active (but the opposite potentiality produces the opposite re-

τἀναντία ποιούσης. ὥστε συμβαίνειν μὴ παρὰ τὰ ἐν οἷς
μόνον, ἀλλὰ καὶ παρὰ τὰ ἐξ ὧν καὶ δι' ὧν [καὶ τὴν τῆς
κινήσεως ἰδιότητα]¹ ποιὰν τὴν κίνησιν καὶ ⟨τὴν τῆς
κινήσεως ἰδιότητα⟩¹ τοιάνδε εἶναι ἐν τοῖς τοιούτοις.

24. Περὶ δὲ τῆς κατὰ τόπον κινήσεως, εἰ τὸ ἄνω
φέρεσθαι τῷ κάτω ἐναντίον, καὶ τὸ κύκλῳ τοῦ ἐπ'
εὐθείας διοίσει, πῶς ἡ διαφορά, οἷον τὸ ὑπὲρ κεφαλῆς
καὶ ὑπὸ πόδας ῥίπτειν; καὶ γὰρ ἡ δύναμις ἡ ὠστικὴ μία·
5 εἰ μή τις ἄλλην τὴν ἄνω ὠθοῦσαν, καὶ ἄλλην λέγοι καὶ
ἄλλως τὴν κάτω πρὸς τὴν ἄνω φοράν, καὶ μάλιστα εἰ
φυσικῶς κινοῖτο, εἰ ἡ μὲν κουφότης εἴη, ἡ δὲ βαρύτης.
ἀλλὰ κοινὸν καὶ τὸ αὐτὸ τὸ εἰς τὸν οἰκεῖον τόπον
φέρεσθαι, ὥστε ἐνταῦθα κινδυνεύειν παρὰ τὰ ἔξω τὴν
10 διαφορὰν γίνεσθαι. ἐπὶ δὲ τῆς κύκλῳ καὶ ἐπ' εὐθείας, εἰ
οἷόν περ ἐπ' εὐθείας καὶ κύκλῳ περιθρέξαιεν, πῶς ἄλλη;
ἢ παρὰ τὸ τῆς πορείας σχῆμα, εἰ μή τις μικτὴν λέγοι
τὴν κύκλῳ, ὡς οὐ παντελῶς οὖσαν κίνησιν οὐδὲ πάντη
ἐξισταμένην. ἀλλ' ἔοικεν ὅλως μία τις εἶναι ἡ τοπικὴ
τοῖς ἔξωθεν τὰς διαφορὰς λαμβάνουσα.

25. Σύγκρισις δὲ καὶ διάκρισις ἐπισκεπτέα πῶς. ἆρ'
ἕτεραι κινήσεις τῶν εἰρημένων, γενέσεως καὶ φθορᾶς,
αὔξης καὶ φθίσεως, τοπικῆς μεταβολῆς, ἀλλοιώσεως, ἢ
εἰς ταύτας αὐτὰς ἀνακτέον, ἢ τούτων τινὰς συγκρίσεις

¹ Igal, H–S².

sult). So it happens that it is not only according to the things in which it is but according to what it comes from and through which it operates that the movement is qualified and the particular character of the movement is of such and such a kind in such and such things.

24. But about local motion, if moving upwards is contrary to moving downwards, and moving in a circle differs from moving in a straight line, how are we to differentiate, for instance, throwing something over the head and under the feet? For the pushful potentiality is one; unless someone says that the push upwards is different, and the push downwards is different and works differently in comparison with the movement upwards, especially if the movement is natural, if one is levity and one is gravity. But moving to one's own place is common and the same for both, so that it is likely that here the differentiation is according to externals. But as for movement in a circle and in a straight line, if running around in a circle is the same sort [of running] as in a straight line, how is it different? It is according to the shape of the course, unless someone says that movement in a circle is mixed, because it is not entirely movement and does not altogether go out of its place. But in general it seems that local movement is one movement taking its differentiations by externals.

25. But we must investigate how it is with composition and dissolution. Are these different movements from those already mentioned, coming-to-be and passing-away, growth and diminution, change of place, and qualitative alteration, or are they to be referred to these, or are some of these to be con-

5 καὶ διακρίσεις θετέον; εἰ μὲν οὖν τοῦτ' ἔχει ἡ σύγκρισις,
πρόσοδον ἑτέρου πρὸς ἕτερον καὶ τὸ πελάζειν, καὶ αὖ
ἀποχώρησιν εἰς τοὐπίσω, τοπικὰς ἄν τις κινήσεις λέγοι
δύο κινούμενα[1] λέγων πρὸς ἕν τι, ἢ ἀποχωροῦντα ἀπ'
ἀλλήλων. εἰ δὲ σύγκρισίν[2] τινα καὶ μίξιν σημαίνουσι
10 καὶ κρᾶσιν καὶ εἰς ἕν ἐξ ἑνὸς σύστασιν τὴν κατὰ τὸ
συνίστασθαι γινομένην, οὐ κατὰ τὸ συνεστάναι ἤδη, εἰς
τίνα ἄν τις ἀνάγοι τῶν εἰρημένων ταύτας; ἄρξει μὲν γὰρ
ἡ τοπικὴ κίνησις, ἕτερον δὲ ἐπ' αὐτῇ τὸ γινόμενον ἂν
εἴη, ὥσπερ καὶ τῆς αὔξης ἄν τις εὕροι ἄρχουσαν μὲν τὴν
15 τοπικήν, ἐπιγινομένην δὲ τὴν κατὰ ⟨τὸ⟩ ποσὸν[3]
κίνησιν· οὕτω δὴ καὶ ἐνταῦθα ἡγεῖται μὲν τὸ κατὰ
τόπον κινηθῆναι, ἔπεται δὲ οὐκ ἐξ ἀνάγκης συγκριθῆναι
οὐδ' αὖ διακριθῆναι, ἀλλὰ γενομένης μὲν συμπλοκῆς
τοῖς ἀπαντήσασι συνεκρίθη, σχισθέντων δὲ τῇ συν-
20 τεύξει διεκρίθη. πολλαχοῦ δ' ἂν καὶ διακρινομένων
ἐφέποιτο ἂν ἡ τοῦ τόπου ἢ ἅμα συμβαίνοι τοῦ πάθους
ἄλλου περὶ τὰ διακρινόμενα, οὐ κατὰ τὸ κινεῖσθαι
τοπικῶς, νοουμένου, ἔν τε τῇ συγκρίσει ἄλλου πάθους
καὶ συστάσεως, ἐπακολουθοῦντος ἑτέρου τῆς τοπικῆς
κινήσεως. ἆρ' οὖν ταύτας μὲν ἐφ' ἑαυτῶν, τὴν δὲ
25 ἀλλοίωσιν εἰς ταύτας ἀνακτέον; πυκνὸν γὰρ γενόμενον
ἠλλοίωται· τοῦτο δὲ ταὐτὸν τῷ "συγκέκριται". μανὸν
δὲ αὖ ἠλλοίωται· τοῦτο δὲ ταὐτὸν τῷ "διακέκριται".
καὶ οἴνου καὶ ὕδατος μιγνυμένων ἄλλο ἢ πρότερον

[1] Kirchhoff: –μένας Enn.
[2] Sleeman, Igal, H–S[2]: –κρασίν Enn.
[3] ⟨τὸ⟩ ποσὸν Creuzer (cf. Arist. Metaph. Λ 2. 1069b11):
ποσὸν EBxUC: τόπον A: ποιὸν A[3mg]: qualitatis Ficinus.

sidered compositions and dissolutions? Well then, if composition is a matter of the approach of one thing to another and coming close, and on the other side [dissolution] of going away back, one could say that they are local movements, saying that two things are moving to one or going away from each other. But if they mean to signify a composition and a mixture, and a coming together into a unity from another unity, which occurs in the actual coming together, not as a result of having come together, to which of the movements already mentioned is one to refer these? Certainly local movement will make the beginning, but what follows upon it will be something else, as one would find that local movement makes the beginning of growth, but quantitative movement follows upon it; so here too local movement takes the lead, but being composed, or again dissolved, does not necessarily follow, but when the parts which meet become interwoven there is composition, and when they are split apart there is dissolution. But often local motion even follows on dissolution or is simultaneous with it, the way what is in process of dissolution is affected being thought of differently, and not as local motion; and in composition another affection, that is a coming together, is thought of, and something else follows, local motion. Should then these be thought of by themselves, and [qualitative] change be referred to them? For when a thing becomes dense it is changed; but this is the same as "it is composed [or compacted]"; but again when it becomes rarefied it is changed; but this is the same as "it is dissolved [or its texture is loosened]". And when wine and water are mixed something else comes into existence different from

ἦν ἑκάτερον ἐγένετο· τοῦτο δὲ σύγκρισις, ἢ πεποίηκε
30 τὴν ἀλλοίωσιν. ἢ φατέον καὶ ἐνταῦθα ἡγεῖσθαι τὰς
συγκρίσεις καὶ διακρίσεις τινῶν ἀλλοιώσεων, ἑτέρας δὲ
αὐτὰς εἶναι συγκρίσεων ἢ διακρίσεων· οὔτε γὰρ τὰς
ἄλλας ἀλλοιώσεις εἶναι τοιαύτας, οὔτε τὴν ἀραίωσιν καὶ
πύκνωσιν σύγκρισιν καὶ διάκρισιν ἢ ἐκ τούτων ὅλως
35 εἶναι· οὕτω γὰρ ἄν τις καὶ κενὸν παραδέχοιτο. ἐπὶ
δὲ μελανίας ἢ λευκότητος πῶς; εἰ δὲ ἐν τούτοις
ἀμφισβητεῖ, πρῶτον μὲν τὰς χρόας καὶ τάχα τὰς
ποιότητας ἀναιρεῖ ἢ τάς γε πλείστας, μᾶλλον δὲ
πάσας· εἰ γὰρ πᾶσαν ἀλλοίωσιν, ἣν λέγομεν κ α τ ὰ
π ο ι ό τ η τ α μ ε τ α β ο λ ή ν, σύγκρισιν καὶ διάκρισιν
40 λέγοι, τὸ γινόμενον οὐδέν ἐστιν ἢ ποιότης, ἀλλὰ ἐγγὺς
κείμενα καὶ διεστῶτα. ἔπειτα τὸ μανθάνειν καὶ τὸ
διδάσκεσθαι πῶς συγκρίσεις;

26. Ἐπισκεπτέον δὴ περὶ τούτων καὶ ἤδη ζητητέον
πάλιν αὖ τῶν κατ᾽ εἴδη λεγομένων κινήσεων οἷον ἐπὶ
τοπικῆς, εἰ μὴ τῷ ἄνω καὶ κάτω καὶ εὐθείᾳ καὶ κύκλῳ,
ὡς ἠπόρηται, ἢ ἐμψύχων καὶ ἀψύχων κινήσει—οὐ γὰρ
5 ὁμοία ἡ κίνησις τούτων—καὶ πάλιν ταύτας τῇ πεζῇ καὶ
τῷ νεῖν καὶ πτήσει. ἢ καὶ τῷ φύσει γε καὶ παρὰ φύσιν
τάχ᾽ ἄν τις διέλοι καθ᾽ ἕκαστον εἶδος· τοῦτο δὲ οὐκ
ἔξωθεν διαφορὰς κινήσεων· ἢ ποιητικαὶ τούτων αὗται,

---

[1] This is a *reductio ad absurdum*. For all ancient
philosophers except Atomists and Epicureans, the
existence of void was the ultimate physical absurdity.

what each of them was previously: and this is composition, which has produced change. Now here too we must assert that compositions and dissolutions take the lead in some changes, but these changes themselves are different from compositions and dissolutions; nor are the other changes of this kind, and rarefaction and condensation are not composition and dissolution and do not in any way result from them; for if they did one would even have to admit the existence of void.[1] But how about blackness or whiteness? But if one raises a doubt about these, first of all he abolishes colours and perhaps qualities, or at any rate most of them—but rather all of them; for if he says that all change, which we say is "alteration in quality", is composition and dissolution, the result is in no way quality but parts close set or widely spaced. Then how are learning and being taught compositions?

26. We should certainly consider these matters, and now we have to enquire again about what are described as specific kinds of movement, for instance in the case of local movement, if it is not to be distinguished by up and down and straight and circular, as the problem was stated,[2] or by the movement of living and non-living things—their movement is not alike—and again these [movements of living things] by walking and swimming and flying. Or one might distinguish movements in each species by whether they are natural or unnatural. But this would mean that the differentiations of movements do not come from outside; now the movements themselves produce these differentiations and

[2] In ch. 24, 1–11.

καὶ οὐκ ἂν ἄνευ τούτων· καὶ ἡ φύσις δὲ ἀρχὴ δοκεῖ
10 τούτων. ἢ τὰς μὲν φύσει, τὰς δὲ τέχνῃ, τὰς δὲ
προαιρέσει· φύσει μὲν αὐξήσεις, φθίσεις, τέχνῃ δὲ
οἰκοδομεῖν, ναυπηγεῖν, προαιρέσει δὲ σκοπεῖσθαι,
μανθάνειν, πολιτεύεσθαι, ὅλως λέγειν, πράττειν. περὶ
αὐξήσεως αὖ καὶ ἀλλοιώσεως καὶ γενέσεως κατὰ φύσιν
παρὰ φύσιν ἢ ὅλως τοῖς ὑποκειμένοις.

27. Περὶ δὲ στάσεως, ὃ ἀντιτέτακται κινήσει, ἢ
ἠρεμίας τί ποτε χρὴ λέγειν; πότερα καὶ αὐτὸ ἕν τι γένος
θετέον ἢ εἴς τι γένος τῶν εἰρημένων ἀνακτέον; βέλτιον
δ᾽ ἴσως στάσιν τοῖς ἐκεῖ ἀποδόντα ἠρεμίαν ἐνταῦθα
5 ζητεῖν. τὴν οὖν ἠρεμίαν ταύτην ζητητέον πρῶτον τί
ποτ᾽ ἐστί. καὶ εἰ μὲν ταὐτὸν φανείη τῇ στάσει, οὐδ᾽
ὀρθῶς ἂν ἐνταῦθα ταύτην ζητοῖ οὐδενὸς ἑστηκότος,
ἀλλὰ τοῦ φαινομένου ἑστάναι σχολαιτέρᾳ τῇ κινήσει
χρωμένου. εἰ δ᾽ ἕτερον ἠρεμίαν στάσεως λέγοιμεν τῷ
10 τὴν μὲν στάσιν περὶ τὸ ἀκίνητον παντελῶς εἶναι, τὴν δὲ
ἠρεμίαν περὶ τὸ ἑστώς, πεφυκὸς δὲ κινεῖσθαι, ὅταν μὴ
κινῆται, εἰ μὲν τὸ ἠρεμίζεσθαι λέγοι τὸ ἠρεμεῖν, κίνησιν
οὔπω παυσαμένην, ἀλλ᾽ ἐνεστῶσαν· εἰ δὲ τὴν οὐκέτι
περὶ τὸ κινούμενον οὖσαν, πρῶτον μὲν ζητητέον, εἴ τί
15 ἐστι μὴ κινούμενον ἐνταῦθα. εἰ δὲ μὴ πάσας οἷόν τέ τι
τὰς κινήσεις κινεῖσθαι, ἀλλὰ δεῖ κινήσεις τινὰς μὴ

could not be without them, and nature appears to be the principle of them. Or [one might distinguish movements] as some natural, some artificial, and some deliberate. Natural would be growths and diminutions, artificial building houses and ships, deliberate inspecting, learning, engaging in politics, and in general speaking and acting. And with growth and change and coming-to-be [one can distinguish] by natural and unnatural or in general by the subjects.

27. But what should one say about rest, the genus which is opposed to motion, or stillness? Should it be posited as itself one genus, or referred to some genus of those already mentioned? But perhaps it would be better to allot rest to the intelligibles there, and to look for stillness here below. We must, therefore, first enquire what this stillness is. And if it should appear that it is the same as rest, it would not be correct to look for it here below, where nothing stands still, but that which seems to stand still is in more leisurely movement. But if we are going to say that stillness is something different from rest, because it applies to what is absolutely unmoved, but rest to what has come to a standstill, but is naturally in movement, when it is not moving, then if one is going to say that being still is becoming still, [one is saying] that it is motion which has not yet come to a stop, but is pausing; but if [one means] that it is a stillness which does not apply to what is in movement, one must enquire first if there is anything here below which is not in movement. But if it is not possible to move with all the movements, but there must be some ways in which there is no movement if it is to be possible to say that what is

κινεῖσθαι, ἵνα καὶ ἐξῇ λέγειν τόδε τὸ κινούμενον εἶναι, τί
ἄλλο χρὴ λέγειν τὸ μὴ κινούμενον κατὰ τόπον, ἀλλ'
ἠρεμοῦν ταύτην τὴν κίνησιν, ἢ ὅτι μὴ κινεῖται;
ἀπόφασις ἄρα ἔσται ἡ ἠρεμία τοῦ κινεῖσθαι· τοῦτο δὲ
20 οὐκ ἐν γένει. ἠρεμεῖ δὲ οὐκ ἄλλο τι ἢ ταύτην τὴν
κίνησιν, οἷον τὴν τοπικήν· τὴν οὖν ἀφαίρεσιν τούτου
λέγει. εἰ δέ τις λέγοι· διὰ τί δ' οὐ τὴν κίνησιν ἀπόφασιν
τῆς στάσεως φήσομεν; ὅτι, φήσομεν, ἥκει τι φέρουσα ἡ
κίνησις καὶ ἔστιν ἄλλο τι ἐνεργοῦν καὶ οἷον ὠθοῦν τὸ
25 ὑποκείμενον καὶ μυρία ἐργαζόμενον αὐτὸ καὶ φθεῖρον, ἡ
δὲ ἠρεμία ἑκάστου οὐδέν ἐστι παρ' αὐτό, ἀλλὰ σημαίνει
μόνον, ὅτι κίνησιν οὐκ ἔχει. τί οὖν οὐ καὶ ἐπὶ τῶν
νοητῶν στάσιν εἴπομεν ἀπόφασιν κινήσεως; ἢ ὅτι οὐδ'
ἔστιν εἰπεῖν ἀναίρεσιν τῆς κινήσεως τὴν στάσιν, ὅτι οὐ
30 παυσαμένης τῆς κινήσεώς ἐστιν, ἀλλ' οὔσης ἐκείνης καὶ
αὕτη ἐστί. καὶ οὐ πεφυκὸς κινεῖσθαι, καθόσον μὴ
κινεῖται, ἡ στάσις ἐκεῖ, ἀλλά, καθὸ στάσις κατείληφεν,
ἔστηκε, καθὸ δέ ἐστι κινούμενον, ἀεὶ κινήσεται· διὸ καὶ
στάσει ἔστηκε καὶ κινήσει κινεῖται. ἐνταῦθα δὲ κινήσει
35 μὲν κινεῖται, ἀπούσης δὲ ἠρεμεῖ ἐστερημένον τῆς
ὀφειλομένης κινήσεως. ἔπειτα δὲ ὁρᾶν δεῖ, τί ἐστιν ἡ
στάσις αὕτη, καὶ οὕτως· ὅταν ἐκ νόσου εἰς ὑγίειαν ἴῃ,
ὑγιάζεται· τί οὖν τῇ ὑγιάνσει ταύτῃ ἠρεμίας εἶδος
ἀντιτάξομεν; εἰ μὲν γὰρ τὸ ἐξ οὗ, νόσος, ἀλλ' οὐ στάσις·
264

moving is this particular thing, what else should one say about that which is not in local movement but is still as regards this movement, except that it is not moving? So stillness will be a negation of movement; and that means, not among the genera. But a thing is still only in regard to this movement, local movement for instance: stillness therefore means only the taking away of this. But if someone were to say "Why are we not going to maintain that movement is a negation of rest?" we shall reply that movement comes bringing something with it, and is something else active and in a way pushing what is subjected to it and doing innumerable things to it and destroying it; but the stillness of each thing is nothing besides the thing, but only indicates that it does not have movement. Why then do we not say that rest is the negation of movement also among the intelligibles? This is because it is impossible to say that rest is the abolition of movement because it does not exist when movement has stopped, but when movement exists rest also exists. And rest there in the intelligible does not consist in the fact that something which is naturally adapted to move is not moving, but in so far as rest has a hold on it, it stands still, but in so far as it is in motion it will always be moving: therefore it stands still by rest and moves by movement. But here below it moves by movement, but when movement is not there it stays still because it is deprived of the movement which it ought to have. Further, we ought to see what this rest here below is in the following way: when one goes from sickness to health, one is becoming healthy; so what form of standstill shall we oppose to this process of becoming healthy? For if it is that from which it

40 εἰ δὲ τὸ εἰς ὅ, ὑγίεια· ὃ οὐ ταὐτὸν τῇ στάσει. εἰ δέ τις
λέγοι τὴν ὑγίειαν ἢ τὴν νόσον τινὰ στάσιν εἶναι, εἴδη
στάσεως τὴν ὑγίειαν καὶ τὴν νόσον εἶναι φήσει· ὅπερ
ἄτοπον. εἰ δὲ συμβεβηκέναι τῇ ὑγιείᾳ τὴν στάσιν, πρὸ
τῆς στάσεως ἡ ὑγίεια οὐχ ὑγίεια ἔσται; ἀλλὰ περὶ μὲν
τούτων, ὅπῃ δοκεῖ ἑκάστῳ.

28. Εἴρηται δ' ὅτι τὸ ποιεῖν καὶ τὸ πάσχειν κινήσεις
λεκτέον, καὶ ἔστι τὰς μὲν τῶν κινήσεων ἀπολύτους, τὰς
δὲ ποιήσεις, τὰς δὲ πείσεις λέγειν. καὶ περὶ τῶν ἄλλων
γενῶν λεγομένων, ὅτι εἰς ταῦτα. καὶ περὶ τοῦ πρός τι,
5 ὅτι ἄλλου πρὸς ἄλλο σχέσις, καὶ ὅτι σύνεισιν ἄμφω καὶ
ἅμα· καὶ τὸ πρός τι δέ, ὅταν σχέσις οὐσίας ποιῇ αὐτό,
οὐχ ᾗ οὐσία ἔσται πρός τι, ἀλλὰ ᾗ καθὸ μέρος τινός—
οἷον χεὶρ ἢ κεφαλὴ—ἢ αἴτιον ἢ ἀρχὴ ἢ στοιχεῖον. ἔστι
δὲ καὶ τὰ πρός τι διαιρεῖν, ὥσπερ διῄρηται τοῖς
10 ἀρχαίοις, τὰ μὲν ὡς ποιητικά, τὰ δὲ ὡς μέτρα, τὰ δ' ἐν
ὑπεροχῇ καὶ ἐλλείψει, τὰ δ' ὅλως χωρίζοντα ὁμοιότησι
καὶ διαφοραῖς. καὶ περὶ μὲν τούτων τῶν γενῶν ταῦτα.

starts, this is sickness, not rest; but if it is that to which it is directed, this is health; and this is not the same as rest. But if someone is going to say that health or sickness is a particular kind of rest, he will be asserting that health and sickness are species of rest: which is absurd. But if rest is incidental to health, will health before rest not be health? But everyone may think as he likes about these questions.

28. It has been said that active doing and making and passive experience are to be called movements, and one can say that some movements are absolute, some actions, and some experiences. And it has been said about the other so-called genera that they are to be referred to these. And about relation, that it is a disposition of one thing in relation to another, and that they enter into it both together and simultaneously; and there is relation when a disposition of a substance produces it; the substance will not be relative as substance, except in so far as it is a part of something—hand or head for instance—or a cause or a principle or an element. It is also possible to divide relation, as the ancients divided it,[1] distinguishing some relations as productive, some as measures, some consisting in excess and deficiency, some in general separating things by likenesses and differences. And so much for these genera.

---

[1] Plotinus seems to have Aristotle *Metaphysics* Δ 15. 1020b26–31 in mind.

ENNEAD VI. 4–5

VI. 4–5. ON THE PRESENCE OF BEING, ONE AND THE SAME, EVERYWHERE AS A WHOLE

Introductory Note

THIS work, the first written by Plotinus after Porphyry joined him (*Life* ch. 5), was divided by Porphyry into two *Ennead* treatises (22 and 23 in the chronological order) at a point where Plotinus himself makes a break and a new start. In VI. 4 the discussion of the omnipresence of real being starts from man's experience of being soul in body. In VI. 5 it starts again from man's common awareness of the presence of God. There is, perhaps, no work in the *Enneads* which it is more necessary to understand if we are really to grasp Plotinus' thought, and all Neoplatonically influenced thought about the nature and presence of spiritual being, in all its depth and breadth. Its influence, direct and indirect, has been very great. Plotinus explains in it, more fully and forcibly than elsewhere, what it means to be incorporeal and how an incorporeal divine being which is fullness of life and thought and power must be present immediately and as a whole in and to everyone and everything here below, at every point in space-time diffusion and dispersion. Because of his concentration on this main theme Plotinus does not make much in this work of the distinctions between the divine hypostases, Soul, Intellect and the One or Good. The boundary between Soul and Intellect is often not very well-defined in the *Enneads*, but it is unusual for so little stress to be laid on the transcendence of the One or Good. The transcendent Good is, however, by no means absent from the work, as a careful reading together of 4, ch. 11 and 5, chs. 1 and 4 will show.

THE PRESENCE OF BEING EVERYWHERE

The unity of the divine, the immediate presence of the higher in the lower, the unbroken continuity of the divine life from its source to its last diffusion (cp. V 2 [11] 2, 24–29) were always essential parts of the thought of Plotinus. This was the side of his thought which Porphyry developed. Iamblichus and his successors, though still maintaining the continuity of divine life and the presence of the higher in the lower, were more inclined to sharpen and harden distinctions and transcendence.

The stress on the unity and omnipresence of spiritual being leads to strong statements of a doctrine which Plotinus always maintains, that of the unity of all souls (especially 4, chs. 4 and 14). It also leads to a powerful critique of emanation-images (4, ch. 7, prepared for by the critique of the common idea of "presence by powers" in ch. 3), which makes it clear that for Plotinus emanation was an inadequate, though necessary, metaphor. The immediacy of the presence of the spiritual or intelligible to the world of sense, and the total dependence of the latter on this presence for such quasi-reality as it has, are well brought out by the important distinction made in 4, ch. 10 between natural images, shadows or reflections, and artificial images, statues or pictures.

The ultimate object of the work, as so often with Plotinus, is not just to solve problems or expound a doctrine but to move its readers to seek liberation or salvation; and in some chapters as powerful as anything in the *Enneads* (4, 14–15; 5, 12) he shows what liberation and salvation means for him: deliverance from the limitations of our petty, empirical ego, the "other man" who has added himself to us, and return to that unity in diversity of the divine All which, at the deepest level, we always are.

THE PRESENCE OF BEING EVERYWHERE

Synopsis

VI. 4

The omnipresence of soul: because it is not a body it is present as a whole everywhere in body (ch. 1). The really existent, intelligible universe is not in anything else, but in itself; its image, the sensible universe, is in the intelligible (ch. 2). Is the intelligible universe only present by its powers? No, where its powers are, it is itself immediately present as a whole, though not in place (ch. 3). The many beings, intellects and souls of which Plato speaks are all one together in the unity of Intellect-Being or of Soul (ch. 4). The greatness of Being is not a matter of material bulk (ch. 5). How many bodies come to and share in the one soul (ch. 6). The unity of immaterial power; critique of emanation-imagery (ch. 7). The participation of the sensible in the intelligible involves no division of the intelligible: it is present to each and every participant as a whole (chs. 8–10). The sense-world is a natural, not an artificial, image of the intelligible (chs. 9–10). Participation according to the capacity of the participant (ch. 11). The one sound or sight and the many hearers or seers; soul does not "come" to body, but body to soul (ch. 12). The extended participates in the unextended (ch. 13). The unity-in-diversity of Intellect and Soul: but who are we? The "other man" who came and attached himself to our true original self, which was and is in the intelligible unity-in-diversity (ch. 14). What approaches is living body, already with a share in soul; our higher and lower self like the Senate and the mob (ch. 15). The "descent" of soul as self-limitation and particularisation; its liberation is return to the whole and separation from its image (ch. 16).

THE PRESENCE OF BEING EVERYWHERE

VI. 5

The common opinion of all men about the One God within us is the firmest of all starting-points. We are one in Being and find our good in it (ch. 1). We must reason about unity and being from appropriate principles (ch. 2). Real Being cannot depart from itself but is present everywhere as a whole (ch. 3). The One God is totally omnipresent: the transcendent One and the One-Being (ch. 4). The image of the centre of the circle and the radii (ch. 5). Unity in multiplicity in the intelligible and sensible worlds (ch. 6). We are all one in the intelligible; many faces, one head (ch. 7). The unity of the one Form in the many particulars (ch. 8). The unity of the sense-world is given it by one unbounded life and soul, present to all the multiplicity as a whole without being possessed by it (ch. 9). The unity which all things desire and on which all things depend, and which gives itself as a whole to each and every thing (ch. 10). The One-Being is present as living power, without extension or size, according to the capacity of the recipients (ch. 11). How to attend to the All and become the All by liberation from the unreal addition of particularity. The One God who is everywhere, to whom all things turn (ch. 12).

1. Ἀρά γε ἡ ψυχὴ πανταχοῦ τῷ παντὶ πάρεστιν, ὅτι
σῶμά ἐστι τοῦ παντὸς τοσόνδε, περὶ τὰ σώματα φύσιν
ἔχουσα μερίζεσθαι; ἢ καὶ παρ' αὑτῆς πανταχοῦ ἐστιν,
οὐχ οὗπερ ἂν ὑπὸ σώματος προαχθῇ, ἀλλὰ σώματος
5 εὑρίσκοντος αὐτὴν πρὸ αὑτοῦ πανταχοῦ οὖσαν, ὥστε,
ὅπου ἂν τεθῇ, ἐκεῖ εὑρίσκειν ψυχὴν οὖσαν πρὶν αὐτὸ
τεθῆναι ἐν μέρει τοῦ παντός, καὶ τὸ ὅλον τοῦ παντὸς
σῶμα τεθῆναι ἐν ψυχῇ οὔσῃ; ἀλλ' εἰ ἔστιν εἰς τοσοῦτον
πρὶν τὸ τοσόνδε σῶμα ἐλθεῖν πληροῦσα τὸ διάστημα
10 πᾶν, πῶς οὐ μέγεθος ἕξει; ἢ τίς τρόπος ἂν εἴη τοῦ εἶναι
ἐν τῷ παντὶ πρὶν τὸ πᾶν γενέσθαι τοῦ παντὸς οὐκ
ὄντος; τό τε ἀμερῆ λεγομένην καὶ ἀμεγέθη εἶναι
πανταχοῦ εἶναι μέγεθος οὐκ ἔχουσαν πῶς ἄν τις
παραδέξαιτο; καὶ εἰ τῷ σώματι λέγοιτο συνεκτείνεσθαι
15 μὴ σῶμα οὖσα, οὐδ' ὡς ἐκφεύγειν ποιεῖ τὴν ἀπορίαν τῷ
κατὰ συμβεβηκὸς τὸ μέγεθος αὐτῇ διδόναι. ὁμοίως γὰρ
ἄν τις καὶ ἐνταῦθα ζητήσειεν εὐλόγως, ὅπως κατὰ
συμβεβηκὸς μεγεθύνεται. οὐ γὰρ δή, ὥσπερ ἡ ποιότης,

VI. 4. ON THE PRESENCE OF BEING, ONE AND THE SAME, EVERYWHERE AS A WHOLE I

1. Is the soul everywhere present to the All because the body of the All is of a certain size and it is naturally divisible in the sphere of bodies[1]? Or is it everywhere on its own, not wherever it may be brought out to by body, but since body finds it existing everywhere before itself, so that wherever a body is placed it finds soul there before it itself is placed in a part of the All, and the whole body of the All is placed in soul already existing? But if it is extended so far, before a body of corresponding size comes, as to fill the whole space, how will it not have size? Or in what way could it be in the All before the All came to be when the All did not exist? How could anyone accept that soul which is said to be something without parts and without size is everywhere when it has no size? And if it was said to be spread out with body though it is not a body, one would not in this way either escape the difficulty by giving it size incidentally. For just the same here too one could reasonably enquire how it acquires size incidentally. For soul is certainly not in the whole body

---

[1] The text of Plato on which this question is based is one of the foundation-texts of the Neoplatonic doctrine of Soul, *Timaeus* 35A1–6 (the composition of the World-Soul by the Demiurge).

οἷον γλυκύτης ἢ χρόα, κατὰ πᾶν τὸ σῶμα, οὕτω καὶ ἡ
ψυχή. τὰ μὲν γὰρ πάθη τῶν σωμάτων, ὥστε πᾶν τὸ
20 πεπονθὸς ἔχειν τὸ πάθος, καὶ μηδὲν εἶναι ἐφ' ἑαυτοῦ
σώματος ὄν τι καὶ γινωσκόμενον τότε· διὸ καὶ ἐξ
ἀνάγκης τοσοῦτον, τό τε ἄλλου μέρους λευκὸν οὐχ
ὁμοπαθὲς τῷ ἄλλου. καὶ ἐπὶ τοῦ λευκοῦ τὸ αὐτὸ μὲν
εἴδει τὸ ἐπ' ἄλλου πρὸς τὸ ἐπ' ἄλλου μέρους, οὐ μὴν
25 ταὐτὸν ἀριθμῷ, ἐπὶ δὲ τῆς ψυχῆς τὸ αὐτὸ ἀριθμῷ τὸ ἐν
τῷ ποδὶ καὶ τῇ χειρὶ ὑπάρχει, ὡς δηλοῦσιν αἱ
ἀντιλήψεις. καὶ ὅλως¹ ἐν μὲν ταῖς ποιότησι τὸ αὐτὸ
μεμερισμένον θεωρεῖται, ἐπὶ δὲ τῆς ψυχῆς τὸ αὐτὸ οὐ
μεμερισμένον, οὕτω δὲ μεμερίσθαι λεγόμενον, ὅτι
πανταχοῦ. λέγωμεν οὖν ἐξ ἀρχῆς περὶ τούτων, εἴ τι
30 ἡμῖν σαφὲς καὶ εὐπαράδεκτον γένοιτο, πῶς ἀσώματος
καὶ ἀμεγέθης οὖσα δύναται εἰς πλεῖστον ἰέναι εἴτε πρὸ
τῶν σωμάτων εἴτ' ἐν τοῖς σώμασι. τάχα δέ, εἰ φανείη
καὶ πρὸ τῶν σωμάτων τοῦτο δύνασθαι, ῥᾴδιον ἂν καὶ
ἐπὶ τῶν σωμάτων παραδέξασθαι τὸ τοιοῦτο γένοιτο.

2. Ἔστι δὴ τὸ μὲν ἀληθινὸν πᾶν, τὸ δὲ τοῦ παντὸς
μίμημα, ἡ τοῦδε τοῦ ὁρατοῦ φύσις. τὸ μὲν οὖν ὄντως
πᾶν ἐν οὐδενί ἐστιν· οὐδὲν γάρ ἐστι πρὸ αὐτοῦ. ὃ δ' ἂν
μετὰ τοῦτο ᾖ, τοῦτο ἤδη ἀνάγκη ἐν τῷ παντὶ εἶναι,
5 εἴπερ ἔσται, καὶ μάλιστα ἐξ ἐκείνου ἠρτημένον καὶ οὐ
δυνάμενον ἄνευ ἐκείνου οὔτε μένειν οὔτε κινεῖσθαι. καὶ
γὰρ εἰ μὴ ὡς ἐν τόπῳ τις τιθεῖτο τὸ τοιοῦτον, τὸν τόπον
νοῶν ἢ π έ ρ α ς σώματος τ ο ῦ π ε ρ ι έ χ ο ν τ ο ς καθὸ

---

¹ Sleeman, Harder, Theiler: ὅμως Enn.

in the same way as quality, sweetness or colour for instance. For these are affections of body, so that the whole of what is affected has the affection, and this is nothing of itself since it is something belonging to a body and known as such when the body is affected; for this reason it is necessarily of a certain size, and the white of one part is not co-affected with the white of another. And with white, the white in one part is the same in form as the white in another, but not the same in number, but with soul, the soul in the foot and the soul in the hand is the same thing in number, as perceptions show. And in general, in qualities the same thing is seen divided into parts, but in soul the same thing is seen not divided into parts, but said to be divided in the sense that it is everywhere. Let us therefore speak about this from the beginning, to see if anything occurs to us which is clear and acceptable about how soul, which is incorporeal and sizeless, is able to reach the greatest extension either before bodies or in bodies. But perhaps if it appeared that it could do this also before bodies, it would become easier to accept that the same sort of thing happens in bodies.

2. There exist certainly both the true All and the representation of the All, the nature of this visible universe. The really existent All is in nothing: for there is nothing before it. But that which comes after it must necessarily then exist in the All, if it is going to exist at all, being as much as possible dependent on it and unable either to stay still or move without it. For even if one does not suppose this kind of being in to be like being in place (considering place either as the boundary or the surrounding body in so far as it surrounds, or as

περιέχει, ἢ δ ι ά σ τ η μ ά τι ὃ πρότερον ἦν τῆς φύσεως
10 τοῦ κενοῦ καὶ ἔτι ἐστίν, ἀλλὰ τῷ γε οἷον ἐρείδεσθαι ἐπ'
αὐτοῦ καὶ ἀναπαύεσθαι πανταχοῦ ὄντος ἐκείνου καὶ
συνέχοντος, τὴν τοῦ ὀνόματος ἀφεὶς κατηγορίαν τῇ
διανοίᾳ τὸ λεγόμενον λαμβανέτω. τοῦτο δὲ ἄλλου χάριν
εἴρηται, ὅτι τὸ πᾶν ἐκεῖνο καὶ πρῶτον καὶ ὂν οὐ ζητεῖ
15 τόπον, οὐδ' ὅλως ἔν τινι. πᾶν δὴ τὸ πᾶν οὐκ ἔστιν ὅπως
ἀπολείπεται ἑαυτοῦ, ἀλλ' ἔστι τε πεπληρωκὸς ἑαυτὸ
καὶ ὂν ἴσον ἑαυτῷ· καὶ οὗ τὸ πᾶν, ἐκεῖ αὐτό· τὸ γὰρ πᾶν
αὐτό ἐστιν. ὅλως τε, εἴ τι ἐν τῷ παντὶ ἱδρύθη ἄλλο ὂν
παρ' ἐκεῖνο, μεταλαμβάνει αὐτοῦ καὶ συντυγχάνει αὐτῷ
20 καὶ ἰσχύει παρ' αὐτοῦ οὐ μερίζον ἐκεῖνο, ἀλλ' εὑρίσκον
αὐτὸ ἐν ἑαυτῷ αὐτὸ προσελθὸν ἐκείνῳ ἐκείνου οὐκ ἔξω
ἑαυτοῦ γενομένου· οὐ γὰρ οἷόν τε ἐν τῷ μὴ ὄντι τὸ ὂν
εἶναι, ἀλλ' εἴπερ, τὸ μὴ ὂν ἐν τῷ ὄντι. ὅλῳ οὖν
ἐντυγχάνει τῷ ὄντι· οὐ γὰρ ἦν ἀποσπᾶσθαι αὐτὸ ἀφ'
ἑαυτοῦ, καὶ τὸ πανταχοῦ δὲ λέγεσθαι εἶναι αὐτὸ δῆλον,
25 ὅτι ἐν τῷ ὄντι· ὥστε ἐν ἑαυτῷ. καὶ οὐδὲν θαυμαστόν, εἰ
τὸ πανταχοῦ ἐν τῷ ὄντι καὶ ἐν ἑαυτῷ· ἤδη γὰρ γίνεται
τὸ πανταχοῦ ἐν ἑνί. ἡμεῖς δὲ τὸ ὂν ἐν αἰσθητῷ θέμενοι
καὶ τὸ πανταχοῦ ἐκεῖ τιθέμεθα, καὶ μέγα νομίζοντες τὸ
αἰσθητὸν ἀπορούμεν, πῶς ἐν μεγάλῳ καὶ τοσούτῳ
30 ἐκείνη ἡ φύσις ἐκτείνεται. τὸ δέ ἐστι τοῦτο τὸ

some extension which formerly belonged, and still belongs, to the nature of the void[1]) but to consist in being in a way based on the true All and resting in it, since that All is everywhere and holds it together, let him abandon the verbal signification and grasp the meaning of what is being said. This has been mentioned for the sake of something else, because that All, the first and the existent, does not go looking for place and is not at all in anything. It is certainly not possible for the All, being all, to fall short of itself, but it exists as self-fulfilled and as a being equal to itself[2]; and where the all is, there is itself: for it is itself the All. And altogether, if anything which is other than that All is set firm in the All, it participates in it and coincides with it and draws its strength from it, not dividing it into parts but finding it in itself as it itself approaches it without that All going outside itself; for it is not possible for being to be in not-being but, if at all, not-being in being. It encounters being, therefore, as a whole; for it was not possible for it to be torn away from itself, and to say that it is everywhere clearly means that it is in being: so, then, in itself. And there is nothing surprising in "everywhere" meaning "in being" and "in itself": for "everywhere" already means "in one". But since we put "being" in the perceptible, we also put "everywhere" there too, and since we think the perceptible is large we are puzzled about how that other nature spreads itself out in a largeness of this extent. But this which is

[1] Plotinus is working here with Aristotle's account of place: cp. *Physics* Δ 4. 212a5–11.

[2] Plotinus is possibly thinking here of Parmenides fr. B 8 23–24 DK.

λεγόμενον μέγα μικρόν· ὃ δὲ νομίζεται μικρόν, ἐκεῖνο
μέγα, εἴ γε ὅλον ἐπὶ πᾶν τούτου μέρος φθάνει, μᾶλλον
δὲ τοῦτο πανταχόθεν τοῖς αὐτοῦ μέρεσιν ἐπ᾽ ἐκεῖνο ἰὸν
εὑρίσκει αὐτὸ πανταχοῦ πᾶν καὶ μεῖζον ἑαυτοῦ. ὅθεν ὡς
35 οὐκ ἐν τῇ ἐκτάσει πλέον τι ληψόμενον—ἔξω γὰρ ἂν καὶ
τοῦ παντὸς ἐγίνετο—περιθεῖν αὐτῷ ἐβουλήθη, οὔτε δὲ
περιλαβεῖν δεδυνημένον οὐδ᾽ αὖ ἐντὸς γενέσθαι
ἠγάπησε τόπον ἔχειν καὶ τάξιν οὗ σῴζοιτο γειτονοῦν
αὐτῷ παρόντι καὶ οὐ παρόντι αὖ· ἔστι γὰρ ἐφ᾽ ἑαυτοῦ
ἐκεῖνο, κἄν τι αὐτῷ ἐθέλῃ παρεῖναι. ὅπου δὴ συνίοι[1] τὸ
40 σῶμα τοῦ παντός, εὑρίσκει τὸ πᾶν, ὥστε μηδὲν ἔτι
δεῖσθαι τοῦ πόρρω, ἀλλὰ στρέφεσθαι ἐν τῷ αὐτῷ, ὡς
παντὸς ὄντος τούτου, οὗ κατὰ πᾶν μέρος αὐτοῦ
ἀπολαύει ὅλου ἐκείνου. εἰ μὲν γὰρ ἐν τόπῳ ἦν ἐκεῖνο
αὐτό, προσχωρεῖν τε ἔδει ἐκεῖ καὶ εὐθυπορεῖν καὶ ἐν
45 ἄλλῳ μέρει αὐτοῦ ἄλλῳ μέρει ἐφάπτεσθαι ἐκείνου καὶ
εἶναι τὸ πόρρω καὶ ἐγγύθεν· εἰ δὲ μήτε τὸ πόρρω μήτε
τὸ ἐγγύθεν, ἀνάγκη ὅλον παρεῖναι, εἴπερ πάρεστι. καὶ
ὅλως ἐστὶν ἐκείνων ἑκάστῳ, οἷς μήτε πόρρωθέν ἐστι
μήτε ἐγγύθεν, δυνατοῖς δὲ δέξασθαί ἐστιν.

3. Ἆρ᾽ οὖν αὐτὸ φήσομεν παρεῖναι, ἢ αὐτὸ μὲν ἐφ᾽
ἑαυτοῦ εἶναι, δυνάμεις δὲ ἀπ᾽ αὐτοῦ ἰέναι ἐπὶ πάντα, καὶ
οὕτως αὐτὸ πανταχοῦ λέγεσθαι εἶναι; οὕτω γὰρ τὰς
ψυχὰς οἷον βολὰς εἶναι λέγουσιν, ὥστε αὐτὸ μὲν
5 ἱδρῦσθαι ἐν αὐτῷ. τὰς δ᾽ ἐκπεμφθείσας κατ᾽ ἄλλο καὶ
κατ᾽ ἄλλο ζῷον γίγνεσθαι. ἢ ἐφ᾽ ὧν μὲν τὸ ἕν, τῷ μὴ

---

[1] Igal, H.-S²: συνιὸν Enn.

---

[1] The idea of presence by power was widespread at the
beginning of our era; cp. Pseudo-Aristotle *On The Cosmos*
6. 397b–398a. For souls as rays of light cp. Plutarch *On the*

called large is little; but what is thought little, that is large, if, as we suppose, it reaches as a whole every part of this [perceptible All]; or rather, this goes from everywhere with its parts to that and finds it everywhere as All and greater than itself. For this reason, because it would not get anything more by extension – for it would come to be outside the All – it wanted to run around it, and, since it was unable to embrace it or, again, get inside it, it was satisfied to have a place and rank where it would be kept safe, bordering upon it, which is present and, again, not present: for that All is on its own, even if something wants to be present to it. And where the body of the All meets it, it finds the All, so that it no longer needs to go further, but turns in the same place, because this [perceptible All] is All where with every part of itself it enjoys the whole of that other. For if that other was itself in a place, it would be necessary to approach it there and go in a straight line, and in one of its own parts to touch one part of that, and there would be far and near; but if there is neither far nor near, it must be present whole if it is present at all. And it is wholly present to each and every one of those for which it is neither far nor near, but they are able to receive it.

3. Are we then going to maintain that it is present itself, or that it is on its own but powers from it come to all things, and this is why it is said to be everywhere? For in this way they say that the souls are like rays, so that it is set firm in itself but the soul-rays sent out come now to one living thing and now to another.[1] Now in those where there is the one

Face which Appears in the Orb of the Moon 28, 943D; *Hermetica* XII 1.

πᾶσαν τὴν φύσιν ἀποσῴζειν τὴν οὖσαν ἐν αὐτῷ ἐκείνῳ,
ἐνταῦθα δύναμιν αὐτοῦ ᾧ πάρεστι παρεῖναι· οὐ μὴν οὐδ᾽
ὡς ἐκεῖνο μὴ ὅλως παρεῖναι, ἐπεὶ καὶ τότε οὐκ
10 ἀποτέτμηται ἐκεῖνο τῆς δυνάμεως αὐτοῦ, ἣν ἔδωκεν
ἐκείνῳ· ἀλλ᾽ ὁ λαβὼν τοσοῦτον ἐδυνήθη λαβεῖν παντὸς
παρόντος. οὗ δὲ πᾶσαι αἱ δυνάμεις, αὐτὸ σαφῶς
πάρεστι χωριστὸν ὅμως ὄν· γενόμενον μὲν γὰρ τοῦδε
εἶδος ἀπέστη ἂν τοῦ τε πᾶν εἶναι τοῦ τε εἶναι ἐν αὐτῷ
πανταχοῦ, κατὰ συμβεβηκὸς δὲ καὶ ἄλλου. μηδενὸς δὲ
15 ὂν τοῦ θέλοντος αὐτοῦ εἶναι, ᾧ ἂν αὐτὸ[1] ἐθέλῃ, ὡς
δύναται πελάζει οὐ γενόμενον ἐκείνου, ἀλλ᾽ ἐκείνου
ἐφιεμένου αὐτοῦ, οὐδ᾽ αὖ ἄλλου. θαυμαστὸν οὖν οὐδὲν
οὕτως ἐν πᾶσιν εἶναι, ὅτι αὖ ἐν οὐδενί ἐστιν αὐτῶν
οὕτως ὡς ἐκείνων εἶναι. διὸ καὶ τὸ κατὰ συμβεβηκὸς
20 οὕτω λέγειν συμπαραθεῖν τῷ σώματι καὶ τὴν ψυχὴν οὐκ
ἄτοπον ἴσως, εἰ αὐτὴ μὲν ἐφ᾽ ἑαυτῆς λέγοιτο εἶναι οὐχ
ὕλης γενομένη οὐδὲ σώματος, τὸ δὲ σῶμα πᾶν κατὰ πᾶν
ἑαυτοῦ οἱονεὶ ἐλλάμποιτο. θαυμάζειν δὲ οὐ δεῖ, εἰ αὐτὸ
μὴ ὂν ἐν τόπῳ παντὶ τῷ ἐν τόπῳ ὄντι πάρεστιν· ἦν γὰρ
25 ἂν τοὐναντίον θαυμαστὸν καὶ ἀδύνατον πρὸς τῷ
θαυμαστῷ, εἰ τόπον καὶ αὐτὸ ἔχον οἰκεῖον παρῆν ἄλλῳ
τῷ ἐν τόπῳ, ἢ ὅλως παρῆν, καὶ παρῆν οὕτως, ὡς τι
ἡμεῖς φαμεν. νῦν δέ φησιν ὁ λόγος, ὡς ἀνάγκη αὐτῷ
τόπον οὐκ εἰληχότι ᾧ πάρεστι τούτῳ ὅλον παρεῖναι,

---

[1] ᾧ ἂν αὐτὸ Igal: ὃ ἂν αὐτῷ H–S: ὃ BxUCz: ᾧ w, Perna: αὐτοῦ
wBJ^pcUCQL^pc: αὐτὸ RJ^acL^ac ("ὃ … δύναται locus nondum
sanatus" H–S).

thing [only], because they do not preserve the whole nature which exists in that true All itself, there a power of it is present to that to which [the true All] is present; though it is not true even so that that is not altogether present, since then too it is not cut off from its power which it gave to that recipient; but the receiver was able to receive only so much, though all was present. But where all the powers are, itself is clearly present, though being all the same separate; for if it became the form of this particular thing it would have departed from being all and being everywhere in itself while belonging incidentally to another. But it belongs to no thing which wishes to belong to it, but, as far as it can, approaches whatever it itself wishes, not by its coming to belong to that, nor again to anything else, but by the desire of that for it. There is nothing, therefore, surprising in its being in all things in this way, because it is also in none of them in such a way as to belong to them. For this reason it is not perhaps inappropriate to say that the soul as well runs along incidentally with the body in this way, if it is said to be itself on its own, not belonging to matter or body, but all body over the whole of itself is in a way illuminated by it. But one should not be surprised if [the true All] itself, which is not in place, is present to everything which is in place; it would on the other hand be surprising, and impossible as well as surprising, if it had itself its own proper place and was present to another thing which was in place, or was present at all, and present in the way in which we say it is. But now the argument says that it is necessary for it, since it has not been allotted a place, to be present as a whole to that to which it is

παντὶ δὲ παρὸν ὡς καὶ ἑκάστῳ ὅλον παρεῖναι. ἢ ἔσται
30 αὐτοῦ τὸ μὲν ὡδί, τὸ δὲ ἄλλοθι· ὥστε μεριστὸν ἔσται
καὶ σῶμα ἔσται. πῶς γὰρ δὴ καὶ μεριεῖς; ἆρά γε τὴν
ζωὴν μεριεῖς; ἀλλ᾽ εἰ τὸ πᾶν ἦν ζωή, τὸ μέρος ζωὴ οὐκ
ἔσται. ἀλλὰ τὸν νοῦν, ἵν᾽ ὁ μὲν ᾖ ἐν ἄλλῳ, ὁ δὲ ἐν ἄλλῳ;
ἀλλ᾽ οὐδέτερος αὐτῶν νοῦς ἔσται. ἀλλὰ τὸ ὂν αὐτοῦ;
35 ἀλλὰ τὸ μέρος οὐκ ὂν ἔσται, εἰ τὸ ὅλον τὸ ὂν ὑπῆρχε. τί
οὖν, εἴ τις λέγοι καὶ τὸ σῶμα μεριζόμενον καὶ τὰ μέρη
ἔχειν σώματα ὄντα; ἢ ὁ μερισμὸς ἦν οὐ σώματος, ἀλλὰ
τοσοῦδε σώματος, καὶ σῶμα ἕκαστον ἐλέγετο τῷ εἴδει
καθὸ σῶμα· τοῦτο δὲ οὐκ εἶχε τὸ "τοσόνδε τι", ἀλλὰ
40 οὐδ᾽ ὁπωσοῦν τοσόνδε.

4. Πῶς οὖν τὸ ὂν καὶ τὰ ὄντα καὶ νοῦς πολλοὺς καὶ
ψυχὰς πολλάς, εἰ τὸ ὂν πανταχοῦ ἓν καὶ μὴ ὡς ὁμοειδές,
καὶ νοῦς εἷς καὶ ψυχὴ μία; καίτοι ἄλλην μὲν τοῦ παντός,
τὰς δὲ ἄλλας. ταῦτά τε γὰρ ἀντιμαρτυρεῖν δοκεῖ καὶ τὰ
5 εἰρημένα, εἴ τινα ἀνάγκην, ἀλλ᾽ οὐ πειθώ γε ἔχει
ἀπίθανον νομιζούσης τῆς ψυχῆς τὸ ἓν οὕτω πανταχοῦ
ταὐτὸν εἶναι. βέλτιον γὰρ ἴσως μερίσαντα τὸ ὅλον ὡς
μηδὲν ἐλαττοῦσθαι ἀφ᾽ οὗ ὁ μερισμὸς γεγένηται, ἢ καὶ
γεννήσαντα ἀπ᾽ αὐτοῦ, ἵνα δὴ βελτίοσι χρώμεθα
10 ὀνόμασιν, οὕτω τὸ μὲν ἐᾶσαι ἐξ αὐτοῦ εἶναι, τὰ δ᾽ οἷον
μέρη γενόμενα, ψυχάς, συμπληροῦν ἤδη τὰ πάντα. ἀλλ᾽

present, and to be present as a whole to an all as well as to each individual. Otherwise some of it will be here, and some elsewhere: so that it will be divisible into parts and will be body. For how indeed are you going to divide it? Will you divide its life? But if the whole was life, the part will not be life. But [will you divide] its intellect, so that one intellect is in one thing and one in another? But neither of them will be intellect. But [will you divide] its being? But the part will not be being, if the whole was being. What then, if someone were to say that the body when it is divided has parts which are bodies? Now the division was not of a body, but of a body of such a size, and each [division] was said to be a body by the form according to which it is body; but this did not have a particular quantity, but was not in any way quantitative.

4. How then [does Plato speak of] being and beings, and many intellects and many souls, if being is everywhere one and not only in the sense of specific unity, and intellect is one and soul is one? And [he does say] that the soul of the All is different from the other souls. This seems to be contrary evidence, and what we have said, even if it has a certain [logical] necessity, is not convincing, since the soul thinks it unconvincing that the one should be everywhere present in this way. Perhaps it would be better to divide the whole in such a way that that from which the division originates is in no way diminished, or, to put it better, to generate from it, and so to allow one thing[, the soul of the All,] to be derived from it, and the ones which have come to be like parts, souls, then to fill up the number of all things. But if that being remains on its own, because

285

εἰ ἐκεῖνο μένει τὸ ὂν ἐφ᾽ ἑαυτοῦ, ὅτι παράδοξον εἶναι
δοκεῖ τὸ ἅμα ὅλον τι πανταχοῦ παρεῖναι, ὁ αὐτὸς λόγος
καὶ ἐπὶ τῶν ψυχῶν ἔσται. ἐν οἷς γὰρ λέγονται σώμασιν
15 ὅλαι ἐν ὅλοις εἶναι, οὐκ ἔσονται, ἀλλ᾽ ἢ μερισθήσονται
ἢ μένουσαι ὅλαι που τοῦ σώματος δύναμιν αὐτῶν
δώσουσιν. ἐφ᾽ ὧν καὶ τῶν δυνάμεων ἡ αὐτὴ ἀπορία
ἔσται ἡ ὅλου πανταχοῦ. καὶ ἔτι τὸ μέν τι ψυχὴν ἕξει τοῦ
σώματος, τὸ δὲ δύναμιν μόνον. ἀλλὰ πῶς ψυχαὶ πολλαὶ
καὶ νοῖ πολλοὶ καὶ τὸ ὂν καὶ τὰ ὄντα; καὶ δὴ καὶ
20 προϊόντα ἐκ τῶν προτέρων ἀριθμοὶ ὄντα, ἀλλ᾽ οὐ
μεγέθη, ὁμοίως ἀπορίαν παρέξουσι πῶς πληροῦσι τὸ
πᾶν. οὐδὲν οὖν ἡμῖν παρὰ τοῦ πλήθους οὕτω προϊόντος
ἐξεύρηται εἰς εὐπορίαν· ἐπεὶ καὶ τὸ ὂν πολλὰ
συγχωροῦμεν εἶναι ἑτερότητι, οὐ τόπῳ. ὁμοῦ γὰρ πᾶν τὸ
25 ὄν, κἂν πολὺ οὕτως ᾖ· ἐ ὸ ν γ ὰ ρ ἐ ό ν τ ι π ε λ ά ζ ε ι,
καὶ π ᾶ ν ὁ μ ο ῦ, καὶ νοῦς πολὺς ἑτερότητι, οὐ τόπῳ,
ὁμοῦ δὲ πᾶς. ἆρ᾽ οὖν καὶ ψυχαί; ἢ καὶ ψυχαί· ἐπεὶ καὶ τὸ
π ε ρ ὶ τ ὰ σ ώ μ α τ α μ ε ρ ι σ τ ὸ ν λέγεται ἀμερὲς
εἶναι τὴν φύσιν, τὰ δὲ σώματα μέγεθος ἔχοντα ταύτης
τῆς ψυχῆς φύσεως αὐτοῖς παρούσης, μᾶλλον δὲ τῶν
30 σωμάτων ἐκεῖ γενομένων, ὅσον ἐστὶ μεμερισμένα, κατὰ
πᾶν μέρος ἐκείνης ἐμφανταζομένης τῆς φύσεως, περὶ
τὰ σώματα οὕτως ἐνομίσθη εἶναι μεριστή. ἐπεί, ὅτι οὐ
συνδιείληπται τοῖς μέρεσιν, ἀλλ᾽ ὅλη πανταχοῦ, φανερὸν
ποιεῖ τὸ ἓν καὶ τὸ ἀμέριστον ὄντως τῆς φύσεως.
35 οὔτ᾽ οὖν τὸ μίαν εἶναι τὰς πολλὰς ἀναιρεῖ, ὥσπερ οὐδὲ

¹ Parmenides fr. B 8 25 and 5 DK.
² Again Timaeus 35A2–3.

it seems contradictory that a whole should be simultaneously present everywhere, the same argument
will apply to the souls. For they will not be in the
bodies in which they are said to be as wholes in
wholes, but they will either be divided or, if they
remain wholes, will be somewhere in the body and
give it their power. And the same difficulty of the
whole everywhere will arise with them and with
their powers. And further, some one part of the body
will have soul, and another only power. But how are
there many souls and many intellects, and being and
beings? And furthermore, since they come forth from
what is before them as numbers, not as magnitudes,
they will cause a difficulty in a similar way about
how they fill the All. So, therefore, we have discovered nothing from a multiplicity proceeding in
this way which helps to a solution; since we shall
agree that being also is many things by difference,
not by place. For being is all together one, even if it
is many things in this way; for "being borders on
being" and "all is together",[1] and intellect is many
by difference, not by place, and all together. Are
souls then also? Yes, souls also; since "what is
divided in the sphere of bodies"[2] means that it is
naturally partless, but, since the bodies have magnitude, and this nature of soul is present to them (or
rather the bodies come to be there in it), in so far as
they are divided into parts, that nature being
imagined present in every part, in this way it was
considered to be divided in the sphere of bodies. For
because it is not divided up along with the parts, but
is everywhere as a whole, it makes clear the unity
and the true indivisibility of the nature. The soul's
being one, then, does not do away with the many

τὸ ὂν τὰ ὄντα, οὔτε μάχεται τὸ πλῆθος ἐκεῖ τῷ ἑνί, οὔτε
τῷ πλήθει συμπληροῦν δεῖ ζωῆς τὰ σώματα, οὔτε διὰ
τὸ μέγεθος τοῦ σώματος δεῖ νομίζειν τὸ πλῆθος τῶν
ψυχῶν γίνεσθαι, ἀλλὰ πρὸ τῶν σωμάτων εἶναι καὶ
40 πολλὰς καὶ μίαν. ἐν γὰρ τῷ ὅλῳ αἱ πολλαὶ ἤδη οὐ
δυνάμει, ἀλλ' ἐνεργείᾳ ἑκάστη· οὔτε γὰρ ἡ μία καὶ[1]
ὅλη κωλύει τὰς πολλὰς ἐν αὐτῇ εἶναι, οὔτε αἱ πολλαὶ
τὴν μίαν. διέστησαν γὰρ οὐ διεστῶσαι καὶ πάρεισιν
ἀλλήλαις οὐκ ἀλλοτριωθεῖσαι· οὐ γὰρ πέρασίν εἰσι
διωρισμέναι, ὥσπερ οὐδὲ ἐπιστῆμαι αἱ πολλαὶ ἐν ψυχῇ
45 μιᾷ, καὶ ἔστιν ἡ μία τοιαύτη, ὥστε ἔχειν ἐν ἑαυτῇ
πάσας. οὕτως ἐστὶν ἄπειρος ἡ τοιαύτη φύσις.

5. Καὶ τὸ μέγα αὐτῆς οὕτω ληπτέον, οὐκ ἐν ὄγκῳ·
τοῦτο γὰρ μικρόν ἐστιν εἰς τὸ μηδὲν ἰόν, εἴ τις ἀφαιροῖ.
ἐκεῖ δὲ οὐδὲ ἀφελεῖν ἔστιν, οὐδ' εἰ ἀφαιρεῖς ἐπιλείψει. εἰ
δὴ "οὐκ ἐπιλείψει", τί δεῖ δεδιέναι, μή τινος ἀποστατῇ;
5 πῶς γὰρ ἀποστατεῖ οὐκ ἐπιλείπουσα, ἀλλ' ἀέννασος
οὖσα φύσις οὐ ῥέουσα; ῥέουσα μὲν γὰρ ἐπὶ τοσοῦτον
ἔρχεται, ἐφ' ὅσον ῥεῖν δύναται, μὴ ῥέουσα δέ—οὐδὲ γὰρ
ἄν, οὐδ' ὅπου ῥεύσειεν ἔχει· τὸ γὰρ πᾶν κατείληφε,
μᾶλλον δὲ αὐτή[2] ἐστι τὸ πᾶν—καὶ μεῖζόν τι οὖσα ἢ
10 κατὰ σώματος φύσιν ὀλίγον γ' ἂν εἰκότως νομίζοιτο τῷ
παντὶ διδόναι, ὅσον δύναται τοῦτο αὐτοῦ φέρειν. δεῖ

---

[1] Porphyrius *Sent.*, Igal, H–S[2]: ἡ Enn.: om. Stobaeus.
[2] Kirchhoff: αὕτη Enn., H–S[1].

souls, any more than being does away with beings,
nor does the multiplicity there in the true All fight
with the one, nor does one need to fill up bodies with
life by the multiplicity, nor ought one to think that
the multitude of souls came into existence because
of bodily magnitude, but souls were both many and
one before the bodies. For the many are already in
the whole, not in potency, but each and every one in
active actuality; for neither does the one and whole
hinder the many from being in it, nor do the many
hinder the one. For they stand apart without standing aloof and are present to each other without
being made other than themselves; for they are not
bounded off [from each other] by limits, as neither
are the many bodies of knowledge in one soul, and
the one is of such a kind as to have all of them in
it. It is in this way that a nature of this kind is
unbounded.

5. And its greatness is to be understood in this
way, not as consisting in bulk; for bulk is a little
thing, going to nothing if one takes away from it.
But there in the true All it is not possible to take
away; and if you do take away, it will not fail. If then
it will not fail, why should one be afraid that it may
depart from anything? For how will it depart when it
does not fail, but is a nature which springs up for
ever and does not flow? For if it flowed, it would
reach as far as it was able to flow, but as it does not
flow – for it could not, and has nowhere it could flow
to: for it has taken hold of the All, or rather is itself
the All – and is something greater than accords with
the nature of the body, it would reasonably be
considered to give little of itself to the [perceptible]
All, only as much of itself as this is able to bear. But

δὲ ἐκεῖνο μήτε ἔλαττον λέγειν, μηδὲ τιθέμενον ἔλαττον
τῷ ὄγκῳ ἀπιστεῖν ἤδη, ὡς οὐ δυνατὸν ἐπὶ τὸ μεῖζον
αὐτοῦ ἰέναι τὸ ἔλαττον. οὔτε γὰρ τὸ ἔλαττον
κατηγορητέον, οὐδὲ παραθετέον ὄγκον πρὸς ἄογκον ἐν
15 μετρήσει—ὅμοιον γὰρ ὡς εἴ τις ἰατρικὴν λέγοι ἐλάττω
εἶναι τοῦ σώματος τοῦ ἰατροῦ—οὐδ' αὖ οὕτως μεῖζον
νομιστέον τῇ ποσοῦ μετρήσει, ἐπεὶ οὐδ' ἐπὶ τῆς ψυχῆς·
οὕτω τὸ μέγα καὶ τὸ μεῖζον τοῦ σώματος. μαρτυρεῖ δὲ
τῷ μεγάλῳ τῆς ψυχῆς καὶ τὸ μείζονος τοῦ ὄγκου
20 γινομένου φθάνειν ἐπὶ πᾶν αὐτοῦ τὴν αὐτὴν ψυχήν, ἢ
ἐπ' ἐλάττονος ὄγκου ἦν. γελοῖον γὰρ πολλαχῇ, εἴ τις
προσθείη καὶ τῇ ψυχῇ ὄγκον.

6. Τί οὖν οὐ καὶ ἐπ' ἄλλο σῶμα ἔρχεται; ἢ ὅτι ἐκεῖνο
δεῖ, εἰ δύναται, προσελθεῖν, τὸ δὲ προσεληλυθὸς καὶ
δεξάμενον ἔχει. τί οὖν; τὸ ἄλλο σῶμα τὴν αὐτὴν ψυχὴν
ἔχει ἔχον καὶ αὐτὸ ἣν ἔχει ψυχήν; τί γὰρ διαφέρει; ἢ καὶ
5 ταῖς προσθήκαις. εἶτα πῶς ἐν ποδὶ καὶ χειρὶ τὴν αὐτήν,
τὴν δὲ ἐν τῷδε τῷ μέρει τοῦ παντὸς οὐ τὴν αὐτὴν τῇ ἐν
τῷδε; εἰ δὲ αἱ αἰσθήσεις διάφοροι, καὶ τὰ πάθη τὰ
συμπίπτοντα διάφορα λεκτέον εἶναι. ἄλλα οὖν ἐστι τὰ
κρινόμενα, οὐ τὸ κρῖνον· ὁ δὲ κρίνων ὁ αὐτὸς δικαστὴς
10 ἐν ἄλλοις καὶ ἄλλοις πάθεσι γινόμενος· καίτοι οὐχ ὁ
πάσχων αὐτός, ἀλλ' ἡ σώματος τοιοῦδε φύσις· καὶ ἔστιν
οἷον εἰ αὐτὸς ἡμῶν καὶ ἡδονὴν κρίνει τὴν περὶ τὸν
δάκτυλον καὶ ἀλγηδόνα τὴν περὶ τὴν κεφαλήν. διὰ τί
οὖν οὐ συναισθάνεται ἡ ἑτέρα τὸ τῆς ἑτέρας κρίμα; ἢ ὅτι

we must not say that this is less, nor, because we assume that it is less in bulk, lose confidence at this stage because it is impossible for the less to extend to what is greater than itself. For "less" should not be predicated of it, nor should one set bulk and the bulkless side by side by measuring them – this would be like saying that the physician's art was less than the body of the physician – nor on the other side should one think that [the true All] is greater in the sense of quantitative measurement, since this does not apply to the soul either: this is how the great and small of body is. But there is evidence of the greatness of soul in the fact that when the bulk becomes greater the same soul reaches to the whole of it which was in the lesser bulk. For it would be ridiculous in many ways if one added bulk to soul as well.

6. Why then does it not also come to another body? It is because that body must approach the soul, if it can, but the one which has approached it and received it has it. Well then, does the other body have the same soul when it itself has the soul which it has? For what is the difference? It lies in the additions. And then, how does it come to pass that it is the same soul in foot and hand, but that the soul in this part of the universe is not the same as the soul in that? But if the perceptions are different, the occurrent experiences must also be said to be different. But then it is what is judged which is different, not what judges; but he who judges is the same judge in a variety of different experiences; yet it is not he who has the experiences, but the nature of a body appropriately qualified; it is as if he judges the pleasure in our finger and the pain in our head. Why then does not one soul share in the perception of what another

15 κρίσις ἐστίν, ἀλλ' οὐ πάθος. εἶτα οὐδ' αὐτὴ ἡ κρίνασα
"κέκρικα" λέγει, ἀλλ' ἔκρινε μόνον· ἐπεὶ οὐδὲ παρ' ἡμῖν
ἡ ὄψις τῇ ἀκοῇ λέγει, καίτοι ἔκριναν ἄμφω, ἀλλὰ ὁ
λογισμὸς ἐπ' ἀμφοῖν· τοῦτο δὲ ἕτερον ἀμφοῖν. πολλαχῇ
δὲ καὶ ὁ λογισμὸς εἶδε τὸ ἐν ἑτέρῳ κρίμα καὶ σύνεσιν
20 ἔσχεν ἑτέρου πάθους. εἴρηται δὲ περὶ τούτου καὶ ἐν
ἄλλοις.

7. Ἀλλὰ πάλιν λέγωμεν πῶς ἐπὶ πάντα ἐστὶ τὸ
αὐτό· τοῦτο δὲ ταὐτόν ἐστι πῶς ἕκαστον τῶν πολλῶν
τῶν αἰσθητῶν οὐκ ἄμοιρον τοῦ αὐτοῦ πολλαχῇ
κείμενον. οὐ γὰρ ἐκεῖνο ὀρθῶς ἔχει ἐκ τῶν εἰρημένων
5 μερίζειν εἰς τὰ πολλά, ἀλλὰ τὰ πολλὰ μεμερισμένα εἰς
τὸ ἓν μᾶλλον ἀνάγειν, κἀκεῖνο οὐκ ἐληλυθέναι πρὸς
ταῦτα, ἀλλὰ ταῦτα ὅτι διέρριπται παρεσχηκέναι δόξαν
ἡμῖν κατὰ ταῦτα κἀκεῖνο διειλῆφθαι, οἷον εἴ τις τὸ
κρατοῦν καὶ συνέχον εἰς ἴσα τῷ κρατουμένῳ διαιροῖ.
10 καίτοι κρατοῖ ἂν καὶ χεὶρ σῶμα ὅλον καὶ ξύλον
πολύπηχυ καὶ ἄλλο τι, καὶ ἐπὶ πᾶν μὲν τὸ κρατοῦν, οὐ
διείληπται δὲ ὅμως εἰς ἴσα τῷ κρατουμένῳ ἐν τῇ χειρί,
καθόσον ἐφάπτεται εἰς τοσοῦτον περιγραφομένης, ὡς
δοκεῖ, τῆς δυνάμεως, ἀλλ' ὅμως τῆς χειρὸς ὁριζομένης
τῷ αὐτῆς ποσῷ, οὐ τῷ τοῦ αἰωρουμένου καὶ
15 κρατουμένου σώματος. καὶ εἰ προσθείης δὲ τῷ
κρατουμένῳ σώματι μῆκος ἄλλο καὶ δύναιτο ἡ χεὶρ
φέρειν, ἡ δύναμις κἀκεῖνο κρατεῖ οὐ διαληφθεῖσα εἰς
τοσαῦτα μέρη, ὅσα τὸ σῶμα ἔχει. τί οὖν, εἴ τις τὸν
ὄγκον τὸν σωματικὸν τῆς χειρὸς ὑποθεῖτο ἀφῃρῆσθαι,

---

[1] The reference is possibly to IV. 9.2–3 (on the unity of
individual souls); IV. 7.6–7 deals with the unity of soul in
the diversity of sense-experiences.

judges? It is because it is a judgement, not an experience. And further, the soul itself which has made a judgement does not say "I have judged", but only judges; since not even in us does our sight say this to our hearing, though both have judged, but the reason over both. But the reason often sees the judgement in another and acquires an understanding of the other's experience. But we have also spoken of this elsewhere.[1]

7. But again let us ask how it is the same which is over all; but this is the same as asking how each and every one of the many perceptible things, though in many different places, is not without a share in the same. For, from what has been said, it is not correct to divide that same up into the many, but rather to bring back the divided many to the one, and that one has not come to these many, but these because they are scattered have given us the impression that also that has been taken apart, as if one were to divide what controls and holds together into parts equal to what is controlled. And yet a hand might control a whole body and a piece of wood many cubits long, or something else, and what controls extends to the whole, but is not all the same divided into parts equal to what is controlled in the hand; the bounds of the power, it appears, extend as far as the grip, but all the same the hand is limited in extent by its own quantity, not by that of the body it lifts and controls. And if you were to add another length to the body which is controlled and the hand was able to bear it, the power would control that too without being divided into as many parts as the body has. Well then, what if someone supposed the corporeal bulk of the hand to be taken away, but left the same

20 καταλείποι δὲ τὴν δύναμιν τὴν αὐτὴν τὴν ἀνέχουσαν καὶ
πρότερον αὐτό, τὴν πρόσθεν ἐν τῇ χειρὶ οὖσαν; ἆρ' οὐκ
ἂν ἡ αὐτὴ ἀμέριστος οὖσα ἐν παντὶ ὡσαύτως κατὰ πᾶν
μέρος εἴη; εἰ δὲ δὴ φωτεινὸν μικρὸν ὄγκον οἷον κέντρον
ποιησάμενος μεῖζόν τι περιθείης σφαιρικὸν σῶμα
25 διαφανές, ὥστε τὸ φῶς τοῦ ἔνδον ἐν παντὶ τῷ
περιέχοντι φαίνειν, οὐκ οὔσης ἄλλοθεν αὐγῆς τῷ ἔξωθεν
ὄγκῳ, ἆρ' οὐκ ἐκεῖνο τὸ ἔνδον φήσομεν αὐτὸ μηδὲν
παθόν, ἀλλὰ μένον ἐπὶ πάντα τὸν ἔξωθεν ὄγκον
ἐληλυθέναι, καὶ τὸ ἐκεῖ ἐνορώμενον ἐν τῷ μικρῷ ὄγκῳ
φῶς κατειληφέναι τὸ ἔξω; ἐπειδὴ τοίνυν οὐ παρὰ τοῦ
30 ὄγκου τοῦ σωματικοῦ τοῦ μικροῦ ἐκείνου ἦν τὸ φῶς—
οὐ γὰρ ᾗ σῶμα ἦν εἶχε τὸ φῶς, ἀλλ' ᾗ φωτεινὸν σῶμα,
ἑτέρᾳ δυνάμει, οὐ σωματικῇ οὔσῃ—φέρε, εἴ τις τὸν
ὄγκον τοῦ σώματος ὑφέλοι, τηροῖ δὲ τὴν τοῦ φωτὸς
δύναμιν, ἆρ' ἂν ἔτι εἴποις που εἶναι τὸ φῶς, ἢ ἐπίσης ἂν
35 εἴη καθ' ὅλην τε τὴν ἔξω σφαῖραν; οὐκέτι δὲ οὐδ'
ἀπερείσῃ τῇ διανοίᾳ ὅπου πρότερον ἦν κείμενον, καὶ
οὔτε ἔτι ἐρεῖς ὅθεν οὔτε ὅπῃ, ἀλλὰ περὶ μὲν τούτου
ἄπορος ἔσῃ ἐν θαύματι ποιούμενος, ἅμα δὲ ὡδὶ τοῦ
σφαιρικοῦ σώματος ἀτενίσας εἴσῃ τὸ φῶς καὶ ὡδὶ
40 αὐτός. ἐπεὶ καὶ ἐπὶ τοῦ ἡλίου ἔχεις μὲν εἰπεῖν ὅθεν τὸ
φῶς ἐπιλάμπει κατὰ πάντα τὸν ἀέρα εἰς τὸ σῶμα τοῦ
ἡλίου βλέπων, τὸ δὲ αὐτὸ ὅμως ὁρᾷς φῶς πανταχοῦ
οὐδὲ τοῦτο μεμερισμένον. δηλοῦσι δὲ αἱ ἀποτομαὶ
ἐπὶ θάτερα ἢ ὅθεν ἐλήλυθεν οὐ διδοῦσαι εἶναι οὐδὲ

power which also before held up what was formerly in the hand? Would not the same power, being without parts, be present in the same way in it all, in every part? And suppose you made a small luminous bulk a kind of centre, and put a larger transparent spherical body round it, so that the light of what was inside shone in the whole of what was round it, and no ray of light from anywhere else came to the outside bulk, shall we not affirm that what is inside has not itself been affected but has reached the whole of the outer bulk while remaining as it is, and that the light seen in the small bulk has taken possession of that outside? Now, since the light does not come from that small bodily bulk – for it is not in that it is body that it has the light, but in that it is luminous body, by another power which is not bodily [1] – suppose that someone took away the bulk of the body but kept the power of the light, would you still say that the light was somewhere, or would it be equally present over the whole outer sphere? You will no longer rest in your thought on the place where it was before, and you will not any more say where it comes from or where it is going, but you will be puzzled and put in amazement when, fixing your gaze now here and now there in the spherical body, you yourself perceive the light. For with the sun also you can say whence the light shines over all the air by looking at the body of the sun, but none the less you see the same light everywhere, and this light is not divided into parts either. And the cuttings-off of light make this clear; they do not allow it to be on the other side of them from that whence it came, but

---

[1] On the incorporeality of light cp. II. 1.7. 26–8; IV. 5.6–7.

μερίζουσαι. καὶ δὴ τοίνυν εἰ δύναμις μόνον ὁ ἥλιος ἦν
45 σώματος χωρὶς οὖσα καὶ φῶς παρεῖχεν, οὐκ ἂν ἐντεῦθεν
ἤρξατο οὐδ᾽ ἂν εἶπες ὅθεν, ἀλλ᾽ ἦν ἂν τὸ φῶς πανταχοῦ
ἓν καὶ ταὐτὸν ὂν οὐκ ἀρξάμενον οὐδ᾽ ἀρχὴν ποθεν ἔχον.

8. Τὸ μὲν οὖν φῶς, ἐπειδὴ σώματός ἐστιν, ὅθεν
ἐλήλυθεν εἰπεῖν ἔχεις ἔχων εἰπεῖν τὸ σῶμα ὅπου ἐστίν,
ἄϋλον δὲ εἴ τί ἐστι καὶ δεῖται οὐδὲν σώματος πρότερον
ὂν τῇ φύσει παντὸς σώματος, ἱδρυμένον αὐτὸ ἐν ἑαυτῷ,
5 μᾶλλον δὲ οὐδὲ ἱδρύσεως δεόμενον οὐδὲ τῆς τοιαύτης,
τοῦτο δὴ τὸ τοιαύτην ἔχον φύσιν οὐκ ἔχον ἀρχὴν ὅθεν
ὁρμηθείη οὔτε ἔκ τινος τόπου οὔτε τινὸς ὂν σώματος,
πῶς αὐτοῦ τὸ μὲν ὡδὶ φήσεις, τὸ δὲ ὡδί; ἤδη γὰρ ἂν καὶ
τὸ ὅθεν ὡρμήθη ἔχοι καὶ τό τινος εἶναι. λείπεται τοίνυν
10 εἰπεῖν ὡς, εἴ τι αὐτοῦ μεταλαμβάνει, τῇ τοῦ ὅλου
δυνάμει μεταλαμβάνειν αὐτοῦ πάσχοντος[1] μηδὲν μήτ᾽
οὖν ἄλλο τι μήτε μεμερισμένου. τῷ μὲν γὰρ σῶμα
ἔχοντι τὸ πάσχειν κἂν κατὰ συμβεβηκὸς ἂν γένοιτο, καὶ
ταύτῃ παθητὸν ἂν λέγοιτο καὶ μεριστόν, ἐπειδὴ
15 σώματός ἐστί τι οἷον πάθος ἢ εἶδος· ὃ δέ ἐστι μηδενὸς
σώματος, ἀλλὰ τὸ σῶμα ἐθέλει αὐτοῦ εἶναι, ἀνάγκη
τοῦτο τά τε ἄλλα πάθη τοῦ σώματος μηδαμῶς αὐτὸ
πάσχειν μερίζεσθαί τε οὐχ οἷόν τε· σώματος γὰρ καὶ
τοῦτο καὶ πρώτως πάθος καὶ ᾗ σῶμα. εἰ δὴ ᾗ σῶμα τὸ
μεριστόν, ᾗ μὴ σῶμα τὸ ἀμέριστον. πῶς γὰρ καὶ

they do not divide it either. And certainly, then, if the sun was only a power which was without a body, and gave light, the light would not have begun from there [where the sun was] and you would not be able to say whence it came, but it would be everywhere as one and the same; it would have no beginning and no starting-point anywhere.

8. Since light, then, belongs to a body you are able to say whence it came because you can say where the body is; but if there is something which is immaterial, and has no need whatever of body because it is naturally prior to body, itself set firm in itself, or rather not in any way needing a setting of this kind, how can you say that some of this is here and some of it there when it has a nature of this kind and has no point from which it started and does not come from any place or belong to any body? For [if you could say this] it would already have a place from which it started and a belonging to some body. It remains, then, to say that if anything participates in it, it participates by the power of the whole, while it itself is not at all affected, either in any other way or by being divided into parts. For that which has a body could be affected, even if only incidentally, and could in this way be called subject to affection and divisible into parts, since it is something like an affection or a form of body; but that which belongs to no body, but the body wishes to belong to it, must necessarily itself in no way be affected by the other bodily affections and cannot be divided into parts: for this is an affection of body, and primarily so, and of body in that it is body. If then the divisible is so in that it is body, the indivisible is so in that it is not body. For how will you divide that which has no

20 μερίσεις οὐκ ἔχον μέγεθος; εἰ οὖν οὐκ ἔχοντος μέγεθος
τὸ ἔχον τὸ μέγεθος ἀμηγέπῃ μεταλαμβάνει, οὐ
μεριζομένου αὐτοῦ ἂν μεταλαμβάνοι· ἢ μέγεθος αὖ
ἕξει[1] πάλιν. ὅταν οὖν ἐν πολλοῖς λέγῃς, οὐκ αὐτὸ πολλὰ
γενόμενον λέγεις, ἀλλὰ τῶν πολλῶν τὸ πάθος
25 περιάπτεις τῷ ἑνὶ ἐκείνῳ ἐν πολλοῖς αὐτὸ ἅμα ὁρῶν. τὸ
δὲ "ἐν αὐτοῖς" οὕτω ληπτέον ὡς οὐκ αὐτῶν γενόμενον
ἑκάστου οὐδ' αὖ τοῦ παντός, ἀλλ' ἐκεῖνο μὲν αὐτοῦ εἶναι
καὶ αὐτὸ εἶναι, αὐτὸ δὲ ὂν οὐκ ἀπολείπεσθαι ἑαυτοῦ.
οὐδ' αὖ τοσοῦτον, ὅσον τὸ πᾶν αἰσθητόν, οὐδ' εἴ τι
30 μέρος τοῦ παντός· ὅλως γὰρ οὐδὲ ποσόν· πῶς ἂν οὖν
τοσοῦτον; σώματι μὲν γὰρ "τοσοῦτον", τῷ δὲ μὴ
σώματι, ἀλλ' ἑτέρας ὄντι φύσεως, οὐδαμῇ δεῖ
προσάπτειν "τοσοῦτον", ὅπου μηδὲ τὸ τοιοῦτον· οὐ
τοίνυν οὐδὲ τὸ ποῦ· οὐ τοίνυν οὐδὲ τὸ ἐνταῦθα καὶ
ἐνταῦθα· ἤδη γὰρ ἂν πολλάκις "ποῦ" εἴη. εἰ τοίνυν ὁ
35 μερισμὸς τοῖς τόποις, ὅταν τὸ μέν τι αὐτοῦ ὡδί, τὸ δὲ
ὡδί, ὅτῳ τὸ ὡδὶ μὴ ὑπάρχει, πῶς ἂν τὸ μερίζεσθαι ἔχοι;
ἀμέριστον ἄρα δεῖ αὐτὸ σὺν αὐτῷ εἶναι, κἂν τὰ πολλὰ
αὐτοῦ ἐφιέμενα τυγχάνῃ. εἰ οὖν τὰ πολλὰ ἐφίεται
αὐτοῦ, δῆλον ὅτι ὅλου ἐφίεται αὐτοῦ· ὥστε εἰ καὶ
40 δύναται μεταλαβεῖν, ὅλου ἂν αὐτοῦ καθόσον δύναται
μεταλαμβάνοι. δεῖ οὖν τὰ μεταλαμβάνοντα αὐτοῦ
οὕτως ἔχειν αὐτοῦ, ὡς οὐ μετέλαβε, μὴ ἰδίου αὐτῶν
ὄντος· οὕτως γὰρ ἂν μένοι αὐτὸ ἐφ' ἑαυτοῦ ὅλον καὶ ἐν
οἷς ὁρᾶται ὅλον. εἰ γὰρ μὴ ὅλον, οὐκ αὐτό, οὐδ' αὖ οὐ

---

[1] H–S²: ἕξει Enn.

298

magnitude? If then what has the magnitude in any way participates in what does not have magnitude it will participate in it without its being divided: or it will again have magnitude. Whenever then you say it is in many things, you are not saying that it has become many, but you are fitting what happens to the many to that one when you see it all at once in the many. But the "in them" must be taken in the sense that it does not come to belong to each one of them, or again to the totality, but it belongs to itself and is itself, and because it is itself does not depart from itself. Nor again is it of the same size as the perceptible All, or of any part of it; for it is altogether not quantitative: how then can it be of any size? For one attributes "of such a size" to body; but one should not in any way attach "of such a size" to what is not body but of another nature; one should not even attach "of such a kind" there; so then not "where" either; so then not "here and there" either; for that would already be "where" many times over. If then division is by places, when one part of it is here and another there, how can what has no "here" be divided? It must then be indivisible, itself with itself, even if the many aspire to and attain it. If then the many aspire to it, it is clear they aspire to it as whole: so that if they are also able to participate in it, they would participate in it as whole in so far as they can. The things therefore which participate in it must be so related to it as if they did not participate, since it is not their private property; for in this way it will remain whole itself by itself and whole in visible things. For if it is not whole, it is not itself, nor again will the partici-

45 ἐφίενται ἡ μετάληψις ἔσται, ἀλλὰ ἄλλου, οὗ ἡ ἔφεσις
οὐκ ἦν.

9. Καὶ γὰρ εἰ τὸ μέρος τὸ γενόμενον ἐν ἑκάστῳ ὅλον
ἦν καὶ αὐτὸ ἕκαστον οἷον τὸ πρῶτον—ἀποτετμημένον
ἀεὶ ἕκαστον—πολλὰ τὰ πρῶτα καὶ ἕκαστον πρῶτον.
εἶτα ταῦτα τὰ πολλὰ πρῶτα τί ἂν εἴη τὸ διεῖργον, ὥστε
5 μὴ ἓν ὁμοῦ πάντα εἶναι; οὐ γὰρ δὴ τὰ σώματα αὐτῶν· οὐ
γὰρ τῶν σωμάτων οἷόν τε ἦν εἴδη αὐτὰ εἶναι, εἴπερ
ὅμοια καὶ ταῦτα ἐκείνῳ τῷ πρώτῳ ἀφ' οὗ. εἰ δὲ
δυνάμεις αὐτοῦ τὰ λεγόμενα μέρη τὰ ἐν τοῖς πολλοῖς,
πρῶτον μὲν οὐκέτι ὅλον ἕκαστον· ἔπειτα πῶς ἦλθον
10 ἀποτμηθεῖσαι καὶ καταλείπουσαι; εἰ γὰρ δὴ καὶ
κατέλιπον, δηλονότι κατέλιπόν που ἰοῦσαι. εἶτα πότερα
ἔτι εἰσὶν ἐν αὐτῷ αἱ δυνάμεις αἱ ἐνταῦθα ἐν τῷ αἰσθητῷ
γεγενημέναι ἢ οὔ; εἰ μὲν γὰρ μή εἰσιν, ἄτοπον
ἐλαττωθῆναι ἐκεῖνο καὶ ἀδύναμον γεγονέναι
ἐστερημένον ὧν πρότερον εἶχε δυνάμεων, χωρίς τε τὰς
15 δυνάμεις εἶναι τῶν οὐσιῶν ἑαυτῶν πῶς ἂν οἷόν τε ἢ
ἀποτετμημένας; εἰ δ' ἐν ἐκείνῳ τέ εἰσι καὶ ἄλλοθι, ἢ
ὅλαι ἢ μέρη αὐτῶν ἐνταῦθα ἔσονται. ἀλλ' εἰ μέρη, κἀκεῖ
τὰ λοιπὰ μέρη. εἰ δὲ ὅλαι, ἤτοι αἵπερ ἐκεῖ καὶ ἐνταῦθα
οὐ μεμερισμέναι, καὶ πάλιν αὖ ἔσται τὸ αὐτὸ πανταχοῦ
20 οὐ μεμερισμένον· ἢ πολλὰ γενόμενον ὅλον ἕκαστον αἱ
δυνάμεις καὶ ὅμοιαι ἀλλήλαις, ὥστε καὶ μετὰ τῆς
οὐσίας ἑκάστης ἡ δύναμις· ἢ μία μόνον ἔσται ἡ συνοῦσα

pation be in what men aspire to but in something else to which the aspiration was not directed.

9. For indeed if the part which came to be in each was a whole, and each individual thing was like the first – each individual thing in a state of continual severance – then the firsts would be many and each individual would be a first. Then what would it be which kept these many firsts apart, so as not to be one thing all together? It would certainly not be their bodies; for it would not be possible for them to be forms of the bodies, assuming that these firsts are like that first from which they came. But if what are called the parts in the many things are the powers of that whole, first of all each is no longer a whole; then how did they come here when they had been cut off from and left that first? For if they really did leave it, they were obviously going somewhere when they left it. Then, are the powers which have come to be here in the perceptible world still in that first or not? For if they are not, it is absurd that it should be diminished and become powerless by being deprived of the powers which it had before; and how would it be possible for the powers to exist separate or cut off from their substances? But if they are both in that first and elsewhere, then either they will be here as wholes or parts of them will be here. But if it is parts, then the other parts will be there [in the true All]. But if they are here as wholes, then either they are here what they are there, not divided, and again there will be the same everywhere, not divided; or the powers will each be one whole thing which has become many, and will be like each other, so that each substance will have its power with it; or the power accompanying substance will only be one,

τῇ οὐσίᾳ, αἱ δ' ἄλλαι δυνάμεις μόνον· καίτοι οὐχ οἷόν τε,
ὥσπερ οὐσίαν ἄνευ δυνάμεως, οὕτως οὐδὲ δύναμιν ἄνευ
25 οὐσίας. ἡ γὰρ δύναμις ἐκεῖ ὑπόστασις καὶ οὐσία ἢ
μεῖζον οὐσίας· εἰ δ' ἕτεραι ὡς ἐλάττους καὶ ἀμυδραὶ
δυνάμεις αἱ ἐξ ἐκείνου, οἱονεὶ φῶς ἐκ φωτὸς ἀμυδρὸν ἐκ
φανοτέρου, καὶ δὴ καὶ οὐσίαι συνοῦσαι ταῖς δυνάμεσι
ταύταις, ἵνα μὴ γίνηται ἄνευ οὐσίας δύναμις, πρῶτον
μὲν καὶ ἐπὶ τῶν τοιούτων δυνάμεων ἀναγκαῖον
30 ὁμοειδῶν πάντως πρὸς ἀλλήλας γινομένων ἢ τὴν αὐτὴν
πανταχοῦ συγχωρεῖν εἶναι, ἢ καί, εἰ μὴ πανταχοῦ, ἀλλ'
οὖν πανταχῇ ἅμα τὴν αὐτὴν ὅλην, οὐ μεμερισμένην, οἷον
ἐν ἑνὶ καὶ τῷ αὐτῷ σώματι· εἰ δὲ τοῦτο, διὰ τί οὐκ ἐν
παντὶ τῷ ὅλῳ; εἰ δέ, μεμερίσθαι ἑκάστην εἰς ἄπειρον,
35 καὶ οὐκέτι οὐδ' αὐτὴ ὅλη, ἀλλὰ τῷ μερισμῷ ἔσται
ἀδυναμία. ἔπειτα ἄλλη κατ' ἄλλο οὖσα οὐ καταλείψει
συναίσθησιν. ἔπειτα δέ, [εἰ] [1] καθάπερ τὸ ἴνδαλμά τινος,
οἷον καὶ τὸ ἀσθενέστερον φῶς, ἀποτεμνόμενον τοῦ παρ'
οὗ ἐστιν οὐκέτ' ἂν εἴη, καὶ ὅλως πᾶν τὸ παρ' ἄλλου τὴν
40 ὑπόστασιν ἔχον ἴνδαλμα ὂν ἐκείνου οὐχ οἷόν τε
ἀποτέμνοντα ἐν ὑποστάσει ποιεῖν εἶναι, οὐδ' ἂν αἱ
δυνάμεις αὗται αἱ ἀπ' ἐκείνου ἐλθοῦσαι ἀποτετμημέναι
ἂν ἐκείνου εἶεν. εἰ δὲ τοῦτο, οὗ εἰσιν αὗται, κἀκεῖνο ὑφ'
οὗ ἐγένοντο ἐκεῖ ἅμα ἔσται, ὥστε πανταχοῦ ἅμα πάλιν
45 αὐτὸ οὐ μεμερισμένον ὅλον ἔσται.

10. Εἰ δέ τις λέγοι, ὡς οὐκ ἀνάγκη τὸ εἴδωλόν του

---

[1] del. Kirchhoff.

and the others will only be powers; and yet, just as it is not possible to have substance without power, so it is not possible to have power without substance. For power there [in the true All] is real existence and substance, or greater than substance. But if the powers from that first are other because they are less and dim, like a dim light from a brighter light, and the same is true of the substances which accompany these powers, that there may not be power without substance, first of all, even with powers of this kind it is necessary, since they are in every way of like form to each other, either to agree that there is one and the same power everywhere, or, if not everywhere, at any rate present at once as a whole in every direction, not divided, as in one and the same body (but if this is so why not in all the whole universe?). But if this is so, each power will be divided to infinity, and will no longer be a whole even for itself, but will by being divided be a powerlessness. Then if one power is in one part and one in another, there will be no room for consciousness. And then further, just as the image of something, like the weaker light, if cut off from that from which it is, would no longer exist, and in general one cannot cut off and make exist [separately] anything at all which derives its existence from something else and is its image, these powers also which came from that first could not exist cut off from it. But if this is so, that from which they derived will be there simultaneously where they are, so that again it will be present itself everywhere all at once undivided as a whole.

10. But if someone were to say that it is not necessary for the image to be dependent on anything

συνηρτῆσθαι τῷ ἀρχετύπῳ—ἔστι γὰρ καὶ εἰκόνα εἶναι
ἀπόντος τοῦ ἀρχετύπου, ἀφ' οὗ ἡ εἰκών, καὶ τοῦ πυρὸς
ἀπελθόντος τὴν θερμότητα εἶναι ἐν τῷ θερμανθέντι—
5 πρῶτον μὲν ἐπὶ τοῦ ἀρχετύπου καὶ τῆς εἰκόνος, εἰ τὴν
παρὰ τοῦ ζωγράφου εἰκόνα λέγοι τις, οὐ τὸ ἀρχέτυπον
φήσομεν τὴν εἰκόνα πεποιηκέναι, ἀλλὰ τὸν ζωγράφον,
οὐκ οὖσαν αὐτοῦ εἰκόνα οὐδ' εἰ αὐτόν τις γράφει· τὸ γὰρ
γράφον ἦν οὐ τὸ σῶμα τοῦ ζωγράφου οὐδὲ τὸ εἶδος τὸ
10 μεμιμημένον· καὶ οὐ τὸν ζωγράφον, ἀλλὰ τὴν θέσιν τὴν
οὑτωσὶ τῶν χρωμάτων λεκτέον ποιεῖν τὴν τοιαύτην
εἰκόνα. οὐδὲ κυρίως ἡ τῆς εἰκόνος καὶ τοῦ ἰνδάλματος
ποίησις οἷον ἐν ὕδασι καὶ κατόπτροις ἢ ἐν σκιαῖς—
ἐνταῦθα ὑφίσταταί τε παρὰ τοῦ προτέρου κυρίως καὶ
15 γίνεται ἀπ' αὐτοῦ καὶ οὐκ ἔστιν ἀφ' ἑαυτοῦ ἀποτετμημένα τὰ γενόμενα εἶναι. τοῦτον δὲ τὸν τρόπον
καὶ τὰς ἀσθενεστέρας δυνάμεις παρὰ τῶν προτέρων
ἀξιώσουσι γίνεσθαι. τὸ δ' ἐπὶ τοῦ πυρὸς λεγόμενον οὐκ
εἰκόνα τὴν θερμότητα τοῦ πυρὸς λεκτέον εἶναι, εἰ μή τις
λέγοι καὶ πῦρ ἐν τῇ θερμότητι εἶναι· εἰ γὰρ τοῦτο, χωρὶς
20 πυρὸς ποιήσει τὴν θερμότητα. εἶτα κἂν εἰ μὴ αὐτίκα, ἀλλ'
οὖν παύεται καὶ ψύχεται τὸ σῶμα τὸ θερμανθὲν ἀπο-
στάντος τοῦ πυρός. εἰ δὲ καὶ οὗτοι ταύτας τὰς δυνάμεις
σβεννύοιεν, πρῶτον μὲν ἓν μόνον ἄφθαρτον φήσουσι,
τὰς δὲ ψυχὰς καὶ τὸν νοῦν φθαρτὰ ποιήσουσιν. εἶτα καὶ
25 οὐκ ἐκ ῥεούσης οὐσίας ῥέοντα τὰ ἐξ αὐτῆς ποιήσουσι.
καίτοι, εἰ μένοι [1] ἱδρυθεὶς ἥλιος ὁπουοῦν, τὸ αὐτὸ φῶς

---

[1] Vitringa: μὲν ὁ Enn.

---

[1] This must be the right sense, as Sleeman saw (*C.Q.* 24,
1930, 78); cp. II. 6.1. 50 and 53 (my translation there is
incorrect).

in the original – for it is possible for a likeness to exist when the original is not there from which the likeness is taken, and, when the fire has gone away, for the heat to exist in what has been heated – first of all, as regards the original and the likeness, if one is talking about the likeness made by the painter, we shall affirm that it is not the original which made the likeness but the painter, since even if some painter makes a self-portrait it is not a likeness of himself; for what made the painting was not the body of the painter or the [bodily] form which was represented; and it is not the painter, but this particular disposition of the colours, which should be said to make this particular likeness. This is not in the strict and proper sense the making of likeness and image as it occurs in pools and mirrors, or in shadows – here the image has its existence in the strict and proper sense from the prior original, and comes to be from it, and it is not possible for what has come to be to exist cut off from it. But they will accept that this is the way in which the weaker powers come from the prior ones. But as for what is said about fire, the heat should not be called a likeness of the fire, unless one is going to say that fire is included in heat; for if this is so [the inclusive form of heat] will produce heat without fire. And then, even if not at once, the heated body does cease to be hot and does grow cold when the fire has gone away. But if these people were going to quench these powers, first of all they will be affirming that only the One is indestructible, and will make the souls and Intellect destructible. And then they will make flow away the things which come from a substance which does not flow away.[1] Yet, if the sun were to stay fixed in any particular

ἂν παρέχοι τοῖς αὐτοῖς τόποις· εἰ δὲ λέγοι τις μὴ τὸ
αὐτό, τούτῳ ἂν πιστῶτο τὸ τὸ σῶμα ῥεῖν τοῦ ἡλίου.
ἀλλ' ὅτι μὲν μὴ φθαρτὰ τὰ παρ' ἐκείνου, ἀθάνατοι δὲ
30 καὶ αἱ ψυχαὶ καὶ νοῦς πᾶς, καὶ ἐν ἄλλοις διὰ πλειόνων
εἴρηται.

11. Ἀλλὰ διὰ τί, εἴπερ ὅλον πανταχοῦ, οὐχ ὅλου
πάντα μεταλαμβάνει τοῦ νοητοῦ; πῶς δὲ τὸ μὲν πρῶτον
ἐκεῖ, τὸ δὲ ἔτι δεύτερον καὶ μετ' ἐκεῖνο ἄλλα; ἢ τὸ παρὸν
ἐπιτηδειότητι τοῦ δεξομένου ⟨παρ⟩εῖναι[1] νομιστέον,
5 καὶ εἶναι μὲν πανταχοῦ τοῦ ὄντος τὸ ὂν οὐκ ἀπο-
λειπόμενον ἑαυτοῦ, παρεῖναι δὲ αὐτῷ τὸ δυνάμενον
παρεῖναι, καὶ καθόσον δύναται κατὰ τοσοῦτον αὐτῷ οὐ
τόπῳ παρεῖναι, οἷον τῷ φωτὶ τὸ διαφανές, τῷ δὲ
τεθολωμένῳ ἡ μετάληψις ἄλλως. καὶ δὴ τὰ πρῶτα καὶ
10 δεύτερα καὶ τρίτα τάξει καὶ δυνάμει καὶ διαφοραῖς, οὐ
τόποις. οὐδὲν γὰρ κωλύει ὁμοῦ εἶναι τὰ διάφορα, οἷον
ψυχήν καὶ νοῦν καὶ πάσας ἐπιστήμας μείζους τε καὶ
ὑφιεμένας. ἐπεὶ καὶ ἀπὸ τοῦ αὐτοῦ ὁ μὲν ὀφθαλμὸς εἶδε
τὸ χρῶμα, ἡ δὲ ὄσφρησις τὸ εὐῶδες, ἄλλη δὲ αἴσθησις
ἄλλο, ὁμοῦ πάντων, ἀλλ' οὐ χωρὶς ὄντων. οὐκοῦν ἐκεῖνο
15 ποικίλον καὶ πολύ; ἢ τὸ ποικίλον ἁπλοῦν αὖ, καὶ τὰ
πολλὰ ἕν. λόγος γὰρ εἷς καὶ πολύς, καὶ πᾶν τὸ ὂν ἕν. καὶ
γὰρ τὸ ἕτερον ἑαυτῷ καὶ ἡ ἑτερότης αὐτοῦ· οὐ γὰρ δὴ
τοῦ μὴ ὄντος. καὶ τὸ ὂν δὲ τοῦ ἑνὸς οὐ κεχωρισμένου,
καὶ ὅπου ἂν ᾖ τὸ ὄν, πάρεστιν αὐτῷ καὶ τὸ αὐτοῦ ἕν,

---

[1] Vitringa, Müller.

place, it would give the same light to the same
regions; but if anybody were to say, not the same
light, he would confirm by this that the body of the
sun was flowing away. But that the things that come
from that first are indestructible, and that the souls
and every intellect are immortal, has been stated at
greater length elsewhere.

11. But why, if the intelligible is everywhere as a
whole, do not all things participate in it as a whole?
And why is there the first there, and the second as
well, and after that others? Now one must suppose
that what is present is present for the capacity of
what is going to receive it, and that being is everywhere in being and does not fall short of itself, but
that is present to it which is able to be present, and is
present to it to the extent of its ability, not spatially;
as the transparent is present to light, but the participation of the turbid is otherwise. And certainly
things are first and second and third in rank and
power and difference, not by their positions. For
nothing prevents different things from being all
together, like soul and intellect and all bodies of
knowledge, major and subordinate. For the eye perceives the colour, the smell the fragrance, and other
different senses different things, coming from the
same body, which exist all together, but not separately. Is that first, then, variegated and many? Yes,
but the variegated is also simple, and the many one.
For it is a rational form which is one and many, and
all being is one. For its other is in itself and its
otherness belongs to itself; for it certainly could not
belong to non-being. And being belongs to the one
which is not separated from it, and wherever being
is, its one is present to it, and the one, again, is in

20 καὶ τὸ ἓν ὂν αὖ ἐφ' ἑαυτοῦ. ἔστι γὰρ καὶ παρεῖναι
χωρὶς ὄν. ἄλλως δὲ τὰ αἰσθητὰ τοῖς νοητοῖς πάρεστιν,
ὅσα πάρεστιν αὐτῶν καὶ οἷς πάρεισιν, ἄλλως τὰ νοητὰ
αὐτοῖς· ἐπεὶ καὶ ἄλλως ψυχῇ σῶμα, ἄλλως ἐπιστήμη
ψυχῇ καὶ ἐπιστήμη ἐπιστήμη ἐν τῷ αὐτῷ ἑκατέρα
25 οὖσα· σῶμα δὲ σώματι παρὰ ταῦτα ἑτέρως.

12. Ὥσπερ δὲ φωνῆς οὔσης κατὰ τὸν ἀέρα πολλάκις
καὶ λόγου ἐν τῇ φωνῇ οὖς μὲν παρὸν ἐδέξατο καὶ
ᾔσθετο, καὶ εἰ ἕτερον θείης μεταξὺ τῆς ἐρημίας, ἦλθε
καὶ πρὸς αὐτὸ ὁ λόγος καὶ ἡ φωνή, μᾶλλον δὲ τὸ οὖς
5 ἦλθε πρὸς τὸν λόγον, καὶ ὀφθαλμοὶ πολλοὶ πρὸς τὸ
αὐτὸ εἶδον καὶ πάντες ἐπλήσθησαν τῆς θέας καίτοι
ἐναφωρισμένου τοῦ θεάματος κειμένου, ὅτι ὁ μὲν
ὀφθαλμός, ὁ δὲ οὖς ἦν, οὕτω τοι καὶ τὸ δυνάμενον ψυχὴν
ἔχειν ἕξει καὶ ἄλλο αὖ καὶ ἕτερον ἀπὸ τοῦ αὐτοῦ. ἦν δὲ ἡ
10 φωνὴ πανταχοῦ τοῦ ἀέρος οὐ μία μεμερισμένη, ἀλλὰ
μία πανταχοῦ ὅλη· καὶ τὸ τῆς ὄψεως δέ, εἰ παθὼν ὁ ἀὴρ
τὴν μορφὴν ἔχει, ἔχει οὐ μεμερισμένην· οὗ γὰρ ἂν ὄψις
τεθῇ, ἔχει ἐκεῖ τὴν μορφήν. ἀλλὰ τοῦτο μὲν οὐ πᾶσα
δόξα συγχωρεῖ, εἰρήσθω δ' οὖν δι' ἐκεῖνο, ὅτι ἀπὸ τοῦ
15 αὐτοῦ ἑνὸς ἡ μετάληψις. τὸ δὲ ἐπὶ τῆς φωνῆς
ἐναργέστερον, ὡς ἐν παντὶ τῷ ἀέρι ὅλον τὸ εἶδός ἐστιν·
οὐ γὰρ ἂν ἤκουσε πᾶς τὸ αὐτὸ μὴ ἑκασταχοῦ ὅλου ὄντος

---

[1] For an even more impressive version of this sound-
image cp. III. 8.9. 26–29.

itself being. For it is possible to be present while being separate. But the beings of the sense-world are present in one way to the intelligibles (those of them which are present, and to the intelligibles to which they are present), and the intelligibles to themselves in another; since also soul is present in one way to body, and a knowledge to soul, and a knowledge to another knowledge, differently, when both are in the same [mind]; and body is present to body in another way besides these.

12. Just as there is often a sound in the air, and a word in the sound, and an ear is there and receives and perceives it; and if you put another ear in the middle of the space between, the word and the sound would come also to it, or rather the ear would come to the word[1]; and many eyes would look towards the same thing and all be filled with the sight of it (though the object of sight would be separate because one was an eye and the other an ear); in this same way that which is able to have soul will have it, and another again and yet another from the same source. But the sound was everywhere in the air and not as one sound divided into parts, but as one whole sound everywhere; and with sight, if the air has the shape by being affected, it has it not divided into parts; for wherever the sight is placed, it has the shape there. But not every way of thinking [about vision] accepts this,[2] but let the mention of it stand, because the participation is of the same one thing. But with the sound it is clearer that the whole form is in all the air: for everyone would not have heard the same thing if the spoken word had not been in

[2] Plotinus himself does not: see IV. 5.6.

τοῦ φωνηθέντος λόγου καὶ ἑκάστης ἀκοῆς τὸ πᾶν
ὁμοίως δεδεγμένης. εἰ δὲ μηδ' ἐνταῦθα ἡ ὅλη φωνὴ
καθ' ὅλον τὸν ἀέρα παρατέταται, ὡς τόδε μὲν τὸ μέρος
20 αὐτῆς τῷδε τῷ μέρει συνεζεῦχθαι, τόδε δὲ τῷδε
συμμεμερίσθαι, τί δεῖ ἀπιστεῖν, εἰ ψυχὴ μὴ μία τέταται
συμμεριζομένη, ἀλλὰ πανταχοῦ οὗ ἂν παρῇ πάρεστι καὶ
ἔστι πανταχοῦ τοῦ παντὸς οὐ μεμερισμένη; καὶ
γενομένη μὲν ἐν σώμασιν, ὡς ἂν γένοιτο, ἀνάλογον ἕξει
25 τῇ ἤδη ἐν τῷ ἀέρι φωνηθείσῃ φωνῇ, πρὸ δὲ τῶν
σωμάτων τῷ φωνοῦντι καὶ φωνήσοντι· καίτοι καὶ
γενομένη ἐν σώματι οὐδ' ὡς ἀπέστη τοῦ κατὰ τὸν
φωνοῦντα εἶναι, ὅστις φωνῶν καὶ ἔχει τὴν φωνὴν καὶ
δίδωσι. τὰ μὲν οὖν τῆς φωνῆς ταὐτότητα μὲν οὐκ ἔχει
τοῖς πρὸς ἃ εἴληπται, ἔχει δ' οὖν ὁμοιότητα κατά τι· τὰ
30 δὲ τῆς ψυχῆς ἅτε καὶ φύσεως ὄντα τῆς ἑτέρας δεῖ
λαμβάνειν ὡς οὐκ ὄντος αὐτῆς τοῦ μὲν ἐν σώμασι, τοῦ
δὲ ἐφ' ἑαυτοῦ, ἀλλὰ ὅλου ἐν αὐτῷ καὶ ἐν πολλοῖς αὖ
φανταζομένου. καὶ αὖ ἦλθεν ἄλλο εἰς τὸ λαβεῖν ψυχὴν
καὶ ἐξ ἀφανοῦς αὖ καὶ τοῦτο ἔχει, ὅπερ ἦν καὶ ἐν τοῖς
35 ἄλλοις. οὐδὲ γὰρ οὕτω προητοίμαστο, ὥστε μέρος
αὐτῆς ὡδὶ κείμενον εἰς τοῦτο ἐλθεῖν, ἀλλὰ τὸ λεγόμενον
ἥκειν ἦν ἐν παντὶ ἐν ἑαυτῷ καὶ ἔστιν ἐν ἑαυτῷ, καίτοι
δοκοῦν ἐνταῦθα ἐλθεῖν. πῶς γὰρ καὶ ἦλθεν; εἰ οὖν μὴ
ἦλθεν, ὤφθη δὲ νῦν παροῦσα καὶ παροῦσα οὐ τῷ
40 ἀναμεῖναι τὸ μεταληψόμενον, δηλονότι οὖσα ἐφ' ἑαυτῆς
πάρεστι καὶ τούτῳ. εἰ δ' οὖσα ἐφ' ἑαυτῆς τούτῳ

each and every place as a whole, and each hearing had not alike received the whole. But if even here the whole sound is not spread over the whole air, because this one part of it is joined to this one part of the air and that other divided up with that other, why should one disbelieve that one soul is not spread out and divided up with the body, but is present everywhere where it is present and is everywhere in the All without being divided? And when it comes to be in bodies, in whatever way it does come to be in them, it will be analogous to the sound already sounded in the air, but before the bodies it will be like what makes or is going to make the sound; yet even when it comes to be in a body it has not even so departed from being like the one who makes the sound and both has it and gives it. Well then, what happens with sound is not exactly the same as that for which it was taken as an example, but it has a certain likeness to it; but what happens with soul, since it belongs to the other nature, must be understood in the sense, not that one part of it is in body and another on its own, but that it is in itself as a whole and, again, is imagined as a whole in many. And again another came to get soul, and again this too has from the unseen what was also in the others. For soul was not made ready before in such a way that a part of it placed here came to this particular thing, but what was said to come was in everything in itself and is in itself, though we think it has come here. For how could it have come? If then it did not come, but was seen now present, and present not by waiting for something to come and participate in it, clearly it is both on its own and present to this thing. But if when it is on its own it is present to this, this

πάρεστι, τοῦτο ἦλθε πρὸς αὐτήν. εἰ δὲ τοῦτο ἔξω ὂν τοῦ
οὕτως ὄντος ἦλθε πρὸς τὸ οὕτως ὂν καὶ ἐγένετο ἐν τῷ
τῆς ζωῆς κόσμῳ, ἦν δὲ ὁ κόσμος ὁ τῆς ζωῆς ἐφ' ἑαυτοῦ,
καὶ πᾶς δὴ ἦν ἐφ' ἑαυτοῦ οὐ διειλημμένος εἰς τὸν ἑαυτοῦ
45 ὄγκον—οὐδὲ γὰρ ὄγκος ἦν—καὶ τὸ ἐληλυθὸς δὲ οὐκ εἰς
ὄγκον ἦλθε· μετέλαβεν ἄρα αὐτοῦ οὐ μέρους [ὅλου] [1]·
ἀλλὰ κἂν ἄλλο ἥκῃ εἰς τὸν τοιοῦτον κόσμον, ὅλου αὐτοῦ
μεταλήψεται. ὁμοίως ἄρα, εἰ λέγοιτο ἐκεῖνος ἐν τούτοις
ὅλος, ἐν παντὶ ἑκάστῳ ἔσται. καὶ πανταχοῦ ἄρα ὁ αὐτὸς
50 εἷς ἀριθμῷ οὐ μεμερισμένος, ἀλλ' ὅλος ἔσται.

13. Πόθεν οὖν ἡ ἔκτασις ἡ ἐπὶ πάντα τὸν οὐρανὸν
καὶ τὰ ζῷα; ἢ οὐκ ἐξετάθη. ἡ μὲν γὰρ αἴσθησις, ᾗ
προσέχοντες ἀπιστοῦμεν τοῖς λεγομένοις, λέγει ὅτι
ὧδε καὶ ὧδε, ὁ δὲ λόγος τὸ ὧδε καὶ ὧδέ φησιν οὐκ
5 ἐκταθεῖσαν ὧδε καὶ ὧδε γεγονέναι, ἀλλὰ τὸ ἐκταθὲν
πᾶν αὐτοῦ μετειληφέναι ὄντος ἀδιαστάτου αὐτοῦ. εἰ
οὖν τι μεταλήψεταί τινος, δῆλον ὅτι οὐχ αὐτοῦ
μεταλήψεται· ἢ οὐ μετειληφὸς ἔσται, ἀλλ' αὐτὸ ἔσται.
δεῖ οὖν σῶμα μεταλαμβάνον τινὸς οὐ σώματος
μεταλαμβάνειν· ἔχει γὰρ ἤδη. σῶμα δὴ οὐ σώματος
10 μεταλήψεται. οὐδὲ μέγεθος τοίνυν μεγέθους
μεταλήψεται· ἔχει γὰρ ἤδη. οὐδὲ γὰρ εἰ προσθήκην
λάβοι, τὸ μέγεθος ἐκεῖνο, ὃ πρότερον ἦν, μεγέθους
μεταλήψεται· οὐ γὰρ τὸ δίπηχυ τρίπηχυ γίνεται, ἀλλὰ
τὸ ὑποκείμενον ἄλλο ποσὸν ἔχον ἄλλο ἔσχεν· ἐπεὶ οὕτω

---

[1] delevimus, ut glossam ad οὐ μέρους.

came to it. But if this thing which was outside this kind of being came to that which exists in this way and came to be in the ordered beauty of life, and this ordered beauty of life was on its own, and was really on its own not divided over its own bulk – for there is no bulk – then what came to it also did not come to bulk; it did not therefore participate in a part of it; but if another thing as well comes to this kind of ordered beauty, it will participate in it as a whole. In the same way, then, if that is said to be present in these [two] things as a whole, it will be present as a whole in each and every thing. And so it will be everywhere, one in number and not divided into parts, but as a whole.

13. What, then, is the origin of its extension over all the heaven and all living things? Now, it is not extended. For it is sense-perception, to which we are paying attention when we disbelieve what is now being said, which says that it is here and there, but reason says that the "here and there" has not come about by its being extended but the whole of what is extended has participated in it, while it is not itself spaced out. If then anything is going to participate in anything, it is clear that it will not be participating in itself: otherwise it will not be a participant, but [just] itself. Body, then, if it participates in anything, cannot participate in body: for it has it already. A body certainly will not participate in a body. Nor, then, will magnitude participate in magnitude: for it has it already. For not even if it receives an addition will that magnitude which was there before participate in magnitude; for it is not the length of two cubits which becomes three cubits long, but the substrate which had one quantity has

15 γε αὐτὰ τὰ δύο τρία ἔσται. εἰ οὖν τὸ διειλημμένον καὶ τὸ
ἐκτεταμένον εἰς τόσον ἄλλου γένους μεταλήψεται ἢ
ὅλως ἄλλου, δεῖ τὸ οὗ μεταλαμβάνει μήτε διειλημμένον
εἶναι μήτε ἐκτεταμένον μήτε ὅλως ποσόν τι εἶναι. ὅλον
ἄρα δεῖ τὸ παρεσόμενον αὐτῷ πανταχοῦ ἀμερὲς ὂν
παρεῖναι, οὐχ οὕτω δὲ ἀμερές, ὡς μικρόν· οὕτω γὰρ
20 οὐδὲν ἧττον καὶ μεριστὸν ἔσται καὶ οὐ παντὶ αὐτῷ
ἐφαρμόσει οὐδ᾽ αὖ αὐξομένῳ τὸ αὐτὸ συνέσται. ἀλλ᾽
οὐδ᾽ οὕτως, ὡς σημεῖον· οὐ γὰρ ἓν σημεῖον ὁ ὄγκος, ἀλλ᾽
ἄπειρα ἐν αὐτῷ· ὥστε καὶ τοῦτο ἄπειρα σημεῖα ἔσται,
εἴπερ ἔσται, καὶ οὐ συνεχές· ὥστε οὐδ᾽ ὡς ἐφαρμόσει. εἰ
25 οὖν ὁ ὄγκος ὁ πᾶς ἕξει αὐτὸ ὅλον, ἕξει αὐτὸ κατὰ πᾶν
ἑαυτοῦ.

14. Ἀλλ᾽ εἰ ἡ αὐτὴ ἑκασταχοῦ ψυχή, πῶς ἰδία
ἑκάστου; καὶ πῶς ἡ μὲν ἀγαθή, ἡ δὲ κακή; ἢ ἐξαρκεῖ καὶ
ἑκάστῳ καὶ πάσας ψυχὰς ἔχει καὶ πάντας νοῦς. καὶ γὰρ
ἕν ἐστι καὶ ἄπειρον αὖ καὶ πάντα ὁμοῦ καὶ ἕκαστον ἔχει
5 διακεκριμένον καὶ αὖ οὐ διακριθὲν χωρίς. πῶς γὰρ ἂν
καὶ ἄπειρον ἢ οὕτω λέγοιτο, ὅτι ὁμοῦ πάντα ἔχει,
πᾶσαν ζωὴν καὶ πᾶσαν ψυχὴν καὶ νοῦν ἅπαντα; ἕκαστον
δὲ αὐτῶν οὐ πέρασιν ἀφώρισται· διὰ τοῦτο αὖ καὶ ἕν. οὐ
γὰρ δὴ μίαν ζωὴν ἔδει αὐτὸ ἔχειν, ἀλλ᾽ ἄπειρον, καὶ αὖ
10 μίαν καὶ τὴν μίαν οὕτω μίαν, ὅτι πάσας ὁμοῦ οὐ
συμφορηθείσας εἰς ἕν, ἀλλ᾽ ἀφ᾽ ἑνὸς ἀρξαμένας καὶ
μενούσας ὅθεν ἤρξαντο, μᾶλλον δὲ οὐδὲ ἤρξαντο, ἀλλ᾽
οὕτως εἶχεν ἀεί· οὐδὲν γὰρ γινόμενον ἐκεῖ· οὐδὲ

another; for [otherwise] the two themselves will be three. If then that which is divided and extended to a certain distance is going to participate in another kind, or in general in something else, that in which it participates must not be divided or extended or in any way quantitative. So that which is going to be present to it must be present to it everywhere as a whole, without parts; but not without parts as being small; for in this way it will none the less be divisible and will not fit the participant, and will not be with it as the same if it grows. But it is not without parts like a point either; for the bulk is not a point, but there are infinitely many points in it; so this too, if it is going to be a point, will be infinitely many points, and not continuous: so that it will not fit in this way either. If then the whole bulk has it as a whole, it will have it in the whole of itself.

14. But if it is the same soul in each and every place, how is it the particular soul of each individual? And how is one soul evil and the other good? Now, it is sufficient for each and contains all souls and all intellects. For it is one and again unbounded and holds all things together and each distinct, and, again, not distinct in separation. For how could it be called unbounded except in this sense, that it has all things together, every life and every soul and every intellect? But each of them is not marked off by boundaries: for this reason, again, it is one. For it did not have to have [only] one life, but a life unbounded and again one, and the one life one in this way, that all the lives are together, not heaped together into one, but beginning from one and remaining where they began; or rather they did not even begin, but it was like this always; for nothing

μεριζόμενον τοίνυν, ἀλλὰ δοκεῖ μερίζεσθαι τῷ λαβόντι.
15 τὸ δὲ ἐκεῖ τὸ ἔκπαλαι καὶ ἐξαρχῆς· τὸ δὲ γινόμενον
πελάζει καὶ συνάπτεσθαι δοκεῖ καὶ ἐξήρτηται ἐκείνου.
ἡμεῖς δέ—τίνες δὲ ἡμεῖς; ἆρα ἐκεῖνο ἢ τὸ πελάζον καὶ
τὸ γινόμενον ἐν χρόνῳ; ἢ καὶ πρὸ τοῦ ταύτην τὴν
γένεσιν γενέσθαι ἦμεν ἐκεῖ ἄνθρωποι ἄλλοι ὄντες καί
τινες καὶ θεοί, ψυχαὶ καθαραὶ καὶ νοῦς συνημμένος τῇ
20 ἀπάσῃ οὐσίᾳ, μέρη ὄντες τοῦ νοητοῦ οὐκ ἀφωρισμένα
οὐδ' ἀποτετμημένα, ἀλλ' ὄντες τοῦ ὅλου· οὐδὲ γὰρ οὐδὲ
νῦν ἀποτετμήμεθα. ἀλλὰ γὰρ νῦν ἐκείνῳ τῷ ἀνθρώπῳ
προσελήλυθεν ἄνθρωπος ἄλλος εἶναι θέλων· καὶ εὑρὼν
ἡμᾶς—ἦμεν γὰρ τοῦ παντὸς οὐκ ἔξω—περιέθηκεν
25 ἑαυτὸν ἡμῖν καὶ προσέθηκεν ἑαυτὸν ἐκείνῳ τῷ
ἀνθρώπῳ τῷ ὃς ἦν ἕκαστος ἡμῶν τότε· οἷον εἰ φωνῆς
οὔσης μιᾶς καὶ λόγου ἑνὸς ἄλλος ἄλλοθεν παραθεὶς τὸ
οὖς ἀκούσειε καὶ δέξαιτο, καὶ γένοιτο κατ' ἐνέργειαν
ἀκοή τις ἔχουσα τὸ ἐνεργοῦν εἰς αὐτὴν παρόν· καὶ
γεγενήμεθα τὸ συνάμφω καὶ οὐ θάτερον, ὃ πρότερον
30 ἦμεν, καὶ θάτερόν ποτε, ὃ ὕστερον προσεθέμεθα
ἀργήσαντος τοῦ προτέρου ἐκείνου καὶ ἄλλον τρόπον οὐ
παρόντος.

15. Ἀλλὰ πῶς προσελήλυθε τὸ προσεληλυθός; ἢ
ἐπειδὴ ἐπιτηδειότης αὐτῷ παρῆν, ἔσχε πρὸς ὃ ἦν
ἐπιτήδειον· ἦν δὲ γενόμενον οὕτως, ὡς δέξασθαι ψυχήν.
τὸ δὲ γίνεται ὡς μὴ δέξασθαι πᾶσαν καίτοι πιμοῦσαν
5 πᾶσαν, ἀλλ' οὐχ αὑτῷ, οἷον καὶ ζῷα τὰ ἄλλα καὶ τὰ
φυτὰ τοσοῦτον ἔχει, ὅσον δύναται λαβεῖν· οἷον φωνῆς
λόγον σημαινούσης τὰ μὲν καὶ τοῦ λόγου μετέσχε μετὰ
τῆς κατὰ φωνὴν ἠχῆς, τὰ δὲ τῆς φωνῆς καὶ τῆς πληγῆς

comes into being there; it is not then divided up into parts, but seems to be so divided to the recipient. But what is there is the primeval, that which was from the beginning; but that which comes to be draws near it and thinks to be joined to it and depends on it. But we – who are we? Are we that which draws near and comes to be in time? No, even before this coming to be came to be we were there, men who were different, and some of us even gods, pure souls and intellect united with the whole of reality; we were parts of the intelligible, not marked off or cut off but belonging to the whole; and we are not cut off even now. But now another man, wishing to exist, approached that man; and when he found us – for we were not outside the All – he wound himself round us and attached himself to that man who was then each one of us (as if there was one voice and one word and one here and another there turned their ears to it and heard and received it, and there came to be a hearing made actual, having that which acted on it present): and we have come to be the pair of them, not the one which we were before – and sometimes just the other one which we added on afterwards, when that prior one is inactive and in another way not present.

15. But how did that which approached approach? Since there was an adaptability present in it, it had that to which it was adapted. But what comes to exist in such a way as not to receive all soul, though all is present, but not to it, like the other animals and the plants receives as much as it can take: as when a voice says a word, and some partake of the word along with the noise of the voice, some only of the voice and its impact. So when a living thing

μόνον. γενομένου δὴ ζῴου, ὃ ἔχει μὲν παροῦσαν αὐτῷ ἐκ
10 τοῦ ὄντος ψυχήν, καθ᾽ ἣν δὴ ἀνήρτηται εἰς πᾶν τὸ ὄν,
παρόντος δὲ καὶ σώματος οὐ κενοῦ οὐδὲ ψυχῆς ἀμοίρου,
ὃ ἔκειτο μὲν οὐδὲ πρότερον ἐν τῷ ἀψύχῳ, ἔτι δὲ μᾶλλον
οἷον ἐγγὺς γενόμενον τῇ ἐπιτηδειότητι, καὶ γενομένου
οὐκέτι σώματος μόνου, ἀλλὰ καὶ ζῶντος σώματος, καὶ
15 τῇ οἷον γειτονείᾳ καρπωσαμένου τι ἴχνος ψυχῆς, οὐκ
ἐκείνης μέρους, ἀλλ᾽ οἷον θερμασίας τινὸς ἢ ἐλλάμψεως
ἐλθούσης, γένεσις ἐπιθυμιῶν καὶ ἡδονῶν καὶ ἀλγηδόνων
ἐν αὐτῷ ἐξέφυ· ἦν δὲ οὐκ ἀλλότριον τὸ σῶμα τοῦ ζῴου
τοῦ γεγενημένου. ἡ μὲν δὴ ἐκ τοῦ θείου ψυχὴ ἥσυχος ἦν
20 κατὰ τὸ ἦθος τὸ ἑαυτῆς ἐφ᾽ ἑαυτῆς βεβῶσα, τὸ δὲ ὑπ᾽
ἀσθενείας τὸ σῶμα θορυβούμενον καὶ ῥέον τε αὐτὸ καὶ
πληγαῖς κρουόμενον ταῖς ἔξω, πρῶτον αὐτὸ εἰς τὸ
κοινὸν τοῦ ζῴου ἐφθέγγετο, καὶ τὴν αὐτοῦ ταραχὴν
ἐδίδου τῷ ὅλῳ. οἷον ἐκκλησίᾳ δημογερόντων
καθημένων ἐφ᾽ ἡσύχῳ συννοίᾳ δῆμος ἄτακτος, τροφῆς
25 δεόμενος καὶ ἄλλα ἃ δὴ πάσχει αἰτιώμενος, τὴν πᾶσαν
ἐκκλησίαν εἰς θόρυβον ἀσχήμονα ἐμβάλλοι. ὅταν μὲν
οὖν ἡσυχίαν ἀγόντων τῶν τοιούτων ἀπὸ τοῦ φρονοῦντος
ἥκῃ εἰς αὐτοὺς λόγος, κατέστη εἰς τάξιν μετρίαν τὸ
πλῆθος, καὶ οὐ κεκράτηκε τὸ χεῖρον· εἰ δὲ μή, κρατεῖ τὸ
30 χεῖρον ἡσυχίαν ἄγοντος τοῦ βελτίονος, ὅτι μὴ ἠδυνήθη
τὸ θορυβοῦν δέξασθαι τὸν ἄνωθεν λόγον, καὶ τοῦτό ἐστι
πόλεως καὶ ἐκκλησίας κακία. τοῦτο δὲ καὶ ἀνθρώπου

---

[1] Plotinus may be thinking here of the Roman Senate: a
number of his circle were senators (Porphyry *Life* ch. 7);

came to be, which had soul present to it from what [really] exists, and was linked by that soul to all reality, but also had a body which is not empty or without a share in soul, which did not lie in the soulless even before, it drew nearer still, one might say, by its adaptability and became no longer merely a body, but also a living body; and by what one might call its neighbourhood it gained a trace of soul, not a part of it, but something like a heating or illumination coming from it, and the coming-to-be of desires and pleasures and pains grew up in it; but the body of the living thing which has come into being was not alien to it. Now the soul which comes from the divine was quiet, standing in itself according to its character; but the body, in a tumult because of its weakness, flowing away itself and battered by the blows from outside, first itself cried out to the community of the living thing and imparted its disturbance to the whole. It is like when in an assembly the elders of the people sit in quiet consideration,[1] and the disorderly populace, demanding food and complaining of other sufferings, throws the whole assembly into an ugly tumult. Now if people like this keep quiet and a speech from a sensible man gets through to them, the multitude settles to a decent order and the worse has not gained the mastery; but if not, the worse is master and the better keeps quiet, because the tumultuous mob could not receive the word from above, and this is the vice of city and assembly. But this is also the vice of man; he too has

but it is not clear that there is a reference to any particular episode in Roman history or passage of Latin literature (Henry and Schwyzer suggest Virgil *Aeneid* 1. 148-53).

κακία αὖ ἔχοντος δῆμον ἐν αὐτῷ ἡδονῶν καὶ ἐπιθυμιῶν
καὶ φόβων κρατησάντων συνδόντος ἑαυτὸν τοῦ
35 τοιούτου ἀνθρώπου δήμῳ τῷ τοιούτῳ· ὃς δ᾽ ἂν τοῦτον
τὸν ὄχλον δουλώσηται καὶ ἀναδράμῃ εἰς ἐκεῖνον, ὃς
ποτε ἦν, κατ᾽ ἐκεῖνόν τε ζῇ καὶ ἔστιν ἐκεῖνος διδοὺς τῷ
σώματι, ὅσα δίδωσιν ὡς ἑτέρῳ ὄντι ἑαυτοῦ· ἄλλος δέ
τις ὁτὲ μὲν οὕτως, ὁτὲ δὲ ἄλλως ζῇ, μικτός τις ἐξ
40 ἀγαθοῦ ἑαυτοῦ καὶ κακοῦ ἑτέρου γεγενημένος.

16. Ἀλλ᾽ εἰ ἐκείνη ἡ φύσις οὐκ ἂν γένοιτο κακὴ καὶ
οὗτος τρόπος ψυχῆς εἰς σῶμα ἰούσης καὶ παρούσης, τίς
ἡ κάθοδος ἡ ἐν περιόδοις καὶ ἄνοδος αὖ καὶ αἱ δίκαι καὶ
αἱ εἰς ἄλλων ζώων σώματα εἰσκρίσεις; ταῦτα γὰρ παρὰ
5 τῶν πάλαι περὶ ψυχῆς ἄριστα πεφιλοσοφηκότων
παρειλήφαμεν, οἷς πειρᾶσθαι προσήκει σύμφωνον ἢ μὴ
διάφωνόν γε ἐπιδεῖξαι τὸν νῦν προκείμενον λόγον.
ἐπειδὴ τοίνυν τὸ μεταλαμβάνειν ἐκείνης τῆς φύσεως ἦν
οὐ τὸ ἐλθεῖν ἐκείνην εἰς τὰ τῇδε ἀποστᾶσαν ἑαυτῆς,
10 ἀλλὰ τὸ τήνδε ἐν ἐκείνῃ γίνεσθαι καὶ μεταλαβεῖν, δῆλον
ὅτι ὃ λέγουσιν ἐκεῖνοι "ἥκειν" λεκτέον εἶναι τὴν
σώματος φύσιν ἐκεῖ γενέσθαι καὶ μεταλαβεῖν ζωῆς καὶ
ψυχῆς, καὶ ὅλως οὐ τοπικῶς τὸ ἥκειν, ἀλλ᾽ ὅστις
τρόπος τῆς τοιαύτης κοινωνίας. ὥστε τὸ μὲν κατελθεῖν
15 τὸ ἐν σώματι γενέσθαι, ὡς φαμεν ψυχὴν ἐν σώματι
γενέσθαι, τὸ τούτῳ δοῦναί τι παρ᾽ αὐτῆς, οὐκ ἐκείνου
γενέσθαι, τὸ δ᾽ ἀπελθεῖν τὸ μηδαμῇ τὸ σῶμα

in himself a populace of pleasures and lusts and fears, which gain the mastery when a man of this kind surrenders himself to a populace of this kind; but whoever enslaves this mob, and runs back up to that man he once was, lives according to that man and is that man and gives what he gives to the body as to something other than himself; but someone else lives now this way and now the other; he has become a person mixed from the good self and the evil other.

16. But if that nature could not become evil, and this is the way of soul's coming and presence to the body, what are the descent at fixed periods, and again the ascent, and the judgements, and the entries into the bodies of other animals? For we have received these from those who in ancient times have philosophised best about the soul; and it is proper to try to show that our present discourse is in agreement, or at least not in disagreement, with them.[1] Since, then, participation in that nature was not its coming to this world and abandoning itself, but this our nature's coming to be in that and participating in it, it is clear that the "coming" those ancient philosophers speak of must mean that the nature of body comes to be there and participates in life and soul, and in general is not meant spatially, but indicates whatever the manner of this kind of communion is. So that "descent" means coming to be in body as we say soul comes to be in body, the giving to this body of something from itself, not coming to belong to it, and "departure" means that body in no

[1] A very firm statement of the traditionalism of Plotinus; the ancient philosophers are of course Plato and, secondarily, the Pythagoreans.

ἐπικοινωνεῖν αὐτῆς· τάξιν δὲ εἶναι τῆς τοιαύτης
κοινωνίας τοῖς τοῦδε τοῦ παντὸς μέρεσι, τὴν δὲ οἷον ἐν
ἐσχάτῳ τῷ νοητῷ τόπῳ πλεονάκις διδόναι ἑαυτῆς ἅτε
20 πλησίον τῇ δυνάμει οὖσαν καὶ ἐν βραχυτέροις
διαστήμασι φύσεως τῆς τοιαύτης νόμῳ· κακὸν δὲ εἶναι
τὴν τοιαύτην κοινωνίαν καὶ ἀγαθὸν τὴν ἀπαλλαγήν. διὰ
τί; ὅτι, κἂν μὴ τοῦδε ᾖ, ἀλλ' οὖν ψυχὴ τοῦδε λεγομένη
ὁπωσοῦν μερική πως ἐκ τοῦ παντὸς γίνεται· ἡ γὰρ
25 ἐνέργεια αὐτῆς οὐκέτι πρὸς τὸ ὅλον καίπερ τοῦ ὅλου
οὔσης, ὥσπερ ἂν εἰ ἐπιστήμης ὅλης οὔσης κατά τι
θεώρημα ὁ ἐπιστήμων ἐνεργεῖ· τὸ δ' ἀγαθὸν αὐτῷ ἦν τῷ
ἐπιστήμονι οὐ κατά τι τῆς ἐπιστήμης, ἀλλὰ κατὰ τὴν
πᾶσαν ἣν ἔχει. καὶ τοίνυν αὕτη τοῦ παντὸς οὖσα κόσμου
νοητοῦ καὶ ἐν τῷ ὅλῳ τὸ μέρος ἀποκρύπτουσα οἷον
30 ἐξέθορεν ἐκ τοῦ παντὸς εἰς μέρος, εἰς ὃ ἐνεργεῖ ἑαυτὴν
μέρος ὄν, οἷον εἰ πῦρ πᾶν καίειν δυνάμενον μικρόν τι
καίειν ἀναγκάζοιτο καίτοι πᾶσαν ἔχον τὴν δύναμιν. ἔστι
γὰρ ἡ ψυχὴ χωρὶς πάντη οὖσα ἑκάστη οὐχ ἑκάστη, ὅταν
δὲ διακριθῇ οὐ τόπῳ, ἀλλ' ἐνεργείᾳ γένηται τὸ
35 καθέκαστον, μοῖρά τίς ἐστιν, οὐ πᾶσα, καίτοι καὶ ὡς
πᾶσα τρόπον ἄλλον· οὐδενὶ δὲ ἐπιστατοῦσα πάντη
πᾶσα, οἷον δυνάμει τότε τὸ μέρος οὖσα. τὸ δὲ εἰς Ἅιδου

way has any community with it; and there is an
order of this kind of communion for the parts of this
All, but soul, which is as it were on the edge of the
intelligible region, often gives them something of
itself since it is close to them by its power and the
distances are shorter by the law of a nature of this
kind; but communion of this kind is an evil [for soul]
and release from it a good. Why? Because, even if it
does not belong to this particular body, yet when it
is said to belong to this body, it in some way or other
comes out of its All to be partial; for its activity is no
longer directed to the whole although it belongs to
the whole, just as if when a whole body of knowledge
is there [in his mind] the one who knows is active
about a particular subject of study; but the good for
the knower himself is not in some particular point of
his knowledge but in the whole body of knowledge
which he has. And so this soul, which belongs to the
whole intelligible universe and hides its part in the
whole, leapt out, we might say, from the whole to a
part, and actualises itself as a part in it, as if a fire
able to burn everything was compelled to burn some
little thing although it had all its power. For the soul
when it is altogether apart is particular without
being particular, but when it is separated – not
spatially, but it becomes each particular thing in its
activity – it is a part, not the whole, though even so
it is in another way the whole; but when it is not in
charge of anything it is altogether the whole, and
then it is a part, one might say, in potency. But as for
going to Hades, if this means in the unseen,[1] it is

---

[1] The word-play here is clear in Greek, but cannot be
rendered in English.

γίνεσθαι, εἰ μὲν ἐν τῷ ἀιδεῖ, τὸ χωρὶς λέγεται· εἰ δέ τινα
χείρω τόπον, τί θαυμαστόν; ἐπεὶ καὶ νῦν, οὗ τὸ σῶμα
ἡμῶν καὶ ἐν ᾧ τόπῳ, κἀκείνη λέγεται ἐκεῖ. ἀλλ' οὐκ
40 ὄντος ἔτι τοῦ σώματος; ἢ τὸ εἴδωλον εἰ μὴ
ἀποσπασθείη, πῶς οὐκ ἐκεῖ, οὗ τὸ εἴδωλον; εἰ δὲ
παντελῶς λύσειε φιλοσοφία, καὶ ἀπέλθοι τὸ εἴδωλον εἰς
τὸν χείρω τόπον μόνον, αὐτὴ δὲ καθαρῶς ἐν τῷ νοητῷ
οὐδενὸς ἐξῃρημένου αὐτῆς. τὸ μὲν οὖν ἐκ τοῦ τοιοῦδε
45 εἴδωλον γενόμενον οὕτως· ὅταν δ' αὐτὴ οἷον ἐλλάμψῃ
πρὸς αὐτήν, τῇ νεύσει τῇ ἐπὶ θάτερα πρὸς τὸ ὅλον
συνέσταλται καὶ οὐκ ἔστιν ἐνεργείᾳ οὐδ' αὖ ἀπόλωλεν.
ἀλλὰ περὶ μὲν τούτων ταῦτα· πάλιν δὲ ἀναλαβόντες τὸν
ἐξαρχῆς λόγον λέγωμεν.

soul's being apart that is spoken of; but if going to
some worse place, what is surprising in that? For
even now, soul too is said to be there in that place
where our body is. But what if the body no longer
exists? If the image has not been torn away from it,
how can it not be there where the image is[1]? But if
philosophy has freed it completely, the image then
too goes to the worse place alone, but the soul itself
is purely in the intelligible without losing anything
of itself. This is how it is with an image produced by
this sort of process; but when the soul itself so to
speak shines upon itself, by its inclination to the
other [higher] side it is concentrated upon the
whole, and it neither exists actually nor, again, does
it perish. But this is enough about these matters: let
us now take up the original discussion.

[1] For the relationship of soul and image or shade,
illustrated by what is said about Heracles and his shade in
Odyssey 11. 601–3, cp. I. 1.12 and IV. 3. 32–4. 1.

VI. 5. (23) ΠΕΡΙ ΤΟΥ ΤΟ ΟΝ ΕΝ ΚΑΙ ΤΑΥΤΟΝ ΟΝ ΑΜΑ ΠΑΝΤΑΧΟΥ ΕΙΝΑΙ ΟΛΟΝ ΔΕΥΤΕΡΟΝ

1. Τὸ ἓν καὶ ταὐτὸν ἀριθμῷ πανταχοῦ ἅμα ὅλον εἶναι
κοινὴ μέν τις ἔννοιά φησιν εἶναι, ὅταν πάντες κινούμενοι
αὐτοφυῶς λέγωσι τὸν ἐν ἑκάστῳ ἡμῶν θεὸν ὡς ἕνα καὶ
τὸν αὐτόν. καὶ εἴ τις αὐτοὺς τὸν τρόπον μὴ ἀπαιτοῖ μηδὲ
5 λόγῳ ἐξετάζειν τὴν δόξαν αὐτῶν ἐθέλοι, οὕτως ἂν καὶ
θεῖντο καὶ ἐνεργοῦντες τοῦτο τῇ διανοίᾳ οὕτως
ἀναπαύοιντο εἰς ἕν πως συνερείδοντες καὶ ταὐτόν, καὶ
οὐδ' ἂν ἐθέλοιεν ταύτης τῆς ἑνότητος ἀποσχίζεσθαι. καὶ
ἔστι πάντων βεβαιοτάτη ἀρχή, ἣν ὥσπερ αἱ ψυχαὶ ἡμῶν
10 φθέγγονται, μὴ ἐκ τῶν καθέκαστα συγκεφαλαιωθεῖσα,
ἀλλὰ πρὸ τῶν καθέκαστα πάντων προελθοῦσα καὶ πρὸ
ἐκείνης τῆς τοῦ ἀγαθοῦ πάντα ὀρέγεσθαι τιθεμένης τε
καὶ λεγούσης. οὕτω γὰρ ἂν αὕτη ἀληθὲς εἴη, εἰ τὰ
πάντα εἰς ἓν σπεύδοι καὶ ἓν εἴη, καὶ τούτου ἡ ὄρεξις εἴη.
15 τὸ γὰρ ἓν τοῦτο προϊὸν μὲν ἐπὶ θάτερα, ἐφ' ὅσον

---

[1] This is one of Plotinus' rare appeals to the common
experience of mankind as a good starting-point for a
philosophical investigation (III. 7. 1 may be compared,
though "we" there probably means "philosophers" rather

VI. 5. ON THE PRESENCE OF BEING, ONE AND THE SAME, EVERYWHERE AS A WHOLE II

1. A general opinion affirms that what is one and the same in number is everywhere present as a whole, when all men are naturally and spontaneously moved to speak of the god who is in each one of us one and the same.[1] And if someone did not ask them how this is and want to examine their opinion rationally, this is what they would assume, and with this active and actual in their thinking they would come to rest in this way somehow supporting themselves on what is one and the same, and they would not wish to be cut away from this unity. And this is the firmest principle of all, which our souls cry out, as it were, not summed up from individual instances, but preceding all the individuals and coming before that principle which lays down and says that all things desire the good. For this latter would be true if all things press on to the one and are one, and their desire is of this. For this one, proceeding to the others as far as, and in the way in which, it can

than "mankind in general"). The way in which he expresses this general consent may remind us of how much the centuries of Christianity and anti-Christianity have changed the common thinking of our own world. What he says here would probably still be true in India.

προελθεῖν αὐτῷ οἷόν τε, πολλὰ ἂν φανείη τε καί πως καὶ
εἴη, ἡ δ᾽ ἀρχαία φύσις καὶ ἡ ὄρεξις τοῦ ἀγαθοῦ, ὅπερ
ἐστὶν αὐτοῦ, εἰς ἓν ὄντως ἄγει, καὶ ἐπὶ τοῦτο σπεύδει
πᾶσα φύσις, ἐφ᾽ ἑαυτήν. τοῦτο γάρ ἐστι τὸ ἀγαθὸν τῇ
μιᾷ ταύτῃ φύσει τὸ εἶναι αὐτῆς καὶ εἶναι αὐτήν· τοῦτο δ᾽
20 ἐστὶ τὸ εἶναι μίαν. οὕτω δὲ καὶ τὸ ἀγαθὸν ὀρθῶς εἶναι
λέγεται οἰκεῖον· διὸ οὐδὲ ἔξω ζητεῖν αὐτὸ δεῖ. ποῦ γὰρ
ἂν εἴη ἔξω τοῦ ὄντος περιπεπτωκός; ἢ πῶς ἄν τις ἐν τῷ
μὴ ὄντι ἐξεύροι αὐτό; ἀλλὰ δηλονότι ἐν τῷ ὄντι οὐκ ὂν
αὐτὸ μὴ ὄν. εἰ δὲ ὂν καὶ ἐν τῷ ὄντι ἐκεῖνο, ἐν ἑαυτῷ ἂν
25 εἴη ἑκάστῳ. οὐκ ἀπέστημεν ἄρα τοῦ ὄντος, ἀλλ᾽ ἐσμὲν
ἐν αὐτῷ, οὐδ᾽ αὖ ἐκεῖνο ἡμῶν· ἓν ἄρα πάντα τὰ ὄντα.

2. Λόγος δὲ ἐπιχειρήσας ἐξέτασιν ποιεῖσθαι τοῦ
λεγομένου οὐχ ἕν τι ὤν, ἀλλά τι μεμερισμένον,
παραλαμβάνων τε εἰς τὴν ζήτησιν τὴν τῶν σωμάτων
φύσιν καὶ ἐντεῦθεν τὰς ἀρχὰς λαμβάνων ἐμέρισέ τε τὴν
5 οὐσίαν τοιαύτην εἶναι νομίσας, καὶ τῇ ἑνότητι
ἠπίστησεν αὐτῆς ἅτε μὴ ἐξ ἀρχῶν τῶν οἰκείων τὴν
ὁρμὴν τῆς ζητήσεως πεποιημένος. ἡμῖν δὲ ληπτέον εἰς
τὸν ὑπὲρ τοῦ ἑνὸς καὶ πάντη ὄντος λόγον οἰκείας εἰς
πίστιν ἀρχάς· τοῦτο δ᾽ ἐστὶ νοητὰς νοητῶν καὶ τῆς
ἀληθινῆς οὐσίας ἐχομένας. ἐπεὶ γὰρ τὸ μέν ἐστι
10 πεφορημένον καὶ παντοίας δεχόμενον μεταβολὰς καὶ εἰς
πάντα τόπον ⟨ἀεὶ⟩[1] διειλημμένον, ὃ δὴ γένεσιν ἂν
προσήκοι ὀνομάζειν, ἀλλ᾽ οὐκ οὐσίαν, τὸ δὲ ὂν ἀεὶ

---

[1] Igal, H–S².

proceed, would appear as many and even, in a sense, be many; but the ancient nature and the desire of the good, that is of itself, leads to what is really one, and every nature presses on to this, to itself. For this is the good to this one nature, belonging to itself and being itself: but this is being one. It is in this sense that the good is rightly said to be our own; therefore one must not seek it outside. For where could it be if it had fallen outside being? Or how could one discover it in non-being? But it is obvious that it is in being, since it is not non-being. But if that good is being and in being, it would clearly be for each individual in himself. We have not, then, departed from being, but are in it, nor has it departed from us: so all things are one.[1]

2. But the reason which tried to make the investigation of what we are talking about, since it is not one thing but something divided and brings along to its enquiry the nature of bodies and takes its principles from them, both divided substance, thinking that it was of this [bodily] kind, and disbelieved in its unity, because it did not take the starting-point of its enquiry from the principles proper to substance. But we must take for our reasoning about the one and altogether existent principles which, being proper to it, will lead to conviction: that is, intelligible principles of intelligibles and those which belong to true substance. For since one [nature] is carried about and accepts every kind of change and is continually divided into every place, which it would be appropriate to call becoming, not substance, but the other

[1] On this passage and ch. 4, 17–24 see *Introductory Note*, pp. 270–271.

[διειλημμένον]¹ ὡσαύτως κατὰ ταὐτὰ ἔχον, οὔτε
γινόμενον οὔτε ἀπολλύμενον οὐδέ τινα χώραν οὐδὲ
15 τόπον οὐδέ τινα ἕδραν ἔχον οὐδ' ἐξιὸν ποθὲν οὐδ' αὖ
εἰσιὸν εἰς ὁτιοῦν, ἀλλ' ἐν αὑτῷ μένον, περὶ μὲν ἐκείνων
λέγων ἄν τις ἐξ ἐκείνης τῆς φύσεως καὶ τῶν ὑπὲρ αὐτῆς
ἀξιουμένων συλλογίζοιτο ἂν εἰκότως δι' εἰκότων
εἰκότας καὶ τοὺς συλλογισμοὺς ποιούμενος. ὅταν δ' αὖ
τοὺς περὶ τῶν νοητῶν λόγους τις ποιῆται, λαμβάνων
20 τὴν τῆς οὐσίας φύσιν περὶ ἧς πραγματεύεται τὰς ἀρχὰς
τῶν λόγων δικαίως ἂν ποιοῖτο μὴ παρεκβαίνων ὥσπερ
ἐπιλελησμένος ἐπ' ἄλλην φύσιν, ἀλλ' ὑπ' αὐτῆς ἐκείνης
περὶ αὐτῆς τὴν κατανόησιν ποιούμενος, ἐπειδὴ
πανταχοῦ τὸ τί ἐστιν ἀρχή, καὶ τοῖς καλῶς ὁρισαμένοις
25 λέγεται καὶ τῶν συμβεβηκότων τὰ πολλὰ γινώσκεσθαι·
οἷς δὲ καὶ πάντα ἐν τῷ τί ἐστιν ὑπάρχει, πολλῷ μᾶλλον
ἐν τούτοις ἔχεσθαι δεῖ τούτου, καὶ εἰς τοῦτο βλεπτέον
καὶ πρὸς τοῦτο πάντα ἀνενεκτέον.

3. Εἰ δὴ τὸ ὂν ὄντως τοῦτο καὶ ὡσαύτως ἔχει καὶ οὐκ
ἐξίσταται αὐτὸ ἑαυτοῦ καὶ γένεσις περὶ αὐτὸ οὐδεμία
οὐδ' ἐν τόπῳ ἐλέγετο εἶναι, ἀνάγκη αὐτὸ οὕτως ἔχον ἀεί
τε σὺν αὑτῷ εἶναι, καὶ μὴ διεστάναι ἀφ' αὑτοῦ μηδὲ
5 αὑτοῦ τὸ μὲν ὡδί, τὸ δὲ ὡδὶ εἶναι, μηδὲ προϊέναι τι ἀπ'
αὑτοῦ· ἤδη γὰρ ἂν ἐν ἄλλῳ καὶ ἄλλῳ εἴη, καὶ ὅλως ἕν

_____
¹ del. Harder.

[nature] is being, always in exactly the same state, neither coming to be nor perishing nor having any space or place or base, nor going out from anywhere nor entering into anything, but remaining in itself, when one was speaking about those things [of the lower world] one would reason logically from that nature and from what is held to be true about it and, reasoning probably by means of probable principles, would frame syllogisms which are also [only] probable. But when, on the other hand, one engages in reasonings about the intelligibles, the right way would be to take the nature of substance about which one is concerned and so establish the principles of one's reasonings, without passing over, as if one had forgotten, to the other nature, but applying one's mind to that intelligible nature by means of itself; since everywhere the "what it is" is the starting-point, and it is said that those who have defined well know most of the incidental accompaniments; but in things where everything is included in the "what it is", one must much more hold fast to this and look to this and refer everything to this.[1]

3. Now if this is real being and remains the same and does not depart from itself and there is no coming-to-be about it and, as was said, it is not in place, it is necessary for it, being in this state, to be always with itself, and not to stand away from itself; one part of it cannot be here and another there, nor can anything come out of it; [for if it did] it would already be in different places, and, in general, would

[1] Plotinus is here developing an Aristotelian thought in a Platonic manner: cp. Aristotle on Socrates, *Metaphysics* M 4, 1078b24–25.

τινι εἴη, καὶ οὐκ ἐφ' ἑαυτοῦ οὐδ' ἀπαθές· πάθοι γὰρ ἄν,
εἰ ἐν ἄλλῳ· εἰ δ' ἐν ἀπαθεῖ ἔσται, οὐκ ἐν ἄλλῳ. εἰ οὖν μὴ
ἀποστὰν ἑαυτοῦ μηδὲ μερισθὲν μηδὲ μεταβάλλον αὐτὸ
10 μηδεμίαν μεταβολὴν ἐν πολλοῖς ἅμα εἴη ἓν ὅλον ἅμα
ἑαυτῷ ὄν, τὸ αὐτὸ ὂν πανταχοῦ ἑαυτῷ τὸ ἐν πολλοῖς
εἶναι ἂν ἔχοι· τοῦτο δέ ἐστιν ἐφ' ἑαυτοῦ ὂν μὴ αὖ ἐφ'
ἑαυτοῦ εἶναι. λείπεται τοίνυν λέγειν αὐτὸ μὲν ἐν οὐδενὶ
εἶναι, τὰ δ' ἄλλα ἐκείνου μεταλαμβάνειν, ὅσα δύναται
15 αὐτῷ παρεῖναι, καὶ καθόσον ἐστὶ δυνατὰ αὐτῷ
παρεῖναι. ἀνάγκη τοίνυν ἢ τὰς ὑποθέσεις καὶ τὰς ἀρχὰς
ἐκείνας ἀναιρεῖν μηδεμίαν εἶναι τοιαύτην φύσιν
λέγοντας ἤ, εἰ τοῦτό ἐστιν ἀδύνατον καὶ ἔστιν
ἐξανάγκης τοιαύτη φύσις καὶ οὐσία, παραδέχεσθαι τὸ
ἐξαρχῆς, τὸ ἓν καὶ ταὐτὸν ἀριθμῷ μὴ μεμερισμένον,
20 ἀλλὰ ὅλον ὄν, τῶν ἄλλων τῶν παρ' αὐτὸ μηδενὸς
ἀποστατεῖν, οὐδὲν τοῦ χεῖσθαι δεηθὲν οὐδὲ τῷ μοίρας
τινὰς ἀπ' αὐτοῦ ἐλθεῖν μηδ' αὖ τῷ αὐτὸ μὲν μεῖναι ἐν
αὑτῷ ὅλον, ἄλλο δέ τι ἀπ' αὐτοῦ γεγονὸς καταλελοιπὸς
αὐτὸ ἥκειν εἰς τὰ ἄλλα πολλαχῇ. ἔσται τε γὰρ οὕτως τὸ
25 μὲν ἄλλοθι, τὸ δ' ἀπ' αὐτοῦ ἄλλοθι, καὶ τόπον ἕξει
διεστηκὸς ἀπὸ τῶν ἀπ' αὐτοῦ. καὶ ἐπ' ἐκείνων αὖ, εἰ
ἕκαστον ὅλον ἢ μέρος—καὶ εἰ μὲν μέρος, οὐ τὴν τοῦ
ὅλου ἀποσώσει φύσιν, ὅπερ δὴ εἴρηται· εἰ δὲ ὅλον
ἕκαστον, ἢ ἕκαστον μεριοῦμεν ἴσα μέρη τῷ ἐν ᾧ ἐστιν ἢ
30 ταὐτὸν ὅλον πανταχοῦ συγχωρήσομεν δύνασθαι εἶναι.

be in something and not on its own or unaffected; for it would be affected if it was in something else; but if it is going to be in a state of freedom from affection, it will not be in something else. If, therefore, without departing from itself or being divided into parts or itself undergoing any change, it is in many things at once, existing at the same time as one whole with itself, then, being the same everywhere, it will have an existence in many things: but this is being on its own and, again, not being on its own. It remains, then, to say that it is itself in nothing, but the other things participate in it, all those which are able to be present to it and in so far as they are able to be present to it. We must then either do away with these hypotheses and principles and say that there is no nature of this kind; or, if this is impossible and there is of necessity a nature and substance of this kind, we must accept what we have been saying from the beginning, that the one and the same in number which is not divided but exists as a whole does not depart from any of the things which exist beside it, with no need of any diffusion either by some portions coming from it or, alternatively, by its remaining as a whole in itself but something else generated from it leaving it and coming to the others in many ways. For in this way it will be in one place and what comes from it in another, and it will have a place separated from what comes from it. And again with the things which come from it, if each is a part or a whole – if it is a part it will not preserve the nature of the whole, as has been said already; but if each is a whole, we shall either divide each one into parts equal to that in which it is, or we shall agree that the same can be everywhere present as a whole. This,

οὗτος δὴ ὁ λόγος ἐξ αὐτοῦ τοῦ πράγματος καὶ τῆς
οὐσίας ἀλλότριον οὐδὲν οὐδ' ἐκ τῆς ἑτέρας φύσεως
ἑλκύσας.

4. Ἴδε δέ, εἰ βούλει, καὶ τόνδε· τὸν θεὸν οὐ πῆ μὲν
εἶναι, πῆ δ' οὐκ εἶναί φαμεν. ἔστι γὰρ ἀξιούμενόν τε
παρὰ πᾶσι τοῖς ἔννοιαν ἔχουσι θεῶν οὐ μόνον περὶ
ἐκείνου, ἀλλὰ καὶ περὶ πάντων λέγειν θεῶν, ὡς
5 πανταχοῦ πάρεισι, καὶ ὁ λόγος δέ φησι δεῖν οὕτω
τίθεσθαι. εἰ οὖν πανταχοῦ, οὐχ οἷόν τε μεμερισμένον· οὐ
γὰρ ἂν ἔτι πανταχοῦ αὐτὸς εἴη, ἀλλ' ἕκαστον αὐτοῦ
μέρος τὸ μὲν ὡδί, τὸ δὲ ὡδὶ ἔσται, αὐτός τε οὐχ εἷς
ἔτι ἔσται, ὥσπερ εἰ τμηθείη τι μέγεθος εἰς πολλά,
ἀπολλύμενόν τε ἔσται καὶ τὰ μέρη πάντα οὐκέτι τὸ ὅλον
10 ἐκεῖνο ἔσται· πρὸς τούτοις δὲ καὶ σῶμα ἔσται. εἰ δὴ
ταῦτα ἀδύνατα, πάλιν αὖ ἀνεφάνη τὸ ἀπιστούμενον ἐν
πάσῃ φύσει ἀνθρώπου ὁμοῦ τῷ θεὸν νομίζειν καὶ
πανταχοῦ τὸ αὐτὸ ἅμα ὅλον εἶναι. πάλιν δέ, εἰ ἄπειρον
λέγομεν ἐκείνην τὴν φύσιν—οὐ γὰρ δὴ πεπερασμένην—
15 τί ἂν ἄλλο εἴη, ἢ ὅτι οὐκ ἐπιλείψει; εἰ δὲ μὴ ἐπιλείψει,
ὅτι πάρεστιν ἑκάστῳ; εἰ γὰρ μὴ δύναιτο παρεῖναι,
ἐπιλείψει τε καὶ ἔσται ὅπου οὔ. καὶ γὰρ εἰ λέγοιμεν ἄλλο
μετ' αὐτὸ τὸ ἕν, ὁμοῦ αὖ αὐτῷ καὶ τὸ μετ' αὐτὸ περὶ
ἐκεῖνο καὶ εἰς ἐκεῖνο καὶ αὐτοῦ οἷον γέννημα συναφὲς
20 ἐκείνῳ, ὥστε τὸ μετέχον τοῦ μετ' αὐτὸ κἀκείνου
μετειληφέναι. πολλῶν γὰρ ὄντων τῶν ἐν τῷ νοητῷ,

certainly, is an argument derived from the thing itself and its substance, dragging in nothing alien or derived from the other nature.

4. But, please, look at this argument also: we deny that God is in one place but not in another. For it is accepted among all who have a notion of gods that one says, not only about that [supreme God] but about all gods, that they are present everywhere, and the argument says that this must be assumed. If then God is everywhere, it is not possible that he should be divided; for then he would not still be everywhere, but each part of him would be one here and another there, and he would not still be one, as, if one cuts a magnitude into many parts, it will be destroyed and all the parts will no longer be that whole; and besides, he will be a body. But if all this is impossible, then again what is disbelieved in has reappeared; in every human nature believing in God goes with believing that the same thing is everywhere as a whole. And again, if we say that that [divine] nature is unbounded – it certainly is not limited – what could this mean other than that he will not fall short? But if he is not going to fall short, does this mean that he is present to each and every thing? Yes, for if he should not be able to be present, he will fall short and there will be somewhere he is not. For even if we may be talking about something else after the One itself, this again will be together with the One itself and what is after it will be around that One and directed to that One and like something generated from it in close touch with it, so that what participates in what comes after it has also participated in that One. For, since there are many things in the intelligible, firsts and seconds and

πρώτων τε καὶ δευτέρων καὶ τρίτων, καὶ οἷον σφαίρας
μιᾶς εἰς ἓν κέντρον ἀνημμένων, οὐ διαστήμασι
διειλημμένων, ἀλλ' ὄντων ὁμοῦ αὐτοῖς ἁπάντων, ὅπου
ἂν παρῇ τὰ τρίτα, καὶ τὰ δεύτερα καὶ τὰ πρῶτα
πάρεστι.

5. Καὶ σαφηνείας μὲν ἕνεκα ὁ λόγος πολλάκις οἷον ἐκ
κέντρου ἑνὸς πολλὰς γραμμὰς ποιήσας εἰς ἔννοιαν τοῦ
πλήθους τοῦ γενομένου ἐθέλει ἄγειν. δεῖ δὲ τηροῦντας
ὁμοῦ πάντα τὰ λεγόμενα πολλὰ γεγονέναι λέγειν,
5 ὡς κἀκεῖ ἐπὶ τοῦ κύκλου οὐκ οὔσας γραμμὰς ἀφωρισ-
μένας ἔστι λαμβάνειν· ἐπίπεδον γὰρ ἕν. οὐ δὲ οὐδὲ κατ'
ἐπίπεδον ἓν διάστημά τι, ἀλλ' ἀδιάστατοι δυνάμεις καὶ
οὐσίαι, πάντα ἂν εἰκότως κατὰ κέντρα λέγοιτο ἐν ἑνὶ
ὁμοῦ κέντρῳ ἡνωμένα, οἷον ἀφέντα τὰς γραμμὰς τὰ
10 πέρατα αὐτῶν τὰ πρὸς τῷ κέντρῳ κείμενα, ὅτε δὴ καὶ
ἕν ἐστι πάντα. πάλιν δέ, εἰ προσθείης τὰς γραμμάς, αἱ
μὲν ἐξάψονται τῶν κέντρων αὐτῶν ἃ κατέλιπον ἑκάστη,
ἔσται γε μὴν οὐδὲν ἧττον κέντρον ἕκαστον οὐκ
ἀποτετμημένον τοῦ ἑνὸς πρώτου κέντρου, ἀλλ' ὁμοῦ
15 ὄντα ἐκείνῳ ἕκαστον αὖ εἶναι, καὶ τοσαῦτα ὅσαι αἱ
γραμμαὶ αἷς ἔδοσαν αὐτὰ πέρατα εἶναι ἐκείνων, ὥστε
ὅσων μὲν ἐφάπτεται γραμμῶν τοσαῦτα φανῆναι, ἓν δὲ
ὁμοῦ πάντα ἐκεῖνα εἶναι. εἰ δ' οὖν κέντροις πολλοῖς
ἀπεικάσαμεν πάντα τὰ νοητὰ [εἶναι]¹ εἰς ἓν κέντρον
ἀναφερομένοις καὶ ἑνουμένοις, πολλὰ δὲ φανεῖσι διὰ τὰς
20 γραμμὰς οὐ τῶν γραμμῶν γεννησασῶν αὐτά, ἀλλὰ
δειξασῶν, αἱ γραμμαὶ παρεχέτωσαν ἡμῖν χρείαν ἐν τῷ

¹ del. Kirchhoff.

thirds, and they are linked like one sphere to its one centre, not disparted by distances, but all existing together with themselves, wherever the thirds are present, the seconds and firsts are present as well.[1]

5. And for the sake of clarity our discourse often, by making, as it were, many lines proceed from one centre, wants to lead to a notion of the multiplicity which has come to be. But one must bear in mind when one says this that the things which are said to become many are all together at once, just as there in the example of the circle one cannot take the lines as being separated: for it is one surface. But where there is not even any spacing out on one surface, but only unspaced powers and substances, all may reasonably be spoken of in terms of their centres all united in one centre, as if their ends located in the centre dropped their lines, and then certainly all are one. But again, if you put the lines on, they are attached to their centres which each of them leaves, and none the less each and every centre will not be cut off from that one first centre, but they will be all together with that and each, again, individual, and they will be as many as the lines to which they gave themselves to be their ends, so that they appear to be as many as the lines with which they are in contact, but all of them are one together. But if we likened all the intelligibles to many centres all going back to and united in one centre, but appearing as many because of their lines – the lines do not generate them but show them – the lines might serve our purpose at present by providing an analogy to the

---

[1] On this passage see *Introductory Note*, pp. 270–271.

παρόντι ἀνάλογον εἶναι ὧν ἐφαπτομένη ἡ νοητὴ φύσις
πολλὰ καὶ πολλαχῇ φαίνεται παρεῖναι.

6. Πολλὰ γὰρ ὄντα τὰ νοητὰ ἕν ἐστι, καὶ ἓν ὄντα τῇ
ἀπείρῳ φύσει πολλά ἐστι, καὶ πολλὰ ἐν ἑνὶ καὶ ἓν ἐπὶ
πολλοῖς καὶ ὁμοῦ πάντα, καὶ ἐνεργεῖ πρὸς τὸ ὅλον μετὰ
τοῦ ὅλου, καὶ ἐνεργεῖ πρὸς τὸ μέρος αὖ μετὰ τοῦ
5 ὅλου. δέχεται δὲ τὸ μέρος εἰς αὐτὸ τὸ ὡς μέρους πρῶτον
ἐνέργημα, ἀκολουθεῖ δὲ τὸ ὅλον· οἷον εἰ ὁ ἄνθρωπος
ἐλθὼν εἰς τόν τινα ἄνθρωπον τὶς ἄνθρωπος γίνοιτο ὢν
αὖ ἄνθρωπος. ὁ μὲν οὖν ἄνθρωπος ὁ ἐν τῇ ὕλῃ ἀφ᾿ ἑνὸς
τοῦ ἀνθρώπου τοῦ κατὰ τὴν ἰδέαν πολλοὺς ἐποίησε τοὺς
10 αὐτοὺς ἀνθρώπους, καὶ ἔστιν ἓν τὸ αὐτὸ ἐν πολλοῖς
οὕτως, ὅτι ἐστὶν ἔν τι οἷον ἐνσφραγιζόμενον ἐν πολλοῖς
αὐτό. αὐτὸ δὲ ἄνθρωπος καὶ αὐτοέκαστον [1] καὶ ὅλον τὸ
πᾶν οὐχ οὕτως ἐν πολλοῖς, ἀλλὰ τὰ πολλὰ ἐν αὐτῷ,
μᾶλλον δὲ περὶ αὐτό. ἄλλον γὰρ τρόπον τὸ λευκὸν
πανταχοῦ καὶ ἡ ψυχὴ ἑκάστου ἐν παντὶ μέρει τοῦ
15 σώματος ἡ αὐτή· οὕτω γὰρ καὶ τὸ ὂν πανταχοῦ.

7. Ἀνάγεται γὰρ καὶ τὸ ἡμέτερον καὶ ἡμεῖς εἰς τὸ
ὄν, καὶ ἀναβαίνομέν τε εἰς ἐκεῖνο καὶ τὸ πρῶτον ἀπ᾿
ἐκείνου, καὶ νοοῦμεν ἐκεῖνα οὐκ εἴδωλα αὐτῶν οὐδὲ
τύπους ἔχοντες. εἰ δὲ μὴ τοῦτο, ὄντες ἐκεῖνα. εἰ οὖν
5 ἀληθινῆς ἐπιστήμης μετέχομεν, ἐκεῖνά ἐσμεν οὐκ
ἀπολαβόντες αὐτὰ ἐν ἡμῖν, ἀλλ᾿ ἡμεῖς ἐν ἐκείνοις ὄντες.
ὄντων δὲ καὶ τῶν ἄλλων, οὐ μόνον ἡμῶν, ἐκεῖνα, πάντες
ἐσμὲν ἐκεῖνα. ὁμοῦ ἄρα ὄντες μετὰ πάντων ἐσμὲν

_____

[1] H–S²: αὐτὸ ἕκαστον Enn.

338

things by contact with which the intelligible nature appears to be present as many and in many places.[1]

6. For the intelligibles are many and they are one, and, being one, they are many by their unbounded nature, and many in one and one over many and all together, and they are active towards the whole with the whole, and active towards the part again with the whole. But the part receives into itself the first activity as that of a part, but the whole follows; as if [the Form of] Man came to a particular man and became a particular man though being on the other hand [the Form of] Man. For the man in the matter made from the one man according to the Idea many men, all the same, and the same thing is one in the many in a way like that in which there is one seal-imprint in many things. But the thing itself, Man, and each thing itself, and the [intelligible] All as a whole are not in many in this way, but the many are in the thing itself, or rather around it. For there is a difference between the way in which the white is everywhere and that in which the soul of each individual is in every part of the body the same; for this latter is the way in which being is everywhere.

7. For we and what is ours go back to real being and ascend to that and to the first which comes from it, and we think the intelligibles; we do not have images or imprints of them. But if we do not, we are the intelligibles. If then we have a part in true knowledge, we are those; we do not apprehend them as distinct within ourselves, but we are within them. For, since the others, and not only ourselves, are those, we are all those. So then, being together with

[1] For the very important image of the circle and its radii in Plotinus see also, e.g., I. 7.1; V. 1.11; VI. 9.8.

ἐκεῖνα· πάντα ἄρα ἐσμὲν ἕν. ἔξω μὲν οὖν ὁρῶντες ἢ ὅθεν
10 ἐξήμμεθα ἀγνοοῦμεν ἓν ὄντες, οἷον πρόσωπα [πολλὰ] [1]
εἰς τὸ ἔξω πολλά,[2] κορυφὴν ἔχοντα εἰς τὸ εἴσω μίαν. εἰ
δέ τις ἐπιστραφῆναι δύναιτο ἢ παρ' αὐτοῦ ἢ τῆς
Ἀθηνᾶς αὐτῆς εὐτυχήσας τῆς ἕλξεως, θεόν τε καὶ
αὐτὸν καὶ τὸ πᾶν ὄψεται· ὄψεται δὲ τὰ μὲν πρῶτα οὐχ
ὡς τὸ πᾶν, εἶτ' οὐκ ἔχων ὅπη αὐτὸν στήσας ὁριεῖ καὶ
15 μέχρι τίνος αὐτός ἐστιν, ἀφεὶς περιγράφειν ἀπὸ τοῦ
ὄντος ἅπαντος αὐτὸν εἰς ἅπαν τὸ πᾶν ἥξει προελθὼν
οὐδαμοῦ, ἀλλ' αὐτοῦ μείνας, οὗ ἵδρυται τὸ πᾶν.

8. Οἶμαι δὲ ἔγωγε καὶ εἴ τις ἐπισκέψαιτο τὴν τῆς
ὕλης τῶν εἰδῶν μετάληψιν, μᾶλλον ἂν εἰς πίστιν ἐλθεῖν
τοῦ λεγομένου καὶ μὴ ἂν ἔτι ὡς ἀδυνάτῳ ἀπιστεῖν ἢ
αὖ ἀπορεῖν. εὔλογον γὰρ καὶ ἀναγκαῖον, οἶμαι, μὴ
5 κειμένων τῶν εἰδῶν χωρὶς καὶ αὖ τῆς ὕλης πόρρωθεν
ἄνωθέν ποθεν τὴν ἔλλαμψιν εἰς αὐτὴν γεγονέναι· μὴ γὰρ
ᾖ κενὸν τοῦτο λεγόμενον· τί γὰρ ἂν εἴη τὸ "πόρρω" ἐν
τούτοις καὶ τὸ "χωρίς"; καὶ οὐκ αὖ τὸ δύσφραστον καὶ
τὸ ἀπορώτατον ἦν τὸ τῆς μεταλήψεως λεγόμενον,
10 ἀλλ' εἴρητο ἂν προχειρότατα γνώριμον ὂν τοῖς παρα-
δείγμασιν. ἀλλὰ κἂν ἔλλαμψιν λέγωμέν ποτε, οὐχ
οὕτως ἐροῦμεν, ὡς ἐπὶ τῶν αἰσθητῶν λέγομεν εἰς
αἰσθητὸν τὰς ἐλλάμψεις· ἀλλ' ἐπεὶ εἴδωλα τὰ ἐν τῇ ὕλῃ,

---

[1] del. H–S[2].
[2] del. Kirchhoff.

---

[1] This is the clearest explanation in the *Enneads* of
Plotinus' statement, which so much annoyed later
Neoplatonists, that we are "each of us an intelligible

all things, we are those: so then, we are all and one.[1]
So therefore when we look outside that on which we
depend we do not know that we are one, like faces
which are many on the outside but have one head
inside. But if someone is able to turn around, either
by himself or having the good luck to have his hair
pulled by Athene herself,[2] he will see God and
himself and the All; at first he will not see as the All
but then, when he has nowhere to set himself and
limit himself and determine how far he himself goes,
he will stop marking himself off from all being and
will come to all the All without going out anywhere,
but remaining there where the All is set firm.

8. But I for my part think that also, if one were to
consider the participation of matter in the Forms,
one would be more inclined to have confidence in
what is being said and not to disbelieve it as impossible or continue to be puzzled about it. For, I think,
it is probable, and indeed necessary, that the ideas
are not placed separately on one side and matter a
long way off on the other and then illumination
comes to matter from somewhere up there: I am
afraid this would be empty words. For what would
"far off" and "separately" mean in this context? And
again, the business of participation would not be
said to be hard to express and extremely perplexing,
but the explanation would be extremely accessible
and well known from the examples. But even if we do
sometimes speak of illumination we do not mean it
in the sense in which we speak of illuminations of a
sense-object in the realm of sense; but, since the
universe" (III. 4.3. 22; cp. IV. 7.10. 34–36) and shows how
literally it is to be taken.

[2] Like Achilles, *Iliad* I. 197–8.

ἀρχετύπων δὲ τάξιν ἔχει τὰ εἴδη, τὸ δὲ τῆς ἐλλάμψεως
τοιοῦτον οἷον χωρὶς ἔχειν τὸ ἐλλαμπόμενον, οὕτω
15 λέγομεν. δεῖ δὲ νῦν ἀκριβέστερον λέγοντας μὴ οὕτω
τίθεσθαι ὡς χωρὶς ὄντος τόπῳ τοῦ εἴδους εἶθ' ὥσπερ ἐν
ὕδατι ἐνορᾶσθαι τῇ ὕλῃ τὴν ἰδέαν, ἀλλὰ τὴν ὕλην
[εἶναι] [1] πανταχόθεν οἷον ἐφαπτομένην καὶ αὖ οὐκ
ἐφαπτομένην τῆς ἰδέας κατὰ πᾶν ἑαυτῆς ἴσχειν παρὰ
20 τοῦ εἴδους τῷ πλησιασμῷ ὅσον δύναται λαβεῖν οὐδενὸς
μεταξὺ ὄντος, οὐ τῆς ἰδέας διὰ πάσης διεξελθούσης καὶ
ἐπιδραμούσης, ἀλλ' ἐν αὐτῇ μενούσης. εἰ γὰρ μὴ ἐν τῇ
ὕλῃ ἐστὶν οἷον πυρὸς ἡ ἰδέα—τὴν γὰρ τοῖς στοιχείοις
ὕλην ὑποβεβλημένην ὁ λόγος λαμβανέτω—αὐτὸ δὴ πῦρ
25 τῇ ὕλῃ οὐκ ἐγγενόμενον αὐτὸ [τῇ ὕλῃ] [2] μορφὴν πυρὸς
κατὰ πᾶσαν τὴν πυρωθεῖσαν ὕλην παρέξεται. ὄγκος δὲ
πολὺς πῦρ τὸ πρῶτον ἔνυλον ὑποκείσθω γενόμενον· ὁ
γὰρ αὐτὸς λόγος καὶ ἐπὶ τῶν ἄλλων τῶν λεγομένων
στοιχείων ἁρμόσει. εἰ οὖν τὸ ἓν ἐκεῖνο πῦρ ᾗ [3] ἰδέα ἐν
πᾶσι θεωρεῖται παρέχον εἰκόνα ἑαυτοῦ ⟨οὐ⟩ [4] κατὰ [5]
30 ⟨τὸ⟩ [4] τόπῳ χωρὶς ὂν οὐ παρέξει ὡς ἡ ἔλλαμψις ἡ
ὁρωμένη· ἤδη γὰρ εἴη που πᾶν ⟨ὅπου ἂν⟩ [6] τοῦτο τὸ
πῦρ τὸ ἐν αἰσθήσει, εἰ πᾶν αὐτὸ πολλὰ ᾖ [7] ἑαυτοῦ τῆς
ἰδέας αὐτῆς μενούσης ἐν ἀτόπῳ αὐτὸ τόπους γεννῆσαν
ἐξ αὐτοῦ ἐπείπερ ἔδει τὸ αὐτὸ πολὺ γενόμενον φυγεῖν
ἀφ' ἑαυτοῦ ἵν' ᾖ πολὺ οὕτως καὶ πολλάκις μεταλάβῃ
35 τοῦ αὐτοῦ. καὶ οὐκ ἔδωκε μὲν ἑαυτῆς οὐδὲν τῇ ὕλῃ ἡ

---

[1] del. Vitringa, Müller.   [4] Igal.
[2] del. H–S.   [5] Igal: καὶ Enn., H–S.
[3] Igal, H S²: ἡ Enn.
[6] πᾶν ⟨ὅπου ἂν⟩ Igal: πᾶν Enn., H–S ("29–33 καὶ—αὐτοῦ
locus nondum sanatus" H–S).
[7] wEBUCz: ᾗ x: εἴη Kirchhoff: ᾖ H–S¹.

things in matter are images, and the Forms hold the rank of archetypes, and illumination is such that it keeps the illuminated object separate, we use the word in this sense. But now we must speak more precisely and not assume that the Form is spatially separate and then the Idea is reflected in matter as if in water, but that matter, from every side grasping (and again not grasping) the Idea, receives from the Form, over the whole of itself, by its drawing near to it all that it can receive, with nothing between; the Idea does not pass through and run over the whole of matter, but remains in itself. For if the Idea of Fire, for instance, is not in matter – let our discourse take the matter underlying the elements as an example – the fire itself which does not come to be in matter will give the character of fire to all the matter made fiery. (Let it be assumed that the first fire in matter comes to be a large bulk.) For the same argument will fit the other elements as they are called. If therefore that one fire in that it is the Idea is seen in all [the fires] giving an image of itself not in the way that it would if it was spatially separate, it will not give its image as the visible illumination does; for it would already be all wherever this fire in the sense-world is,[1] if [that one fire] was itself many as all, since, while the Idea itself of itself remained in the placeless, it would generate places out of itself if it was necessary for the same, having become many, to escape from itself that there might be many in this way and participate often in the same. And the Idea, not being scattered [like this], gave nothing of itself

[1] I adopt Igal's text and interpretation in this very difficult passage.

ἰδέα ἀσκέδαστος οὖσα, οὐ μὴν ἀδύνατος γέγονεν ἐν
οὖσα τὸ μὴ ἓν τῷ ἑνὶ αὐτῆς μορφῶσαι καὶ παντὶ αὐτοῦ
οὕτω τοι παρεῖναι, ὡς ⟨μὴ⟩ [1] ἄλλῳ μὲν μέρει αὐτῆς
τόδε, ἄλλῳ δὲ ἄλλο μορφῶσαι, ἀλλὰ παντὶ ἕκαστον καὶ
40 πᾶν. γελοῖον γὰρ τὸ πολλὰς ἰδέας πυρὸς ἐπεισφέρειν, ἵν'
ἕκαστον πῦρ ὑφ' ἑκάστης ἄλλης, τὸ δὲ ἄλλης, μορφοῖτο·
ἄπειροι γὰρ οὕτως ἔσονται αἱ ἰδέαι. εἶτα πῶς καὶ
μεριεῖς τὰ γινόμενα συνεχοῦς ἑνὸς πυρὸς ὄντος; καὶ εἰ
προσθείημεν τῇ ὕλῃ ταύτῃ ἄλλο πῦρ μεῖζον ποιήσαντες
45 αὐτό, καὶ κατ' ἐκεῖνο αὖ τὸ μέρος τῆς ὕλης φατέον τὴν
αὐτὴν ἰδέαν τὰ αὐτὰ εἰργάσθαι· οὐ γὰρ δὴ ἄλλην.

9. Καὶ τοίνυν εἰ πάντα γενόμενα ἤδη τὰ στοιχεῖα τῷ
λόγῳ τις εἰς ἓν σφαιρικὸν σχῆμα ἄγοι, οὐ πολλοὺς
φατέον τὴν σφαῖραν ποιεῖν κατὰ μέρη ἄλλον ἄλλῃ
ἀποτεμνόμενον αὐτῷ εἰς τὸ ποιεῖν μέρος, ἀλλ' ἓν εἶναι
5 τὸ αἴτιον τῆς ποιήσεως ὅλῳ ἑαυτῷ ποιοῦν οὐ μέρους
αὐτοῦ ἄλλου ἄλλο ποιοῦντος· οὕτω γὰρ ἂν πάλιν πολλοὶ
εἶεν, εἰ μὴ εἰς ἓν ἀμερὲς ἀναφέροις τὴν ποίησιν, μᾶλλον
δ' εἰ ἓν ἀμερὲς τὸ ποιοῦν τὴν σφαῖραν εἴη οὐκ αὐτοῦ
χυθέντος εἰς τὴν σφαῖραν τοῦ ποιοῦντος, ἀλλὰ τῆς

[1] Kirchhoff.

[1] Plotinus, like practically all ancient Platonists except
his friend and colleague Amelius, maintained firmly that
the number of the Ideas was finite; for Amelius' view that
they were infinite in number see Syrianus *In Met.* 147. 2–6.
For the bearing of this passage on the much-disputed
question about Ideas of individuals in Plotinus see, in the

to the matter, but was certainly not incapable, being
one thing, of forming what is not one by its one and
being present to all of it in the way that it is not this
piece of it which forms one part and that other
another, but it forms each part with the whole of it
and as a whole. For it would be absurd to introduce
many Ideas of fire in order that each individual fire
might be formed by a different one; for in this way
the Ideas will be infinite in number.[1] And then how
are you going to divide up the fires which have come
into existence if there is one continuous fire? And if
we were to apply another fire to this matter by
making the fire bigger, we must say that again in
this part of matter the same Idea is doing the same
things: for it certainly could not be another one.

9. And further, if, when all the elements had come
into existence, someone brought them in thought
into one spherical figure, one would have to say that
it was not many makers who made the sphere part by
part, one cutting off a piece for himself in one place
and one in another to make a part with, but that the
cause of the making was one, making with the whole
of itself, not one part of it making one part and one
another; for in this way again the makers would be
many, if you do not bring the making back to one
partless thing, or, to put it better, unless it is one
partless thing which makes the sphere, without the
maker being diffused through the sphere,[2] but with

first instance, my "Form, Individual and Person in
Plotinus" (*Dionysius* I, 1977, 49-68 = *Plotinian and
Christian Studies* XX), where references are given to other
literature.

[2] An allusion to the Stoic doctrine of "complete
transfusion", which Plotinus discusses fully in II. 7.

10 σφαίρας ὅλης εἰς τὸ ποιοῦν ἀνηρτημένης. καὶ ζωὴ
τοίνυν μία τὴν σφαῖραν ἔχει ἡ αὐτή, τῆς σφαίρας αὐτῆς
τεθείσης ἐν ζωῇ μιᾷ· καὶ τὰ ἐν τῇ σφαίρᾳ τοίνυν πάντα
εἰς μίαν ζωήν· καὶ πᾶσαι αἱ ψυχαὶ τοίνυν μία, οὕτω δὲ
μία, ὡς ἄπειρος αὖ. διὸ καὶ οἱ μὲν ἀριθμὸν ἔλεγον, οἱ δὲ
15 ⟨λόγον⟩ [1] αὐτὸν αὔξοντα τὴν φύσιν αὐτῆς,
φαντασθέντες ταύτῃ ἴσως, ὡς οὐδενὶ ἐπιλείπει, ἀλλ᾽ ἐπὶ
πάντα εἰσὶν ὅ ἐστι μένουσα, καὶ εἰ πλείων ὁ κόσμος ἦν,
οὐκ ἂν ἐπέλιπεν ἡ δύναμις μὴ οὐκ ἐπὶ πάντα αὖ ἐλθεῖν,
μᾶλλον δὲ τοῦτον ἐν πάσῃ αὐτῇ εἶναι. δεῖ δῆτα λαβεῖν τὸ
"αὔξων" [2] οὐχ ὡς τῷ ῥήματι λέγεται, ἀλλ᾽ ὅτι οὐκ
20 ἐπιλείπει εἰς τὸ πανταχοῦ ἓν οὖσα· τοιοῦτον γὰρ αὐτῆς
τὸ ἓν ὡς μὴ τοιοῦτον εἶναι οἷον μεμετρῆσθαι ὅσον·
τοῦτο γὰρ φύσεως ἄλλης τῆς τὸ ἓν ψευδομένης καὶ
μεταλήψει ἓν φανταζομένης. τὸ δ᾽ ἀληθείας ἐχόμενον ἓν
οἷον μήτε συγκεῖσθαι ἐκ πολλῶν ἕν, ἵν᾽ ἀφαιρεθέντος
25 τινὸς ἀπ᾽ αὐτοῦ ἀπολωλὸς ᾖ ἐκεῖνο τὸ ὅλον ἕν, μήτε
διειλῆφθαι πέρασιν, ἵνα μὴ ἐναρμοζομένων αὐτῷ τῶν
ἄλλων ἢ ἐλαττοῖτο αὐτῶν μειζόνων ὄντων ἢ διασπῷτο
βουλόμενον ἐπὶ πάντα ἰέναι, παρῇ τε οὐχ ὅλον πᾶσιν,
ἀλλὰ μέρεσιν αὐτοῦ μέρεσιν ἐκείνων· καὶ τὸ λεγόμενον
30 δὴ τοῦτο ἀγνοεῖ ὅπου ἐστὶ γῆς εἰς μίαν τινὰ συντέλειαν
οὐ δυνάμενον ἰέναι ἅτε διεσπασμένον ἑαυτοῦ. εἴπερ οὖν

[1] Roussos.
[2] Roussos: αὖξον Enn.

the whole sphere dependent on the maker. And so
one and the same life holds the sphere, and the
sphere itself is set in one life; and so all things in the
sphere depend on one life; and so all the souls are
one, but so one that it is also an unbounded soul.
This is the reason why some people called it a
"number" and some said that its nature was "a
rational principle augmenting itself",[1] perhaps
imagining it in this way, that it does not fail anything, but, remaining what it is, reaches to everything, and if the universe was larger its power would
not fail to reach again to everything, or rather this
universe would be in the whole of it. One must then
not take the "augmenting" literally, but [under-
stand that it means] that it does not fail in being
everywhere one: for its one is of such a kind as not
to be the kind of thing the size of which can be
measured: for this belongs to another nature which
feigns the one and is imagined as one by its participation. But the one which possesses truth is the kind
which is not a one composed from many, so that if
something was taken away from it the whole one
would be destroyed, nor divided by boundaries, so
that when other things fit themselves into it it would
be diminished because they are too big for it, or torn
apart because it wants to reach all, and would not be
present as a whole to all, but with parts of itself to
parts of those things; as the saying goes, it does not
know where on earth it is since it is not able to come
into one perfect whole because it is torn apart from
itself. If therefore this one is going to be truly one,

[1] The allusions are to Xenocrates (fr. 60 Heinze) and
Heraclitus (fr. B 115 DK).

ἀληθεύσει τὸ ἓν τοῦτο, καθ' οὗ δὴ καὶ κατηγορεῖν ἐστιν
ὡς οὐσίας τὸ ἕν, δεῖ αὐτὸ φανῆναι τρόπον τινὰ τὴν
ἐναντίαν αὐτῷ φύσιν ἔχον τὴν τοῦ πλήθους ἐν τῇ
δυνάμει, τῷ δὲ μὴ ἔξωθεν αὖ τὸ πλῆθος τοῦτο ἔχειν,
35 ἀλλὰ παρ' αὐτοῦ καὶ ἐξ αὐτοῦ, τούτῳ ἓν ὄντως εἶναι,
καὶ ἐν τῷ ἑνὶ ἔχειν τὸ εἶναι ἄπειρόν τε καὶ πλῆθος,
τοιοῦτον δὲ ὂν πανταχοῦ ὅλον φαίνεσθαι ἕνα λόγον ὄντα
ἑαυτὸν περιέχοντα, καὶ τὸν περιέχοντα αὐτὸν εἶναι [καὶ
τὸν περιέχοντα αὐτὸν]¹ οὐδαμοῦ αὐτοῦ ἀποστατοῦντα,
40 ἀλλ' ἐν αὐτῷ πανταχοῦ ὄντα. οὐ δή ἐστιν αὐτὸ οὕτω
ἄλλου τόπῳ διειλημμένον· πρὸ γὰρ τῶν ἐν τόπῳ
ἁπάντων ἦν καὶ οὐδὲν ἐδεῖτο αὐτὸ τούτων, ἀλλὰ ταῦτα
ἐκείνου, ἵνα ἱδρυθῇ. ἱδρυθέντα δὲ οὐκ ἀπέστησεν ἐκεῖνο
τῆς αὐτοῦ ἐν αὐτῷ ἕδρας· κινηθείσης γὰρ ἐκείνης
45 ἀπώλετο ἂν αὐτὰ ἀπολομένης αὐτῶν τῆς βάσεως καὶ
τοῦ στηρίζοντος αὐτά, οὐδ' αὖ ἐκεῖνο οὕτως ἀνόητον ἦν,
ὥστε ἀπαλλαγὲν αὐτὸ ἑαυτοῦ διασπασθῆναι καὶ
σωζόμενον ἐν ἑαυτῷ ἀπίστῳ δοῦναι ἑαυτὸ τόπῳ τῷ
αὐτοῦ πρὸς τὸ σώζεσθαι δεομένῳ.

10. Μένει οὖν ἐν ἑαυτῷ σωφρονοῦν καὶ οὐκ ἂν ἐν
ἄλλῳ γένοιτο· ἐκεῖνα δὲ τὰ ἄλλα ἀνήρτηται εἰς αὐτὸ
ὥσπερ οὗ ἐστι πόθῳ ἐξευρόντα. καὶ οὗτός ἐστιν ὁ
θυραυλῶν Ἔρως παρὼν ἔξωθεν ἀεὶ καὶ ἐφιέμενος τοῦ
5 καλοῦ καὶ ἀγαπῶν εἰ ² οὕτως [ὡς] ³ δύναιτο μετασχεῖν·
ἐπεὶ καὶ ὁ ἐνταῦθα ἐραστὴς οὐ δεχόμενος τὸ κάλλος,
ἀλλὰ παρακείμενος οὕτως ἔχει. τὸ δὲ ἐφ' ἑαυτοῦ μένει,

¹ del. Kirchhoff.
² Theiler, H–S²: ἀεὶ Enn.
³ del. Theiler, H–S².

about which it is possible to predicate the one as of substance, it must appear as in some way having the opposite nature to itself, that of multiplicity, in its power, but by not having this multiplicity from outside, but by itself and from itself, and in this way being really one, and in its one having unbounded-ness and multiplicity; and since it is like this it must appear everywhere as a whole, a single rational principle encompassing itself, and the encompassing principle must be nowhere parted from itself, but everywhere in itself. It certainly does not belong to another in the sense of being spatially divided; for it was before all the things in space and had no need of them, but they needed it, that they might be es-tablished. But in their establishment they did not move that one out of its seat in itself; for if that seat was moved they would perish with the perishing of their foundation and that which sets them firm, and on the other hand that one was not so stupid as to separate itself from itself and be torn to pieces, or, being kept safe in itself, to deliver itself to the untrustworthiness of place which needs it to be kept safe.

10. It has the good sense, then, to remain in itself, and would not come to be in another; but those other things hang from it as if by their longing they had found where it is. And this is "Love camping on the doorstep",[1] even coming from outside into the pre-sence of beauty and longing for it, and satisfied if in this way he can have a part in it; since the lover here below also has beauty in this way, not by receiving it [into himself] but by lying with it. But that [one

[1] Cp. Plato *Symposium* 203C6–D3.

καὶ οἱ ἑνὸς ἐρασταὶ πολλοὶ ὅλου ἐρῶντες ὅλον ἔχουσιν
οὕτως, ὅταν ἔχωσι· τὸ γὰρ ὅλον ἦν τὸ ἐρώμενον. πῶς ἂν
10 οὖν ἐκεῖνο οὐκ ἂν πᾶσιν ἀρκοῖ μένον; ἐπεὶ καὶ διὰ τοῦτο
ἀρκεῖ, ὅτι μένει, καὶ καλόν, ὅτι πᾶσιν ὅλον. καὶ γὰρ καὶ
τὸ φρονεῖν πᾶσιν ὅλον· διὸ καὶ ξ υ ν ὸ ν τ ὸ φ ρ ο ν ε ῖ ν,
οὐ τὸ μὲν ὧδε, τὸ δὲ ὡδὶ ὄν· γελοῖον γάρ, καὶ τόπου
δεόμενον τὸ φρονεῖν ἔσται. καὶ οὐχ οὕτω τὸ φρονεῖν, ὡς
15 τὸ λευκόν· οὐ γὰρ σώματος τὸ φρονεῖν· ἀλλ᾽ εἴπερ
ὄντως μετέχομεν τοῦ φρονεῖν, ἓν δεῖ[1] εἶναι[2] τὸ αὐτὸ
πᾶν ἑαυτῷ συνόν. καὶ οὕτως ἐκεῖθεν, οὐ μοίρας αὐτοῦ
λαβόντες, οὐδὲ ὅλον ἐγώ, ὅλον δὲ καὶ σύ, ἀποσπασθὲν
ἑκάτερον ἑκατέρου. μιμοῦνται δὲ καὶ ἐκκλησίαι καὶ
πᾶσα σύνοδος ὡς εἰς ἓν τὸ φρονεῖν ἰόντων· καὶ χωρὶς
20 ἕκαστος εἰς τὸ φρονεῖν ἀσθενής, συμβάλλων δὲ εἰς ἓν
πᾶς ἐν τῇ συνόδῳ καὶ τῇ ὡς ἀληθῶς συνέσει τὸ φρονεῖν
ἐγέννησε καὶ εὗρε· τί γὰρ δὴ καὶ διείρξει, ὡς μὴ ἐν τῷ
αὐτῷ εἶναι νοῦν ἀπ᾽ ἄλλου; ἀλλ᾽ ὁμοῦ ὄντες ἡμῖν οὐχ
ὁμοῦ δοκοῦσιν εἶναι· οἷον εἴ τις πολλοῖς τοῖς δακτύλοις
25 ἐφαπτόμενος τοῦ αὐτοῦ ἄλλου καὶ ἄλλου ἐφάπτεσθαι
νομίζοι, ἢ τὴν αὐτὴν χορδὴν μὴ ὁρῶν κρούοι. καίτοι καὶ
ταῖς ψυχαῖς ὡς ἐφαπτόμεθα τοῦ ἀγαθοῦ ἐχρῆν
ἐνθυμεῖσθαι. οὐ γὰρ ἄλλου μὲν ἐγώ, ἄλλου δὲ σὺ
ἐφάπτῃ, ἀλλὰ τοῦ αὐτοῦ, οὐδὲ τοῦ αὐτοῦ μέν,
30 προσελθόντος δέ μοι ῥεύματος ἐκεῖθεν ἄλλου, σοὶ δὲ

[1] wEBUC: δὴ x.
[2] coniecimus: εἰς wEBxUC: om. z.

beauty] remains by itself, and the many lovers of the one love the whole and have the whole like this, when they have it: for it was the whole that they loved. How, then, should that in its abiding not be sufficient for all? For it is for this reason that it suffices, because it abides, and it is beautiful because it is whole for all. For thought also is whole for all, that is why "thought is common",[1] not one thought here and another there: for that would be ridiculous, and thought would need space. And thought is not like white; for thought does not belong to the body; but if we truly have a part in thought, it must be one and the same, all together with itself. And so we have our part in it from thence, not receiving portions of it, nor I one whole and you another, each torn apart from each. Assemblies of the people imitate this, and all meetings, being of people moving to a unity of thought; and each member is weak in thought but when everyone in the meeting, and the true meeting of minds, comes together into one, he generates and finds [true] thought; for what will keep them apart, so that the minds of one and another do not meet in the same? But though they are together, they do not seem so to us; as if someone touching the same thing with a number of fingers thought that he was touching one thing after another, or if, without seeing it, he plucked the same string. And besides, we ought to have borne in mind how with our souls we touch the Good. For I do not touch one good and you another, but the same, and not the same in such a way that one stream comes from it to me and another to you, so that it is

[1] Heraclitus fr. B 113 DK.

ἄλλου, ὥστε τὸ μὲν εἶναί που ἄνω, τὰ δὲ παρ' αὐτοῦ
ἐνταῦθα. καὶ ⟨δίδωσι⟩ [1] τὸ διδὸν τοῖς λαμβάνουσιν, ἵνα
ὄντως λαμβάνωσι, [καὶ δίδωσι τὸ διδὸν] [1] οὐ τοῖς
ἀλλοτρίοις, ἀλλὰ τοῖς ἑαυτοῦ. ἐπεὶ οὐ πόμπιος ἡ νοερὰ
35 δόσις. ἐπεὶ καὶ ἐν τοῖς διεστηκόσιν ἀπ' ἀλλήλων τοῖς
τόποις σώμασιν ἡ δόσις ἄλλου ἄλλου συγγενής, καὶ εἰς
αὐτὸ ἡ δόσις καὶ ἡ ποίησις, καὶ τό γε σωματικὸν τοῦ
παντὸς δρᾷ καὶ πάσχει ἐν αὑτῷ, καὶ οὐδὲν ἔξωθεν εἰς
αὐτό. εἰ δὴ ἐπὶ σώματος οὐδὲν ἔξωθεν τοῦ ἐκ φύσεως
40 οἷον φεύγοντος ἑαυτό, ἐπὶ πράγματος ἀδιαστάτου πῶς
τὸ ἔξωθεν; ἐν τῷ αὐτῷ ἄρα ὄντες καὶ ὁρῶμεν τἀγαθὸν
καὶ ἐφαπτόμεθα αὐτοῦ ὁμοῦ ὄντες τοῖς ἡμετέροις
νοητοῖς. καὶ κόσμος εἷς πολὺ μᾶλλον ἐκεῖ· ἢ δύο κόσμοι
αἰσθητοὶ ἔσονται ὅμοια μεμερισμένοι, καὶ ἡ σφαῖρα
ἡ νοητή, εἰ οὕτως ἕν, ὡς αὕτη· ὥστε διοίσει ἢ [2]
45 γελοιοτέρα ἔσται, εἴπερ τῇ μὲν ἐξανάγκης ὄγκος καὶ
εὔλογος, ἡ δὲ μηδὲν δεομένη ἐκτενεῖ ἑαυτὴν καὶ ἑαυτῆς
ἐκστήσεται. τί δὲ καὶ ἐμπόδιον τοῦ εἰς ἕν; οὐ γὰρ δὴ τὸ
ἕτερον ἀπωθεῖ θάτερον τόπον οὐ παρέχον—ὥσπερ οὐχ
ὁρῶντες πᾶν μάθημα καὶ θεώρημα καὶ ὅλως ἐπιστήμας
50 πάσας ἐπὶ ψυχῆς οὐ στενοχωρουμένας. ἀλλ' ἐπὶ οὐσιῶν
φήσει τις οὐ δυνατόν. ἀλλ' οὐ δυνατὸν ἦν ἄν, εἴπερ ὄγκοι
ἦσαν αἱ ἀληθιναὶ οὐσίαι.

11. Ἀλλὰ πῶς τὸ ἀδιάστατον παρήκει παρὰ πᾶν
σῶμα μέγεθος τοσοῦτον ἔχον; καὶ πῶς οὐ διασπᾶται ἓν
ὂν καὶ ταὐτό; ὃ πολλάκις ἠπόρηται, παύειν τοῦ λόγου
τὸ ἄπορον τῆς διανοίας περιττῇ προθυμίᾳ βουλομένου.

---

[1] Kleist, *Studien* 91.
[2] scripsi: ἢ wEBRᵖᶜUCz, H–S: ἡ RᵃᶜJ.

somewhere up there and what comes from it down
here. And what gives gives to the recipients so that
they may really receive, not to alien recipients, but
to its own. For intelligible giving is not pro-
cessional. For even in bodies distant from each other
in their places, the giving of one is related to another, and the giving and making go to the same; and
the bodily part of the All acts and is affected in itself,
and nothing comes into it from outside. If then with
body, which by nature in a way flees from itself,
nothing comes from outside, how can there be anything from outside in a thing unspaced? We are,
then, in the same with the Good and see it and touch
it being together with our own intelligibles. And the
universe there is far more one; otherwise there will
be two universes perceived by sense, divided in the
same way, and the intelligible sphere, if it is one in
this way, will be like this one; so that it will differ in
that it will be more ridiculous, if this one here has
bulk of necessity and reasonably, but the other is
going to stretch itself out and go outside itself when
it has no need. But what can stand in the way of its
unification? For certainly one will not push away
the other by giving it no room – as if we do not see
that every subject of study and observation and in
general all bodies of knowledge are in the soul
without being crowded. But, someone will say, this
is not possible with substances. No, it would not be
possible if true substances were bulks.

11. But how can the unspaced stretch over all
body, which has so great a size? And how, being one
and the same, is it not torn apart? This difficulty has
often been raised, when the argument was excess-
ively anxious to end the discursive reason's dif-

PLOTINUS: ENNEAD VI. 5.

5 ἀποδέδεικται μὲν οὖν ἤδη πολλαχῇ, ὅτι οὕτως· δεῖ δέ
τινων καὶ παραμυθίων, καίτοι οὐκ ἐλάχιστον, ἀλλὰ
μέγιστον εἰς πειθὼ ἦν ἐκείνη ἡ φύσις οἷα ἐστὶ
διδαχθεῖσα, ὅτι οὐκ ἔστιν οἷα λίθος, οἷον κύβος τις
μέγας κείμενος οὗ κεῖται τοσοῦτον ἐπέχων, ὅσος ἐστίν,
10 ἐκβαίνειν οὐκ ἔχων τοὺς αὐτοῦ ὅρους μετρηθεὶς ἐπὶ
τοσοῦτον καὶ τῷ ὄγκῳ καὶ τῇ συμπεριγραφείσῃ ἐν
αὐτῷ τῇ τοῦ λίθου δυνάμει. ἀλλὰ οὖσα πρώτη φύσις καὶ
οὐ μετρηθεῖσα οὐδὲ ὁρισθεῖσα ὁπόσον δεῖ εἶναι—ταύτῃ
γὰρ αὖ ἑτέρα[1] μετρηθήσεται—πᾶσά ἐστι δύναμις
15 οὐδαμοῦ τοσήδε. διὸ οὐδ᾽ ἐν χρόνῳ, ἀλλὰ παντὸς χρόνου
ἔξω, τοῦ μὲν χρόνου σκιδναμένου ἀεὶ πρὸς διάστασιν,
τοῦ δ᾽ αἰῶνος ἐν τῷ αὐτῷ μένοντος καὶ κρατοῦντος καὶ
πλείονος ὄντος δυνάμει ἀιδίῳ τοῦ ἐπὶ πολλὰ δοκοῦντος
ἰέναι χρόνου, οἷον εἰ γραμμῆς εἰς ἄπειρον ἰέναι
δοκούσης εἰς σημεῖον ἀνηρτημένης καὶ περὶ αὐτὸ
20 θεούσης πανταχῇ οὗ ἂν δράμῃ τοῦ σημείου αὐτῇ
ἐμφανταζομένου αὐτοῦ οὐ θέοντος, ἀλλὰ περὶ αὐτὸ
ἐκείνης κυκλουμένης. εἰ τοίνυν χρόνος πρὸς τὸ ἐν τῷ
αὐτῷ μένον ἐν οὐσίᾳ ἔχει τὴν ἀναλογίαν, ἔστι δὲ ἐκείνη
ἡ φύσις οὐ μόνον τῷ ἀεὶ ἄπειρος, ἀλλὰ καὶ τῇ δυνάμει,
25 χρὴ καὶ πρὸς ταύτην τὴν ἀπειρίαν τῆς δυνάμεως
ἀντιπαραθέουσαν ἀποδοῦναι φύσιν ἀνταιωρουμένην καὶ
ἐξηρτημένην ἐκείνης· ταύτης τὰ ἴσα πως τῷ χρόνῳ
θεούσης πρὸς μένουσαν δύναμιν πλείω οὖσαν τῷ ποιεῖν,
ἐκείνη ἐστὶν ὅσον παρετάθη ἡτισοῦν[2] αὕτη ἐστὶν ἡ
30 μεταλαμβάνουσα ταύτης τῆς φύσεως καθόσον οἷόν τε
αὐτῇ μεταλαβεῖν, πάσης μὲν παρούσης, οὐ παντὶ δὲ

[1] Igal, H–S²: ἑτέρα Enn.
[2] Theiler, H–S: τίς οὖν Enn.

354

ficulty. Well, it has already been demonstrated in many ways that it is so; but a bit of encouragement is required, though not the least but the greatest reason for confidence is that nature expounded as it is; it is not like a stone, like a great squared block of stone lying where it is and extending to the size it is, unable to exceed its bounds because it has been measured to this particular size both by its bulk and by the stone-power limited along with it. But since it is the first nature and is not measured or bounded to the size it ought to be – for in this way it would be again measured by another nature – it is all power, nowhere of this particular size. For this reason it is not in time either, but outside all time, for time is continually dispersed into distancing, but eternity abides in the same and has the mastery and is greater by its everlasting power than time which seems to go so far; it is like a line which seems to go on unlimitedly, but depends on a point, and as it runs round it the point is in the picture everywhere the line runs to, though the point does not run, but the line circles round it. If, then, time is related by analogy to that which abides in the same in substance, but that nature is not only unbounded because it is always but unbounded in power, one must also grant besides this unboundedness of power a nature running along over against it, swinging alongside that nature as it hangs from it; this nature runs, somehow in step with time, to the abiding power which is greater [than it] by making [it], and whatever it is is somewhat extended along it and participates in this nature as far as it is possible for it to participate; it is all present, but not all of it is seen in everything because of the incapacity of the

355

πάσης ἐνορωμένης ἀδυναμίᾳ τοῦ ὑποκειμένου. πάρεστι
δὲ ⟨ἀριθμῷ⟩ [1] ταὐτὸν πάντα, οὐχ ὡς τὸ ἔνυλον
τρίγωνον ἐν πολλοῖς πλείω ὂν [ἀριθμῷ ταὐτόν],[1] ἀλλ᾽
ὡς τὸ ἄυλον αὐτό, ἀφ᾽ οὗ καὶ τὰ ἐν ὕλῃ. διὰ τί οὖν οὐ
35 πανταχοῦ τρίγωνον ἔνυλον, εἴπερ πανταχοῦ τὸ ἄυλον;
ὅτι οὐ πᾶσα μετέσχεν ὕλη, ἀλλὰ ἄλλο τι ἔχει, καὶ οὐ
πᾶσα πρὸς πᾶν. ἐπεὶ οὐδὲ ἡ πρώτη πᾶσα πρὸς πᾶν,
ἀλλὰ πρὸς τὰ πρῶτα τῶν γενῶν, εἶτ᾽ ἐπὶ τούτοις ἄλλα.
παρῆν μέν τι παντί.

12. Πάρεστιν οὖν πῶς; ὡς ζωὴ μία· οὐ γὰρ μέχρι
τινὸς ἐν ζῴῳ ἡ ζωή, εἶτ᾽ οὐ δύναται εἰς ἅπαν φθάσαι,
ἀλλὰ πανταχοῦ. εἰ δέ τις ζητεῖ πάλιν πῶς, ἀνα-
μνησθήτω τῆς δυνάμεως, ὅτι μὴ ποσή, ἀλλ᾽ εἰς
5 ἄπειρον διαιρῶν τῇ διανοίᾳ ἀεὶ ἔχει δύναμιν τὴν αὐτὴν
βυσσόθεν ἄπειρον· οὐ γὰρ ἐκεῖ ὕλην,[2] ἵνα τῷ μεγέθει
τοῦ ὄγκου συνεπιλείπῃ εἰς μικρὸν ἐλθοῦσα. ἐὰν οὖν
λάβῃς ἀέναον ἐν αὐτῇ ἀπειρίαν, φύσιν ἀκάματον καὶ
ἄτρυτον καὶ οὐδαμῇ ἐλλείπουσαν ἐν αὐτῇ, οἷον
10 ὑπερζέουσαν ζωή, ἤ που ἐπιβαλὼν ἢ πρός τι ἀτενίσας
οὐχ εὑρήσεις ἐκεῖ, τοὐναντίον δ᾽ ἄν σοι γένοιτο. οὐ γὰρ
σύ γε ὑπερβήσῃ παρελθὼν οὐδὲ αὖ στήσῃ εἰς μικρὸν ὡς
οὐκέτι ἐχούσης διδόναι ἐν τῷ κατὰ μικρὸν ἐπιλιπεῖν·
ἀλλ᾽ ἢ συνθεῖν δυνηθείς, μᾶλλον δὲ ἐν τῷ παντὶ
γενόμενος οὐδὲν ἔτι ζητήσεις, ἢ ἀπειπὼν παρεκβήσῃ εἰς

---

[1] Theiler, H–S².
[2] ἐκεῖ ὕλην (sc. ἔχει) Igal· ἔνει (ε– B) ὕλην (–υν U) BUC, H–S
("locus nondum sanatus"): ἐνὶ ὕλην E: ἐν + lac. 4 lltt. + ὕλην Λ:
ἐν ἑαυτῇ ἔχει ὕλην A³ (= Ficinus) E, Kirchhoff.

underlying recipient. But it is present the same in number everywhere, not like the triangle in matter which is multiplied by being in many, but like the immaterial triangle itself from which those in matter derive. Why then is not the triangle in matter everywhere, if the immaterial triangle is everywhere? Because not every matter participates in it, but every matter has something different, and not every matter is suitable for every Form. For even prime matter is not all adapted to every Form, but to the primary kinds [of bodily Form] and then others upon them. Form is certainly in some way present to everything.

12. How then is it present? As one life: for life in a living being does not reach only so far, and then is unable to extend over the whole, but it is everywhere. But if someone again enquires how, let him call to mind its power, that there is not a certain quantity of it, but if he divides it endlessly in his discursive thought he always has the same power, endless in depth; for it does not have matter there in the intelligible, that it might fall short along with the size of its bulk and come to little. If then you grasp the endlessness for ever welling up in it, the unwearying and unwearing nature which in no way falls short in it, boiling over with life, we may say, if you concentrate your attention somewhere or fix your gaze on a particular point you will not find it there, but the opposite will happen to you. For you will most certainly not step out of it and go past it, and again you will not stop at a littleness as if it had no more to give in its falling short little by little; but you will be able to run along with it, or rather come to be in All and seek nothing any more, or you will

15 ἄλλο καὶ πεσῇ παρὸν οὐκ ἰδὼν τῷ εἰς ἄλλον βλέπειν.
ἀλλ' εἰ "οὐδὲν ἔτι ζητήσεις", πῶς ποτε τοῦτο πείσει; ἢ
ὅτι παντὶ προσῆλθες καὶ οὐκ ἔμεινας ἐν μέρει αὐτοῦ οὐδ'
εἶπας οὐδὲ σὺ "τοσοῦτός εἰμι", ἀφεὶς δὲ τὸ "τοσοῦτος"
γέγονας πᾶς, καίτοι καὶ πρότερον ἦσθα πᾶς· ἀλλ' ὅτι
20 καὶ ἄλλο τι προσῆν σοι μετὰ τὸ "πᾶς", ἐλάττων ἐγίνου
τῇ προσθήκῃ· οὐ γὰρ ἐκ τοῦ ὄντος ἦν ἡ προσθήκη—
οὐδὲν γὰρ ἐκείνῳ προσθήσεις—ἀλλὰ τοῦ μὴ ὄντος.[1]
γενόμενος δέ τις καὶ ἐκ τοῦ μὴ ὄντος ἐστὶν οὐ πᾶς, ἀλλ'
ὅταν τὸ μὴ ὂν ἀφῇ. αὔξεις τοίνυν σεαυτὸν ἀφεὶς τὰ ἄλλα
25 καὶ πάρεστί σοι τὸ πᾶν ἀφέντι· εἰ δὲ πάρεστι μὲν
ἀφέντι, μετὰ δὲ ἄλλων ὄντι οὐ φαίνεται, οὐκ ἦλθεν, ἵνα
παρῇ, ἀλλὰ σὺ ἀπῆλθες, ὅτε οὐ πάρεστιν. εἰ δ' ἀπῆλθες,
οὐκ ἀπ' αὐτοῦ—αὐτὸ γὰρ πάρεστιν—οὐδὲ τότε
ἀπῆλθες, ἀλλὰ παρὼν ἐπὶ τὰ ἐναντία ἐστράφης. οὕτω
30 γὰρ καὶ οἱ ἄλλοι θεοὶ πολλῶν παρόντων ἑνὶ φαίνονται
πολλάκις, ὅτι ὁ εἷς ἐκεῖνος μόνος δύναται βλέπειν. ἀλλ'
οὗτοι μὲν οἱ θεοί, ὅτι π α ν τ ο ῖ ο ι τ ε λ έ θ ο ν τ ε ς
ἐ π ι σ τ ρ ω φ ῶ σ ι τ ὰ ς π ό λ ε ι ς, εἰς ἐκεῖνον δὲ αἱ
πόλεις ἐπιστρέφονται καὶ πᾶσα γῆ καὶ πᾶς οὐρανός,
πανταχοῦ ἐπ' αὐτοῦ καὶ ἐν αὐτῷ μένοντα καὶ ἔχοντα ἐξ
35 αὐτοῦ τὸ ὂν καὶ τὰ ἀληθῶς ὄντα μέχρι ψυχῆς καὶ ζωῆς
ἐξηρτημένα καὶ εἰς ἓν ἄπειρον ἰόντα ἀμεγέθει τῷ
ἀπείρῳ.

[1] Kirchhoff: παντός Enn.

give up and pass out of it to something else and fall by not seeing what is present because you are looking at another. But if "you will seek nothing any more", however will this happen to you? Now it is because you approached the All and did not remain in a part of it, and you did not even say of yourself "I am just so much", but by rejecting the "so much" you have become all – yet even before this you were all; but because something else came to you after the "all" you became less by the addition: for the addition did not come from being – you will add nothing to that – but from non-being. And when someone has come to be also from non-being he is not all except when he rejects the non-being. You will increase yourself then by rejecting all else, and the All will be present to you in your rejection; but if it is present in your rejection and does not appear when you are with the other things, it did not come in order to be present, but you went away when it was not present. But if you went away, it was not from it – for it is present – and you did not even go away then, but were present and turned the opposite way. For in this way the other gods also when many are present often appear to one, because that one alone is able to see them. But these are the gods who "in many forms travel round our cities" [1]; but to that god the cities turn, and all the earth and all the sky, who everywhere abides by himself and in himself and has from himself being and the things which really are down to soul and life depending on him and moving to an unbounded unity by his sizeless unboundedness.

[1] Homer *Odyssey* 17. 486, quoted (with disapproval) by Plato *Republic* II 381D4.